The Rough
Gay & Lesbian Australia

There are more than two hundred Rough Guide titles covering
destinations from Alaska to Zimbabwe and subjects from
Acoustic Guitar to Travel Health

Forthcoming travel guides include
Argentina • Devon & Cornwall • Ibiza • Iceland • Malta • Vancouver

Forthcoming reference guides include
Cuban Music • Hip-Hop • Personal Computers • Trumpet & Trombone

Rough Guides online
www.roughguides.com

ROUGH GUIDE CREDITS

Text editors: Alison Cowan and Heather Cam
Series editor: Mark Ellingham
Design: Melissa Fraser
Production: Leah Maarse

Cartography: Country Cartographics
Text illustrations: Louisa Hamilton White
Picture research: Melissa Fraser and Sophie Ambrose

··

ACKNOWLEDGEMENTS

Huge thanks to all those whose diverse expertise has contributed to this guide – including Bruno Bouchet, Tim Mansour, Anthony Rich and Sinead Roarty (New South Wales); Stephen Carleton (Northern Territory); Jamie Bramwell, Nicole Corbett, Leonie Debnam and Paul Fede (Western Australia); Brenton Geyer and Greg Mackie (South Australia); Michael Broderick, Chris Malden and Louise Titcombe (Victoria); Rodney Croome (Tasmania); Lisa Anderson, Craig Judd, Suzi McConaghy, Leigh Raymond, Jane Schneider and Chris Sims (Contexts); and the formidable dragsters Brenton Geyer, Luke Cutler, John Sadlier, Lance St Leopard, Simone Simons and Pencil Vania.

Special thanks also to the many people across this wide brown land who helped in numerous and hospitable ways with the compilation of this guide: Cliff Anderson, Arcane Bookshop, The Bookshop Darlinghurst, Andrew (Nurse) Brown, Tim Errington, Margie Fischer, Tony Green, Hares & Hyenas, Joshua Higgins, Imprints Bookshop, Daryl Kosch, Patrick McGee, David Nair, Rowland Thomson and Crusader Hillis, Christos Tsiolkas, Sara Waylen, Phil Walcott.

··

PUBLISHING INFORMATION

This edition published 2001 by Rough Guides Ltd, 62–70 Shorts Gardens, London WC2H 9AB.
Distributed by the Penguin Group:
Penguin Books Australia Ltd, 487 Maroondah Highway, PO Box 257, Ringwood, Victoria 3134, Australia
Penguin Books Ltd, Harmondsworth, Middlesex, England
Penguin Putnam Inc., 375 Hudson Street, New York, New York 10014, USA
Penguin Books Canada Limited, 10 Alcorn Avenue, Toronto, Ontario, Canada M4V 3B2
Penguin Books (NZ) Ltd, Cnr Rosedale and Airborne Roads, Albany, Auckland, New Zealand
Penguin Books (South Africa) (Pty) Ltd, 5 Watkins Street, Denver Ext 4, 2094, South Africa
Penguin Books India (P) Ltd, 11, Community Centre, Panchsheel Park, New Delhi 110 017, India
10 9 8 7 6 5 4 3 2 1
Copyright © Neal Drinnan, 2001
The moral right of the author has been asserted
Cover design: Melissa Fraser and React
Front cover photo: Garry Moore/Tony Stone Images
Back-cover photos: Mirror ball, Tony Stone Images; Kata Tjuta (Olgas) in the 'Red Centre', Nick Rains

Typeset in Franklin Gothic by Post Pre-press Group, Brisbane
Printed and bound in Australia by Australian Print Group, Maryborough

National Library of Australia
Cataloguing-in-Publication data:
Drinnan, Neal.
The Rough Guide to gay and lesbian Australia.
Includes index.
ISBN 1 85828 832 0 (pbk.).
1. Gays – Travel – Australia – Guidebooks. 2. Gays – Services for – Australia – Directories. 3. Australia – Guidebooks. I. Title. II. Title : Gay and lesbian Australia.
919.4047

The publishers and authors have done their best to ensure the accuracy and currency of all information in The Rough Guide to Gay & Lesbian Australia; however, they can accept no responsibility for any loss, injury or inconvenience sustained by any traveller as a result of information or advice contained in the guide.

The Rough Guide to
Gay & Lesbian
Australia

Edited by

Neal Drinnan

with contributions by

Lisa Anderson, Bruno Bouchet, Stephen Carleton,
Nicole Corbett, Rodney Croome, Luke Cutler, Leonie Debnam,
Paul Fede, Brenton Geyer, Craig Judd, Suzi McConaghy,
Greg Mackie, Chris Malden, Tim Mansour, Leigh Raymond,
Sinead Roarty, Lance St Leopard, Jane Schneider and Chris Sims

ROUGH
GUIDES

THE ROUGH GUIDES

TRAVEL GUIDES • PHRASEBOOKS • MUSIC AND REFERENCE GUIDES

 We set out to do something different when the first Rough Guide was published in 1982. Mark Ellingham, just out of university, was travelling in Greece. He brought along the popular guides of the day, but found they were all lacking in some way. They were either strong on ruins and museums but went on for pages without mentioning a beach or taverna. Or they were so conscious of the need to save money that they lost sight of Greece's cultural and historical significance. Also, none of the books told him anything about Greece's contemporary life – its politics, its culture, its people, and how they lived.

So with no job in prospect, Mark decided to write his own guidebook, one which aimed to provide practical information that was second to none, detailing the best beaches and the hottest clubs and restaurants, while also giving hard-hitting accounts of every sight, both famous and obscure, and providing up-to-the-minute information on contemporary culture. It was a guide that encouraged independent travellers to find the best of Greece, and was a great success, getting shortlisted for the Thomas Cook travel guide award, and encouraging Mark, along with three friends, to expand the series.

The Rough Guide list grew rapidly and the letters flooded in, indicating a much broader readership than had been anticipated, but one which uniformly appreciated the Rough Guide mix of practical detail and humour, irreverence and enthusiasm. Things haven't changed. The same four friends who began the series are still the caretakers of the Rough Guide mission today: to provide the most reliable, up-to-date and entertaining information to independent-minded travellers of all ages, on all budgets.

We now publish more than 150 titles and have offices in London and New York. The travel guides are written and researched by a dedicated team of more than 100 authors, based in Britain, Europe, the USA and Australia. We have also created a unique series of phrasebooks to accompany the travel series, along with an acclaimed series of music guides, and a best-selling pocket guide to the Internet and World Wide Web. We also publish comprehensive travel information on our Web site:

www.roughguides.com

HELP US UPDATE

We've gone to a lot of effort to ensure that this first edition of *The Rough Guide to Gay & Lesbian Australia* is as accurate as possible. However, if you find we've missed something good or covered something which has now disappeared without trace, then please let us know: suggestions, comments or corrections are much appreciated.
Please send email to glguide@mail.com or mail@roughguides.co.uk.

THE EDITOR

Neal Drinnan is a seasoned traveller and the author of three of Australia's most popular gay novels: *Glove Puppet*, *Pussy's Bow* and *Quill*. He has worked in publishing and journalism for many years. He lives in Sydney.

contents

MAP SYMBOLS

▨▨▨	Pedestrianised street	■	Building
]═════[	Underpass or Tunnel	Ⓗ	Hospital
═╪═	Bridge	ⓘ ⓘ	Tourist office
●━◆━●	Train station & line	✉	Post office
─ ─	Tramline	⬭	Stadium/Sports Centre
～～～	River	🏊	Swimming Pool
🏔	Mountain range	⛳	Golf course
▲	Peak	▨	National Park
✲	Viewpoint	▨	Park
◉	Accommodation	⣿	Beach
▣	Café or restaurant	﴾﴿	Reef
⚠	Bar or club	✈	Airport
■	Bus Station		

list of maps

Introduction

Australia is a weird and often wonderful place. In spite of all its rigid **sexual stereotypes** ('the men are tough and the women are even tougher'), Australian society has become renowned for its tolerance of diverse cultural groups, and of diverse sexualities.

Perhaps because its colonial origins are steeped in 'morally reprehensible' behaviour – being used by the British largely as a dumping ground for petty thieves, whores and sodomites who had somehow avoided the noose – Australia has since developed a certain immunity to zealotry and puritanism. In most states of Australia, there are **anti-discrimination laws** to prevent people from being denied employment or housing on the grounds of race or sexuality (although Western Australia and the Northern Territory still have some way to go on these issues).

Literally and metaphorically turning their backs on the continent's relatively arid interior, 80 per cent of Australians choose to live on the coastal rim. Contemporary Australia also counts itself among the most **urbanized** nations in the world, with 85 per cent living in urban areas, in stark contrast to the indigenous people who thrived throughout this harsh land for at least 400,000 years.

While the bigger cities provide a large number of targeted services to gay men and lesbians, such **specialized services** and venues thin out fast as you travel to remote rural areas. Travellers

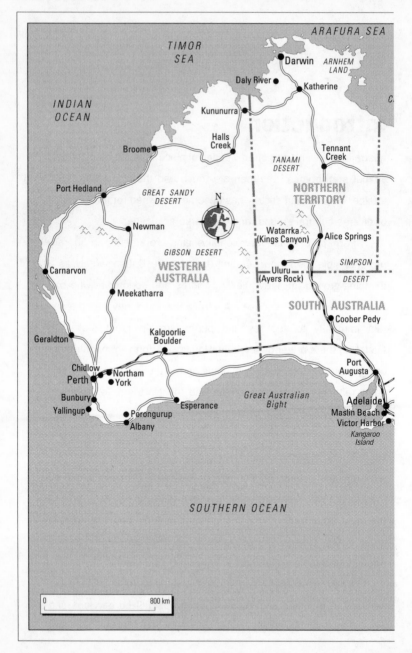

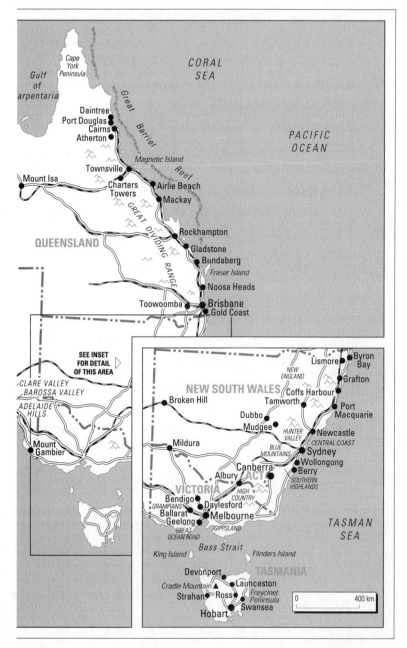

should be aware that Australia is not like the United States or Europe – it is often hundreds, even thousands, of kilometres between towns and the infrastructure in many of these locations is nothing like you would find in more densely populated parts of the world. If you want the **outback** adventure or the **small-town** experience you will find it far more enjoyable if you are patient and don't bring big-city expectations with you. Homosexuality is not a highly regarded human attribute in much of small-town Australia! And your sexuality is possibly not something to advertise in such places. You might be surprised to discover that even the most outspokenly political gays and lesbians in Australia can turn into shrinking violets when they return home to their small-town origins.

Having said that, **holidays** are precious times and we'd all be a good deal happier if we didn't spend the first day in a new city or town hunting down the newspapers which tell us of places where *people like us* can go. Young and not-so-young people coming to terms with their sexuality also need a book that helps to inform them and enables them to get in touch with **the queer community** in their area. It's not always easy to access information in Australia and many people living in smaller communities are still compelled to lead closeted lives. With all this in mind, we hope *The Rough Guide to Gay & Lesbian Australia* will be a great help to Australians and visitors alike.

About this book ... and Australia

This guide is not intended to be the ultimate touring guide to Australia; rather the aim is to enhance your experience of gay and lesbian Australia – and to highlight those places where you'll be able to relax and be sure of a warm welcome. (For detailed coverage of the sights and how best to see them, you could do a lot worse than pick-up a copy of *The Rough Guide to Australia*.)

OUT AND PROUD

Gay and lesbian pride is now celebrated in every capital city, most famously at the Sydney Gay and Lesbian Mardi Gras, held throughout February and into the first week of March, and **legislation** has been dragged along in its wake. South Australia was first to legalize homosexual acts in the 1970s, while Queensland and Tasmania finally changed their laws in the 1990s.

Annual pride **marches**, along with **festivals** such as Midsumma in Melbourne, FEAST in Adelaide and Pride in Brisbane and Perth, aim to raise community awareness of the presence of lesbians and gays in all walks of Australian life. While the focus of these events is on unity and entertainment, the process of obtaining access to city streets and parks for the events is a way of gently insisting that government (and society at large) acknowledge the growing presence and self-determination of the alternative sexualities in their midst.

Despite growing recognition of the power of 'the pink dollar', the community wants to be seen as more than just a powerful economic force, and the **lobbying** for legal recognition of same-sex relationships, equal access to in vitro fertility (IVF) programs, and the right to adopt or care for foster children continues.

THE QUEER COMMUNITY

The history of the political **alliance** between the gay and lesbian communities over the last 30 years has been a bumpy one.

While much activism in the 1970s was undertaken as a joint venture, fuelled by the socialist/feminist zeitgeist, it was not long before the two communities realized that they often had vastly different agendas.

As Quentin Crisp once inflammatorily said, 'gays want to have fun, lesbians want to be right'. And so the forces of division seemed to split many groups, the media and the body politic down the middle – until **AIDS** shook everything up in the 1980s. Since those dark days, lesbians (and women in general) have played a huge part in the national battle against a virus that was once perceived as a 'gay plague', and the demand for equal representa-

tion of gays and lesbians has grown correspondingly.

One great point of gay/ lesbian pride in Australia is that – unlike the male-dominated Stateside scene – the big parties Down Under are truly mixed and go out of their way to cater for all genders, including transgender. Unfortunately, the jury is still out on **bisexuality**, so if you are bisexual and get questioned about your sexuality when buying party tickets (and yes, this sort of questioning does go on), you'd be well-advised to say you're gay or lesbian, just to sidestep having to justify yourself for hours. Your holiday is doubtless too short for you to become embroiled in this perennial debate!

Directory of Australia-wide contacts

ACCOMMODATION AND TRAVEL
GALA
100–104 Reynolds St, Balmain NSW 2041
Web www.gala.net.au
On-line information, travel, entertainment and booking service of the Gay and Lesbian Alliance.

qbeds
Web www.qbeds.com and www.qbeds.com/lesbian
Gender Mixed
qbeds is a comprehensive online travel directory of gay/lesbian/queer/transgender-friendly accommodation: just click on the Web sites' map of Australia and qbeds will list whatever is available in that area.

ARTS AND MEDIA

Lesbian Network

PO Box 7194, Hutt St, Adelaide SA 5001

Phone 08/8227 0072

Email lemon@yahoo.com

Gender Mixed

This is a national lesbian feminist quarterly magazine.

Cost $30 annual subscription

Qstage Digest

7/163 Devonshire St, Surry Hills NSW 2010

Phone 02/8399 0540 or 0419 483 305

Email dpj@loom.net.au

Web www1.loom.net.au/home/dpj

Qstage is a mailing list providing news, reviews and information about theatre, video, film, music and entertainment events in Sydney and beyond. Moderated by dramatist David Paul Jobling, the service is free and the list sometimes has special offers of tickets to shows etc. If you are a traveller, this is a good way of checking out what's on around Sydney and Australia before you arrive.

COMMUNITY

AIDS Trust of Australia

64 Cooper St, Surry Hills NSW 2010

Phone 02 9310 1066 or 1800 689 188 **Fax** 02 9310 1656

Email info@aidstrust.com.au

Web www.aidstrust.com.au

Australia's only national AIDS charity.

Open Mon–Fri 9am–5pm

Country Network

PO Box 236, Rozelle NSW 2039

Australia-wide social organization for isolated gay men and women needing support and social contact. They can offer contact in most states of Australia.

Pinkfind

Web www.pinkfind.com

Gender Mixed

A gay/lesbian resource site.

Regional Pride

Web www.regionalpride.com

Gender Mixed

A national Web resource for rural gay/lesbian community groups throughout Australia.

Women in the Bush

PO Box 244, Panania NSW 2213

Gender Women

Network for women in rural areas.

Wrestling/Mat Men

Mat Men PO Box 578, Dee Why NSW 2099

Phone Derek 02 9971 8336

Email mat_men@hotmail.com

Gender Mostly men

Australia-wide gay and lesbian wrestling contact club, with members in all states – and around the world. *Mat Men* also arranges outdoor activities, including bushwalking and canoeing, at a modest cost. A contact magazine is available ($28).

MAKING CONTACT

While it is undeniably true that there are more gay male **venues** than lesbian ones in Australia, there are powerful and interesting women's **networks** listed in the 'Community' sections of the *Guide*. Many of these are to be found in rural areas because in the last ten years gay and lesbian groups have felt more confident about consolidating their existence in regions of Australia where they previously lived under a shroud of secrecy. Many of these **contacts** and groups are well worth chasing up before you arrive at your Australian destination or if you are planning to travel to Australia's more rural locales. As with any listings of this kind, things change, so always check the contacts first.

ACCOMMODATION

In the *Guide* we have focused primarily on **gay- or lesbian-owned** and -operated establishments. There are some locations where these plain don't exist, but there are many gay/lesbian-friendly businesses where you should not encounter prejudice or discrimination – and these too have been included where appropriate.

There is gay/lesbian accommodation available for as little as $50 per person per night. For those on shoestring budgets, we have also listed some decent **hostels** with rates as low as $25 per person per night – although these are not specifically gay or lesbian, they are often located in areas close to gay and lesbian venues.

The big four- and five-star hotels have generally not been listed in this guide unless they are specifically gay or lesbian or of specific interest and quality. It tends to be the case that money softens the heart of the toughest bigots and expensive hotels are nothing if not discreet. Major **hotel chains** providing luxury accommodation are the same the world over and they are unlikely to make same-sex couples feel uncomfortable if they are prepared to spend hundreds of dollars on a night's accommodation.

We've attempted to set out what the **amenities** are in simple uncluttered language. Many of the listed establishments and organizations have Web sites you can visit for more information. Others may need a quick phone call or email for you to decide whether or not they are suited to your needs. Price is usually a fair indicator of what you can expect: $50 a night is very cheap and you should not expect too much in the way of facilities, let alone room service and in-house movies; for $300 a night, you can expect luxury.

The gentle art of checking-in

I remember going to a country motel with a male 'friend' a few years back and asking the proprietress for a double room. She looked at my male companion and smiled at my mistake.

'No love, ya double's a double bed. You'd be wanting a twin.'

'No, we'd like a double please.' She smiled again but was tiring of how thick I seemed to be.

'No love, I said your double is a double bed, your twin is two singles.'

'That's right,' I said, my pride shrinking and faltering as hetero' heads began to stare from the nearby bar. We *want* a double.'

In that instant her face went ashen as the terrible truth dawned.

'We haven't got any.' And she slammed the keys to a twin on the counter. This scenario has stayed with me and perhaps provided the ongoing inspiration to create a guide such as this. My sorry little anecdote is one we'd all like to avoid . . .

This guide does not 'rate' establishments, as our communities are still too small for that type of comparison or criticism – but it will give you the most comprehensive gay/lesbian-friendly accommodation listings to date.

BARS AND LICENSING

One little Australian idiosyncrasy that international visitors should be aware of is that in some states **licensing laws** require that liquor may be served only if you eat at the establishment as well. New South Wales in particular has curious laws on this matter. This is particularly relevant in Sydney where if you visit a licensed restaurant or one with a bar and only want a drink, you will be asked if you intend to dine. The answer to this question is always 'yes', regardless of whether or not you eat there; if you say 'no', they are forced by law to refuse you alcohol. However, if you have a couple of drinks and decide not to eat after all, well, at least you had the **intention** originally (get it?). It's very silly really, but it is a game played by most Sydneysiders from time to time. This law, of course, does not apply to bars and pubs.

BYO (Bring Your Own) restaurants, where you are welcome to take your own wine or beer to drink with your meal, are very popular in Australia. Most are unlicensed, but some licensed restaurants will also allow you to bring your own wine. However, there is an increasing trend towards charging a corkage fee (either per bottle or per person), and these can sometimes make the wine more expensive than if you'd bought it at the restaurant to begin with. Check when booking.

SMOKING

Statistically at least, gays and lesbians have a reputation for being smokers. If you're among these, be warned that smoking is becoming an increasingly unacceptable habit in Australia. It is now completely banned in restaurants in Sydney, Perth, Adelaide and Canberra. Melbourne

---

The information contained in this guide was believed to be true and accurate at the time of publication. However, the **café, bar and club scene** can be particularly **mercurial**, so phone before you set out or check the local gay or lesbian newspapers for up-to-the-minute bar and club information (these are listed at the beginning of each chapter).

and Brisbane are all trying to go the same way by late 2001. Likewise, many accommodation providers listed in this guide specify that smoking is permitted 'outside only'. Smoking is usually allowed in outside dining areas and, for the time being, it is still permissible in bars and clubs.

DRUGS . . .

Australia, being an island continent, is very protective and guarded about what may, or may not, be brought into the country. '**Forbidden fruit**' extends to fresh produce, flora (including some wooden articles) and animal products, let alone anything stronger. If you have any of these on arrival, they must be declared.

Drugs of any kind, with the exception of prescription drugs that have been specifically prescribed to the person in possession of them, are **illegal**. Marijuana for personal use has been decriminalized in South Australia and the Australian Capital Territory, but this is still a long way from being legal: on-the-spot fines of $500 or more can be imposed on people found to be in possession of any quantity considered to be more than that required for personal use. Higher penalties and criminal charges can be laid against people found to be dealing or in possession of larger quantities.

Bringing drugs into the country is extremely foolish as all international airports employ thorough customs officers, luggage x-rays and sniffer dogs. Even **carrying drugs** from state to state is risky – especially to locations such as Cairns and Darwin, where much of the drug and customs training takes place and dogs sometimes 'practise' on domestic baggage.

. . . AND THE PARTY SCENE

Be that as it may, it would be naive to maintain that drugs play no part in the gay and lesbian party culture of major cities. The most popular illegal party drug in Australia today is ecstasy (Eeees, Eckies, pills, Dame Ednas, disco biscuits, bikkies, snacks, etc): if you hear someone say they are snacking down on some disco biscuits, they are not talking about being served hors d'oeuvres. While ecstasy is highly illegal and criminal charges and gaol sentences can be imposed on people found to be dealing or in possession, it is a major part of Australia's clubbing and party culture. Although some nightclubs may expect you to go through a metal detector, they are not entitled to **search** your person. Large

11

For those who need **syringes** and fit kits, they are available at most chemists in packs or can be obtained through AIDS Council offices across the country (these are listed in the *Guide*). Swabs and distilled water can also be obtained from these locations.

parties such as Sleaze Ball and Mardi Gras *do* have all bags searched though, so be warned.

Because of ecstasy's illegality, all users and buyers do so at their own **risk**. Ecstasy tablets are not controlled substances, so their strength and quality vary wildly. While ecstasy fatalities in Australia have been few, every year people suffer adverse effects requiring hospital treatment. Ecstasy sales are usually done discreetly and illegally in nightclubs and if you are planning on taking some, make sure you are with someone who knows what you've taken and whom you obtained it from.

A very dangerous drug called **GBH** (grievous bodily harm) or GHB is known to be sold as 'liquid ecstasy' or 'G', but should not be confused with the pill variety of ecstasy. People are frequently hospitalized from the effects of GBH and some have died. It is potentially lethal when combined with alcohol and other substances. Gay and lesbian groups all over the country have appealed to people not to take this substance at our clubs or parties, since its

effects not only put your life at risk but also jeopardize the future of hard-won community events, as well as the licences of venues. Other drugs in frequent, if illegal, circulation in Australia are **marijuana**, **amphetamine** (speed, goey) and **crystal** or **base** (highly concentrated amphetamine), **ketamine** (Special K), **LSD** (acid, trips, holidays), cocaine, heroin and MDA.

Amyl nitrate (poppers, rush, vibes) is sold in most adult shops and sex clubs, and is not technically illegal because it is sold as 'liquid aroma', but once again it should not be carried in luggage – if it leaks, the smell alone should be enough to put you off that idea.

SAFE SEX

Australia was internationally praised for its prompt and successful safe-sex **campaigns**: the national response to the AIDS epidemic was swift and effective, with explicit and often controversial campaigns being launched by the AIDS Councils and other organizations. In the larger cities there are outreach programs for young people coming to terms with their sexuality, as well as **counselling** services for parents and **health services** designed to meet the specific needs of the gay/lesbian/bisexual/transgender communities.

More recently, with the advent of combination therapies for HIV-positive people, there has been an alarming increase in the number of people engaging in **unprotected sex**. However free-spirited and easy-going Australia may seem to visitors, HIV and AIDS are still major **health concerns** and it is a matter of basic human respect between partners that casual sex takes place as safely as possible. The party spirit and laissez-faire sexuality of many gay festivals has a way of tempting people to forget about the dangers of unprotected sex, but remember: just because you're on holiday and are having a great time and feel *really* connected with someone and like the way they dance

does not mean that it is OK to dispense with safe-sex protocol. If you like someone that much, the least you can do is offer to be safe with them.

CRUISING

For those in a cruisey mood, there are numerous **cruise clubs** in larger cities – and especially around Oxford Street in Sydney, with admission at around $10. Safe sex is actively encouraged, and all venues provide free condoms and lube. Remember to hold onto your valuables if you go to places without lockers, or leave your wallet at the counter or in your hotel. We have not listed escort agencies or telephone sex services, because these are well and truly covered in the free gay newspapers that are widely distributed in Australia's major cities.

Also, we haven't listed **beats** (apart from gay beaches, which

Age of consent

The age of consent for homosexuals varies across Australia.

New South Wales: gay 18; lesbian 16

Australian Capital Territory: gay 16; lesbian 16

Queensland: gay – 16 for oral sex, 18 for anal sex; lesbian 16

Northern Territory: gay 18; lesbian 16

Western Australia: gay 21; lesbian 18

South Australia: gay 17; lesbian 17

Victoria: gay 16; lesbian 16

Tasmania: gay 17; lesbian 17

tend to be more relaxed and open at least during daylight), as their locations are often changeable, not always easily accessible and frankly, **dangerous**. Even more so to those who are strangers to them. In no state of Australia is it legal to have sex (perform indecent acts) in a public place and, however frolicsome some of the **beaches** may appear to be, it is still against the law to engage in lewd or indecent behaviour. The police have been known to be involved in entrapment campaigns, so be very careful when you're cruising for adventure in the great outdoors. Nothing would ruin your holiday faster than a trip to the police station with a homophobic member of the constabulary.

PART ONE

the guide

New South Wales

New South Wales was the first part of Australia to be settled by Europeans, in 1788, and is still the most densely populated state. Its naming can only be attributed to an act of British sentimentality because there are very few similarities between the state's terrain and that of the south of Wales. It is also considerably larger than its namesake, occupying approximately 1000km of Australia's eastern seaboard and traversing another 1000km inland. The state's climate varies from subtropical in the north to temperate in the south, where Australia's highest mountains are located.

Sydney is the state's capital city – and is also the epicentre of gay and lesbian Australia. Within a couple of hours' drive are the Southern Highlands, the perfect place to experience the gentler side of Australian wilderness, and the dramatic outcrops of the Blue Mountains, which offer fantastic walks, wildlife, sightseeing and plenty of gay/lesbian-friendly accommodation options. If you simply must have an **outback** experience, keep driving west for 10 hours and you'll find the mining town of Broken Hill, as dubiously depicted in *The Adventures of Priscilla, Queen of the Desert*. Other attractions, however, lie along the **coast** and there are many locations worth a detour, both north and south of Sydney.

Sydney

There can be no doubt that Sydney is the **gay and lesbian capital** of Australia, with charms to soften the hardest of hearts. Situated on one of the world's most spectacular harbours, Sydney has dozens of beautiful waterways to explore. Stunning views are the city's hard currency and can be enjoyed from the giddy heights of the Harbour Bridge and various other vantage points around the city, or at closer quarters from the deck of a ferry.

Nestled at the base of the southern end of the Harbour Bridge, **The Rocks** is the oldest part of the city, a maze of steep streets filled with historic pubs, souvenir shops and restaurants. Circular Quay, between The Rocks and the Opera House, is the central port for Sydney's ferries and cruise ships. It is also home to the Museum of Contemporary Art (MCA) and its promenade offers a circus of street theatre, busking and ice-cream licking. While most of The Rocks is well preserved and offers a certain 'olde worlde' charm, the businesses are mostly designed to ensure tourists and their money are quickly parted. There is a craft market here on Saturdays, but it all tends towards the twee. (Far better to explore the Paddington Market on Saturdays, with its stalls clustered in the grounds of the church at 395 Oxford Street.) For a respite from the hubbub, take a stroll around the Botanical Gardens, which are right next to the Opera House – and the **Opera House** itself, well you can't miss that.

The climate is mild and as a rule it's warm from October through May, putting the harbour and **beaches** firmly at the centre of Sydney's summer lifestyle. If you like swimming, sunbathing or just watching the world go by, the beach is the place to do it (just don't forget the sunscreen!). The beaches are relatively clean too, considering they're attached to a city of nearly 4 million people – though you might want to give some beaches, especially harbour ones, a wide berth for a couple of days after heavy rain, to avoid unpleasant encounters with stormwater overflows. If your preference is for still water rather than crashing waves, there are also sea pools and tranquil harbourside beaches.

The golden curve of **Bondi**, 5km south-east of the CBD, lures visitors in droves and offers a wide variety of dining and recreational pursuits. One of the most popular gay male beaches is

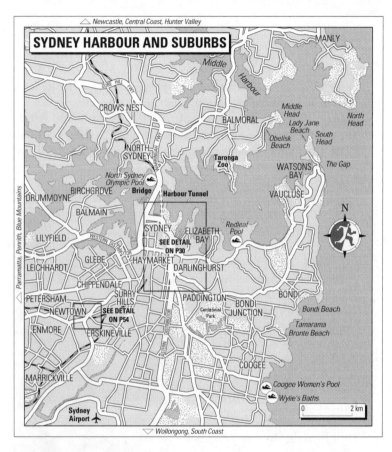

Newcastle, Central Coast, Hunter Valley

SYDNEY HARBOUR AND SUBURBS

MANLY

Middle Harbour

Parramatta, Penrith, Blue Mountains

GORE HILL HWY

CROWS NEST

BALMORAL

Middle Head

Lady Jane Beach

North Head

Obelisk Beach

South Head

NORTH SYDNEY

WARRINGAH HWY

Taronga Zoo

WATSONS BAY

The Gap

North Sydney Olympic Pool

DRUMMOYNE

BIRCHGROVE

Bridge

Harbour Tunnel

VAUCLUSE

N

BALMAIN

SYDNEY

ELIZABETH BAY

Redleaf Pool

LILYFIELD

WESTERN DISTRIBUTOR

SEE DETAIL ON P30

LEICHHARDT

GLEBE

HAYMARKET

DARLINGHURST

CHIPPENDALE

PETERSHAM

SURRY HILLS

PADDINGTON

BONDI JUNCTION

BONDI

NEWTOWN

SEE DETAIL ON P54

Centennial Park

Bondi Beach

ENMORE

ERSKINEVILLE

EASTERN DISTRIBUTOR

Tamarama Bronte Beach

MARRICKVILLE

COOGEE

Coogee Women's Pool

Wylie's Baths

0   2 km

Sydney Airport ✈

Wollongong, South Coast

Tamarama (often called 'Glamarama'), a pleasant 15-minute cliff-top walk south from Bondi Beach. It is also the most 'sceney' of the gay-frequented beaches – the ideal place to view the muscle-bound boys Sydney is so good at producing. Other **eastern beaches** worth visiting (while not necessarily gay) are Bronte, Coogee and Clovelly. **Women** should not miss the opportunity to visit Coogee's famous 'Women's Pool', a space exclusively for women to swim, sunbake and relax. For those not keen on the surf, all of these beaches have sea pools with water that changes with the tide – and lanes for lap swimmers. Alternatively, catch the ferry over to **Manly**, from where you can easily walk to

19

several beaches: the harbour beach is next to the ferry wharf, but if you stroll around past the aquarium (at the far end of that beach) you'll find a string of small coves that are perfect for swimming and snorkelling, plus a saltwater pool. The surf beach is a six-minute walk through the main shopping mall opposite the ferry terminal. For those wishing to frolic naked, there are two beaches to try. Lady Jane Beach, popular with both male and female **naturists**, is nestled into the South Head of Sydney Harbour. The other nude beach very popular with gay men is Obelisk, on the north shore of the harbour. This is a bit further away but well worth a visit. It is surrounded by natural bushland which, not surprisingly, operates as one of Sydney's biggest daytime beats. (See pp.65–68 for the full queer lowdown on the city's beaches and pools.)

Peter J. Mark

Walks around the harbourside eastern suburbs of Elizabeth Bay and Rushcutters Bay or Vaucluse and Watsons Bay are also well worth doing. The Gap at Watsons Bay is a rugged, sheer cliff that guards the entrance to the harbour; its vertigo-inducing cliffs are a popular suicide location for the city's disillusioned. (So is the Harbour Bridge, but we don't talk about that.)

Sydney's charming **ferries** are perfect for romantic, inexpensive sightseeing excursions. The trip to Manly is the classic ferry ride, but Balmain, Watsons Bay and Taronga Zoo are also worth a look – during Mardi Gras, Sisters from the Order of Perpetual Indulgence (see p.78) even offer special guided tours of the zoo. You should, of course, feel free to spreadeagle yourself on the foredeck of the ferry and perform either Barbra Streisand's 'Don't Rain on My Parade' or Leonardo DiCaprio's 'king of the world' speech from *Titanic*. I know which I prefer.

The two main **lesbian and gay districts** are Oxford Street and the surrounding areas of **Darlinghurst**, spilling over into **Kings Cross** and **Potts Point** to the east and **Surry Hills** to the west; and King Street in **Newtown**, together with the adjoining **inner western suburbs** of Erskineville, Enmore and Leichhardt. While Newtown is about 3km south-west of the city centre, it and the rest of the inner west are served by frequent train and bus services (see box on p.23). The **Oxford Street** strip (or 'golden mile', as it is often called), stretches out from the southeastern tip of the CBD. It is the starting point of the famous Sydney Gay and Lesbian Mardi Gras Parade, which ends the almost month-long Mardi Gras Festival during February (see pp.23–26), and is where most of the gay clubs are. The women's scene extends well into the Newtown side of town, but there are plenty of comfortably mixed venues in and around Oxford Street for women, as well as specific women's nights at various clubs and bars. Most of the **gay/lesbian-friendly accommodation** is on the Oxford Street side of town.

Sydney highlights and hot-spots

- Starting at the top, Bridge Climb offers fully supervised climbs up Sydney Harbour Bridge ($117–164; for bookings phone 02/9252 0077, email admin@bridgeclimb.com or visit www.bridgeclimb.com). Note that you'll be breathalysed, so a few nerve-steadying stiff drinks beforehand ain't such a good idea.

- Some of Sydney's best restaurants are gay- or lesbian-run. In The Rocks, David Thompson's *Sailors Thai* (see p.38) has long been regarded as one of the country's best Thai restaurants, and *Water on Sunday* (see p.42) makes a fine choice for an indulgent modern Australian feast with some of your closest friend(s).

- A Saturday shopping excursion to King Street, Newtown, is the perfect way to see funkier Sydneysiders relaxing in their natural habitat. King Street is full of interesting shops and cafés – and when you've worked up a thirst, you can adjourn to the *Bank* or *Newtown* hotels (see pp.52 & 53), or even Erskineville's *Imperial Hotel* (very Priscilla) for a beer.

- Across town in Paddington, Oxford Street offers the chance to see lots of beautiful people on parade. And if you can't find the perfect accessories, there's always the consolation of cocktail hour, which is taken very seriously at *Gilligans*, *Stonewall* and many of the other gay bars. An Oxford Smash at *Gilligans* (see p.45) will take the sting out of your tired feet (and everywhere else while it's at it).

- Ferries at sunset can be a fine thing, as can picnics by the beach in the warm summer months. The park at Bronte Beach has lots of gas barbecues, as well as nearby cafés if you don't feel like cooking. Other superb picnic locations include the Botanic Gardens and the pretty coves west of Watsons Bay – Parsley Bay and Shark Bay.

- In summer, movies are shown outdoors on a screen that rises magically from Farm Cove at dusk. Food and drink is available – and if the film gets boring, you can always gaze at the floodlit sails of the Opera House instead.

The most helpful sources of information you can arm yourself with – in addition to this guide, of course – are the **free lesbian and gay newspapers**; *Sydney Star Observer*, *Capital Q* and *Lesbians on The Loose* (see pp.63–65). These offer weekly updates on venues and events, as well as lots of gossip to help initiate you into the 'Sydney way'. These papers are available at most of the bars and shops listed below – and if you are travelling on to other states it is worth knowing that *The Bookshop, Darlinghurst* (see p.62) also has a good range of gay/lesbian newspapers from other capital cities.

For all its spectacular scenery and easygoing nature, Sydney does have its **darker side**: Kings Cross, Oxford Street and King Street are like busy inner-city areas anywhere in the world, and you should be on your guard. It is sad but true that, statistically, there are more hate crimes directed against gays and lesbians in the vicinity of Oxford Street than anywhere else in the entire country. The city end of Oxford Street is taken over by straight clubbers on Friday and Saturday nights, and gangs of youths or men in cars cruise the strip looking for girls and drugs – and then resort to violence when they fail to 'score'. We don't want to be unnecessarily alarmist, but neither do we want you to be seduced into taking unnecessary risks by the golden mile's openness and the generally tolerant atmosphere.

For information on **buses, trains and ferries**, phone 13 1500 (daily 6am–10pm). This service also provides detailed instructions on how to get where you want to go by public transport from any specific point of departure.

Taxi companies include Legion 13 1451, Premiere 13 1017, RSL 13 1581 and Taxis Combined 02/8332 8888.

If you are on your own, get a taxi or try to avoid the quieter back streets. Carry a whistle when you're out at night. Most importantly, avoid walking through Hyde Park at night, where attacks and robberies are commonplace even in the early evening.

SYDNEY GAY AND LESBIAN MARDI GRAS

The annual **Sydney Gay and Lesbian Mardi Gras** is unique among Australian festivals and special events in using celebration and the arts to promote community, political and social objectives. Every year, in February, members of the gay and lesbian community from all over the world assemble in Sydney for a month-long celebration of lesbian and gay pride and culture. Theatre, visual arts, music, dance, comedy, literary, sporting and community events combine to make this the largest lesbian and gay **arts festival** in the world, culminating in the **parade** that is Mardi Gras's heart and soul. The Mardi Gras parade is undoubtedly the lesbian and gay community's most important event, bringing together individuals, organizations and businesses in a spirit of celebration and cooperation. It is our joyous demonstration of pride in who we are. Drawing a bigger crowd than any other event in Australia, it is a human rights demonstration unequalled in colour, drama, spectacle and wit.

The Sydney Gay and Lesbian Mardi Gras began in 1978, when a group of protesters and speakers congregated outside Hyde Park, then marched down William Street and ended their protest at the Alamein Fountain in Kings Cross. It was here that the protesters encountered considerable police brutality.

Mardi Gras

Peter J. Mark

Some were severely injured and the remaining protesters were herded up and gaoled in the nearby police station. The annual parade and party have come to symbolize that early struggle for gay and lesbian rights in New South Wales – and Australia as a whole. The legal status of homosexuals in New South Wales did not formally change until 1983.

Sydney Gay and Lesbian Mardi Gras (SGLMG) is a community-owned, non-profit, incorporated company. Funding for Mardi Gras comes largely from ticket sales to the after-parade party and to an equally famous party held in October called Sleaze Ball. Tickets to the **post-parade party** are usually well and truly sold out by the end of January so it is always best to book them well in advance. Interstate visitors need to have associate memberships, which

Peter J. Mark

entitle them to purchase one ticket each. International travellers should consult their tour operators when organizing their travel arrangements, as there is a special category of ticketing especially for overseas visitors. Needless to say, **accommodation** for Mardi Gras should be booked as far in advance as possible.

SGLMG publishes a free Mardi Gras guide each year, which is available at bars, clubs, bookshops, AIDS councils and businesses throughout inner Sydney as well as the SGLMG offices and gay/lesbian businesses around the country.

Sydney Gay and Lesbian Mardi Gras
21–23 Erskineville Rd, Newtown NSW 2042
Phone 02/9557 4332
Fax 02/9516 4446
Email mardigras@mardigras.com.au
Web www.mardigras.com.au

For bookings to Mardi Gras Festival events, call 02/9266 4822.

For updates on events, visit the Mardi Gras Web site, and for bookings point your browser to www.ticketek.com.au (a credit card is required and a booking fee will be charged on each ticket).

Peter J. Mark

Open Mon–Fri 10am–6pm

Cost Memberships are available for lesbians and gays who live within 150km of Sydney; the cost is $44 ($19 concessions) and this entitles members to purchase three party tickets to Mardi Gras or Sleaze Ball. Associate memberships are available in all states of Australia for $35 and entitle the purchase of one ticket. Overseas memberships cost $60 and also allow one ticket per person.

Payment methods AmEx, Bankcard, MasterCard, Visa; cheque

Also held during the festival is an event called **Harbour Party**, which traditionally takes place the week prior to the parade. It is held in the afternoon from 4pm until 10pm and offers participants the chance to dance on the harbour's edge as the sun sets. The location is Mrs Macquaries Road, at the northern end of the Botanic Gardens. This popular event requires early booking, as all 5000 tickets invariably sell out immediately on release (people queue all night to be first in line). Tickets can be obtained at *The Toolshed* (see p.59), on Oxford Street. Once again, international visitors should consult their tour operators – better still, if you have contacts in Sydney, get them to organize tickets for you.

Mardi Gras Speak

This particular collection of lingo seems to circulate as an email every year around the time of Mardi Gras. What can we say, except forewarned is forearmed . . .

What they say	What they mean
Welcome to Sydney	You're cute
Happy Mardi Gras	I'm gay
G'day mate	I'm straight

Mardi Gras Speak

What they say	What they mean
Hello darling	I've forgotten your name
Is it your first time in Sydney?	Hopefully they won't know what a slut I am
What do you think of Sydney so far?	Do you fancy me?
I'll show you around town	I'm not letting anyone else near you
It's your shout	My friends and I want you to buy us a drink
I'm a jackaroo	I was in an Aussie porno film
Is that an American accent?	Can I marry you and get a green card?
I prefer classical music myself	Why don't they play Diana Ross anymore?
Let's go to your hotel	My partner's at home
I don't have sex on the first date	I've got crabs
Maybe I'll see you at the party	Have a nice life
I'm over the Mardi Gras Party	I couldn't get a ticket
The recoveries are better anyway	God I wish I'd had a ticket
Darling, that outfit is *outrageous*	Love, you look shocking!
I love you	My ecstasy has just kicked in
I love your pink elephant	My LSD has just kicked in
I #*#@%~!	My Special K has just kicked in
You gays really know how to party!	Suck me off before my girlfriend gets back?
I've been looking for you for ages	I've been in the toilets having sex
I never stay until the end of the party	I'm not so pretty in daylight
I think I'm going to be sick	I think I'm going to be sick
I'm going home to sleep before the recoveries	I'm going to the sauna
Here, have an ecstasy!	I really, really, really like you
The music was just that vile thump thump	I'm over 35
The party was too straight	I didn't manage to pick up
I'm over it	My drugs have worn off

Peter J. Mark

ACCOMMODATION

We have listed accommodation from **budget** through mid-range to **luxury**. The international hotels listed here are not specifically gay or lesbian, but neither are they known to have discriminatory policies. Many of the large hotels at the city end of Oxford Street have decent views of the Mardi Gras parade route – a highly sought-after commodity. Accommodation for **Mardi Gras** should be booked as far in advance as possible – many prime spots are booked out a year or more in advance.

CITY CENTRE

Aarons Hotel
37 Ultimo Rd
Haymarket NSW 2000
Phone 02/9281 5555
Fax 02/9281 2666
Email aarons@acay.com.au
Web www.aaronshotel.citysearch.com.au
Gender Mixed
Aarons Hotel occupies a fantastic location right in the heart of Chinatown, so it's ideal if you like Asian food and markets. It is also handy to the CBD and Central Station. All rooms have air-conditioning, ensuite, TV, refrigerator. The hotel offers a tour-booking service, guest laundry and 24-hour reception.
Cost From $137 per room
Payment AmEx, Bankcard, Diners, EFTPOS, MasterCard, Visa

Hyde Park Plaza
38 College St
Sydney NSW 2000
Phone 02/9331 6933
Fax 02/9331 6022

Email hydeparkplaza@mirvachotel.com.au
Gender Mixed
The *Hyde Park Plaza* has a great position, with many of its rooms providing views of the Mardi Gras parade route. In addition to stylish rooms, there are one-, two- and three-bedroom apartments; special rates are available for corporate guests and for members of motoring organisations.
Cost $190–495 per room
Payment AmEx, Bankcard, Diners, MasterCard, Visa

Marriott Hotel
36 College St
Sydney NSW 2000
Phone 02/9361 8400
Fax 02/9361 8599
Web www.marriott.com
Gender Mixed
Located opposite Hyde Park, this hotel provides the luxury you'd expect from this price bracket, and is popular with business people and tourists. Although this isn't

specifically gay/lesbian accommodation, it's included here for its ideal location a short walk from Oxford Street and the city centre.
Cost $235–385
Payment AmEx, Bankcard, Diners, EFTPOS, MasterCard, Visa

Sydney Central Youth Hostel
Cnr Pitt St and Rawson Place
Sydney NSW 2000
Phone 02/9281 9111
Fax 02/9281 9199
Email sydcentral@yhansw.org.au
Gender Mixed
Directly across the road from Central Station (served by Airport Express buses), Sydney's main youth hostel is clean and modern. It's right next to Chinatown and just 15 minutes' walk to Oxford Street or a 10-minute train ride to Newtown. Those looking for budget accommodation could do a lot worse than here.
Cost Dorm accommodation from $29

per person for YHA members, $36 for non-members; rooms (for members only) $68–78
Payment Bankcard, EFTPOS, MasterCard, Visa

YWCA Sydney Y on the Park
5–11 Wentworth Ave
Sydney NSW 2000
Phone 02/9264 2451
Fax 02/9285 6265
Email y-hotel@zip.com.au
Web www.ywca-syd.com.au
Gender Mixed
Located opposite Hyde Park, the Y provides budget accommodation in a very central location – close to the city, within walking distance to Oxford Street and handy to the Airport Express bus. Facilities for the disabled are available.
Cost Dorm accommodation from $27 per person; rooms $82–145
Payment AmEx, Bankcard, EFTPOS, MasterCard, Visa

DARLINGHURST AND EAST SYDNEY

All Seasons on Crown
302 Crown St
Darlinghurst NSW 2010
Phone 02/9360 1133
Fax 02/9380 8989
Email allseasonsoncrown@bigpond.com.au
Gender Mixed
Handy to all Oxford Street's nightlife, the *All Seasons* is a modern tourist-class hotel with reasonable rates.
Cost $150–175 per room
Payment AmEx, Bankcard, MasterCard, Visa

Hotel Altamont
207 Darlinghurst Rd
Darlinghurst NSW 2010
Phone 02/9360 6000
Fax 02/9360 7096
Web www.altamont.com.au
Gender Mixed
This friendly hotel abounds with Indonesian teak decor, is air-conditioned and close to Oxford Street. Every room has an ensuite and cable TV, and guest facilities include a roof garden, bar and lounge.
Cost From $150 per room (discounts

for multiple-night stays, weekly rates
up to 40 per cent cheaper)
Payment AmEx, Bankcard, Diners,
EFTPOS, MasterCard, Visa

The Barracks Sydney

13 Palmer Lane
East Sydney NSW 2010
Phone 02/9360 5823
Fax 02/9358 4996
Email barracks@chilli.net.au
Gender Mostly men
Comfortable rooms with shared
bathrooms; continental breakfast
included in room rates. A minute's
walk to Oxford Street and venues but
in a quiet locale. Guest facilities
include a private courtyard and a TV
lounge. Gay-owned and -operated
Cost From $66 per room
Payment Bankcard, EFTPOS,
MasterCard, Visa

Chelsea Guest House

49 Womerah Ave
Darlinghurst NSW 2010
Phone 02/9380 5994
Fax 02/9332 2491
Email xchelsea@ozemail.com.au
Web www.chelsea.citysearch.com.au
Gender Mixed
Just minutes from Oxford Street, this
charming European-style guesthouse
has French provincial decor. Bathrooms
are shared, but all rooms have a hand
basin, bar fridge and TV (some with
cable). Continental breakfast, served in
the courtyard, is included in room
rates. Smoking only permitted in
outside areas. Gay-operated.
Cost $88 single, $99 double, $110
queen, $120 king

Payment AmEx, Bankcard,
MasterCard, Visa

L'otel

114 Darlinghurst Rd
Darlinghurst NSW 2010
Phone 02/9360 6868
Fax 02/9331 4536
Web www.lotel.com.au
Gender Mixed
These rooms are individually
decorated to be as modern and
comfortable as possible. The hotel is
located in the heart of Darlinghurst's
restaurant district – and its own very
good restaurant and bar occupy the
ground floor.
Cost $150–275 per room
Payment AmEx, Bankcard, Diners,
EFTPOS, MasterCard, Visa

Manor House

86 Flinders St
Darlinghurst NSW 2010
Phone 02/9380 6633
Fax 02/9380 5016
Email info@manorhouse.com.au
Web www.manorhouse.com.au
Gender Mostly men
Gay-owned and -operated, the *Manor
House* (circa 1850) has been
beautifully restored to reflect its
former glory as the residence of
Sydney's first Lord Mayor. The hotel
comprises 19 well-appointed rooms,
as well as a cocktail lounge and
wooden decks overlooking a central
courtyard, small heated pool and spa.
Very close to Oxford Street.
Cost $130–230 per room
Payment AmEx, Bankcard, Diners,
EFTPOS, MasterCard, Visa

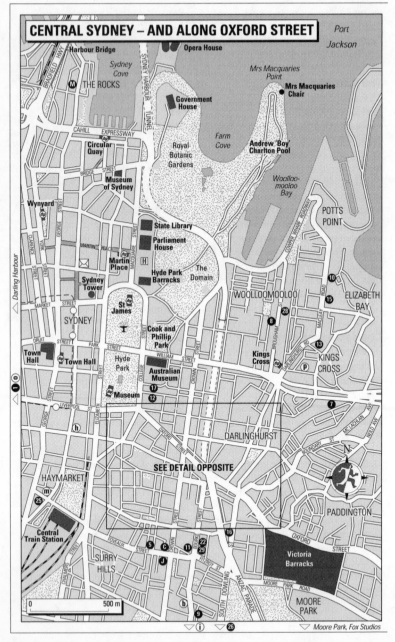

CENTRAL SYDNEY – AND ALONG OXFORD STREET

Port
Jackson

Harbour Bridge
Opera House

Sydney
Cove

BRADFIELD HWY

SYDNEY HARBOUR TUNNEL

M THE ROCKS

Mrs Macquaries
Point

Mrs Macquaries
Chair

CAHILL EXPRESSWAY

Government
House

Circular
Quay

BRIDGE STREET

Museum
of Sydney

Farm
Cove

Royal
Botanic
Gardens

Andrew 'Boy'
Charlton Pool

Woolloo-
mooloo
Bay

Wynyard

GEORGE STREET

CLARENCE STREET

YORK STREET

MARTIN PLACE

MACQUARIE STREET

State Library

Parliament
House

H

Martin
Place

Sydney
Tower

Hyde Park
Barracks

The
Domain

COWPER WHARF ROADWAY

POTTS
POINT

Darling Harbour

MARKET STREET

SYDNEY

St
James

Cook and
Phillip
Park

WOOLLOOMOOLOO

28

8

MACLEAY STREET

10

15

ELIZABETH
BAY

DRUITT STREET

Town
Hall

Town Hall

PARK STREET

Hyde
Park

WILLIAM STREET

Australian
Museum

17

Kings
Cross

BROUGHAM ST

DARLINGHURST RD

13

P

KINGS
CROSS

MCLACHLAN AVE

Museum

12

LIVERPOOL ST

7

NELL AVE

h

OXFORD STREET

DARLINGHURST

BOUNDARY ST

N

SEE DETAIL OPPOSITE

HAYMARKET

m

25

Central
Train Station

FOVEAUX STREET

CROWN STREET

5

C

11

22
29

16

FITZROY ST

PADDINGTON

Victoria
Barracks

OXFORD STREET

SURRY
HILLS

J

b

ANZAC PARADE

SOUTH DOWLING ST

MOORE PARK ROAD

MOORE
PARK

0   500 m

9

i   26   ▽ Moore Park, Fox Studios

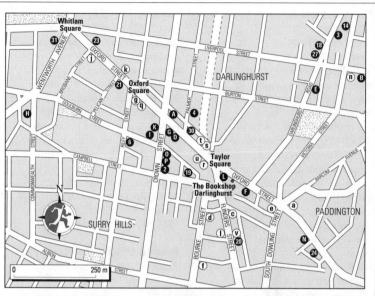

ACCOMMODATION

Aarons Hotel	1
All Seasons on Crown	2
Hotel Altamont	3
The Barracks Sydney	4
Brickfield Hill B&B	5
Cambridge Park Inn	6
Chelsea Guest House	7
Cross Court	8
Cuffs	9
De Vere Hotel	10
Governors on Fitzroy	11
Hyde Park Plaza	12
Kingsview	13
L'otel	14
Macleay Serviced Apartment Hotel	15
Manor House	16
Marriott Hotel	17
Medusa Hotel	18
Meers Serviced Apartments	19
Oasis on Flinders	20
Oxford Koala Hotel	21
Pelican Private Hotel	22
Saville Park Suites	23
Sullivans Hotel	24
Sydney Central Youth Hostel	25
Sydney Park Lodge Hotel	26
Sydney Star Accommodation	27
Victoria Court	28
Villa Private Hotel	29
Wattle Private Hotel	30
YWCA Sydney Y on the Park	31

CAFÉS & RESTAURANTS

Betty's Soup Kitchen	A
bills	B
bills 2	C
Cafe Comity	D
Govinda's	E
Green Park Diner	F
Kink	G
Longrain	H
Pablo's Vice	I
Prasits Northside	J
Roo Bar	K
Sadé	L
Sailors Thai	M
Verona Restaurant	N
Water on Sunday	O
Yipiyiyo	P

BARS & CLUBS

Albury Hotel	a
Annie's Bar	b
ARQ	c
Barracks Bar	d
Beauchamp Hotel	e
Beresford Hotel	f
Bright'n up Bar	g
Civic Hotel	h
Bar Cleveland	i
DCM	j
Exchange Hotel (Lizard Lounge & Phoenix)	k
Flinders Hotel	l
GAS	m
Green Park Hotel	n
Home	o
Icebox	p
Midnight Shift (& Shift Video Bar)	q
NV	r
Oxford Hotel (Gilligans, Gingers & Oxford Bar)	s
Palms	t
Stonewall	u
Taxi Club	v

Wynyard CityRail Underground Station

—◯— Monorail and Station

Medusa Hotel

267 Darlinghurst Rd
Darlinghurst NSW 2010
Phone 02/9331 1000
Fax 02/9380 6901
Email info@medusa.com.au
Web www.medusa.com.au
Gender Mixed
This boutique hotel combines
cutting-edge design with truly sleek
service. The rooms are glamorous and
the staff wear Armani. Built around a
tiled courtyard, the *Medusa* is a sister
hotel to the *Kirketon*, a few doors
down. For those who can't bear to
leave Fido home alone, pooch-
friendly rooms are available (ask when
booking).
Cost $270–385 per room
Payment AmEx, Bankcard, Diners,
EFTPOS, MasterCard, Visa

Oasis on Flinders

106 Flinders St
Darlinghurst NSW 2010
Phone 02/9331 8791
Fax 02/9332 2247
Email admin@oasisonflinders.com.au
Web www.oasisonflinders.com.au
Gender Men
At this gay-owned and -operated
inner-city retreat for male naturists,
year-round nudity is the order of
every day. All three rooms in the large
Victorian terrace have TVs and fans,
and one has an ensuite. There is also a
spa and sundeck.
Cost From $110 per room
Payment Bankcard, MasterCard, Visa

Oxford Koala Hotel

Cnr Oxford and Pelican streets
(enter from Pelican St)
Darlinghurst NSW 2010
Phone 02/9269 0645
Fax 02/9283 2741
Email emailsimon@oxfordkoala.
com.au
Web www.oxfordkoala.com.au
Gender Mixed
This huge hotel is popular at Mardi
Gras because it's right on Oxford
Street – guests staying during Mardi
Gras can purchase tickets to view the
parade from the hotel terrace. All
rooms have a TV and ensuite;
apartments are also available.
Cost $120–165 per room
Payment AmEx, Bankcard, Diners,
MasterCard, Visa; cheque

Pelican Private Hotel

411 Bourke St
Darlinghurst NSW 2010
Phone 02/9331 5344
Fax 02/9331 5344
Gender Mixed
One of Sydney's oldest gay-owned
and -operated guesthouses, the *Pelican*
offers relaxed and comfortable
accommodation; facilities are shared,
and there's a sundeck and courtyard.
Continental breakfast included in
tariff.
Cost From $60 per room
Payment AmEx, Bankcard, EFTPOS,
MasterCard, Visa

Saville Park Suites

16–32 Oxford St
Darlinghurst NSW 2010
Phone 02/9331 7728
Fax 02/8268 2599
Email sydney@shg.com.au
Gender Mixed
While not specifically gay or lesbian
(though it is popular with families and
larger groups), the self-contained

apartments here offer one or two bedrooms and kitchen and laundry facilities. Southside balconies are prime viewing spots for the Mardi Gras parade.

Cost $190–340 per apartment
Payment AmEx, Bankcard, Diners, MasterCard, Visa

Sydney Star Accommodation

275 Darlinghurst Rd
Darlinghurst NSW 2010
Phone 02/9232 4455 or 1800/134 455
Fax 02/9233 6399
Email stay@sydneystar.com.au
Gender Mixed

Centrally located 'home away from home'. Each room is equipped with a mini-kitchen in the manner of European pensions, and there are shared bathrooms on every floor.

Cost From $77 per room
Payment AmEx, Bankcard, Diners, MasterCard, Visa

Villa Private Hotel

413 Bourke St
Darlinghurst NSW 2010
Phone 02/9331 3602
Fax 02/9331 2101
Gender Mixed

This large Victorian house offers boutique accommodation in leafy Bourke Street, close to Taylor Square and all the Oxford Street venues. A range of rooms and suites are available, all with ensuite, TV, stereo, internet access and complimentary Aveda toiletries. There is a courtyard and library of books and CDs for guests' use. Smoking permitted in courtyard only.

Cost From $165 per room, reduced rates for longer stays
Payment AmEx, Bankcard, Diners, MasterCard, Visa

Wattle Private Hotel

Cnr Oxford and Palmer streets
Darlinghurst NSW 2010
Phone 02/9332 4118
Fax 02/9331 2074
Email wattlehotel@yahoo.com.au
Gender Mixed

Close to all the action, each room in this hotel has TV, air-conditioning, ensuite and tea and coffee making facilities. Tariff includes continental breakfast.

Cost $97 single, $105 double, $120 twin
Payment Bankcard, MasterCard, Visa

Hotel rooms in the **city centre** (including Kings Cross) are subject to a **10 per cent bed tax**, which is not included in the rates shown here; hostels are exempt from the tax.

KINGS CROSS AND POTTS POINT

Cross Court

203 Brougham St
Kings Cross NSW 2011
Phone 02/9368 1822
Fax 02/9358 2595
Email res@crosscourthotel.com.au
Web www.crosscourthotel.com.au
Gender Mixed

Pension-style hotel offering a range of affordable rooms and suites in a very convenient, central location. All rooms have bar fridge, TV, queen-size beds and modern decor, and some have city views. No smoking. Gay-owned and -operated.
Cost From $65 single, $75 double, $115 suite; special weekly rates
Payment AmEx, Bankcard, MasterCard, Visa

De Vere Hotel

44 Macleay St
Potts Point NSW 2011
Phone 02/9358 1211 or freecall 1800/818 790
Fax 02/9358 4685
Email info@devere.com.au
Web www.devere.com.au
Gender Mixed
Bright, clean ensuite rooms or self-contained studios in a very handsome part of Sydney and only 10 minutes' walk from Oxford Street. All rooms have air-conditioning, TV, hairdryer. Breakfast included.
Cost From $105 per room, $130 for studio ($30 extra for third person in same room)
Payment AmEx, Bankcard, Diners, MasterCard, Visa

Kingsview

30 Darlinghurst Rd
Kings Cross NSW 2011
Phone 02/9358 5599
Fax 02/9357 3185
Email kingsyd@fc.hotel.com.av
Gender Mixed
Budget motel-style accommodation in the heart of the nightlife district.

All rooms have a bathroom, and parking is available for $10 extra.
Cost From $80 per room
Payment AmEx, Bankcard, Diners, MasterCard, Visa

Macleay Serviced Apartment Hotel

28 Macleay St
Potts Point NSW 2011
Phone 02/9358 2400
Fax 02/9357 7233
Email macleay@nectar.com.au
Web www.themacleay.com
Gender Mixed
Fully self-contained studio apartments, many with harbour views. Clean, well-appointed and freshly renovated. Breakfast available.
Cost $130–150 per apartment
Payment AmEx, Bankcard, Diners, EFTPOS, MasterCard, Visa

Victoria Court

122 Victoria St
Potts Point NSW 2011
Phone 02/9357 3200
Fax 02/9357 7606
Email info@victoriacourt.com.au
Web www.victoriacourt.com.au
Gender Mixed
A Victorian-style hotel offering a range of rooms from basic to luxury, all with a continental breakfast included. All rooms have ensuites, TV, air-conditioning. A lounge and courtyard are available for guests' use. No smoking is permitted in public areas.
Cost $105–275 per room
Payment AmEx, Bankcard, Diners, MasterCard, Visa

SURRY HILLS AND PADDINGTON

Brickfield Hill B&B

403 Riley St
Surry Hills NSW 2010
Phone 02/9211 4886
Fax 02/9212 2556
Email fields@zip.com.au
Web www.zip.com.au/~fields
Gender Mostly men
Elegant gay-owned and -operated
guesthouse in a restored terrace six
minutes' walk from Oxford Street.
Rooms have Victorian decor, with
four-poster beds; some have an ensuite
and all have TV and hairdryer. The
communal drawing room has a phone,
library, piano and CD selection, and
there is also a shared dining room and
balcony. Full breakfast is included in
the tariff, and afternoon tea is
available. Smoking outside only.
Cost From $105 single, $155 double
Payment Bankcard, MasterCard, Visa

Cambridge Park Inn

212 Riley St
Surry Hills NSW 2010
Phone 02/9212 1111
Fax 02/9281 1981
Email campi@mira.net
Web www.parkplaza.com.au
Gender Mixed
This pleasant modern hotel, just off
Oxford Street's main drag, is a popular
conference venue. All rooms have an
ensuite and TV; facilities include a
bar, restaurant, pool, sauna and gym.
Cost From $148 per room,
$170 per suite
Payment AmEx, Bankcard, Diners,
EFTPOS, MasterCard, Visa

Cuffs

524 Bourke St
Surry Hills NSW 2010
Phone 02/9380 5037 (Peter)
Email cuffs@starrworld.net
Web www.cuffs.com.au
Gender Male
Cuffs offers casual, comfortable
accommodation to guys who are into
bondage. Equipment is available to
guests. Shared bathrooms and guest
lounge and continental breakfast
included. They also offer contacts and
information for visitors keen to
participate in the SM scene.
Cost $80 single, $120 double
(discount for longer stays)
Payment Cash or cheque

Governors on Fitzroy

64 Fitzroy St
Surry Hills NSW 2010
Phone 02/9331 4652
Fax 02/9361 5094
Email governor@zip.com.au
Web www.governor.zip.com.au
Gender Mostly men
Only a two-minute walk from
Oxford Street, this guesthouse has
been serving the gay and lesbian
visitor to Sydney since 1987.
Bathroom facilities are shared, but
rooms are spacious, comfortable and
equipped with hand basins. Tariff
includes full breakfast. There is a
courtyard and spa, and smoking is
permitted in outside areas only.
Cost $85 single, $110 double
Payment AmEx, Bankcard, Diners,
EFTPOS, MasterCard, Visa

Meers Serviced Apartments

103/200 Campbell St
Surry Hills NSW 2010
Phone 02/9361 4220
Fax 02/9361 4220
Gender Mixed
Right on Taylor Square, these gay-owned and -operated, fully self-contained studio apartments come with dishwasher, laundry facilities, TV and CD player, and the complex has a gym and pool. Smoking permitted outside only.
Cost $125 per apartment (weekly discounts available)
Payment Bankcard, MasterCard, Visa

Sullivans Hotel

21 Oxford St
Paddington NSW 2021
Phone 02/9361 0211
Fax 02/9360 3735
Email sydney@sullivans.com.au
Web www.sullivans.com.au
Gender Mixed
Sullivans is a boutique hotel with a swimming pool and courtyard. All rooms have modern decor, ensuites and free in-house movies. Room safes, modem connections, undercover security parking and free use of bicycles are also available. Breakfast can be taken at *Sullivans* café, which is attached to the hotel. Buses to the city stop outside the door.
Cost $128–145 per room
Payment AmEx, Bankcard, Diners, EFTPOS, MasterCard, Visa

Sydney Park Lodge Hotel

747 South Dowling St
Moore Park NSW 2016
Phone 02/9318 2393
Fax 02/9318 2513
Email pklodge@parklodgehotel.com
Web www.parklodgesydney.com
Gender Mixed
This friendly, gay-owned and -operated, 20-room boutique hotel offers stylish traditional surroundings with modern bathrooms. It is located within easy walking distance of Oxford Street.
Cost $80–198 per room
Payment AmEx, Bankcard, Diners, EFTPOS, MasterCard, Visa

EASTERN BEACHES

Coogee Sands Apartments

161 Dolphin St
Coogee NSW 2034
Phone 02/9665 8588 or freecall
1800/819 403
Fax 02/9664 1406
Email info@coogeesands.com.au
Web www.coogeesands.com.au
Gender Mixed
Modern boutique accommodation with sundeck directly overlooking the beach. Studio and one-bedroom apartments come with kitchen facilities and ocean views, and there are plenty of restaurants and cafés nearby. Romantic weekend packages or Mardi Gras recovery packages are available, as are room-service breakfasts.
Cost From $170 per room
Payment AmEx, Bankcard, Diners, MasterCard, Visa

INNER WEST

Sojourners Sydney

PO Box 250
Enmore NSW 2042
Phone 02/9516 3221
Fax 02/9516 3221
Email sjnrsyd@hotmail.com
Gender Mostly women

Peaceful renovated home offering a welcoming, smoke- and drug-free environment to women of diverse cultural backgrounds. Spacious double rooms with high ceilings and fully equipped kitchen are available for stays of a few days or a year. Newtown station is four minutes' walk away, and the location is handy for Sydney University. There is a shared laundry and garden. Spanish, German and French are spoken. Children are welcome.

Cost From $130 per room (considerable reductions for longer stays)
Payment Cheque

Flatshare agencies

If you plan to stay in Sydney long-term, or find you just can't tear yourself away, do yourself a favour and find a queer-friendly flatshare.

Share-A-Home

Address on enquiry
Phone 02/9267 9824
Email sharemates@bigpond.com
Web www.gayshare.xrs.net
Gender Mixed

In operation for 10 years, *Share-A-Home* offers a matching service for share-seekers and tenants, with all interviewing done by the agency. Clients may remain on books for up to six months.
Open Mon–Sat 10am–6.30pm
Cost on enquiry
Payment AmEx, Bankcard, MasterCard, Visa

Sharespace

Level 1 263 Oxford St, Darlinghurst NSW 2010
Phone 02/9360 7744   **Fax** 02/9361 3729
Email service@sharespace.com.au
Web www.sharespace.com.au
Gender Mixed

Gay/lesbian share accommodation service for medium-term visitors and permanent residence-seekers. Using profiles of households and accommodation-seekers, *Sharespace* matches prospective tenants to compatible households or flatmates.

Open Mon–Fri 10am–6pm, Sat 10am–3pm

Cost $75 for those seeking or offering accommodation within inner-city suburbs, $55 outside central area; student discount available

Payment AmEx, Bankcard, Diners, EFTPOS, MasterCard, Visa; cheque

CAFÉS AND RESTAURANTS

You'll never go hungry or short of caffeine in Sydney. In the major **'eat streets'** every shopfront seems to be a restaurant or café – and everywhere from book superstores to the local supermarket and the swimming pool seems to have an **espresso** machine. Faced with such abundance, not to mention the fickle and fleeting nature of the Sydney dining scene, we've limited our selection to gay/lesbian-operated or -frequented cafés and restaurants. Never fear: within hours of arriving, you'll be inundated with recommendations for the coolest cafés and most happening restaurants.

CITY CENTRE

Sailors Thai

106 George St, The Rocks
Sydney NSW 2000
Phone 02/9251 2466
Fax 02/9251 2610

One of Sydney's most famous Thai restaurants, *Sailors Thai* offers elegance, excellent service and a post-modern Thai culinary experience. Choose between the exotic, sophisticated flavours of Royal Thai cuisine in the downstairs restaurant or more casual dining upstairs in the canteen, where traditional hawker-style food is served to diners seated at a long stainless-steel table. Restaurant specialities include miang parcels with crispy trout, shallots, chilis and palm sugar sauce or aromatic curry of roast duck and sweet potato accompanied by papaya relish.

Open Restaurant Mon–Fri noon–2pm & Mon–Sat 6pm–10pm; canteen daily noon–8pm

Cost $45 per person in restaurant, $25 in canteen (both licensed, no BYO)

Payment AmEx, Bankcard, Diners, EFTPOS, MasterCard, Visa

DARLINGHURST

Betty's Soup Kitchen

84 Oxford St
Darlinghurst NSW 2010
Phone 02/9360 9698
Frequented by an arty, studenty crowd, this cosy BYO diner offers hearty food with a serve-yourself salad bar; it's a sure place for the budget-conscious to get their money's worth. Street-level access for wheelchairs.
Open Daily noon–11pm
Cost $5–10
Payment Cash only

bills

433 Liverpool St
Darlinghurst NSW 2010
Phone 02/9360 9631
bills is a fresh, bright BYO café set back from the Darlinghurst chaos and is a superb daytime spot, serving all sorts of delicious breakfast and lunch dishes. Street-level access for wheelchairs.
Open Mon–Sat 7.30am–4pm
Cost $10–20 per person
Payment AmEx, Bankcard, Diners, MasterCard, Visa

Café Comity

139 Oxford St
Darlinghurst NSW 2010
Phone 02/9331 2424
Fax 02/9332 3014
Web www.eatme.com.au
Café Comity is one of the better café/restaurants in Oxford Street, and a great place for watching the passing parade. There's a full breakfast menu all day, as well as a main menu with daily specials. Popular dishes include crispy salmon fillet with roasted capsicum, beans, pesto sauce and ragged potatoes, or chargrilled kangaroo fillet with baby eggplant, haloumi cheese, sweet potato chips and red wine sauce. Home-made desserts and coffee are also on the bill. *Comity* is fully licensed and you are free to drink there without ordering food.
Open Daily 10am–3am
Cost $10–20 per person
Payment AmEx, Bankcard, MasterCard, Visa

Govinda's

112 Darlinghurst Rd
Darlinghurst NSW 2010
Phone 02/9380 5155
Fax 02/9360 1736
Email jaxa@ozemail.com.au
Web www.citysearch.com.au/syd/govindas
This remarkable Hare Krishna-owned establishment offers a dinner and movie package every night of the week. The movies are generally art-house or cult films and the vegetarian food is simple, tasty and great value. A night at *Govinda's* gives you 'supper and a show' for less than $15.
Open Daily 6pm–11pm
Cost $10.90 per person for dinner, $14.90 dinner and movie
Payment AmEx, Bankcard, Diners, MasterCard, Visa

Green Park Diner

219 Oxford St
Darlinghurst NSW 2010
Phone 02/9361 6171
This BYO café has stood the test of time and doubles as a gallery for local artists. A good, casual, open and airy

café for a quick meal or coffee and cake. Open to the street for easy wheelchair access.

Open Mon–Fri 10.30am–11pm, Sat & Sun 9.30am–midnight
Cost $10–15 per person
Payment AmEx, Bankcard, Diners, MasterCard, Visa

Kink

137 Oxford St
Darlinghurst NSW 2010
Phone 02/9380 6949

Popular indoor/outdoor café that attracts a groovy crowd and makes another great vantage point to witness the passing parade from. Serves breakfast, lunch and dinner (fully licensed).

Open Daily early–late
Cost $10–20 per person
Payment Bankcard, MasterCard, Visa

Pablo's Vice

Cnr Crown and Goulburn streets, Darlinghurst NSW 2010
Phone 02/9332 3047

Damn fine coffee – probably the best in the Oxford Street area. Good breakfasts and lunch at this altogether groovy little nook.

Open Mon–Sat 7.30am–6pm
Cost $6–10 per person

Roo Bar

253 Crown St
Darlinghurst NSW 2010
Phone 02/9361 5846

Very popular with the hip gay men and dykes, *Roo Bar* is always full of tattoos, piercings and great bodies. A good range of freshly squeezed juices,

snacks and decent coffee is served.
Open Daily 8am–6pm
Cost $7–12 per person

Sadé

191 Oxford St
Darlinghurst NSW 2010
Phone 02/9331 1818
Fax 02/9331 0555
Web www.sade.com.au

Sadé is the most central gay café, located on Taylor Square. It is fully licensed and offers lots of fresh innovative modern Australian dishes featuring pastas, seafood and a host of specials and desserts. The breakfast menu is also interesting, featuring free-range eggs.

Open Mon–Thurs 8am–1am, Fri–Sun 8am–3am
Cost Breakfast $10–15, lunch $15–20, dinner $30–40
Payment AmEx, Bankcard, MasterCard, Visa

Yipiyiyo

290 Crown St
Darlinghurst NSW 2010
Phone 02/9332 3114

Mexican/Greek fusion food takes the flavours way beyond tacos and keeps many loyal diners coming back. Popular for group meals, this place is BYO and reasonably priced. Specialities include Atlantic salmon and rocket spring rolls and quesadilla with chili king-prawn, basil, cheese and tomato.

Open Daily 6.30pm–10pm (or later)
Cost $20–30 per person
Payment AmEx, Bankcard, MasterCard, Visa

SURRY HILLS AND PADDINGTON

bills 2

359 Crown St
Surry Hills NSW 2010
Phone 02/9360 4762

This stylish, modern, BYO café serves the best breakfasts in town and while it is a little more expensive than others in the area it is a great escape from some of the more tawdry dives on Oxford Street. The second of Bill Grainger's restaurants, this one is open for all meals and is highly recommended – if you can get a table (get there before 10am on weekends and you'll have a much better chance). The ricotta hotcakes are exquisite and addictive. Street-level access for wheelchairs.
Open Mon–Sat 7am–10pm, Sun 7am–4pm
Cost $10–20 per person
Payment AmEx, Bankcard, MasterCard, Visa

Longrain

85 Commonwealth St
Surry Hills NSW 2010
Phone 02/9280 2888
Fax 02/9280 2887

One of Sydney's most fashionable restaurant/bars, with a stark, modern interior and three huge communal dining tables. The dishes are inspired, drawing on the entire spectrum of Asian culinary traditions. The kitchen uses really fresh produce, and it shows – try their betel leaf appetizers or salt and pepper calamari. The bar's speciality is a delicious and rather lethal concoction of crushed limes, sugar and vodka (at least 3 standard measures to each drink – you'd better believe it!). Smoking in bar areas only.
Open Tues–Fri noon–3pm & Tues–Sun 6pm–late
Cost Lunch from $20 per person, dinner from $30
Payment AmEx, Bankcard, Diners, MasterCard, Visa

Prasits Northside

415 Crown St, Surry Hills
Surry Hills NSW 2010
Phone 02/9319 0748 or 02/9332 1792

There are many great Thai restaurants, but few match *Prasits* for innovation and mouth-watering spiciness. Eat in at the restaurant or head up the road to number 395 (both BYO), where you can perch at a table or get take out. Be prepared to like it hot.
Open lunch Thurs–Fri noon–3pm, dinner Mon–Sat 6pm–11pm
Cost From $15 per person in takeaway, $35 in restaurant
Payment AmEx, Bankcard, Diners, MasterCard, Visa

Verona Restaurant

17 Oxford St
Paddington NSW 2021
Phone 02/9360 3266
Fax 02/9360 9933

Very smart bar and restaurant situated in one of Sydney's best art-house cinema complexes. A great place for a stylish nosh-up or just a coffee and a drink, the *Verona* is situated at the smarter Paddington end of Oxford Street. Fully licensed.

Open Daily noon–late
Cost $15–30 per person
Payment AmEx, Bankcard, Diners,
MasterCard, Visa

Water on Sunday
312 Crown St
Surry Hills NSW 2010
Phone 02/9361 6965
Fax 02/9361 6965
Very reasonably priced, gay-owned

and -operated BYO restaurant that's
perfect for an intimate dinner.
Modern Australian menu includes
seared kangaroo with a beetroot relish
and some wicked desserts including
Belgian-chocolate mousse with a
raspberry coulis. Party rooms available.
Open Tues–Sun 6.30pm–late
Cost $20–30 per person
Payment AmEx, Bankcard, Diners,
MasterCard, Visa

EASTERN BEACHES

Café Momento
479 Bronte Rd
Bronte NSW 2024
Phone 02/9389 1613
Fax 02/9389 1613
This gay-owned and -operated café
overlooking Bronte Beach has
outdoor tables, beach views and an

all-day breakfast. Breakfast consists of
home-made muesli, full cooked
breakfast and fresh juices. Lunch is
pasta, wraps, vegan burgers, rissottos
and salads.
Open Daily 7am–early evening
Cost $10–15 per person
Payment Bankcard, MasterCard, Visa

INNER WEST

Bacigalupo
284 King St
Newtown NSW 2042
Phone 02/9565 5238
Opposite the Dendy cinema, this
Italian café is a glamorous place to
watch the passing parade. Good-
looking crowd, with food to match.
Disabled facilities.
Open Mon 8am–5pm, Tues–Sun
8am–10.30pm
Cost $10–20 per person

Inside-Out on King
232 King St
Newtown NSW 2042
Phone 02/9517 1556

Fax 02/9517 1556
A glossy café/restaurant with good
buzz factor. Scrummy blackboard
specials and great burgers. Food
served until late into the night.
Open Mon & Wed–Sun 8am–late,
Tues 8am–6pm
Cost $10–20 per person
Payment AmEx, Bankcard, EFTPOS,
MasterCard, Visa

Linda's Backstage
174 King St, rear of Newtown Hotel
(enter from Watkin St)
Newtown NSW 2042
Phone 02/9550 6015
Fully licensed pub restaurant, serving

modern Australian food and always providing an entertaining experience. Disabled facilities.

Open Tues–Sat 6pm–late,
Sun noon–3pm
Cost $10–20 per person
Payment AmEx, Bankcard,
MasterCard, Visa

Thai Pothong
294 King St
Newtown NSW 2042
Phone 02/9550 6277
Fax 02/9519 8050

Email thaipothong@bigpond.com.au
Web www.thaipothong.com.au
Gay and lesbian staff and clientele, plus generous portions and glamorous surroundings, raise this restauraunt (licensed and BYO) above the usual local-Thai scene. Daily specials and the grill items are particularly popular. Disabled access.

Open Sun–Thurs 6.30pm–10.30pm,
Fri–Sat 6pm–11pm
Cost $15–25 per person
Payment AmEx, Bankcard, Diners,
EFTPOS, MasterCard, Visa

BARS AND CLUBS

Before you set off to prowl the jungle of Sydney's bar scene, here are a few pointers. The best **mixed bars** are *ARQ*, *Stonewall*, *Gilligans*, the *Albury*, the *Beresford* and the *Imperial*. The most popular **girls' nights** are 'Milkbar' at the *Icebox* and 'Spicy Friday' at the *Lansdowne* – both on Fridays (strictly speaking, both are mixed, but there tends to be more girls than boys). The most popular **boy bars** are the *Beauchamp*, *Midnight Shift*, the *Newtown Hotel*, the *Oxford Bar*, the *Flinders Hotel*, and the exclusively men-only *Barracks*.

For hot nights of dancing and clubbing, look out for 'Hey Homo', Sunday nights at *Home*, *ARQ*, *Gas* and any party nights called 'Frisky' or 'Ffierce'. Sydney has a huge mobile **dance-party scene** and you can guarantee if there's a big gay/lesbian party in town one of these groups will stage a recovery somewhere. *Capital Q* and *Sydney Star Observer* always have plenty of ads for these big nights.

CITY CENTRE

Civic Hotel
Cnr Goulburn and Pitt streets
Sydney NSW 2000
Phone 02/8267 3186
Gender Mixed

Comfortably mixed pub that's also host to some very groovy gay/lesbian nights – 'Lush Velour' on Sundays and 'Club Continental' on Saturdays. Very popular with the more sophisticated

crowd. Check papers for special events.
Open Daily 5pm–late
Admission Mostly free; cover charge
applies on weekend nights
Payment EFTPOS

GAS

477 Pitt St
Haymarket NSW 2000
Phone 02/9211 8777 – for cabaret
bookings only
Gender Mixed
Loads of well-seasoned party boys,
baby dykes and straight friends
flock to this cavernous and groovy
dance bar, which is set on two levels
in the basement of an office building,
opposite Central Station. Sunday is
the popular queer night at this club,
with plenty of guest DJs. *Bohem*
restaurant, part of the same complex,
also hosts the popular Le Club
Cabaret on Sundays.
Open Sun 9pm–late, Sun cabaret
from 6pm

Admission Cover charge may apply
later in the evening or for special
events; cabaret free
Payment Cash only

Home

Cockle Bay Wharf
Sydney NSW 2000
Phone 02/266 0600 or 02/9267 0674
Email homesexual@bigbeat.com.au
Web www.homecorp.com
Sydney's biggest and most amazing
dance venue is on several levels, with
a large dancefloor, lots of hiding
places, a balcony overlooking Darling
Harbour and incredibly designed
toilets! It attracts a young and
fashionable crowd – straight on
Saturday, more gay on Sunday. The
first Friday of every month is 'Hey
Homo' (11pm–6am).
Open Sun 8pm–7am
Admission Up to $20, depending
on the night
Payment Cash only

DARLINGHURST AND KINGS CROSS

ARQ

16 Flinders St
Darlinghurst NSW 2010
Phone 02/9380 8700
Fax 02/9380 8711
Email ray@arqsydney.com.au
Web www.arqsydney.com.au
Gender Mixed
Sydney's coolest 'super club' hosts
cocktails after 5pm and then works its
way into the night as one of the
funkiest dance spots in town. Spread
over two floors, *ARQ* offers full-on
dance upstairs and smoother grooves

downstairs, with lots of chill-out
couches and neat little conversation
nooks. They host girls' nights and
boys' nights, though there is no
exclusive door policy. Admission is
charged on Friday, Saturday and
Sunday; there is often a queue after
11.30pm, so the earlier you get there
the quicker you'll get in.
Open Tues–Sun 5pm–late
Admission $10–15 Fri–Sun; cover
charge may apply for special events
Payment AmEx, Bankcard, EFTPOS,
MasterCard, Visa

Beauchamp Hotel

267 Oxford St
Darlinghurst NSW 2010
Phone 02/9331 2575
Gender Mostly men

Very popular on Sundays and over the summer months, when drinkers spill out onto the street, *Beauchamp* (pronounced 'Beecham') is an easygoing, friendly pub for gay men of all types and ages. Drawing a real mixed bunch – from young men to 'gay pioneers' – this is a place to drink beer and bop on the spot: an essential Sydney experience. And if the music and smoke start to get to you, you can always head for the dark little cave of the Base Bar downstairs.

Open Sun–Wed noon–midnight;
Thurs–Sat noon–1am
Admission Free
Payment AmEx, Bankcard, Diners, EFTPOS, MasterCard, Visa

Bright'n up Bar

Upstairs, 77 Oxford St
Darlinghurst NSW 2010
Phone 02/9360 3125
Gender Mixed

Lots of retro dance faves and crazy cabaret goes down in this refurbished, pleasant and friendly cocktail bar with a small dancefloor. Speciality Fridays alternate between 'Toast' (gay and lesbian, but especially lesbian) and 'Rainbow Room', an evening for gay and lesbian Asians and their friends.

Open Wed–Sat 9pm–late
Admission Free
Payment Cash only

DCM

33 Oxford St
Darlinghurst NSW 2010
Phone 02/9267 7036
Fax 02/9267 2691
Email sue@dcm.com
Gender Mixed

DCM specializes in muscles, bigger muscles and designer labels – the look is gym-honed, young and pumped. Huge gay and straight crowds Friday to Sunday and a long queue on Saturdays, all clamouring to get at the three bars and onto the dancefloor and podiums.

Open Fri–Sun 11pm–late
Admission Varies
Payment EFTPOS

Gilligans/Gingers

Upstairs, Oxford Hotel, 134 Oxford St
Darlinghurst NSW 2010
Phone 02/9331 3467
Fax 02/9331 3566
Gender Mixed

Hang-out of 'the beautiful poofs and dykes' – and a favourite meeting place for 'fashionable friends', beautiful bods

Peter J. Mark

and the A-list – *Gilligans* is a Sydney institution. The name refers to 'Gilligan's Island', the patch of grass with palm trees in the middle of Taylor Square, opposite the hotel. They definitely make the best cocktails in Oxford Street and after a couple you'll find yourself chatting away to some gorgeous creature and daring yourself to have another. For an even more glamorous experience head upstairs to *Gingers* on the top floor.
Open Sun–Tues 5pm–midnight, Wed–Thurs 5pm–1am, Fri–Sat 5pm–2am; happy hour 5pm–7pm
Admission Free
Payment AmEx, Bankcard, Diners, MasterCard, Visa

Green Park Hotel

360 Victoria St (cnr Liverpool St)
Darlinghurst NSW 2010
Phone 02/9380 5311
Gender Mixed
Not technically a gay or lesbian pub, but a very relaxed mix, the *Green Park Hotel* is one of those truly civilized Darlinghurst locals that attracts sophisticates and bohemians alike. Pool tables included, of course.
Open Mon–Sat 10am–1am, Sun 10am–midnight
Admission Free
Payment Bankcard, EFTPOS, MasterCard, Visa

Icebox

2 Kellet St
Kings Cross NSW 2011
Phone 02/9331 0058
Fax 02/9331 0065
Email theiceboxnightclub@ bigpond.com.au

Gender Mixed
A hip, easygoing queer club with a good 50/50 mix of lesbians and gays. This chi-chi spot pushes camp to a higher altitude; lots of hip chicks, groovy boys and aging glamour pusses. Very Armistead Maupin, with loads of disco and handbag. Friday nights are called 'Milkbar' and Saturday nights 'Fishtank'.
Open Fri 9pm–late, Sat 9pm–late
Admission $5
Payment Cash only

Lizard Lounge

Upstairs, Exchange Hotel, 34 Oxford St
Darlinghurst NSW 2010
Phone 02/9331 1936
Fax 02/9360 9704
Gender Mixed
A great place for after-work drinks and socializing, this is popular with the arty crowd, but very straight on Friday and Saturday nights.
Open Daily noon–late (happy hour 5pm–8pm)
Admission Cover charge may apply later
Payment AmEx, Bankcard, EFTPOS, MasterCard, Visa

Midnight Shift

Upstairs, 85 Oxford St
Darlinghurst NSW 2010
Phone 02/9360 4319
Fax 02/9332 3887
Email midnightshift@bigpond.com
Gender Mostly men
A favourite with the shirt-off, whistle-blowing dance queens, this is one of Sydney's oldest gay clubs. It's a place for a boys' night out and is a real dance temple with a fully equipped cocktail

lounge. There's a show on Thursdays and 'Boys Own' every Saturday night.
Open Thurs 10pm–late, Fri 11pm–dawn, Sat midnight–dawn, Sun 10pm–dawn
Admission $10–15 Saturdays only
Payment Cash only

NV
163 Oxford St
Darlinghurst NSW 2010
Phone 02/9360 5666
Fax 02/9360 6955
Email nvclub@ozemail.com.au
Web www.nv.com.au
Gender Mixed
Thursday and Sunday at *NV* are most popular with gay men and lesbians: Sunday night is OUT, which is very popular with 'party girls'. *NV* offers lots of special nights, guest DJs and a boppy crowd. Memberships are available and give reduced admission.
Open Wed–Sun 9pm–late
Admission $5–20, depending on night
Payment AmEx, Bankcard, Diners, EFTPOS, MasterCard, Visa

Oxford Bar
134 Oxford St
Darlinghurst NSW 2010
Phone 02/9331 3467
Fax 02/9331 3566
Gender Mostly men
Cruisey bar right on Taylor Square, with DJ and flashing lights. Find a corner or circulate. Wheelchair access.
Open Mon–Tues 4pm–midnight, Wed–Thurs 4pm–1am, Fri–Sat 4pm–2am, Sun 4pm–midnight
Admission Free
Payment AmEx, Bankcard, Diners, MasterCard, Visa

Palms
Downstairs, 124 Oxford St,
Darlinghurst NSW 2010
Phone 02/9357 4166
Fax 02/9357 4167
Gender Mixed
Palms offers an intimate environment with booths and a dancefloor, and holds regular talent nights for would-be stars. The nightclub and cabaret offer drag and live entertainment most nights to a mixed crowd of gays, lesbians and friends.
Open Daily 8pm–3am (closed Mon & Tues in winter)
Payment EFTPOS

Phoenix
Basement, Exchange Hotel, 34 Oxford St
Darlinghurst NSW 2010
Phone 02/9331 1936
Fax 02/9360 9704
Gender Mostly men
This downstairs bar can get very crowded but it's always a lively scene full of party people. Crisco Kitchen is a popular mens' night – use your imagination. Sunday recoveries are in fact an opportunity to do *anything but* recover.
Open Wed–Sun 10pm–late; also Sun 11am for recovery party
Admission Free
Payment AmEx, Bankcard, EFTPOS, MasterCard, Visa

Shift Video Bar
85 Oxford St
Darlinghurst NSW 2010
Phone 02/9360 4319
Fax 02/9332 3887
Email midnightshift@bigpond.com
Gender Mostly men

The main bar offers thumping music, drinks and gaming machines, while the Locker Room has pool tables and competitions. A good cruisey bar that's open until very late most nights and is popular with men of all ages and scenes.

Open Mon–Fri noon–late,
Sat noon–6am, Sun noon–5am
Admission Free
Payment Cash only

Stonewall

175 Oxford St
Darlinghurst NSW 2010
Phone 02/9360 1963
Fax 02/9331 4733
Gender Mixed
Stonewall offers three separate floors

of fun. At street level it's a friendly walk-in bar, upstairs is a cosy cocktail lounge and the top floor is the dance floor, where the DJs play good commercial dance. The ground floor has a lunchtime bistro and opens onto the street, which makes it very nice for getting some fresh air on Sydney's more humid summer evenings. Mostly men fill the street-level bar, but the cocktail bar and dance club are quite mixed most nights; popular with lesbians on Thursday nights.

Open Daily noon–5am
Admission Cover charge upstairs some nights
Payment AmEx, Bankcard, Diners, EFTPOS, MasterCard, Visa

SURRY HILLS AND PADDINGTON

Albury Hotel

6 Oxford St
Paddington NSW 2011
Phone 02/9361 6555
Fax 02/9361 6669
Gender Mixed

This famous gay icon is a must to visit while you're in Sydney – you just never know what will be happening in there. The *Albury* occupies the most fantastic Art Deco building: there are drag shows every night in the main bar (which also has an ATM in case you get caught short); and the back bar has a cocktail lounge with live singers and DJs. Although mostly gay, the *Albury* is popular with the young crowd and attracts straight tourists.

Open Mon–Thurs 2pm–1am,
Fri–Sat 2pm–2am, Sun 2pm–midnight;

cocktail lounge daily from 6.30pm
Admission Free
Payment Cash only

Annie's Bar

Rear of Carrington Hotel
Cnr Bourke and Arthur streets
Surry Hills NSW 2010
Phone 02/9360 4714
Gender Mixed

Drag shows most nights – Sydney's best – attract a comfortable, kooky crowd. Reminiscent of 1980s discos, this venue makes a fun escape from Oxford Street. Weekend recoveries and day parties are specialities.

Open Mon 8am–noon,
Thurs 7am–midnight, Fri 8am–1pm,
Sat 7am–noon, Sun 10am–midnight
Admission Free
Payment EFTPOS

Sydney's Drag Queens

Sydney is a city famous for many things and many people. Its glamorous harbour, the razzle-dazzle and tawdriness of Kings Cross and – let's get down to brass tacks – its drag queens.

Am I daring to declare that Sydney boasts the most magnificent drag queens in the world? That before, during and after the phenomenon that was *The Adventures of Priscilla, Queen of the Desert*, these gals were entertaining audiences (often for lousy amounts of loot), perfecting their art, giving their all and generally celebrating their spillage of sheer talent by presenting each other with

Peter J. Mark

glittering gold statuettes at a star-studded evening known as the Diva Awards? Yes, I am – and I oughta know.

As the editor of *Showgirls*, a photographic column devoted to all matters drag in Sydney's *Capital Q* weekly, I've come across (not literally, mind you) most of the Emerald City's premier drag. I now offer you a guided tour of some of the showgirls you really shouldn't miss while visiting Sydney Town.

Firstly of course, there are the legends. And what becomes a legend most? Feathers! You'll find them all over the magnificent **Carlotta**, star of the original Les Girls. Carlotta was Australia's first sex change – a timeless celebrity and currently the star of Australian television's 'Beauty and the Beast', as well as doing numbers all over town too. She's like that.

Peter J. Mark

Then there's the red-headed charms of the buxom and bawdy broad, **Robyn Lee Squint**. One more drink and you're watching Ann-Margret. You'll often find her in cahoots with the acid-tongued and beautifully coiffed **Simone Troy**, whose name is whispered in even the highest of circles. **Monique St John** (is that Raquel Welch?) is always a thrill, as is **Carmen**; when she 'Begins the Beguine', you know about it.

Then we have what some refer to as the **Robo Drags**. It's because these showstoppers can dance in unison, in matching costumes. Names like Trudi Valentine, Wyness Mongrel-Bitch, Amelia Airhead and Mitzi MacIntosh pop into my fevered mind.

Sydney is also home of the 'personality drag': unique performers with microphone in hand are favourites. **Vanessa Wagner** is the grrrl you just can't ignore; she's a dose of tough love who at the end of the day knows what's good for you. You be good to Vanessa and Vanessa'll be good to you! Her face (and hairy bikini-clad body) crops up all over the place, even in the straight press. Other personality drags include **Claire de Lune**, who is as French as her name, and the lovely **Chelsea Bun**, who runs a wildly successful drag emporium called the House of Priscilla when she's not selling it on stage at *Annie's Bar* or hosting karaoke at the *Stonewall Hotel*. You gotta love Chelsea.

Peter J. Mark

I do have favourites of my own – after all, I'm only human. **Victoria Bitter**, for instance, sports a great set of legs and only sings live. **Black Eena** and **Maria Misere** complement each other fabulously on keyboards and violin. **Portia Turbo** and **Tess Tickle** I simply will not do without. **Polly Petrie** deserves an honourable mention for starting off many of these beauties at Pollie's Follies on Sunday nights at the *Albury Hotel*, which is always chockers! **Maude Boate** can only be described as Disney on acid and **Verushka Darling** brings out the Faye Dunaway in Joan Crawford.

So many names, so little time. How can you lose?

Lance St Leopard

Bar Cleveland

Cnr Bourke and Cleveland streets
Surry Hills NSW 2010
Phone 02/9698 1908
Gender Mixed
A rotating roster of queer DJs on Friday,
Saturday and Sunday nights pulls a great
mixed crowd of the young and the hip.
Great cocktail lounge with pool tables
and comps. Disabled facilities
downstairs.
Open Daily; check papers for special
events and opening times
Admission Free
Payment AmEx, Bankcard, Diners,
EFTPOS, MasterCard, Visa

Barracks Bar

Cnr Bourke and Flinders streets
(enter from Patterson Lane at rear)
Surry Hills NSW 2010
Phone 02/9360 6373
Gender Men
Popular with all types of gay men –
especially leather men of all ages,
bears, Levis boots, etc – this bar is a
true 'dungeon experience', with pool
tables and competitions, peanuts in
troughs and wall-to-wall men.
Upstairs has a dancefloor with guest
DJs, and a *little* more light.
Open Varies: usually Mon–Sat
5pm–3am, Sun noon–1am
Admission Free
Payment Cash only

Beresford Hotel ('The Laneway')

354 Bourke St
Surry Hills NSW 2010
Phone 02/9331 1045
Gender Mixed
A popular recovery spot with the

party people, who dance and drink
here on Sundays and Mondays, this
pleasant pub has lots of thumping
music and a sunny beer garden. For
those who'd prefer to pretend it's still
night time, there is a darkened annexe
and dancefloor at the rear. Regular
pool comps, with $100 prize money;
Thursday night is 'Rack It', a
women's pool comp.
Open From 5.30am Mon & Fri–Sun,
2pm Tues–Thurs (closing times vary;
not always open in the evenings)
Admission Free
Payment Cash only

Flinders Hotel

63 Flinders St
Surry Hills NSW 2010
Phone 02/9360 4929
Gender Mostly men
The *Flinders* has traditionally offered
plenty of bop and 'handbag' with a
pool table out back. The crowd is
mostly young gay boys and their
friends – both male and female. Also a
popular recovery spot during the day.
Open Varies: usually Mon–Thurs
noon–10pm, Fri–Sun 24 hours
Admission Free
Payment AmEx, Bankcard, Diners,
EFTPOS, MasterCard, Visa

Taxi Club

Upstairs, The Grosvenor Club
40–42 Flinders St
Surry Hills NSW 2010
Phone 02/9331 4256
Fax 02/9331 7252
Email taxi@primus.com.au
Web www.taxiclub@citysearch.
com.au
Gender Mixed

Often compared to the bar in *Star Wars*, this legendary club has been tarted up in recent times, but is still a last stop for many revellers – gay, straight, transgendered and transfigured. Given how trashed people are when they arrive, you'd have to wonder why they bothered – and, as mother always said, 'you can't make a silk purse out of a sow's ear'. Not that anyone was complaining too loudly in this sow's ear . . . The *Taxi Club* is one of Sydney's more bizarre institutions and everyone seems to have wound up here at some time or another to dance the night away.

Some say it's called the *Taxi Club* because it's where you go when you really ought to be calling a taxi to take you home. If you truly want to witness Sydney's demimonde, this is the place to do it. You will have to sign yourself in, so do try and get there while you can still write your name. Apart from the upstairs dance club, there is a bistro and lots of poker machines.
Open Daily 24 hours; dance club Fri, Sat & public holidays only
Admission $5 members, $10 non-members
Payment EFTPOS

INNER WEST

Bank Hotel
324 King St
Newtown NSW 2042
Phone 02/9557 1692
Gender Mixed
Join a serious school of sapphic sharks upstairs at Wednesday's pool comps (7.30pm), with prize money of $50. Then spend your winnings downstairs at the pub's *Sumalee Thai* restaurant, where you can have a fiery feast in a beautiful bamboo-lined courtyard for between $15 and $30.
Open Daily 11am–1.30am
Admission Free
Payment Bankcard, EFTPOS, MasterCard, Visa

Caesar's Bar
92–94 Parramatta Rd
Camperdown NSW 2050
Phone 02/9550 2411
Gender Mixed

A very happy mix of gays and lesbians congregate at this club with a beer garden and barbecues in summer. Away from the main strips of Oxford and King streets, it offers a comfortable alternative to the frantic Darlinghurst scene.
Open Fri–Sat 5pm–3am
Payment Cash only

Hellfire Club
Blackmarket Hotel, 111 Regent St
Chippendale NSW 2008
Phone 02/9698 8863
Gender Mixed
Popular fetish venue for men and women – straight, bi or queer – who have a taste for whips and wickedness. Guest DJs, lots of leather and rubber, and plenty of discipline. Please Miss, may I have some more?
Open Fri 11pm–4am
Admission $10–15
Payment Cash only

Imperial Hotel

35 Erskineville Rd
Erskineville NSW 2043
Phone 02/9519 9899
Fax 02/9565 1804
Gender Mixed

Casual and easygoing, with lots of women, the *Imperial* has three bars to choose from, so there's always something happening here. The front bar has poker machines, pool tables and events most nights, while the cabaret bar has frequent drag shows. The basement has a dancefloor that really 'goes off'and is an excellent place for queers of all genders to go dancing. Deservedly popular gay and lesbian club on weekends.

Open Mon–Thurs 11am–2am, Fri–Sat 11am–5am
Admission Free
Payment Cash only

old pub is a bit of a playground for the bawdy and sporty gals. Naturally there's pool to be played, and the courtyard bistro is open Tuesday through Sunday for lunch and dinner.

Open Sun–Tues noon–10pm, Wed–Sat 10am–midnight
Admission Free
Payment EFTPOS

Newtown Hotel

Cnr King and Watkin streets
Newtown NSW 2042
Phone 02/9557 1329
Fax 02/9565 1804
Gender Mixed

A real mixture of Newtown lesbians and gays frequent this legendary lesbian-owned, gay-run establishment. With drag shows from Tuesday through Sunday, there is never a dull moment here. Next door

Peter J. Mark

Leichhardt Hotel

126 Balmain Rd
Leichhardt NSW 2040
Phone 02/9569 1217
Fax 02/9560 0318
Gender Mixed

Located in the centre of what is often called 'Dyke-heart', this relaxed, cute

and upstairs is *Bar 2*, offering a more relaxed drinking environment as well as pool tables.

Open Mon–Thurs 11am–noon, Fri–Sat 11am–1am, Sun 10am–10pm; *Bar 2* Tues–Sat from 6pm
Admission Free
Payment Cash only

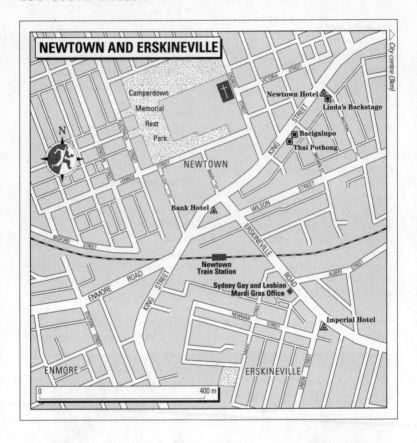

Spicy Friday

Lansdowne Hotel
Cnr City Rd and Broadway
Chippendale NSW 2008
Phone 02/9211 2325
Gender Mostly women
This is a really fun, groovy and queer
night, attracting about 70 per cent
women and 30 per cent men, and
featuring funk and soul music.

Cabaret acts showcase Sydney's most
eccentric and notorious performers.
With pool tables and an upstairs chill-
out lounge, this is a great place for
those who find the Sydney scene a
little lacking in coalitionist venues and
groovy queers of both genders.
Open Fri 8pm–3am
Admission $5
Payment EFTPOS

PARRAMATTA

Castaways

Paramatta Club, 37 Hunter St
Parramatta NSW 2150
Phone 02/9674 5903
Fax 02/9674 5903
Email castaways-c@hotmail.com
Gender Mixed
Popular night with the gay and lesbian crowd from the western suburbs and beyond. Friendly fun crowd with no attitude means a good time had by all. The organiser makes hilarious announcements over the mike and there are regular shows. Venue includes a bistro and a restaurant, and drinks are at club prices. Proceeds support those living with HIV/AIDS.
Open Sat 8pm–4am
Admission $5.50
Payment EFTPOS

SEX CLUBS AND SAUNAS

Adult World

124a Oxford St
Darlinghurst NSW 2010
Phone 02/9360 8527
Gender Men
Video booths, lounge and back room with cruise space and cubicles. There are two lounges – one showing straight porn, the other gay porn. Also stockists of toys, videos, magazines and vibes.
Open Mon–Wed 10am–2am,
Thurs–Sun 24 hours
Admission $10 to video lounge
Payment AmEx, Bankcard, EFTPOS, MasterCard, Visa

Bodyline

10 Taylor St
Darlinghurst NSW 2010
Phone 02/9360 1006
Web www.bodylinesydney.com
Gender Men
Located just off Taylor Square (first left past *Sadé*), this venue boasts a brilliant spa and is all very new and clean. It offers dry and wet saunas in the basement and cruise space on the top floor with porn lounge. The ground floor has a coffee lounge, and the regulars are mostly quite sexy.
Open Mon–Thurs noon–7am,
Fri–Sun 24 hours
Admission $12–18
Payment AmEx, Bankcard, EFTPOS, MasterCard, Visa

Club X Sydney

380 Pitt St
Sydney NSW 2000
Phone 02/9264 3249
Gender Men
Adult bookshop with 'Ram Lounge' offering adult movies and back-room activities. Lube and condoms are provided.
Open Mon–Sat 9am–2am,
Sun 9am–1am
Admission $10 all-day pass
Payment AmEx, Bankcard, Diners, EFTPOS, MasterCard, Visa

Den

Upstairs, 97 Oxford St
Darlinghurst NSW 2010
Phone 02/9332 3402

Web www.deninternational.com
Gender Men
Cruise club full of all sorts of guys, with pool tables, porn movies, showers, private cubicles, free coffee, large maze and grope rooms. Located right next to the *Midnight Shift*.
Open Mon–Thurs 8pm–late, Fri–Sun 24 hours
Admission $12
Payment AmEx, Bankcard, MasterCard, Visa

Fantasy Lane
Upstairs, 320 King St
Newtown NSW 2042
Phone 02/9557 0069
Gender Men
Cruise lounge and porn videos, as well as adult bookshop stocking toys, magazines and fetish wear.
Open Mon–Sat 8.30am–2am, Sun 10am–2am
Admission $10
Payment AmEx, Bankcard, EFTPOS, MasterCard, Visa

Headquarters
273 Crown St
Darlinghurst NSW 2010
Phone 02/9331 6217
Web www.headquarters.com.au
Gender Men
This three-storey 'boys' own' adventureland has all sorts of play things to explore – from swinging chain bridges to mineshafts, barber's chairs, gaol cells, slings, bondage facilities and porn movies shown in underground 'mines'. It also has a coffee bar serving refreshments and non-porn movies on a large screen upstairs. Special nights include 'Night of the Dragon', a popular Asian night, and 'Lock-up' on Wednesdays for heavy-duty stuff with rubber, leather and uniforms (check papers for other special nights).
Open Mon–Thurs noon–7am, Fri–Sun 24 hours
Admission $10 before 7pm, $13.50 after
Payment Cash only

Ken's of Kensington
83 Anzac Parade
Kensington NSW 2033
Phone 02/9662 1359
Gender Mostly men
Ken's – or KKK, as it is often called because of its earlier, euphemistic name of Ken's Karate Klub – is the flagship of Sydney saunas. Although not on the main drag, it is worth a taxi ($7–12) from Taylor Square. *Ken's* main feature is the glass-floored coffee shop which overlooks the swimming pool below. *Ken's* has a Romanesque steam room, a dry sauna, spa and porn video lounge, as well as a regular movie lounge. It seems to be a popular spot for some of Sydney's more gorgeous men and gets very, very crowded; after big parties, there's often a queue snaking out the door. *Ken's* also hosts 'Wet Girls', a girls-only night, several times a year.
Open Mon–Fri noon–6am, Fri–Sun 24 hours
Admission $16.50 weekdays, $18.50 weekends
Payment Cash only

Kingsteam
First floor, 38–42 Oxford St
Darlinghurst NSW 2010
Phone 02/9360 3431
Fax 02/9550 1116

Gender Men

Popular with bears and the more mature crowd, this clean, central sauna at the city end of Oxford Street has all the usual features – dry sauna, wet sauna and spa – plus a gym, coffee bar and video lounge.

Open Mon–Thurs 10am–6am, Fri–Sun 24 hours

Admission $20, plus $5 key deposit

Payment Cash only

Numbers

95 Oxford St
Darlinghurst NSW 2010
Phone 02/9331 6099

Gender Men

Numbers boasts a wide range of different vibes, adult toys, books and a dark cruise club with a male-porn video lounge. Not the most glamorous of venues but right at the meat of things.

Open 24 hours, 7 days a week

Admission $10 all-day pass

Payment AmEx, Bankcard, Diners, EFTPOS, MasterCard, Visa

Pleasure Chest

Upstairs, 56 Darlinghurst Rd
Kings Cross NSW 2011
Phone 02/9356 3640

with branches at:

161 Oxford St
Darlinghurst NSW 2010
Phone 02/9332 2667

382A Pitt St
Sydney NSW 2000
Phone 02/9283 2194

705 George St
Haymarket NSW 2000
Phone 02/9212 6440

Gender Mostly men

The *Pleasure Chest* 'formula' consists of very dark cruising venues (usually upstairs), with cubicles and porn videos, attracting a truly bizarre mix – the Kings Cross branch in particular attracts gay men, straight men and the occasional trannie. The lounge of the Haymarket location shows straight porn videos to an all-male viewing audience – straight porn in a gay sex venue. Go figure! The ever-popular suckatorium is a signature feature of all *Pleasure Chests*, as are toys, videos and vibes for sale. The video lounge and cruise club in the Kings Cross *Pleasure Chest* has to be one of the wierdest, sleaziest joints in The Cross. Outside there are rentable booths for liasons with ladies (and trannies) of the night and it seems like almost anything goes in this club. It might just be the place to score that unattainable 'straight' man of your dreams. Not for the faint-hearted or those obsessed with venue cleanliness, this place. And hold onto your valuables.

Open Kings Cross and Darlinghurst 24 hours, 7 days a week; city and Haymarket daily 10am–1am (later on weekends)

Admission $10

Payment AmEx, Bankcard, EFTPOS, MasterCard, Visa

Probe

159 Oxford St
Darlinghurst NSW 2010
Phone 02/9361 5924

Gender Men

This curious upstairs club offers male peep shows from private or shared cubicles, plus private video booths.

There is a bookshop stocking a wide range of porn from all over the world, and tokens can be purchased to watch boys doing their thing through glass windows – check the billboard on the street for 'showtimes'.

Open Mon–Thurs 9am–1am, Fri–Sun 24 hours
Admission $10
Payment AmEx, Bankcard, Diners, EFTPOS, Mastercard, Visa

Signal

2nd floor, Cnr Riley St and Arnold Place
Darlinghurst NSW 2010
Phone 02/9331 8830
Web www.toolshed.com.au
Gender Men

This venue is a cleaner, newer sex venue, offering some interesting cruise spaces and non-stop porn videos. It also has a coffee bar and non-porn large-screen television and Internet. Situated just around the corner from Oxford Street, you'll see the 'Signal' sign as soon as you turn the corner into Riley Street: take the lift to the 2nd floor, or enter through *The Toolshed*. Occasional special nights like '8 or more, free at the door' – show 'em 8 inches and you're in for free. Phone for information about 'special nights'.

Open Mon–Thurs 11am–3am, Fri–Sun 24 hours
Admission $10 before 10pm, $12.50 after
Payment Cash only

ADULT SHOPS, PARTY AND FETISH WEAR

Aussie Boys

102/Oxford St
Darlinghurst NSW 2010
Phone 02/9360 7011
Gender Mostly men

Male clothing and accessories; loads of skimpy party outfits, as well as underwear and swimwear.

Open Mon–Fri 10am–7pm, Sat 9am–7pm, Sun noon–6pm
Payment AmEx, Bankcard, Diners, EFTPOS, MasterCard, Visa

Daly Male

28 Oxford St
Paddington NSW 2021
Phone 02/9361 0331
Gender Men

Stockist of casual and party wear. Lots of flashy and trashy one-night-wear outfits, shorts and cobweb tops for parties and play.

Open Mon–Fri 10am–6pm, Sat 10am–6am, Sun noon–5pm
Payment AmEx, Bankcard, Diners, EFTPOS, MasterCard, Visa

Drag Bag

Upstairs, 185 Oxford St
Darlinghurst NSW 2010
Phone 02/9380 8222
Web www.dragbag.com.au
Clientele Transvestites, transsexuals, and drag queens, as well as women seeking something way over the top

Clothes and accessories for crossdressers, party boys and girls. Large sizes available and lots of stunning designs, with imported and custom-made frocks or special costumes to

order. Loads of shoes, jewellery, boys'
party wear and theatrical make up.
Also home to *Wig World*, a huge
emporium of wigs.
Open Mon–Sat 10.30am–6pm
Payment Bankcard, EFTPOS,
MasterCard, Visa

House of Fetish
93 Oxford St
Darlinghurst NSW 2010
Phone 02/9380 9042
Email hos@eternia.net
Gender Mixed
Stockists of leather, rubber, PVC,
fetish clothing, chainmail, classic
Victoriana, elaborate jewellery for
piercings, corsetry. Certain
garments can be custom made and
they have a lifestyle emporium also.
Specialties include rubber nurses
uniforms and lethally spikey dog
collars.
Open Mon–Sat 10am–6pm,
Thurs 10am–8pm, Sun 1pm–5pm
Payment AmEx, Bankcard, Diners,
EFTPOS, MasterCard, Visa

Mephisto Leather
135 Oxford St
Darlinghurst NSW 2010
Phone 02/9332 3218
Fax 02/9360 6436
Email mephistoleather@ozemail.
com.au
Web www.mephisto.com.au
Gender Mixed
Leather clothing, latex, PVC and
leather goods and specialty fetish
wear. Piercing jewellery and plenty of
bondage gear.
Open Mon–Wed & Fri 10am–6pm,
Thurs 10am–9pm, Sat 10am–5pm,
Sun noon–5pm

Payment AmEx, Bankcard, EFTPOS,
MasterCard, Visa

Pile Up
83 Oxford St
Darlinghurst NSW 2010
Phone 02/9360 1279
Gender Mixed
Specialist in both gorgeous and
outrageous party wear, with lots of
extravagent designs for girls and guys. It
may not be cheap, but it's very pretty.
Open Mon–Wed & Fri–Sun
10am–7pm, Thurs 10am–9pm
Payment AmEx, Bankcard, EFTPOS,
MasterCard, Visa

Sax Leather
110 Oxford St
Darlinghurst NSW 2010
Phone 02/9331 6105
Fax 02/9331 6105
Email shop@saxleather.com.au
Web www.saxleather.com.au
Gender Mixed
Stockists of leather wear, bondage
gear, restraints and accessories.
Open Mon–Wed & Fri 10am–6pm,
Thurs 10am–5pm, Sat 10am–5pm
Payment AmEx, Bankcard, Diners,
EFTPOS, MasterCard, Visa

Toolshed
81 Oxford St
Darlinghurst NSW 2010
Phone 02/9332 2792

with branches at:

191 Oxford St
Darlinghurst
Phone 02/9360 1100

198 King St
Newtown NSW 2042
Phone 02/9565 1599

Web www.toolshed.com.au
Gender Mixed
Toolsheds are two parts sex shop, one part community centre – well shaken. They attract a much less sleazy crowd than some of the other adult bookshops; women won't feel uncomfortable in here. Drop in to peruse a huge range of adult products, greeting cards, party wear and removable tattoos. Lesbians are seriously catered for at all three *Toolsheds*.
Open Darlinghurst 24 hours, 7 days a week; Newtown Thurs–Sat 10am–2.30am, Sun–Wed 10am–1.30am
Payment AmEx, Bankcard, Diners, EFTPOS, MasterCard, Visa

ARTS

Queer Screen
PO Box 1081
Darlinghurst NSW 1300
Phone 02/9332 4938
Fax 02/9331 2988
Email info@queerscreen.com.au
Web www.queerscreen.com.au
Gender Mixed
Queer Screen is a non-profit incorporated organization set up in 1993 to organize Sydney's annual lesbian & gay film festival and to actively promote queer film culture. The festival, held each February as part of the month-long Sydney Gay and Lesbian Mardi Gras Arts Festival, is regarded as one of the top five gay/lesbian film festivals in the world. An important component of the festival is the 'My Queer Career' competition for queer Australian and New Zealand short films. A festival guide is available from early January and can be found at many gay/lesbian venues including *ACON* and *Bookshop Darlinghurst*. *Queer Screen* also holds events throughout the year, such as film premieres and previews, and supports gay and lesbian film festivals in other states and countries.

Members receive discounted tickets to many events during the festival and throughout the year, and are encouraged to become active in the organization.
Open Mon–Fri 10am–6pm
Cost membership $25, plus $5 joining fee.
Payment Bankcard, MasterCard, Visa; cheque

Sydney Gay and Lesbian Choir
PO Box 649
Darlinghurst NSW 1300
Phone 02/9360 7439
Fax 02/9360 7439
Email vlmac@hotmail.com
Web www.eagles.bbs.net.au/~sglc
Gender Mixed
Sydney Gay and Lesbian Choir is open to anyone wanting to raise their voice in song. It has a solid core of members who meet for rehearsals every Thursday at 7pm in Hefron Hall, on the corner of Burton and Palmer streets, in East Sydney. The choir is a highly acclaimed and visible part of the the gay and lesbian community and is involved in all major arts festivals and gay games.

Women's Library

8–10 Brown St
Newtown NSW 2042
Phone 02/9557 7060
Fax 02/9557 5720
Email twl2@bigpond.com
Gender Mostly women
Voluntarily funded and operated resource library offering a wide range of literary and theoretical texts by and about women. The library has an excellent range of lesbian crime, travel guides and works dealing with sexuality, health and identity. Computers are available for members' use and there is a small video collection. Postal lending services are available for members who don't live locally.
Open Tues–Fri 11am–8pm,
Sat 11am–5pm
Cost $50 institutions, $30 individuals, $20 concessions
Payment Bankcard, MasterCard, Visa; cheque

BOOKSHOPS

Ariel

42–44 Oxford St (cnr West St)
Paddington NSW 2010
Phone 02/9332 4581
Fax 02/9360 9398
with a smaller branch at:
103 George St, The Rocks
Sydney NSW 2000
Phone 02/9241 5622
Fax 02/9241 5930

Ariel is one of Sydney's best upmarket bookshops and though not particulary gay, it does carry many relevant titles. Street-level entrance for wheelchairs.
Open Daily 9am–midnight
Payment AmEx, Bankcard, Diners, EFTPOS, MasterCard, Visa; cheque

Berkelouw

19 Oxford St
Paddington NSW 2021
Phone 02/9360 3200
Fax 02/9360 3124
with another branch at:
70 Norton St
Leichhardt, NSW 2040
Phone 02/9560 3200
Email books@berkelouw.com.au
Web www.berkelouw.com.au
These beautiful bookshops stock both new and secondhand titles, and boast delightful coffee shops overlooking the street scene. A great place to find a treasured limited edition or just enjoy a coffee and a browse.
Open Daily 10am–midnight
Payment AmEx, Bankcard, EFTPOS, MasterCard, Visa

Better Read than Dead

265 King St
Newtown NSW 2042
Phone 02/9557 8700
Fax 02/9557 8560
Email derek@betterread.com.au
Web www.betterread.com.au
Wide range of gay and lesbian titles, with regular author events. Customer loyalty program and Mardi Gras discounts apply.
Open Mon–Thurs 9.30am–9pm,
Fri–Sat 9.30am–10pm,
Sun 9.30am–9pm
Payment AmEx, Bankcard, Diners, EFTPOS, MasterCard, Visa

Books on Oxford

37 Oxford St
Darlinghurst NSW 2010
Phone 02/9267 4405
Although not strictly speaking a
gay/lesbian bookshop, this cosy little
shop at the city end of Oxford Street
does stock many gay and lesbian titles.
Open Mon–Fri 9am–7pm,
Sat 9am–5pm, Sun 1pm–6pm
Payment AmEx, Bankcard, EFTPOS,
MasterCard, Visa

The Bookshop Darlinghurst

207 Oxford St
Darlinghurst NSW 2010
Phone 02/9331 1103
Fax 02/9331 7021
Email info@thebookshop.com.au
Web www.thebookshop.com.au
The Bookshop Darlinghurst is
Australia's original gay and lesbian
bookshop, making it an ideal first
stop to pick up all your reading
needs, as well as gay magazines and
videos from all around the world, free
newspapers and tourist information.
The staff are always helpful with any
questions you might have. The
bookshop also stocks loads of
imported gay and lesbian titles – any
gay/lesbian books they don't have in
stock, they'll happily order for you.
They also offer a national and
international mailing service and a
quarterly free magazine, *GR*, which
fills you in on the latest releases.
Open Mon–Wed 10am–11pm,
Thurs–Sat 10am–midnight,
Sun 11am–midnight
Payment AmEx, Bankcard, Diners,
EFTPOS, MasterCard, Visa

The Feminist Bookshop

Shop 9, Orange Grove Plaza, Balmain Rd
Lilyfield NSW 2040
Phone 02/9810 2666
Fax 02/9818 5745
In operation since 1974, *The Feminist
Bookshop* offers 'books for a changing
world' – a great selection of works
that often cannot be found elsewhere,
along with cards, posters, T-shirts and
gifts. The shop also provides a
women's resouce centre, all the
national lesbian magazines, a
noticeboard and accommodation
listings service, and up-to-date news
on Sydney happenings, including
Mardi Gras. The friendly staff also
handle ticket sales for popular
community arts events.
Open Mon–Fri 10.30am–6pm,
Sat 10.30am–4pm
Payment AmEx, Bankcard, EFTPOS,
MasterCard, Visa

Gleebooks

49 Glebe Point Rd
Glebe NSW 2037
Phone 02/9660 2333
Fax 02/9660 3597
Email books@gleebooks.com.au
Web www.gleebooks.com.au
Gleebooks, situated in a popular
'alternative' neighbourhood, is one of
Sydney's finest bookshops, offering a
good range of upmarket literature
including gay, lesbian and queer-theory
stuff. They also have a second-hand
bookshop at 191 Glebe Point Road for
those with antiquarian interests.
Open Daily 8am–9pm
Payment AmEx, Bankcard, Diners,
EFTPOS, MasterCard, Visa

NEWSPAPERS AND MAGAZINES

blue

Studio Publications,
Level 3, 101–111 William St
Sydney NSW 2000
Phone 02/9360 1422
Fax 02/9360 9550
Email ed@studio.com.au
Gender Mostly men

Available at most newsagents, *blue* is a bimonthly visual arts and popular culture magazine with a strong accent on male nude photography. This delectably stylish magazine enjoys pride of place on many gay households' coffee tables. The journalistic content is snappy and sophisticated, with lots of smart, fresh stories, but on bad days you may just want to look at the pictures – everyone else does. *blue*'s high production values and network of correspondents around the globe make it one of the most admired and collected gay magazines on the planet.
Cost $12.95 per issue, $110 annual subscription
Payment AmEx, Bankcard, MasterCard, Visa; cheque

Capital Q (relaunched as G)

PO Box 236
Vaucluse NSW 2030
Phone Anthony 0401 439 699
Fax 02/9380 5104
Email editor@capitalq.com.au
Web www.capitalq.com.au
Gender Mixed

Out every Friday, *Capital Q* offers lots of gossip, news, arts and gay/lesbian-related services information, as well as a venue guide. It is distributed to most gay/lesbian businesses and organizations in Sydney.
Cost Free street distribution, $108 annual subscription
Payment AmEx, Bankcard, MasterCard, Visa; cheque

DNA

PO Box 400
Kings Cross NSW 1340
Phone 02/9380 4211
Fax 02/9380 4288
Email andrew@dna.com.au
Gender Mostly men

DNA is Australia's newest gay glossy and its prime directive is that gays should have more fun being gay – and that they should do it with style, verve and wit. Lots of hot boys wearing, well, not much at all really. Witty interviews across all areas of the arts, a little in-depth cultural probing, a hint of retro and a stab at some neo-gay iconoclasm.
Cost $7.60 per issue, $79 annual subscription
Payment Bankcard, MasterCard, Visa; cheque

HIV Herald

PO Box 876
Darlinghurst NSW 1300
Phone 02/9281 1999
Fax 02/9281 1044

Email jsergeant@afao.org.au
Web www.afao.org.au
Gender Mixed
Provides reliable information on treatment options for people living with HIV/AIDS. Includes latest news and clinical trials from around the world, as well as articles on health maintenance and complementry therapies. Available from *ACON* (see p.74)
Cost Free

Lesbians on the Loose (LOTL)

PO Box 1099
Darlinghurst NSW 1300
Phone 02/9380 6528
Fax 02/9380 6529
Email lotl@lotl.com
Web www.lotl.com
Gender Women
Published monthly in Sydney (and quite Sydney-focused), this is required reading for every lesbian in the land. *LOTL* is filled with news, events, arts, personals, goss and up-to-date listings of women's groups and organizations. Available at most gay/lesbian businesses in the Darlinghurst/Newtown areas or by subscription.
Cost Free street distribution, $44 annual subscription
Payment MasterCard, Visa; cheque

National AIDS Bulletin

PO Box 876
Darlinghurst NSW 1300
Phone 02/9281 1999
Fax 02/9281 1044
Web www.afao.org.au
National journal providing news, analysis, information and comment on issues of interest to anyone affected by HIV/AIDS. Published six times a year.

Cost $50 annual subscription (concessions available)
Payment Cheque

Outrage

PO Box 981
Darlinghurst NSW 1300
Phone 02/9332 4988
Fax 02/9380 5104
Email outrage_editor@ satellitemedia.com.au
Gender Mostly men
Australia's best selling gay glossy magazine is a monthly publication full of glamour, news, politics and lifestyle articles. It also carries a large personals section catering to just about any gay man's romantic needs. It runs regular features on travel, music, books and eating out and is usually on newsstands in the last week of the month.
Cost $7.50 per issue, $86.40 annual subscription
Payment AmEx, Bankcard, Diners, MasterCard, Visa; cheque

Positive Living

PO Box 876
Darlinghurst NSW 1300
Phone 02/9281 1999
Fax 02/9281 1044
Email kmachon@afao.org.au
Web www.afao.org.au
Gender Mostly men
A publication outlining treatment options for people living with HIV/AIDS, together with details of the latest research and clinical trials around the world. Published every six weeks as an insert in *Sydney Star Observer* (see below).
Cost Free

Sydney Star Observer

PO Box 939
Darlinghurst NSW 2010
Phone 02/9380 5577
Fax 02/9331 2118
Email mail@ssonet.com.au
Web www.ssonet.com.au
Gender Mixed

Established in 1979, the *Sydney Star Observer* is Australia's oldest and most widely distributed gay and lesbian newspaper, with a circulation in the region of 30,000. *SSO* provides a unique range of news, arts and scene coverage; it is run as a non-profit company of community shareholders with a fierce commitment to independence and a proud tradition of original and extensive news coverage. Its Web site not only provides a Web-based version of weekly features and news but also has a range of interactive features, such as chat rooms and an online database of gay/lesbian community groups and venues. The print version is published weekly on Thursday, and is available throughout Sydney in cafés, major department stores, music stores and gay/lesbian venues (major distribution points are listed, by suburb, on *SSO*'s Web site).
Cost Free street distribution, $66 annual subscription

Talkabout

PO Box 831
Darlinghurst NSW 1300
Phone 02/9361 6750
Fax 02/9360 3504
Email feonas@plwha.org.au
Gender Mixed

Monthly magazine for AIDS/HIV communities. News, views and information for positive people. Get it monthly at all gay-friendly outlets.
Cost Free street distribution, free for people on benefits, $30 annual subscription

BEACHES AND POOLS

Andrew 'Boy' Charlton Pool

Mrs Macquaries Rd, The Domain
Sydney NSW 2000
Phone 02/9358 6686
Gender Mixed

An outdoor saltwater pool with a utilitarian simplicity. Nestled by the harbour, its convenient location means that office types pound up and down at lunchtime, while the boys take over in the afternoon and at weekends. Chat to old friends, make new ones, sunbake and enjoy the views. You can even swim here.
Open Nov–April only: Mon–Thurs 6.30am–8pm, Fri 6.30am–7pm, Sat & Sun 6.30am–8pm
Cost $2.75, concessions $1.30; $66 30-visit pass, concessions $27.50

Bondi Beach

Bondi Beach Rd
Bondi NSW 2026
Gender Mixed

Bondi Beach needs little introduction. Popular with everyone, this surf beach is patrolled by lifeguards year-round – and there's a seawater pool at the southern end for those wanting to do laps. Backing the beach is a long promenade with lots of restaurants, cafés and pubs. Take bus #380, #82 or #L82 from Circular Quay, Central Station or Taylor Square.

Coogee Women's Pool

Grant Reserve
Coogee NSW 2034
Gender Women

If lesbian heaven were in Sydney, it would be here. Originally established to provide Coogee's Muslim women with an escape from the evil eye, it has long since been subverted for more sapphic lounging. This beautiful ocean pool has decking for sunbathing and great views as far as the eye can see. To find this idyllic spot, head for the southernmost end of Coogee Beach, where you'll find Grant Reserve. About 100m along the path that veers left towards the cliff-top there's a discreet entrance on your left and a sign saying 'Women's Pool'. Entry is by donation and women only are allowed, though small children accompanied by women are permitted. Bus #372 or #374 from Circular Quay or Surry Hills.
Open Daily dawn–dusk
Cost Donation box, 20c

Wet Grrrls

A fortnightly women's summer event worth catching is 'Wet Grrrls' at **South Maroubra Beach** from November through April. Wet Grrrls meet on the first and third Sunday of each month from noon onwards. This is a fun day for women who like surfing, women who like watching women surfing, or women who like just hanging out with the other gals. Catch the #376 **bus** from Railway Square or the #377 from Circular Quay or Taylor Square (eastbound on Oxford Street). For more **information**, contact Lea 02/9519 6903, or Lisa on 02/9130 1367. Take a towel and join the fun.

Cook and Phillip Park

4 College St (cnr William St)
Sydney NSW 2000
Phone 02/9326 0444
Fax 02/9326 0599
Email cookandphillip@connect.net.au
Gender Mixed

This 50m pool and fully equipped gym also has a hydrotherapy pool and children's activity pool with wave machine. Cook and Phillip (or 'Cock and Pullet', as it's cheekily become known) is the closest pool to the CBD and is very handy to Oxford Street. There is an outdoor area for sunbaking and the centre organises basketball, water polo, aerobics and gym classes and a whole range of other activities.
Open Mon–Fri 6am–10pm, Sat 7am–7pm, Sun 7am–9pm
Cost $4.40 swim, $11 gym and swim; memberships and multi-passes available
Payment MasterCard, Bankcard, Visa

Lady Jane Beach
Lady Bay, South Head
Watsons Bay NSW 2030
Gender Mixed
This, one of Sydney's oldest, most popular nude beaches is situated right near the mouth of the harbour. Catch the #324 or #325 bus from Circular Quay, via William Street, to Watsons Bay, then walk through the Sydney Harbour National Park. The rocks at the southern end are very popular with gay men.

North Sydney Olympic Pool
Alfred St
Milsons Point NSW 2061
Phone 02/9955 2309
Gender Mixed
Situated in the shadow of the Harbour Bridge, there is no other pool in Australia that can boast such a view. A long-time favourite training spot for Olympic champions, this pool has just been redeveloped and offers a whole range of health and fitness services. Catch a train to Milsons Point, then walk down to the harbour and you can't miss it.
Open Mon–Fri 5.30am–9pm, Sat–Sun 7am–7pm
Cost $3.50, student $2.75, child $1.65, seniors free
Payment Bankcard, EFTPOS, MasterCard, Visa

Obelisk Beach
Chowder Bay Rd
Mosman NSW 2088
Gender Mostly men
Clientele Almost exclusively gay during the week
This beautiful harbour beach is set amidst hectares of national park and subtropical rainforest. Sheltered from weather and peering eyes, it makes a perfect setting for nude bathing and boy watching. Weekends tend to be more mixed, with lots of nude families present as well. The surrounding bushland offers some extraordinary sights throughout the summer – it's a bit like Alice in Wonderland. You'll meet people who set up camp in the bush and cruise all day. Parking tickets are freely given out here, so check signs carefully. Obelisk Beach is tricky to get to by public transport, but if you're determined catch a #175, #178 or #180 bus or the express #L88 or #L90 services from Wynyard or Town Hall, then change at Neutral Bay or Spit Junction. Take the #247 or #257 to Balmoral and from there you can walk to the beach in about 20 minutes. (Don't walk too far, you might find yourself in the military reserve – an illegal alien.) On summer weekends, a ferry service runs to Balmoral Beach, which makes for an easier journey.

Redleaf Pool
New South Head Rd
Woollahra NSW 2025
Gender Mixed
Clientele You may be safe from the aquatic variety of sharks, but the beached gay variety can be quite vicious here
This charming harbourside public sea-pool is very popular with Sydney's body-beautiful boys who sun themselves on the shore or pontoon. It is also a local swimming spot for families, so everyone is welcome. Redleaf Pool is next to Woollahra

Library, about 400m past Double Bay shopping centre heading away from the city (bus #324 or #325). Enter from Woollahra Council offices and follow the path down to the pool. Facilities include a kiosk and lawns, as well as a sandy beach.

Open Daily dawn–dusk

Cost Free

Tamarama

Cnr Tamarama St and Pacific Ave
Tamarama NSW 2026

Gender Mixed

One of the most 'sceney' of Sydney's surf beaches, Tamarama (aka 'Glamarama') attracts the most magnificently enhanced examples of the male physique. Are they all on steroids? Are those tans for real? Ask no questions and you'll be told no lies. Catch bus #380 from Circular Quay via Oxford Street or follow the cliff walk at the south end of Bondi Beach (about 15 minutes). Tamarama

also boasts a nice little café and in true Mediterranean style, reclining lounges can be rented by the hour. Be warned – there can be some tricky currents in the water here.

Wylie's Baths

Grant Reserve
Coogee NSW 2034

Gender Mixed

This 50m sea-pool in an exquisite cliffside location still has all the original pavilions, as well as a kiosk with a shiny new espresso machine. Sensational views of Wedding Cake Island and the coast, with lots of rocky nooks to plant your towel. Wylie's Baths is situated about a five-minute walk to the south of Coogee's main beach (bus #372 or #374): enter from the far corner of Grant Reserve. One of Sydney's best kept secrets – ooops, I guess it's not anymore.

Open Daily dawn–dusk

Cost $2.20

Bayswater Fitness

33 Bayswater Rd
Kings Cross NSW 2011

Phone 02/9356 2555

Fax 02/9356 2185

Gender Mixed

Air-conditioned, clean and modern gym right in the heart of Kings Cross. Regular step and other classes.

Open Mon–Thurs 6am–midnight, Fri 6am–11pm, Sat–Sun 7am–9pm

Cost $15 casual visit

Payment AmEx, Bankcard, EFTPOS, MasterCard, Visa

Bees Knees

399 Liverpool St
Darlinghurst NSW 2010

Phone 02/9361 4888

Gender Mixed

This establishment offers a whole range of beauty treatments and body waxing, as well as piercings, massage and tattoos. Bookings essential.

Payment Bankcard, MasterCard, Visa

City Gym

107 Crown St
East Sydney NSW 2010

Phone 02/9360 6247
Fax 02/9361 0347
Gender Mixed
A huge gym that's very popular with gay men and lesbians. The gym is well equipped, with multiples of all machines, as well as a sauna.
Open Mon–Fri 24 hours, Sat–Sun 8am–10pm
Cost $12.50 casual visit, $85 10-visit pass
Payment AmEx, Bankcard, MasterCard, Visa

Fitness Network
256 Riley St
Surry Hills NSW 2010
Phone 02/9211 2799 or 9211 0354
Fax 02/9211 6382
Gender Mixed
Clean and airy gym with a substantial gay and lesbian clientele offering an extensive range of machines and free weights, as well as classes in step, circuit and yoga for all levels of expertise. Dry sauna (mixed) and steam room (women only).
Open Mon–Fri 6am–9.30pm, Sat 8am–8pm, Sun 2pm–8pm
Cost $13.20 casual visit
Payment AmEx, Bankcard, EFTPOS, MasterCard, Visa

Ginseng Bath House and Relaxation Centre
Crest Hotel, 111 Darlinghurst Rd
Kings Cross NSW 2011
Phone 02/9368 1442
Gender Mixed
This bath house in the heart of Kings Cross is a true delight, with separate men's and women's baths, ginseng baths, spas, hot pool, cold pool, wet sauna, dry sauna, gymnasium, grooming facilities and body scrubs, as well as massages (phone for appointment). They even have a barber who does facials. This temple of god and goddesses is an ideal place for both men and women to unwind. Note this is not a gay or lesbian venue, though it is popular with both – but guys be warned, this is a lot more civilized than the other saunas listed in the guide.
Open Daily 10am–10pm
Cost $22 use of bath house facilities, treatments extra
Payment AmEx, Bankcard, Diners, EFTPOS, MasterCard, Visa

Newtown Gym
Level 1, 294 King St
Newtown NSW 2042
Phone 02/9519 6969
Fax 02/9519 6317
Email newtowngym@optusnet.com.au
Web www.newtownetwork.com
Gender Mixed
The whole gamut of fitness regimes are available at this queer-owned and -run gym: step, stretch, yoga and pump classes, weights, personal trainers, solarium, sauna and childcare facilities. Popular with lesbians.
Open Mon–Fri 6am–10pm, Sat–Sun 8am–8pm
Cost $8 casual visit
Payment AmEx, Bankcard, Diners, EFTPOS, MasterCard, Visa

Piercing Urge
Shop 3, 322 Bourke St
Darlinghurst NSW 2010
Phone 02/9360 3179
Web www.thepiercingurge.com.au

Gender Mixed

A popular piercing salon freqented by queer boys and girls, and neo-primitives. Bookings advisable on weekends.

Open Mon–Fri 10am–8pm, Sat 10am–6pm, Sun noon–6pm

Payment AmEx, Bankcard, Diners, EFTPOS, MasterCard, Visa

Team Sydney

c/- Pride, 26 Hutchinson St Surry Hills NSW 2010

Phone men 02/9558 2909, women 02/9818 2543

Fax 02/9331 1199

Email teamsyd@ozemail.com.au

Web www.teamsydney.org.au

Gender Mixed

The main lesbian and gay sports body in New South Wales and the Host Team for the 2002/Gay Games, *Team Sydney* plays a coordinating role in all major gay and lesbian sports events. *Team Sydney* recently adopted the slogan, 'Out Doing It' – and indeed they are! *Team Sydney* organizes the Australian Gaymes, a national gay and lesbian sports festival held annually at Easter, as well as the sports festival which forms an important part of the annual Sydney Gay and Lesbian Mardi Gras. Membership benefits include discounts on sports clothing and products, gym memberships, access to coaching and training, plus serious and social sporting events. Check out *Team Sydney*'s quarterly *Warm Up*, as well as gay/lesbian newspapers for details of specific gay and lesbian sporting groups.

Cost Membership $15 individual, club memberships available

Gay Games VI 2002

Sydney 2002/Gay Games VI Sport & Cultural Festival

GPO Box 2763, Sydney NSW 2000

Phone 02/9380 8202   **Fax** 02/9360 1220

Email admin2002@gaygamesvi.org.au

Web www.gaygamesvi.org.au

Gender Mixed

Every four years, the Gay Games are held somewhere in the world. A vast gathering of people participating in sport and cultural activities, with more competitors than the Olympic games, the Gay Games are about inclusion and participation – a celebration of friendship, support and sporting achievement. Anyone can enter, regardless of sexuality or ability. The next Gay Games are to be held in 2002, in Sydney, from 25 October to 9 November, and it will be an exciting and exhilarating time to experience the city.

Cost Registration fee yet to be confirmed; registration opens March 2001. Stay tuned to the Web site for more information.

Payment AmEx, Bankcard, MasterCard, Visa; cheque

Ultimate Gym Newtown

Level 2, 328–338 King St
Newtown NSW 2042
Phone 02/9557 2219
Fax 02/9516 1190
Gender Mixed

This gay-owned and -operated gym has been providing a friendly environment for gays, lesbians and transgender people for 10 years. The emphasis is on creating an inviting atmosphere, and there's even an area set aside for easy training. Facilities include weights, aerobics, yoga, dance, sauna, solarium, masseur, acupuncturist, Chinese medical practitioner, naturopath, homeopath and child-minding facilities.
Open Mon 6am–Sat 10pm (24 hours), Sun 8am–10pm
Cost $8 casual visit
Payment AmEx, Bankcard, EFTPOS, MasterCard, Visa

MEDICAL

Holdsworth House

1/32A Oxford St
Darlinghurst NSW 2010
Phone 02/9331 7228
Fax 02/9360 9232
Email reception1@hhgp.com.au
Web www.hhgp.com.au
Gender Mixed

A private, upmarket practice of four male doctors, with part-time female doctors available, which employs specialists in sexual health and travel immunisation. There are also a dietician, counsellors and psychologists on staff. Wheelchair access. Bulk billing is available to Medicare card holders.
Open Mon–Fri 8am–7pm, Sat 9am–2pm
Cost $60 per consultation
Payment AmEx, Bankcard, MasterCard, Visa

Immediate Health Care and Dental

257 Oxford St
Darlinghurst NSW 2010
Phone 02/9360 2666
Gender Mixed

Convenient medical clinic offering bulk billing to Medicare card holders and after-hours phone referrals. Easy access for wheelchairs.
Open Mon–Fri 9am–10pm, Sat–Sun 9am–8pm
Cost $33 per consultation
Payment AmEx, Bankcard, Diners, EFTPOS, MasterCard, Visa

Leichhardt Women's Community Health Centre

55 Thornley St
Leichhardt NSW 2040
Phone 02/9560 3011
Fax 02/9569 5098
Email lwchc@aussiemail.com.au
Gender Women

This women-only centre prioritizes services to disadvantaged women but willingly serves all women; it is staffed by lesbian and non-lesbian women. Services (by appointment only) include consultations with general practitioners and clinical nurses,

general counselling, drug and alcohol counselling, acupuncture, information on artificial insemination, naturopathy, group sessions and targeted information nights – some conducted in Chinese or Vietnamese. Disabled facilities available by prior arrangement.
Open Mon 9.30am–5.30pm, Tues 9.30am–7.30pm, Thurs 9.30am–7.30pm, Fri 9.30am–5.30pm
Cost Varies according to income

Livingstone Road Sexual Health Centre
182 Livingstone Rd
Marrickville NSW 2204
Phone 02/9560 3057
Fax 02/9568 3335
Email trand@rpamail.cs.nsw.gov.au
Screening and clinical care for HIV and sexually transmitted diseases (STDs); pap smears, vaccinations against hepatitis A and B, hepatitis C information and referrals. Thai- and Vietnamese-speaking health workers and interpreters are available and there's a counselling service for men and women. Appointments preferred; no Medicare card required.
Open Mon–Fri 9am–5pm, Tues 9am–7.30pm, Wed 9am–7.30pm, Thurs 9am–7.30pm, Fri 9am–5pm
Cost Free

Manly Sexual Health Service
8/18 Whistler St
Manly NSW 2095
Phone 02/9977 3288
Fax 02/9977 3347
Full range of free and totally confidential STD/HIV services,

counselling, practical support, needle exchange and referrals. No Medicare card required.
Open Mon 2pm–6pm, Tues 2pm–5pm, Wed 3pm–6pm, Thurs 4pm–8pm, Fri 9am–noon
Cost Free

Multicultural HIV/AIDS Service
Level 5, Queen Mary Building
Grose St, Camperdown NSW 2050
Phone 02/9515 3098
Fax 02/9550 6815
Email clerical@hiv.rpa.cs.nsw.gov.au
Bilingual/bicultural workers who provide emotional support and information to people from non-English-speaking backgrounds and families dealing with HIV/AIDS or hepatitis C. No Medicare card or identification required.
Open Mon–Fri 9am–5pm
Cost Free

Nepean Sexual Health and HIV Clinic
Nepean Hospital, The Annexe
Somerset St
Penrith NSW 2751
Phone 02/4734 2507
Fax 02/4734 2620
A complete sexual health clinic with friendly staff and confidential service. *Nepean Sexual Health Clinic* offers HIV testing and counselling, treatment and management; hepatitis C testing, monitoring and referrals; contraception information and emergency contraception; pap smears; sexuality counselling. No Medicare card required.
Open Mon–Fri 8.30am–5pm (appointments preferred)

Oxford Square Medical Centre
10–14 Oxford Square
Darlinghurst NSW 2010
Phone 02/9361 6151
Gender Mixed
Both male and female doctors are available at this centrally located clinic, which also offers bulk billing for Medicare card holders.
Open Mon–Fri 7.30am–8pm,
Sat 8.30am–3pm
Cost $44 per consultation
Payment Bankcard, MasterCard, Visa

Parramatta Sexual Health Clinic
Cnr George and Marsden streets
Parramatta NSW 2150
Phone 02/9843 3124
Fax 02/9893 7103
Provides a full range of walk-in STD medical services, with no Medicare card required.
Open Mon–Wed 9am–4pm,
Thurs 4pm–7.30pm, Fri 9am–4pm
Cost Free

Sydney Sexual Health Service
Nightingale Ward, 3rd floor,
Sydney Hospital, Macquarie St
Sydney NSW 2001
Phone 02/9382 7440

Fax 02/9382 7475
Gender Mixed
A specialist clinic dealing with STDs. Treatment is confidential, and you can use a false name if you wish. Disabled facilities available. Telephone counselling and information also available.
Open Mon–Tues 8.30am–6pm,
Wed 2.30pm–6pm, Thurs–Fri
8.30am–6pm
Cost Free

Taylor Square Clinic
302/Bourke St
Darlinghurst NSW 2010
Phone 02/9331 6151
Fax 02/9331 3943
Email tspc@clinipath.com.au
Gender Mixed
A practice of male and female general practitioners offering bulk billing to Medicare card holders. Street-level entrance for wheelchair access. A popular clinic for both gay men and lesbians.
Open Mon–Fri 8am–8pm,
Sat 10am–noon
Cost From $40 per consultation
Payment Bankcard, MasterCard, Visa

COMMUNITY

Acceptance For Catholics
St Canice's Church, 28 Roslyn St
Elizabeth Bay NSW 2011
Phone 02/9568 4433
Web sites.netscape.net/acceptsyd/
index.html
Gender Mixed
Organization for gay- and lesbian-

identifying Catholics wishing to celebrate their faith in a safe, non-threatening environment. Masses are held at 8pm on Fridays at St Canice's Church, followed by coffee and informal discussion. Counselling and liturgy groups are also on offer.

AIDS Council of New South Wales (ACON)

9 Commonwealth St
Surry Hills NSW 2010
Phone freecall 1800/063 060 or
02/9206 2000, TTY 02/9283 2088
Fax 02/9206 2069
Email mailbox@acon.org.au
Web www.acon.org.au
Gender Mixed
ACON is the largest government-
funded community organization
catering to the physical and mental
health needs of all gay and lesbian
communities. It provides a
counselling service, in-house referrals
to specialists, education services,
youth workshops, esteem-building
groups, community workshops,
information services and safe-sex
programs. They also handle ticket
sales for *ACON* fundraising events
and parties. *ACON* is a good place to
start if you are trying to locate specific
community organizations that might
be relevant to you; *ACON* also carries
a wide range of free printed
information, as well as gay/lesbian
newspapers.
Open Mon–Fri 10am–6pm

AIDS Council of Western Sydney

1st floor, 81 George St
Parramatta NSW 2150
Phone 02/9204 2400; 'Fun and
Esteem West', Kent 02/9204 2405
Fax 02/9891 2088
Email aconwest@acon.org.au
Gender Mixed
Provides education and support
programs, plus condom and lube
sales, and needle exchange. The

council has a small library that carries
gay newspapers and other
publications, and also runs 'Fun and
Esteem West', a self-esteem program
for gays and lesbian under-26s in the
Liverpool and Parramatta areas, and a
Community Support Network that
trains volunteers in home-based care
for people living with HIV/AIDS.
It also offers referrals and regular
workshops dealing with safe sex,
relationships, coming out and
homophobia.
Open Mon–Fri 9am–5pm

ANKALI Project

150 Albion St
Surry Hills NSW 2010
Phone 02/9332 9742
Fax 02/9360 3243
Email ankali@sesahs.nsw.gov.au
Web www.sesahs.nsw.gov.au/
albionstcentre
Gender Mixed
The *ANKALI Project* is an emotional
support service for people living with
and affected by HIV/AIDS. It
provides professional and one-to-one
volunteer support and referral.
Open Mon–Fri 9am–5pm

Australian Federation of AIDS Organisations (AFAO)

PO Box 876
Darlinghurst NSW 1300
Phone 02/9281 1999
Fax 02/9281 1044
Email afao@rainbow.net.au
Web www.afao.org.au
National AIDS organization
responsible for formulating national
AIDS policies. Publishers of *National
AIDS Bulletin*, *HIV/AIDS Legal Link*,

HIV Herald and *Positive Living*.
Provides current treatment
information through the National
Treatments Project.
Open Mon–Fri 9am–5pm

Bobby Goldsmith Foundation (BGF)

PO Box 97
Darlinghurst NSW 1300
Phone 02/9283 8666,
freecall 1800/651 011
Fax 02/9283 8288
Email georgina.harman@bgf.org.au
Web www.bgf.org.au
BGF's mission is to assist people
directly disadvantaged by HIV and
AIDS to maintain a reasonable quality
of life through the provision of
financial assistance, financial
counselling and supported housing.
Their vision is that no-one should live
in poverty because they live with
HIV/AIDS. The foundation helps to
bridge the gap between public
funding and private need. *BGF* also
organizes reserved seating at the
Sydney Gay and Lesbian Mardi Gras
Parade – the only guaranteed view of
the parade! Tickets usually go on sale
at the end of January.
Open Mon–Fri 9.30am–5.30pm

Dayenu Jewish Gay and Lesbian Group

10/300B Burns Bay Rd
Lane Cove NSW 2066
Phone Malcolm 0413 444 208
Web www.dayenu.homestead.com
Social and support group for Jewish
gays and lesbians. Friday night services
and suppers are held weekly, and there
are regular social events and workshops.

HIV support and the services of
Reform Rabbis are also available.

Deaf Lesbian and Gay Association

PO Box 1641
Potts Point NSW 2011
Gender Mixed
Social club for deaf gays and lesbians.

Dykes on Bikes

PO Box 634
Newtown NSW 2042
Phone Louise 02/9913 8759 or
Sasha 0416 046 730
Web www.researchbydesign.com.au/
dob.html
Gender Women
Australia's largest lesbian motor-
cycling club. Meets regularly at the
clubhouse – the Leichhardt Hotel,
Balmain Road, Leichhardt. Contact
for details of rides and meetings.

GAMMA

197 Albion St
Surry Hills NSW 2010
Phone 02/9360 9810 or
freecall 1800/804 617
Web www.gamma.queer.org.au
Gender Men
GAMMA is a self-help group for men
who are married or in a long-term
heterosexual relationship and who
feel emotionally and/or sexually
attracted to other men. Meetings are
held on the first and third Wednesday
of each month at 8pm.

Gay and Lesbian Business Association (GLBA)

PO Box 394
Darlinghurst NSW 2010

Phone 02/9552 2000
Fax 02/9225 9096
Email sglba@iname.com
Gender Mixed

GLBA host a monthly dinner for business people of all professions, with guest speakers. They also hold regular informal drinks meetings for gay men (aka 'Fruits in Suits') on the first Thursday of the month at centrally located venues. The women's gathering is called 'Lemons with a Twist', and is held on the first Friday of every month. Phone for details of get-togethers and membership.
Open Mon–Thurs 9am–5pm
Cost Monthly dinners $50 for members, $60 non-members;'Fruits in Suits'/'Lemons with a Twist' gatherings free for members, $5 non-members.

Gay and Lesbian Counselling Service

Sydney NSW 2000
Phone 02/9207 2800 or freecall 1800/805379
Fax 02/9207 2828
Gender Mixed
Statewide information and referrals on all issues of concern to gays, lesbians and queers.
Open Daily 4pm–midnight

Gay and Lesbian Rights Lobby

PO Box 9
Darlinghurst NSW 1300
Phone 02/9360 6650
Fax 02/9331 7963
Email glrl@rainbow.net.au
Web www.rainbow.net.au/~glrl
Gender Mixed
The *Gay and Lesbian Rights Lobby* is the successor to the Gay Rights Lobby, which was formed in the late 1970s but ceased to exist after the decriminalisation of male homosexuality in New South Wales in 1984. In the 10 years since the *Gay and Lesbian Rights Lobby* was formed it has been most active in campaigning for legislative change and fighting discrimination in a variety of areas.

Gay and Lesbian Youth Support Network (GLYSSN)

Locked Bag 3
Beaconsfield NSW 2014
Phone Barry 02/9382 8336 or Sally 02/9382 8346
Fax 02/9382 8158
Email edwardsb@sesahs.nsw.gov.au
Gender Mixed
A support network for gay/lesbian/bisexual/transgender under-25s in Sydney's southern suburbs. Offers opportunities to meet friends and access health and community information. Meetings on the first and third Wednesdays of every month.

Gender Centre

75 Morgan St
Petersham NSW 2049
Phone 02/9569 2366
Fax 02/9569 1176
Email gendercentre@one.net.au
Gender Transgender
Counselling, support and housing for people with gender issues. The gender centre has a full-time residential worker as well as an outreach program and several accommodation projects specifically targeted towards those dealing with aspects of the transgender process. Social activities are regularly organized, and medical

referrals are available.
Open Mon & Thurs 10am–midnight,
Tues, Wed & Fri 10am–5.30pm

Irish Lesbian and Gay Group (*Amach*)

PO Box 422
Darlinghurst NSW 1300
Phone 02/9360 3616
Fax 9332 3326
Email fod@dot.net.au
Web www.fod.com.net.au
Gender Mixed
Social group for Irish gay/lesbian
people who need social and cultural
support in Australia. Group organises
weekends away and an entry in the
annual Mardi Gras parade.

Lesbian and Gay Anti-Violence Project (AVP)

PO Box 1178
Paddington NSW 2010
Phone 02/9360 6687 or
freecall 1800/637 360
Fax 02/9380 5848
Email avp@kbdnet.net.au
The *AVP*'s mission is to eliminate hate-
related violence against lesbians and gay
men. Its 'Homophobia: what are you
scared of?' campaign encouraged young
people to take a stand against
homophobia, and won a Violence
Protection Award. The organization
also provides a reporting and
information service, as well as offering
support to survivors of violence.
Open Mon–Fri 9am–5pm

Lesbian and Gay Legal Rights Service

Inner City Legal Centre
Level 2, 94 Oxford St
Darlinghurst NSW 2010
Phone 02/9332 1966
Fax 02/9360 5941
Email inner_city@fcl.fl.asn.au
This is a project run out of and in
conjunction with the Inner City
Legal Centre, providing legal advice
to gay men and lesbians; it initiated
the successful campaign to extend de
facto rights to same-sex couples.
Individual assistance is given in a
variety of areas, particularly legal
inequality, discrimination and hate-
related violence, as well as family and
relationships law. The service is free;
however, matters such as
conveyancing, property aquisition or
immigration are not handled.
Open Wed (by appointment only)

Lezbiz

PO Box 1445
Darlinghurst NSW 2010
Phone 02/9380 6244
Email lezbiz@silkes.com.au
Gender Women
Lezbiz is the national business
association for lesbians. They host
regular events and monthly dinners
with prominent lesbian speakers –
great for networking and socialising
when you're in town.
Open Mon–Fri 9am–5pm

Long Yang Club

PO Box 25
Haymarket NSW 1240
Phone 02/9587 1246
Email ogeditor@ozemail.com.au or
sydney@longyangclub.org
Web www.longyangclub.org/sydney
Gender Men
The *Long Yang Club* arranges monthly

social activities for gay Asian men and their Caucasian friends/partners away from the bars, clubs and nightlife of Oxford Sreet. The club is part of a worldwide network of East–West clubs.

Cost Membership $30 couples, $20 singles, $15 students (membership form on Web site)

Metropolitan Community Church of Sydney

96 Crystal St
Petersham NSW 2049
Phone Rev Greg Smith 02/9569 5122
Fax 02/9569 5144
Email mcc@eagles.bbs.net.au
Web www.mccsydney.org.au
Gender Mixed
A church offering worship services to everyone, but especially to gay, lesbian, bisexual and transgender people. Services 10am and 7.30pm on Sundays. Special AIDS memorial services held on the first Sunday of each month.

Northern Beaches Gay and Lesbian Social Club

PO Box 27
Manly NSW 2095
Phone Club Hotline 02/9990 5637
(recorded information) or president
0500 803 300
Email nbglsc@surf.to
Web www.surf.to/nbglsc
Gender Mixed
The *NBGLSC* is a friendly social group for the gays and lesbians of Sydney's northern beaches. The club runs a weekly social get-together at a gay-friendly pub in Manly on Thursday nights, as well as organizing

activities and events ranging from roller-skating and movies to nightclubbing and regular Gay Community Forum meetings with guest speakers.
Cost Membership $20

The Open Door

Community Centre, 717 Laycock St
Mount Pleasant NSW 2749
Phone Sue Palmer, pastoral minister
02/4730 4833 or 0419 434 735
Fax 02/4730 4833
Email opendoor@tpgi.com.au
Gender Mixed
The Open Door welcomes the whole gay, lesbian, bisexual and transgender community and their friends. It provides an interdenominational, safe and friendly place to worship, with the emphasis on celebrating the diversity of God's creation. Sunday service at 7pm.

Order of Perpetual Indulgence

PO 426 Grosvenor Place
Sydney NSW 2000
The Australian branch of the famous Sisters of Perpetual Indulgence, roaming 'nuns' who redefine the scriptures to suit their own hedonistic and charitable philosophy.

Out of the Closet Emporium

523 King St
Newtown NSW 2042
Phone 02/9557 7032
Email mcc@eagles.bbs.net.au
Sells secondhand goods, including books, electricals, furniture and clothes. Owned and operated by the Metropolitan Community Church, with all proceeds going to support

gay/lesbian/bisexual/transgender people in need.
Open Wed–Sun 10am–4pm

Over 45s
Gladesville, NSW
Phone 02/9817 5304
Gender Women
Lesbian get-togethers every fortnight, with restaurant nights, trips away and a calendar of events.

OWLS
PO Box 610
Petersham NSW 2049
Social get-togethers and discussion groups for lesbians over 30.

Parents and Friends of Lesbians and Gays (PFLAG)
PO Box 1488
Darlinghurst NSW 1300
Gender Mixed
Support group for families and friends of gays and lesbians who hold regular discussion groups and meetings. Contact *ACON* (*AIDS Council of New South Wales*) to be put in touch with your nearest group. Groups are also listed in the free gay/lesbian newspapers (see pp.63–65).

Pastoral Care
1–5 Marion St
Blacktown NSW 2148
Phone Marie Lavis 02/9671 4100
Fax 02/9622 7469
Provides emotional, practical and spiritual support for people living with HIV/AIDS and their families and friends. Pastoral care also offers counselling and can help families deal with coming-out issues. HIV

education programs are also available to a diverse range of communities.
Open Mon–Fri 9am–5pm

People Living with HIV and AIDS (PLWHA)
PO Box 831
Darlinghurst NSW 1300
Room 5, Level 1, 94 Oxford St
Phone 02/9361 6011 or freecall 1800/245 677
Fax 02/9360 3504
Email admin@plwha.org.au
Web www.plwha.org.au
Gender Mixed
Community organization providing support and advocacy for those living with HIV/AIDS. They publish *Talkabout* magazine and *Contacts*, with listings of vital services and the current state of HIV/AIDS research and action. Both publications are available from *The Bookshop Darlinghurst* (see p.62) and many other local distributors. *PLWHA* offers a phone referral service to other organisations and services – and also operates the positive speakers bureau for NSW, which gives schools, communities and professional groups the opportunity to hear the personal experience of people living with HIV/AIDS and the issues they face.
Open Mon–Fri 10am–6pm

Positive Living Centre
703 Bourke St
Darlinghurst NSW 2010
Phone 02/9699 8756
Fax 02/9699 8956
Provides transport, meals, social support, complementary therapies, free internet access and drop-in centre

for all people living with HIV/AIDS.
The centre also offers a wide range of
community resources.
Open Tues–Fri 10am–3pm

PRIDE

26 Hutchinson St
Surry Hills NSW 2010
Phone 02/9331 1333
Fax 02/9331 1199
Email mail@pridecentre.com.au
Web www.pridecentre.com.au
Gender Mixed
Catering to lesbian, gay, queer,
transgender and bisexual individuals,
PRIDE puts out a monthly newsletter
of political and social news relevent to
all their communities. Appropriate
groups can hire space at the Pride
Centre, which also sells tickets for
some of Sydney's most important
PRIDE parties, such as Leather Pride
and New Year's Eve.
Open Mon–Sat 10am–6pm

Queer Dharma

c/- Pride Centre, 26 Hutchinson St
Surry Hills NSW 2010
Phone 02/9554 6874
Email queerdharma@geocities.com
Web www.come.to/queerdharma
Gender Mixed
Meeting weekly on Tuesday nights,
Queer Dharma is a Buddhist group
which organizes group meditations,
dharma talks, weekend retreats and
social events. It is non-sectarian and is
open to beginners and experienced
meditators alike.

Quilt Project

PO Box 862
Darlinghurst NSW 1300

Phone 02/9360 7669
Fax 02/9331 7628
The *Quilt Project* commemorates the
lives of those who have died from
AIDS. It is a volunteer-based
organisation and workshop hours vary.
The quilt is used in NSW schools to
help promote AIDS awareness.

Seahorse Society of NSW Inc

PO Box 168
Westgate NSW 2048
Phone 0401 007894 or 02/9716 9459
Fax 02/9716 9459
Email seahorsesoc@hotmail.com
Web www.geocities.com/
WestHollywood/2888
This is an incorporated, non-profit
self-help group funded entirely by
members. Membership is open to all
cross-dressers (and their relatives and
friends). Fortnightly meetings, regular
social outings, contact with other
cross-dressers, information service
and monthly newsletter.
Cost Membership $40

Sex, Fun and Esteem

9 Commonwealth St
Surry Hills NSW 2010
Phone 02/9206 2077, or
freecall 1800/063 060
Fax 02/9206 2092
Gender Men
Support group for young gays and
bisexuals between 16 and 26 years
old, which operates under the
auspices of the *AIDS Council of NSW*
(*ACON;* see p.74). This esteem-
building program promotes friendship
and communication between young
people in a non-threatening
environment.

Silk Road

AIDS Council of New South Wales
PO Box 350
Darlinghurst NSW 1300
Phone 02/9206 2080
Fax 02/9206 2069
Email asia@acon.org.au
Gender Men
A confidential support group for
Asian gay men and bisexuals. Meet
other gay Asian men, have fun and
share your experiences. Regular
group discussions deal with self-
esteem, cultural identity, friendships,
sexual health, coming out and
relationships. There are also
workshops, forums, lectures and film
screenings.
Open Mon–Fri 10am–6pm

Southern Beaches Gay and Lesbian Group

PO Box 810
Cronulla NSW 2230
Phone Joseph 0419 639 264
Social group for gays and lesbians of
all ages in the Cronulla and St George
region. Meets once a month on a
Sunday downstairs at the Brass
Monkey, 115A Cronulla St, Cronulla.

Sydney Bisexual Network (SBN)

PO Box 281
Broadway NSW 1400
Phone 02/9565 4281 recorded infoline
Web bi.org/~sbn/
Gender Mixed
Regular social events and a float in
the annual Mardi Gras parade are
organised by the group. Drinks are
held on the third Sunday of each
month at the Bank Hotel, Newtown;
check the Web site for details.

Sydney Gay and Lesbian Immigration Task Force (GLITF)

PO Box 400
Darlinghurst NSW 1300
Phone 02/9380 5950
Fax 02/9569 1661
Email glitf@dot.net.au
Web www.glitf.org.au
Gender Mixed
Support and information for overseas
partners of Australian gays and lesbians
who are seeking to stay in Australia.
The phone is only attended on Monday
evenings between 7pm and 9pm but
there is a recorded information message
at other times. A guidebook for couples
is also available ($20).
Open Mon 7.30pm–9.30pm

20/10 Lesbian and Gay Youth Service

PO Box 213
Glebe NSW 2037
Phone 02/9552 6130 or
freecall 1800/652 010
Fax 02/9552 6324
Email 20ten@rainbow.net.au
Web www.rainbow.net.au/~twenty10/
Gender Mixed
Offers a range of services to all
gay/lesbian under-25s, including
information and referral; semi-
supported and independent housing.
Also offers assistance with employment,
education, training and family support.
Open Mon–Fri 10am–6pm

Women Out West

PO Box 79
Toongabbie NSW 2146
Phone Tracy 02/9671 1327
Gender Women
Social group meeting regularly in

members' homes, with events including poetry and song afternoons.

Women's Coming Out Group
197 Albion St
Surry Hills NSW 2010
Phone 02/9207 2800
Gender Women
Meets the second and fourth Thursday of each month at 7pm.

Young Lesbian Support Group
Macarthur NSW 2560
Phone 02/4625 2525
Gender Women
Group offers social support for lesbians, and women who are questioning their sexuality, in the Macarthur region of Sydney. Group meets fortnightly.

 TRAVEL SERVICES

Australian Gay and Lesbian Tourism Association (AGLTA)
PO Box 208
Darlinghurst NSW 2018
Phone 02/9351 5561
Email info@aglta.asn.au
Web www.aglta.asn.au
A national network of tourism professionals dedicated to the welfare and satisfaction of all gay and lesbian travellers to, from and within Australia. *AGLTA* works with governments, corporations, businesses and individuals to increase awareness of gay and lesbian travellers and their needs. The *AGLTA* logo indicates that a business has signed the *AGLTA* code of ethics. *AGLTA* produces various free travel brochures and accommodation listings.

Beyond the Blue
685–687 South Dowling St
Surry Hills NSW 2016
Phone 02/8399 0070
Fax 02/8394 8467
Email sales@beyondtheblue.net
Web www.beyondtheblue.net/gay
Beyond the Blue is a major accredited

Australian provider of gay travel packages to Australian and overseas clients, specializing in tours to Australia for Mardi Gras, Sleaze and Leather Pride and recoveries at Noosa, Cairns, Daydream Island, Byron Bay and Cairns. They also offer international packages to Pride events all over the world.
Open Mon–Fri 9am–5.30am
Payment AmEx, Bankcard, Diners, EFTPOS, MasterCard, Visa; cheque

Flight Centre
Shop 3, 18–32 Oxford St
Darlinghurst NSW 2010
Phone 02/9331 0993
Fax 02/9331 0112
Email sue_bohme.7ka7@
flightcentre.com
Flight Centre is located right in the heart of Sydney's 'Golden Mile' and is staffed by friendly and helpful gay/lesbian consultants. They are also very good when it comes to securing the cheapest fares.
Open Mon–Sat 9am–5pm
Payment AmEx, Bankcard, EFTPOS, MasterCard, Visa; cheque

Friends of Dorothy Travel

77 Oxford St
Darlinghurst NSW 2010
Phone 02/9360 3616
Fax 02/933 23326
Email fod@dot.net.au
Web www.fod.com.au
This gay-owned and -operated
business offers tours specially designed
for gays and lesbians.
Open Mon–Wed 9am–5.30pm,
Thurs–Fri 9am–7pm, Sat 9am–noon
Payment AmEx, Bankcard, Diners,
EFTPOS, MasterCard, Visa

Gay Maps

PO Box 1401
Bondi Junction NSW 1355
Phone 02/9369 2738
Fax 02/9389 5450
Email gma@tma.com.au
Web www.tma.com.au/gaymaps
Publishers of gay and lesbian maps of
Sydney, which come out at the
beginning of each year and list many
of the gay and lesbian businesses along
Oxford Street.

gay.travel.com.au

76–80 Clarence St
Sydney NSW 2000
Phone 02/9249 5483
Fax 02/9262 3525
Email cindy@travel.com.au
Web www.travel.com.au/gay
Experienced organizers of
Australian and international gay
travel, with discount airfares and
rental car bookings.
Open Mon–Fri 9am–5.30pm (on-line
bookings 24 hours)
Payment AmEx, Bankcard, Diners,
EFTPOS, MasterCard, Visa; cheque

Gentry Travel

11–15 Falcon St (PO Box 193)
Crows Nest NSW 1585
Phone 02/9906 7000
Fax 02/9906 5129
Email gentrytraveland@aussiemail.
com.au
The North Shore's longest-established
gay and lesbian travel agency, special-
izing in personal and corporate travel
requirements.
Open Mon–Sat 9am–5pm
Payment AmEx, Bankcard, Diners,
EFTPOS, MasterCard, Visa; cheque

Global Gossip

108 Oxford St
Darlinghurst NSW 2010
Phone 02/9380 4588
Fax 02/9380 4599

with branches at:

111 Darlinghurst Rd
Kings Cross NSW 2011
Phone 02/9326 9777
Fax 02/9326 9755

317 Glebe Point Rd
Glebe NSW 2037
Phone 02/9552 6966
Fax 02/9552 6933

770 George St
Sydney NSW 2000
Phone 02/9212 1466
Fax 02/9212 1499

14 Wentworth Ave
Sydney NSW 2000
Phone 02/9263 0400
Fax 02/9263 0404

Gay-owned chain of internet and
communication centres, offering
email, internet, chat, cheap phone
calls, employment services, copying,
faxing and mailbox rental.

Open Daily 8am–midnight (Kings Cross until 1am, Wentworth Ave only until 9pm)
Payment Bankcard, EFTPOS, MasterCard, Visa; cheque

International Gay and Lesbian Travel Association (IGLTA)

Sydney NSW 2000
Phone 02/9818 6669
Email rhopkins@iglta.org
Web www.iglta.org
IGLTA is dedicated to elevating the standards of the hospitality/travel industry and supporting the businesses and professional organizations serving the needs of gay and lesbian travellers. Membership is open to any individual, association, corporation or partnership directly or indirectly involved with the gay and lesbian travel industry.
Open Mon–Fri 9am–5pm

Jornada

Level 1, 263 Liverpool St
Darlinghurst NSW 2010
Phone 02/9360 9611
Fax 02/9326 0199
Email justask@jornada.com.au
Web www.jornada.com.au
Offers a wide range of tailor-made packages for gays and lesbians.
Open Mon–Fri 9am–5.30pm
Payment AmEx, Bankcard, Diners, MasterCard, Visa; cheque

Mardi Gras Travel

Level 10,130 Elizabeth St
Sydney NSW 2000
Phone 02/92682188
Fax 02/9267 9733
Email lynne@ats-pacific.com.au

Web www.mardigras.com.au or www.redoyster.com
Mardi Gras Travel is the official travel agency for the Sydney Gay and Lesbian Mardi Gras, and for year-round gay/lesbian travel to Australia. Specialities include Mardi Gras recovery weeks in Cairns, the SPIN-FX dance party in the Central Australian deserts and Sensational Women – lesbian adventure travel, which includes horse riding, snow skiing and 4WD tours.
Open Mon–Fri 9.30am–5.30pm
Payment AmEx, Bankcard, Diners, MasterCard, Visa; cheque

Out Around Oz

PO Box 824
Darlinghurst NSW 2010
Phone 0500/803300
Fax 0500/804400
Email speedo@html.com.au
Web www.outaroundoz.com.au
Out Around Oz is a comprehensive and independent on-line resource for gay travellers who wish to explore not only the well-known gay tourism meccas of the major cities and resorts, but also regional Australia, its country towns and lesser-known attractions. Its comprehensive database lists every business and service around Australia that caters to the gay traveller.

Silke's Travel

Level 1, 263 Oxford St
Darlinghurst NSW 2010
Phone 02/9380 6244 or freecall 1800/807 860
Fax 02/9361 3729
Email info@silkes.com.au

Web www.silkes.com.au
Gender Mixed
Silke's provides tailor-made holiday arrangements for lesbians and gays, and is sure to have a queer holiday

package to suit anyone. Lesbian-owned and -operated.
Open Mon–Fri 9am–5pm
Payment Bankcard, MasterCard, Visa; cheque

Escape from sweltering Sydney

Summer in Sydney's cling-wrap humidity wears down the least humble of souls. So go *somewhere else*! Palm Beach is divine, but summer makes a crush of it. Drive a little further and be thrilled twice. Head north for Woy Woy. Follow the signs to **Pearl Beach**, a secret enclave of wealth, inaccessible to cars until relatively recently. The beach is precious, the homes exquisite and discreet (mostly). You'd never guess how much they cost. Legend has it that the rich once hid their less-than-perfect offspring there. Déjà vu? Now they want it all for themselves. Enjoy the beach, pine for the luxury and just when you spot the expensive little restaurant on the beach, *Get back in the car kids!* Drive on for 10 more minutes to **Patonga** and soak up the simple charm of this little fishing hamlet. Go to the fish and chip shop, buy all the fresh seafood you can eat (and some chips, because vegetables are important) then venture around the corner to the general store-cum-post office-cum-bottle shop (there are only two shops here – you won't get lost) and buy beer or wine. Sit under the seaside pines, squeeze lemon, pop cork, eat, drink and marvel that life could be so bloody grand. Patonga is just over an hour from the city.

If what the doctor ordered is a whole **weekend away**, then look no further than the **Blue Mountains** (see below), the **Hunter Valley** (see p.92) or the **Southern Highlands** (see p.100) – all within a couple of hours' drive of Sydney, and all with gay/lesbian-friendly accommodation. Just remember that these destinations can get pretty booked up on weekends, that rates rise accordingly on Friday and Saturday nights, and that some places stipulate a two-night minimum stay over a weekend.

Blue Mountains

Just two hours by car or train from Sydney, the Blue Mountains really *are* blue (a trick of the light reflecting off droplets of eucalyptus oil in the air). The walks are to die for – and from, if you don't watch your footing on the breathtaking promenades and zany stairways. **Katoomba** is the main centre, attracting a deluge of tourists every weekend. To give the crowds a wider berth, head for the smaller villages along the ridge (**Leura**, Medlow Bath, **Blackheath** and Mount Victoria) or stay in the **lower mountains** at Glenbrook or Faulconbridge.

ACCOMMODATION

Agapanthus Cottage and Camellia Cottage

Address on enquiry
(Blackheath NSW 2785)
Phone Sara 02/4787 6662
Fax 02/4787 6662
Web www.agapanthus.com.au
Email mahish@bigpond.com
Gender Mixed
Set in secluded Pope's Glen, these two fully self-contained cottages each have a double spa, polished wooden floors, log fire, TV, CD player and bush views. Stroll to village or national parks. Breakfast provisions supplied.
Cost From $365 per cottage for a weekend (two nights), midweek specials available
Payment AmEx, Bankcard, EFTPOS, MasterCard, Visa

Allendale Cottages

Pope's Glen
Blackheath NSW 2785
Phone 02/4787 8270
Email allendale@pnc.com.au
Web www.bluemts.com.au/allendale
Gender Mixed
Set in rambling gardens, each cottage has a fireplace, CD player, sundeck and double spa with floor-to-ceiling windows looking out onto bush

views. Privacy is assured in these romantic hideways, and continental breakfast is included. Town is a short stroll away, via a duck pond, and walking tracks lead into national parks from the property. Gay-owned and -operated.
Cost From $144 per cottage midweek, $430 for a weekend (two nights)
Payment AmEx, Bankcard, EFTPOS, MasterCard, Visa

Balmoral Guest House

196 Bathurst Rd
Katoomba NSW 2780
Phone 02/4782 2264
Fax 02/4782 6008
Email balmoral@pnc.com.au
Web www.bluemts.com.au/balmoral
Gender Mixed
This is the oldest guesthouse in the Blue Mountains, established in 1876. *Balmoral* offers Victorian decor, brass beds and traditional gardens. There is an outdoor spa, as well as spa baths in some rooms.
Cost $110 per room midweek (bed and breakfast), $110 per person at weekends (dinner, bed and breakfast)
Payment AmEx, Bankcard, Diners, EFTPOS, MasterCard, Visa

Blue Gum Cottage

1322 Mountain Lagoon via Bilpin
Bilpin NSW 2758
Phone 02/4567 1184 or 0409 248 993
Fax 02/4567 1184
Web www.qbeds.cjb.com
Gender Mixed
Located on the northern edge of the
Blue Mountains and set in tranquil
gardens, *Blue Gum Cottage* has two
bedrooms and a fully equipped
kitchen. A breakfast basket is supplied
daily, and there is a summer house with
a barbecue area adjacent to the cottage.
Cost $144 per night midweek; $165
per night at weekends for two people,
$55 each extra person (sleeps a
maximum of four)
Payment Cheque

Bygone Beautys Cottages

c/- 20–22 Grose St
Leura NSW 2780
Phone 02/4784 3117
Fax 02/4784 3078
Email info@bygonebeautys.com.au
Web www.bygonebeautys.com.au
Gender Mixed
Bygone Beautys offers a range of
cottages to accommodate between
two and 10 people. Four-poster beds
and old-world charm abound, and
some cottages have spa baths. Tariff
includes a full cooked breakfast
platter, chocolates, fruit, log fires and
Devonshire teas.
Cost $66–144 per person per night
(minimum two-night stay at
weekends)
Payment AmEx, Bankcard, EFTPOS,
MasterCard, Visa

Caraloon

Address on enquiry
(Glenbrook NSW 2773)
Phone Sarah and Jo 02/4739 6769
Email caraloon@pnc.com.au
Web www.bluemts.com.au/caraloon
Gender Mixed
This lesbian–owned and –operated
guesthouse offers upstairs
accommodation with ensuite, double
spa bath, library and garden views.
Afternoon tea is served on arrival,
dinner is available for guests, and
there are romance packages which
include chocolates, champagne and
all meals.
Cost $105–165 per room; romance
package $280 per couple
Payment Bankcard, MasterCard, Visa

Hydro Majestic Hotel

Great Western Highway
Medlow Bath NSW 2780
Phone 02/4788 1002
Fax 02/4788 1063
Email sales@hydromajestic.com.au
Web www.hydromajestic.com.au
Gender Mixed
This vast Art Deco extravaganza is
probably the most famous hotel
in the Blue Mountains – not least for
the sweeping views it commands.
The hotel has several restaurants and
bars, a gym and swimming pool,
and offers a wide range of mountain
activities. Ideal for midweek getaways
but can be a little over-run on
weekends.
Cost From $190 per room
Payment AmEx, Bankcard, Diners,
MasterCard, Visa

Kanangra Lodge

9 Belvidere Ave
Blackheath NSW 2785
Phone Margaret 02/4787 8715
Fax 02/4787 8748
Email info@kanlodge.com.au
Web www.kanlodge.com.au
Gender Mixed

Kanangra Lodge is a traditional bed
and breakfast offering guests an
elegant home-like environment in a
quiet location, surrounded by
tranquil gardens. There are spacious
living areas and all bedrooms have
private facilities and kitchenette with
microwave; a full breakfast is
included in room rates. Smoking
outside only.
Cost $110 single, $165 double
Payment Bankcard, EFTPOS,
MasterCard, Visa; cheque

Leura House

7 Britain St
Leura NSW 2780
Phone John 02/4784 2035
Fax 02/4784 3329
Web www.bluemts.com.au/
leurahouse
Gender Mixed

Just four minutes' walk from the
station, this 1880 guesthouse boasts
great views of Leura valley and
village. Luxurious accommodation
and spacious gardens surround the
main house, which has 12 guest
rooms, most with ensuites. There are
also three cottages available, sleeping
up to 10 people.
Cost $75–85 per person midweek
(bed and breakfast), $280–320
weekend package (dinner, bed and

breakfast for two nights)
Payment AmEx, Bankcard, Diners,
EFTPOS, MasterCard, Visa

Park West

84 Great Western Hwy
Mount Victoria NSW 2786
Phone 02/4787 1112
Fax 02/4787 1711
Email parkwest@dnd.com.au
Web www.bluemts.com.au/parkwest
Gender Mixed

This sophisticated, gay-owned and
-operated Blue Mountains resort
offers total recovery weekends with
massages, facials, relaxation and
exercise. All rooms have ensuites and
TV, and some have spas. There is an
elegant bar and restaurant for guests
and visitors; smoking permitted in
bar only.
Cost $155–205 per room midweek,
$205–290 weekends
Payment AmEx, Bankcard, Diners,
EFTPOS, MasterCard, Visa; cheque

Sirens Bed and Breakfast

3 Duff St
Katoomba NSW 2780
Phone 02/4782 9386
Fax 02/4782 9576
Email sirenskatoomba@iname.com
Web www.hermes.net.au/sirens
Gender Mixed

Edwardian House with four
bedrooms, each with double brass bed
and ensuite. All rooms have TV and
there is a piano for guests' use;
breakfast is included in room rates.
Smoking outside only.
Cost From $130 per room
Payment Bankcard, MasterCard, Visa

Theodora's Hideaway

Address on enquiry
(Faulconbridge NSW 2776)
Phone 02/4751 9270
Fax 02/47511186
Email theo@pnc.com.au
Web www.bluemts.com.au/theodoras
Gender Mixed
All rooms have king-size four-poster
bed, mirrored ceiling, double spa, TV,
video, CD player and kitchenette.

And for that extra frisson, choose one
of the themed suites – Heritage or
French Bordello. A two-bedroom
cottage with private spa is also
available. All tariffs include breakfast,
and there's a swimming pool in the
grounds.
Cost $165 per room midweek,
$450–495 weekends (two nights)
Payment AmEx, Bankcard, EFTPOS,
MasterCard, Visa

CAFÉS AND RESTAURANTS

Cleopatra

118 Cleopatra St
Blackheath NSW 2785
Phone 02/4787 8456
Fax 02/4787 6238
Email cleopat@ozemail.com.au
Set in extensive gardens designed by
the late Paul Sorensen, this elegant,
French Provincial-style restaurant and
guesthouse offers respite from the
stresses of modern life. Chef Damien
Pignolet's cuisine is French and
flavourful, perfectly suited to the brisk
mountain air, with a menu that makes
the most of fresh seasonal produce.
Open Lunch Sun from 1pm, dinner
daily from 7.30pm
Cost $66–88 per person
Payment AmEx, Bankcard, Diners,
MasterCard, Visa

Vulcans

33 Govetts Leap Rd
Blackheath NSW 2785
Phone 02/4787 6899
Warmed by the yeasty breath of a
wood-fired oven and the buzz of
happy diners, this former bakery
conjures up some of the tastiest
dishes in the mountains, with slow-
roasted comfort food given extra
pizazz by Asian spicing. Save some
room for Philip Searle's signature
dessert, a chequerboard of anise,
pineapple and licorice ice cream.
Open Fri–Sun noon–3pm &
6pm–11pm
Cost $35–40 per person
Payment AmEx, Bankcard, Diners,
MasterCard, Visa

COMMUNITY

Blue Mountains PLWHA Centre

rear, 2 Station St (PO Box 187)
Katoomba NSW 2780
Phone Julie 02/4782 2119

Gender Mixed
Lunches, social contact, massage,
natural therapies, newsletters,
computer equipment, gym, HIV

treatment information are all available at this friendly drop-in centre.
Open Wed 11.30am–3pm, Fri 11.30am–3pm

Blue Mountains Sexual Health and HIV Clinic

Katoomba Hospital
Great Western Highway
Katoomba NSW 2780
Phone 02/4780 6060
Fax 02/4782 4659
Free STD testing, treatment and counselling, by appointment. No Medicare card required.
Open Mon 9am–3.30am, Wed 8.30am–12.30pm

Mountain Lesbian News

PO Box 2
Katoomba NSW 2780
Phone Jocelyn 02/4757 2990
Email gemces@ozemail.com.au
Mountain Lesbian News is a bi-monthly magazine put out by lesbians in the Blue Mountains. It includes stories and poetry, news and articles. *Mountain Lesbian News* also organizes

social activies, including dances, dinners, bushwalks and games nights.
Cost $4 per issue, $20 annual subscription

Three Sisters Social Group Inc.

PO Box 74
Leura NSW 2780
Phone 0414 865 372
Gender Men
Gay social network for men living in the Blue Mountains. Meets the second Tuesday of each month for dinner; other social functions are held throughout the year.

Young Lesbian Group

PO Box 51
Katoomba NSW 2780
Phone 02/4782 2875
Email umyc@hotmail.com
Gender Women
Lesbian group for girls and women up to the age of 24 exploring social issues, sharing social activities and offering support to those in the Blue Mountains region.

Mudgee District

Further west, on the far side of the Great Dividing Range from the Blue Mountains and some 300km from Sydney, is **Mudgee**, the heart of a youthful but very promising wine region surrounded by unspoilt countryside.

High Tweeters Holiday Farmstay

High Tweeters, Nullo Mountain
Rylstone NSW 2849
Phone 02/6379 6253
Fax 02/6379 6253

Gender Mixed
Set among pristine bush and nature reserves southeast of Mudgee, *High Tweeters* boasts great views and total seclusion. There are dams on the property where you can

swim, and plenty of wildlife. Motel-style rooms are fully equipped with cooking facilities; bathrooms are shared. Barbecue facilities are provided, and breakfast is available on request. Clothing is optional.

Cost $55 per room
Payment Cash only

Parkview Guest House
99 Market St
Mudgee NSW 2850
Phone 02/6372 4477
Fax 02/6372 4477

Gender Mixed

Victorian house with large rooms opening onto a wide veranda. Rooms have four-poster beds, ensuites and open fires, and there's a cosy guest lounge and library with games, and complimentary port and sherry. One block from the centre of Mudgee. A cooked breakfast is included in the tariff, and evening meals are available by arrangement. Smoking outside only.

Cost $120–155 per room
Payment Bankcard, EFTPOS, MasterCard, Visa; cheque

The Hawkesbury and the Central Coast

Barely an hour out of Sydney is the Hawkesbury river region, with its maze of waterways and bush-clad headlands and islands. The stretch of coast between here and Newcastle, called the Central Coast, is renowned for its lakes and beaches. The main tourist resort is family-oriented **Terrigal**, just north of Broken Bay, where the Hawkesbury finally spills into the sea.

ACCOMMODATION

Lavender Homestead
60 Victoria St
Teralba NSW 2284
Phone 02/4958 6579 or 0417 675 849
Fax 02/4958 6579
Gender Mixed

Near Lake Macquarie and Newcastle, *Lavender Homestead* is a Federation house with three bedrooms, all with French doors opening onto a veranda and period furnishings, including claw-foot baths and brass beds. Set in a lakeside valley with walking and cycling tracks, this is an ideal house for a group getaway. Commitment ceremonies, either catered or self-catered, are a speciality. *Lavender Homestead* can accommodate groups of up to 17 people, with two separate cottages sleeping four and seven in addition to rooms in the main house. Dog kennels and breakfast can be arranged.

Cost From $550 per weekend (two nights)
Payment Cash only

Sails

6 Marroomba Rd
Terrigal NSW 2260
Phone 02/4384 7444
Fax 02/4384 7222
Gender Mixed
Located in the heart of Terrigal,
a minute from the beach, *Sails* offers
executive one-bedroom units with
spas, and studio units, all with mini-
kitchens. No smoking.
Cost $160–180 per unit
Payment AmEx, Bankcard, EFTPOS,
MasterCard, Visa

COMMUNITY

Hawkesbury Sexual Health Clinic

108 March St
Richmond NSW 2753
Phone 02/4578 1622
Fax 02/4588 5085
Confidential and free service offering
STD diagnosis and treatment, HIV
testing and treatment for people living
with HIV/AIDS, hepatitis C testing
and information, as well as pap
smears. The clinic also offers a wide
variety of resources and counselling
for sexually related issues. No
Medicare card required.
Open Tuesdays only (appointments
preferred)

Newcastle and the Hunter Valley

Heading upstream from its mouth at the industrial port city of
Newcastle, the Hunter River winds its way past former mining
villages to the wineries of the Hunter Valley, where you can
indulge in wine tastings and fine dining.

ACCOMMODATION

Eaglereach Wilderness Resort

Summer Hill Rd
Vacy NSW 2421
Phone 02/4938 8233
Fax 02/4938 8234
Email info@eaglereach.com.au
Web www.eaglereach.com.au
Gender Mixed
Located north of the Hunter Valley, just
over two hours from Sydney by road,
the lodges at this resort vary in size
from one- to five-bedroom and all are
very private, with spectacular views.
The wild scenery of the Barrington
Tops National Park and state forests are
close by. Gourmet picnic hampers are
available and there's a la carte dining at
Treetops restaurant – or a chef can be
arranged to cater for you in your lodge.
Tariff includes breakfast.
Cost From $210 per couple per night
(two-night minimum stay)
Payment AmEx, Bankcard, Diners,
MasterCard, Visa

Hunter Resort Country Estate

Hermitage Rd
Pokolbin NSW 2320
Phone 02/4998 7777
Fax 02/49987787
Email resort@huntervalley.com.au
Web www.HunterResort.com.au
Gender Mixed

Surrounded by 30-year-old vineyards, the *Hunter Resort* posesses its own winery, a wine school, restaurant and café. The hotel itself has tennis courts, pool, heated spa and mountain bikes for guests' use. Choose between Hunter rooms, spa suites or the two-bedroom cottage. Nearby attractions include golf courses, horse and carriage rides, hot air ballooning, tandem skydiving – and over 70 wineries to visit!

Cost From $155 per room
Payment AmEx, Bankcard, Diners, MasterCard, Visa

Peppers Anchorage

Corlette Point Rd
Corlette NSW 2315
Phone 02/4984 2555
Fax 02/4984 0300
Email papsres@peppers.com.au
Web www.peppers.com.au
Gender Mixed

The luxurious *Peppers Anchorage* is a popular weekend escape for wealthy Sydneysiders. Set on Port Stephens marina, about 75km north of Newcastle, it offers a range of rooms and suites, all with balconies and ensuites. Room rates include buffet breakfast, and some packages include all meals and French champagne on arrival. *Merrett's* restaurant is famous for its à la carte menu and is open to the public.

Cost From $285 per room midweek, $635 weekends
Payment AmEx, Bankcard, Diners, MasterCard, Visa; cheque

Pokolbin Village Resort and Conference Centre

188 Broke Rd
Pokolbin NSW 2320
Phone 02/4998 7670
Fax 02/4998 7377
Email info@pokolbinvillage.com.au
Web www.pokolbinvillage.com.au
Gender Mixed

Right in the heart of the Hunter Valley wine district, the gay-owned and -operated *Pokolbin Village Resort* has two restaurants, a swimming pool, plus tennis and volleyball courts. All rooms have private veranda, mini-bar and microwave oven.

Cost $165–265 per room
Payment AmEx, Bankcard, Diners, MasterCard, Visa

Splinters Guest House

617 Hermitage Rd
Pokolbin NSW 2335
Phone David 02/65 747 118
Fax 02/65 747 280
Email splinters@hunterlink.net.au
Web www.splinters.com.au
Gender Mixed

Splinters offers comfortable rooms with ensuites or self-contained lodges nestled among NSW's best wineries. Guest facilities include a swimming pool and bicycles, and there's complimentary continental breakfast, wine, cheese, port and chocolates.

Cost From $95 per room
Payment AmEx, Bankcard, EFTPOS, MasterCard, Visa; cheque

Club g Newcastle
139 Maitland Rd
Islington NSW 2296
Phone 02/4969 1848
Email kinsair2@hotmail.com
Gender Mixed
Very friendly 1920s pub located in an inner suburb of Newcastle that

promises loads of fun without the attitude. *Club g* mixes gays, lesbians, queers and 'queer straights' into a great time. Phone for details of special men's and women's nights, karaoke competitions, drag shows etc.
Open Daily 10am–late
Admission Cover charge at weekends

ACON (AIDS Council of NSW) Hunter Region
129 Maitland Rd
Islington NSW 2296
Phone 02/4927 6808
Fax 02/4927 6485
Email hunter@acon.org.au

Gender Mixed
Information and support for those living with HIV/AIDS, lovers, family and friends. Also needle exchange service, safe sex supplies, information and guidance.
Open Mon–Fri 9am–5pm

Mid-North Coast

North of Newcastle, the coast unfurls into the boating paradise of **Port Stephens**, where dolphins abound in the deep blue water. Further north are the resorts of **Port Macquarie** and **Coffs Harbour**, the latter marking the transition to subtropical climes – tackily announced by the vision in yellow that is the Big Banana (don't ask).

Aanuka Beach Resort
Firman Drive (PO Box 6069)
Coffs Harbour NSW 2450
Phone 02/6652 7555
Fax 02/6650 2565
Email reservations@aanuka.com.au or brad@aanuka.com.au

Web www.aanuka.com.au
Gender Mixed
Set in lush tropical gardens that go right down to its own surfing beach, *Aanuka* has a choice of suites or villas, all featuring two-person spas and 24-hour room service. The resort is 7km

from the centre of Coffs Harbour, and ten minutes' drive from the airport, with complimentary airport transfers for guests. Breakfast is included in the tariff, and guest facilities include two restaurants, a cocktail bar with live entertainment, tennis courts, gym and on-site masseuse.

Cost $210–365 per room
Payment AmEx, Bankcard, Diners, EFTPOS, MasterCard, Visa

Azura Beach House
109 Pacific Drive
Port Macquarie NSW 2444

Phone 02/6582 2700
Fax 02/6582 2700
Email hosts@azura.com.au
Web www.azura.com.au
Gender Mixed
Modern, private retreat in the heart of Port Macquarie, opposite the beach. All rooms have ensuite bathrooms, TV and video, and breakfast is included. There is also a heated pool, spa and hot tub, barbecue area and shared lounge. Smoking outside only.
Cost From $105 single, $120 double
Payment Bankcard, MasterCard, Visa

BEACHES AND POOLS

Little Diggers Beach
turn off opposite the Big Banana
Coffs Harbour NSW 2450

The northern end of this nude beach is popular with gays.

COMMUNITY

ACON (AIDS Council of NSW) Mid-North Coast
PO Box 1329
Port Macquarie NSW 2444
Phone 02/6584 0943
Fax 02/6583 3810
Email aconmnc@midcoast.com.au
Web www.acon.org.au

Gender Mixed
Information and support for those living with HIV/AIDS, plus needle exchange, safe sex supplies and information, counselling and guidance. They also offer information on surrounding gay and lesbian groups.
Open Mon–Fri 9am–5pm

Byron Bay and Hinterland

At the top end of the state you can't go past **Byron Bay** (the most easterly point in Australia) for its beaches, cafés and relaxed attitudes. Nestled in the hills of the hinterland, about 45 minutes' drive from Byron, **Lismore** is the region's main centre and has become a haven for artists, with plenty of small galleries and craft shops to explore – not to mention the extraordinary *Winsome Hotel*. About 20 minutes' drive north is the counter-cultural town of **Nimbin**, which has clung on to the reputation it gained in the heady 1970s as the alternative-lifestyle capital of Australia. Right up near the Queensland border, **Murwillumbah** is the main town in the lush farming country of the Tweed Valley.

ACCOMMODATION

Andi's B&B

PO Box 306
Bangalow NSW 2479
Phone 02/6687 1192
Email andi@nor.com.au
Gender Women
Andi's B&B is situated in the North Coast hinterland, 15 minutes' drive from Byron Bay and 5 minutes from Bangalow, where there are some excellent restaurants and cafés. The house is surrounded by trees and is very private. Accommodation is homestay-style, with private access and a large deck. Continental breakfast and the services of a massage therapist can be arranged.
Cost $66 single, $88 double (discount for longer stays)
Payment Cheque

Black Sheep Guest House

449a Gungas Rd
Nimbin NSW 2480
Phone 02/6689 1095
Fax 02/6689 1095
Email blackmac@blacksheepfarm.com.au
Web www.blacksheepfarm.com.au
Gender Mixed

A private retreat with pool and sauna in a secluded valley 6km from Nimbin. The accommodation is fully self-contained and has an open fire.
Cost $155 per unit (sleeps three to six) per night, $825 weekly
Payment Cheque

Byron Bay Rainforest Resort

39–75 Broken Head Rd
Byron Bay NSW 2481
Phone Murray and Catherine
02/6685 6139
Fax 02/6685 8754
Email thewheel@nor.com.au
Web www.byron-bay.com
/rainforestresort/index.html
Gender Mixed
Take a private cabin or a room in the guesthouse and enjoy the luxury of 35 acres of wilderness. It's not too far from civilization and is just a short distance from town and beaches. This resort is dog-friendly, and there's a council-approved pet exercise beach a 10-minute walk away.
Cost From $130 per room
Payment Bankcard, EFTPOS, MasterCard, Visa

Middle Reef Beachhouse

13 Marvel St
Byron Bay NSW 2481
Phone 02/6685 5118
Fax 02/6680 9430
Email byronaccom@ozemail.com.au
Web www.byronaccommodation.com
Gender Mixed

Homestay-style clean and friendly accommodation in the heart of Byron Bay, 200m from the beach. *Middle Reef* operates as a shared house, with guests sharing the kitchen and bathrooms of this old Queenslander-style house.
Cost From $33 single, $66 double per room
Payment AmEx, Bankcard, Diners, EFTPOS, MasterCard, Visa; cheque

Oasis Resort

End of Scott St (PO Box 367)
Byron Bay NSW 2481
Phone 02/6685 7390
Fax 02/6685 8290
Email oasis@amrupe.com.au
Web www.byronbay.net.au/oasis
Gender Mixed

These fully self-contained apartments and eccentric treetop houses sleep up to six adults. The complex, which is located between the centre of Byron Bay and the popular nude/gay Kingshead Beach, contains a pool, spa, sauna, gym and tennis court.
Cost $135–330 per room
Payment AmEx, Bankcard, Diners, MasterCard, Visa

Winsome Hotel

11 Bridge St
Lismore NSW 2480
Phone 02/6621 2283
Fax 02/6622 6458
Email ljrich@lis.net.au
Gender Mixed

This rambling pub offers single, double or twin accommodation in large rooms with shared facilities, in the traditional Aussie pub style; a continental breakfast is included in the tariff. Bookings are advised during peak holiday periods – especially at New Year, when the town hosts the famous Tropical Fruits party. Gay and lesbian-owned and -operated.
Cost From $33 single, $50 double (minimum four-night stay during peak periods)
Payment AmEx, Bankcard, EFTPOS, MasterCard, Visa

CAFÉS AND RESTAURANTS

Dr Juice Bar

142 Keen St
Lismore NSW 2480
Phone 02/6622 4440

Vegan and vegetarian delights including burgers, falafel and daily specials, as well as cakes, juices and coffee. Lesbian-owned and -operated.
Open Mon–Fri 9.30am–4pm
Cost $5–10 per person
Payment Cash only

Winsome Hotel

11 Bridge St
Lismore NSW 2480
Phone 02/6621 2283

Fax 02/6622 6458
Email ljrich@lis.net.au
This huge old Federation pub beside
Wilsons River is the only gay/lesbian
venue for miles around, so it attracts a
unique mix of gays and lesbians,
queers and ferals, plus a few friendly
locals. There are three dining options:
the stylish *Two Bridges Eatery* (daily
noon–3pm & 6pm–10pm, $20–30
per person); the *Verandah Bistro*
($10–20 per person); and a bar menu,
with all meals under $10. Every

Friday night there's a disco, and then
the first Saturday of the month is
Boys' Party and the third Saturday is
Girls' Party. At New Year, the hotel is
the gathering point for the famous
Tropical Fruits party. Gay and lesbian-
owned and -operated.
Open Daily noon–midnight
(sometimes later), Fri until 3am (party
night and disco)
Payment AmEx, Bankcard, EFTPOS,
MasterCard, Visa

BEACHES AND POOLS

Kingshead Beach
Seven Mile Beach Rd
Byron Bay NSW 2481
This popular gay and nudist beach is
set beneath some beautiful rainforest
7km south of Byron Bay off Broken
Head Road. You'll need to take a left

turn onto the Seven Mile Beach
Road and park in the first car park
south of Broken Head Beach. Walk
through the rainforest and you'll soon
discover that the southern end of the
beach is popular with the gay
fraternity.

COMMUNITY

ACON (AIDS Council of NSW) Northern Rivers
27 Uralba St
Lismore NSW 2480
Phone 02/6622 1555 or
freecall 1800/633 637
Fax 02/6622 1520
Gender Mixed
Information and support for those
living with HIV/AIDS, lovers, family
and friends. Also safe-sex supplies and
information, gay/lesbian newspapers
(including the local *Rainbow
Newsletter*), counselling and guidance.
Dispenses vitamin supplements for

people living with HIV.
Open Mon–Fri 9am–5pm

Radical Faeries
PO Box 1220
Lismore NSW 2480
Gender Mixed
Network of gay and lesbian folk who
have established an alternative
community.

Tropical Fruits
PO Box 771
Lismore NSW 2480
Phone 02/6622 4353 FruitLine

(recorded information)
Email fruits@byron-bay.com
Web www.tropicalfruits.org.au
Gender Mixed
The New South Wales Northern
Rivers Connection organizes great
parties, memberships and newsletters
for those around the Byron
Bay/Lismore area. Great for making
contact – email adresses as follows:
fruitsec@nor.com.au (general
enquiries, ticket sales, membership);
juiced@nor.com.au (editor of *Fruit
Juice* newsletter, for contributions,
advertising, listings, news);
lbertram@ozemail.com.au
(chairperson – Lynne Bertram).

Tweed Shire Women's Group
5 Queen St
Murwillumbah NSW 2484
Phone 07 6672 4188
Fax 02/6672 5279
Email tswomen@norex.com.au
Web www.norex.com.au/
~tswomen/index.htm
Gender Women
Women's resource centre and library,
providing referral and activities for
women and their children.
Open Mon–Fri 10am–4pm

New England

This plateau country in the north of the state is renowned for its
gemstones, with the route linking the towns of Tamworth, Inverell
and Glen Innes dubbed 'The Fossickers' Way'. The trail passes
through **Bingara**, so keep your eyes peeled when you stay at the
The Hill Homestead and you might even leave a little richer . . .

The Hill Homestead
Kiora Rd
Bingara NSW 2404
Phone 02/6724 1686
Fax 02/6724 1381
Email thehill@northnet.com.au
Web thehillhomestead@hotmail.com
Gender Mixed
Two hours' drive northwest of
Tamworth, *The Hill Homestead* is a gay-
owned and -operated, rather grand

guesthouse in a beautiful valley full of
wildlife. It is a member of *AGLTA* and
IGLTA and is very popular with gay
men and nudists. There's a pool, sauna,
video library, pool table and plenty of
home-cooked food. Bushwalking and
horse riding are also available.
Cost From $10 camping to $105 per
person (full board)
Payment AmEx, Bankcard, Diners,
EFTPOS, MasterCard, Visa

The Southern Highlands – and west to capital country

A couple of hours' drive southwest of Sydney, the manicured English–style gardens and untamed National Parks of the Southern Highlands make a cool and tranquil retreat from the city – or a welcome diversion on the way to the 'Capital Country' surrounding Canberra and the Snowy Mountains.

Adelong's Beaufort House

77 Tumut St
Adelong NSW 2729
Phone 02/6946 2273
Fax 02/6946 2553
Email beaufort@dragnet.com.au
Web www.beaufort.dragnet.com.au
Gender Mixed

This historic gay–owned and –operated hotel on the western side of the Snowy Mountains, just off the Hume Highway, offers old–fashioned hospitality and a restaurant. Rooms are individually decorated, with private or shared facilities.
Cost From $95 single, $165 double
Payment AmEx, Bankcard, MasterCard, Visa

The Carrington of Bungendore

21 Malbon St
Bungendore NSW 2621
Phone 02/6238 1044
Fax 02/6238 1036
Email carrington39@hotmail.com
Web www.thecarrington.com
Gender Mixed

Luxury motel–style accommodation in a garden setting, 40 minutes' drive from Canberra. Next door is the *Carrington* restaurant, a fully restored historic Cobb & Co coach house with open fireplaces and bar. Some rooms have spa baths, full breakfast is included in the tariff, and dinner bed and breakfast packages are also available.
Cost From $185 per room
Payment AmEx, Bankcard, Diners, EFTPOS, MasterCard, Visa; cheque

Idle-A-Wile

2 Penrose Rd
Bundanoon NSW 2578
Phone 02/4883 6822
Fax 02/4883 6969
Email stefanev@highnetdosnet.au
Web www.highlandsnsw.com.au/idleawile.html
Gender Mixed

Lovely country guesthouse with gardens next to Morton National Park, in the Southern Highlands. Gay–owned and –operated, with superb food and homely feel. April sees lots of men in skirts parading through the streets of Bundanoon – don't jump to conclusions – it's just the pipers in the annual Highlands Festival, Brigadoon. *Idle-A-Wile* is walking distance from Bundanoon station. Group bookings of up to 10 welcome.
Cost $99 per person midweek (bed and breakfast), $286 weekends (dinner, bed and breakfast for two nights)
Payment Cheque

Wollongong and the South Coast

On the coast south of Sydney, the city of **Wollongong** and the vast steel works at Port Kembla loom large. Beyond this point, the South Coast eases into its stride, its pristine beaches backed by eucalypt trees and rolling pastures. Within a couple of hours' drive from Sydney is **Kiama**, which is famous for its blowhole, and **Berry**, with its main street full of antique and craft shops. Further south, the dazzling white sands of **Jervis Bay** and the wilderness of the south-east forests beckon.

ACCOMMODATION

The Beach House
Address on enquiry
(Kiama NSW 2533)
Phone Lyndall or Kelli 02/4232 2140
Fax 02/4232 4179
Email bear@1earth.net.au
Gender Mixed
Beachfront house and apartment in Kiama, with ocean and mountain views; breakfast hamper provided.
Cost $130–150 per couple per night
Payment Cheque

Broughton Mill Farm Guesthouse
78 Woodhill Mountain Rd
Berry NSW 2535
Phone 02/4464 2446
Fax 02/4464 1621
Email info@broughtonmillfarm.com.au
Web www.broughtonmillfarm.com.au
Gender Mixed
Guesthouse set in extensive gardens with tennis court, solar pool, spa and petanque court. Five guest suites sleep up to four, with private bathroom and sitting room, TV and sound system; all suites open onto garden. Full breakfast is included, dinners by arrangement, drinks and function rooms available. Smoking outside only.
Cost $135–170 per room midweek, $195–230 weekends (two-night minimum stay)
Payment Bankcard, MasterCard, Visa

Far Meadow Lodge
199 Coolangatta Rd
Berry NSW 2535
Phone 02/4448 5500
Fax 02/4448 5500
Email candya@ozemail.com.au
Web www.farmeadowlodge.com.au
Gender Mixed
Plenty of space and tranquillity with rural and ocean views, 6km from Berry but with restaurants nearby. All suites have log fires, private lounges, spa baths and champagne on arrival; smoking outside only. Full breakfast included in tariff, and there's a saltwater pool and barbecue available for guests' use. A self-contained cottage is also available.
Cost $140–175 per suite
Payment Bankcard, MasterCard, Visa; cheque

Riverglen Lodge
Address on enquiry
(Nimmitabel NSW 2631)
Phone 02/6458 5272
Fax 02/6253 5523
Email monkswa@aol.com
Gender Mixed
Located in the magnificent south-east
forests, this remote hideaway offers a
complete break from all things urban.
Riverglen Lodge is an old farmhouse
sleeping up to six, with one double
bed and four bunks. The lodge has a
fully equipped kitchen, open
fireplace, barbecue area and
wraparound verandas. Breakfast is
optional ($11 per person). The house
fronts onto the river which is ideal for
swimming and backs onto a wildlife
reserve ideal for birdwatching and
native wildlife encounters. Dogs
allowed outside. No smoking inside.
Cost $100 per night
Payment AmEx, Bankcard, Diners,
MasterCard, Visa

South Coast Holiday Cottages
Sanctuary Point
Jervis Bay NSW 2540
Phone 02/4443 7665

Fax 02/4443 7627
Email christine@shoalhaven.net.au
Web www.machelp.com.au/
cottages.html
Gender Mixed
Self-contained waterfront cottages
sleeping two to twelve. Close to white-
sand beaches, national parks, restaurants,
Sanctuary Point and Jervis Bay.
Cost $61–154 per unit
Payment Bankcard, MasterCard, Visa;
cheque

Spotted Gums Cottage
Address on enquiry
(Berry NSW 2535)
Phone 02/4464 1779
Email spotgum@shoalhaven.net.au
Gender Mixed
Self-contained garden cottage with
spa, TV, CD player, barbecue and a
terrace with a view. Champagne on
arrival and breakfast basket in the
morning; bicycles available for
borrowing. Smoking outside only.
Cost $130 first night, $110 each extra
night (two-night minimum stay at
weekends)
Payment Bankcard, MasterCard, Visa;
cheque

BARS AND CLUBS

Chequers
341 Crown St
Wollongong NSW 2500
Phone 02/4226 3788
Gender Mixed
Basically, there is just one 'specific
club' in Wollongong – and it's on top

of a car park! Bar, dance area and an
awful lot of mirror balls to dance away
the night under.
Open Wed–Sat 8pm–late
Admission Free
Payment Cash only

Riverina

For many, the prime agricultural land of New South Wales' south-western plains is little more than a blur of fields, seen through the car window en route between Sydney and Melbourne, but the main centres of **Wagga Wagga** and **Albury** are sizeable communities in their own right. And you may well find yourself stopping in the area, if only to break the journey.

ACCOMMODATION

Tocumwal Motel
11 Murray St
Tocumwal NSW 2714
Phone 03 5874 3022
Fax 03 5874 3438
Gender Mixed
Regular motel-style accommodation right on the border – a fine gay/lesbian-friendly place to break the long drive between Sydney and Melbourne. All rooms have ensuite, VCR, and access to the pool and barbecue. A light breakfast is included in the room rate.
Cost $55–88 per room
Payment AmEx, Bankcard, Diners, MasterCard, Visa

COMMUNITY

Albury Wodonga Lesbian Group
Albury Wodonga Women's Centre
643 Olive St
Albury NSW 2640
Phone 02/6041 1977
Fax 02/6041 1726
Email womenscentre@hotkey.net.au
Gender Women
Organizes dinners, social functions, support, networking and discussion groups for women.

Wagga Wagga Women's Women
1 Osborne Ave
Kooringal NSW 2650
Phone Eunice 02/6922 5233
Email eunicejroberts@aussiemail.com.au
Gender Women
Social support group for lesbians in the Wagga Wagga region. Monthly dinners and occasional outings.

Australian Capital Territory

The **Australian Capital Territory** is 80km from north to south and about 30km wide. It was carved out of the central section of New South Wales in 1909, and largely owes its existence to the fact that neither Melbourne nor Sydney would agree to let the other be the 'capital city' of the newly formed Federal Government in 1901. In the end, a provision in the *Constitution Act* decreed that the **seat of government** be in the state of New South Wales and not less than 100 miles from Sydney. The Australian Capital Territory (ACT) was the result.

The territory's nexus, **Canberra**, was designed by Walter Burley Griffin to be a garden city of the future, but its promise has never been entirely fulfilled. A lake was created as the focus of the city and named – you guessed it – Lake Burley Griffin. Several **satellite suburbs** radiate out from the city centre, linked by green-swathed roadways.

The ACT's inland location and its elevation of 600m above sea level means it experiences four distinct **seasons**. Winter nights frequently drop to or below freezing and even the summer nights can be quite cool.

Canberra

The **capital of Australia** is a truly unique and slightly bizarre city. Because its raison d'être is as the seat of Federal Parliament, Canberra's 350,000 citizens consist largely of politicians, civil servants and their families. The first thing visitors to Canberra should know is while it may be the capital of the country it is home to a only a small population and sometimes it seems as if all those people are locked inside their homes and offices. Some would describe Canberra as 'neat as a pin', while others are more likely to say it is sterile. At night you may feel you are the only person out on the street and this can have a disconcerting effect; however Canberra does not have a reputation for being particularly dangerous.

Canberra can feel deserted on weekends when many of the politicians return to the cities they really live in and **public transport** services are drastically reduced (it can be 30 minutes to an hour between buses). For **information** on public bus services, phone 02/6207 7611 or 13 1710.
   The number to ring for a **taxi** is 02/6285 9222.

Gay men will soon discover that Canberra has a lively beat scene (where there's a park, there's a beat – and there are plenty of parks). And **women** will find their sisters playing pool and shooting the breeze in the *Meridian Club*. There is an active gay and lesbian scene on the weekend, which usually involves forays to *Heaven* nightclub and the *Meridian Club*. The latter is owned and run by members of the gay/lesbian community and its central location makes it a handy place to find out what's happening in the city. The **scene** is a low-key one, and although there is a gay sauna in town, there's no gay district or ghetto as such.

While on the one hand, Canberra prides itself on being civic-minded and espouses wholesome family values, some weird loophole of Federal law also allows it to be the unlikely centre of Australia's **pornography** industry. One industrial suburb, Fyshwick, has a number of sex supermarkets where shoppers casually fill trolleys with videos and marital aids; some of these porn palaces have sex clubs attached.

Finally, it's worth noting that Canberra is not a friendly place for smokers. No restaurants and few hotels will allow you to smoke inside, though nightclubs (with the exception of the gay one) are usually more easygoing. The laws on **smoking** are very strict and it's one of those places where you will feel like a freak of nature with a cigarette in your hand. This is particularly difficult for smokers in winter, since Canberra gets very cold, situated as it is beneath Australia's highest mountains.

Canberra highlights and hot-spots

- New **Parliament House**, built into Capital Hill itself and visible from almost anywhere in the city, is a magnificent example of modern civic architecture. You are welcome to wander around, look at the section of the Magna Carta that resides here or feast your eyes on the Australian arts and crafts that adorn its interior. You can observe parliamentary debates or stand on the grassed-over summit and indulge in delusions of grandeur. And it's all free.

- The **National Gallery of Australia** houses the lion's share of Australia's art treasures and also plays host to some of the most spectacular travelling exhibitions from all over the world. Situated on the shores of Lake Burley Griffin, the gallery also incorporates a beautiful sculpture garden with an ethereal Japanese mist-making machine.

- The **Hyatt Hotel Canberra** is one of the city's earliest hotels. Built in the colonial tradition of hotels such as Raffles Singapore, it dates back to 1924, when the city was still being built. While it's expensive to stay in (see p.108), the hotel's public areas have some quaint historical exhibits (such as the original city plan submissions or the menus for royal dinners in days gone by) and it serves 'high' afternoon teas.

- The **Meridian Club** (see pp.111–112) is an essential first stop. Don't expect a club scene like you'd find in Sydney or Melbourne, but you will encounter a friendly mix of gays and lesbians who are only too pleased to give you the rundown on the local scene.

- A totally queer thing to do is take a drive around **Fyshwick** to visit the sex supermarkets. Passing rows of car yards and furniture warehouses while searching out the lurid flashing lights of these bizarre establishments might not be everyone's idea of a night out, but for consumers of erotic movies and sex toys – believe it or not – this is Australia's mecca.

Capital Executive Apartment Hotel

108 Northbourne Ave
Braddon ACT 2612
Phone 02/6243 8333
Fax 02/6248 8011
Email mail@ceahotel.com.au
Web www.ceahotel.com.au
Gender Mixed
A centrally located place with all mod cons in its apartments, including kitchenette, air-conditioning, TV with free in-house movies, mini-bar, room service, hairdryer, iron and ironing board. Other hotel amenities are 24-hour check-in, secure parking, a sauna, spa pool, and the Haig Italian Restaurant.
Cost $127–182 per room
Payment AmEx, Bankcard, Diners, EFTPOS, MasterCard, Visa; cheque

Forrest Inn and Apartments

30 National Circuit
Forrest ACT 2603
Phone Freecall 1800/676 372 or 02/6295 3433
Fax 02/6295 2119
Email reservations@forrestinn.com.au
Web www.forrestinn.com.au
Gender Mixed
Close to Parliament House and just a short walk to cafés and restaurants, this complex combines a 76-room motel with 26 serviced apartments. Services include a restaurant and bar, a guest laundry and business services. The tariff includes breakfast.
Cost $109 per room
Payment AmEx, Bankcard, Diners, EFTPOS, MasterCard, Visa; cheque

Hyatt Hotel Canberra

Commonwealth Ave
Yarralumla ACT 2600
Phone 02/6270 1234
Fax 02/6281 5998
Web www.canberra@hyatt.com.au
Gender Mixed
This beautifully restored 1920s art deco hotel right on the shores of Lake Burley Griffin is set in landscaped gardens. This is where the politicians, socialites and foreign dignitaries stay, so not surprisingly there is an atmosphere of relaxed indulgence with a gym, pool, sauna and spa, and sporting facilities. There are two restaurants, a smoking bar and the irresistibly camp but stylish Tea Lounge.
Cost From $237 per room; weekend packages available
Payment AmEx, Bankcard, Diners, EFTPOS, MasterCard, Visa

Northbourne Lodge

522 Northbourne Ave
Downer ACT 2602
Phone 02/6257 2599
Fax 02/6248 0442
Email norlodge@wxc.com.au
Gender Mixed
Situated on the main road into Canberra from the Hume Highway, this gay-owned and -operated guesthouse has ten bright clean rooms all with private bathrooms. Tariff includes breakfast. The management is helpful and will make restaurant recommendations and reservations.
Cost $90 single, $110 double
Payment AmEx, Bankcard, MasterCard, Visa

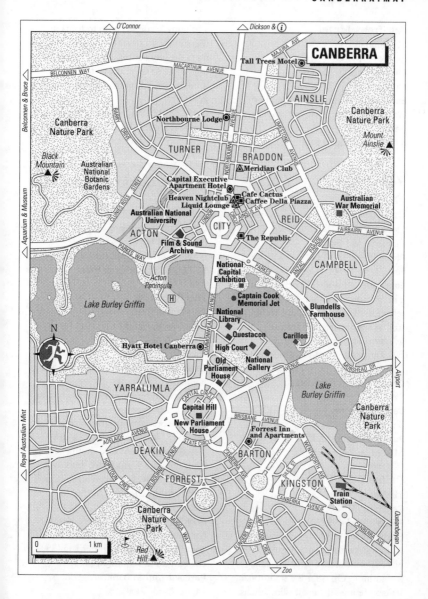

Tall Trees Motel

21 Stephens St
Ainslie ACT 2602
Phone 02/6247 9200
Fax 02/6257 4479
Email talltreesmotel@bigpond.com
Web www.bestwestern.com.au/talltrees
Gender Mixed
There is a range of rooms (some have

a balcony, some sleep up to four) in this motel in a quiet location 3km from the city centre. Breakfast is not included but there is a restaurant. Smoking and non-smoking rooms are available.
Cost $83–122 single, $94–132 double
Payment AmEx, Bankcard, Diners, EFTPOS, MasterCard, Visa

CAFÉS AND RESTAURANTS

Cafe Cactus

Cinema Centre, Garema Place, Civic
Canberra ACT 2600
Phone 02/6248 0449
Fax 02/6248 0449
Email cafecactus@webone.com.au
This gay-owned café has a wide selection of bagels and sandwiches, as well as main meals and a great selection of homemade cakes. It's BYO and indoor and outdoor seating is available, as is Internet access.
Open Mon–Fri 8am–late,
Sat–Sun 10am–late
Cost Breakfast & lunch $5–10,
dinner $10–20
Payment Bankcard, EFTPOS,
MasterCard, Visa

Caffee Della Piazza

19 Garema Place, Civic
Canberra ACT 2600
Phone 02/6248 9711
Fax 02/6249 1238
Although not exclusively gay, this place is not called 'Caffee Della Fag' for nothing. On offer is a traditional Italian menu and a great wine list, as

well as lighter meals, such as foccacia.
Open Daily 10am–late
Cost $15–30 per person
Payment AmEx, Bankcard, Diners, EFTPOS, MasterCard, Visa

The Republic

20 Allara St Civic
Canberra ACT 2600
Phone 02/6247 1717
Fax 02/6247 9988
Email paulsmith@republicrestaurant.com.au
Web www.republic-restaurant.com.au
An excellent restaurant with a contemporary menu specializing in seafood. *The Republic* carries a vast selection of wines based on the best from the local region and, with over 20 available by the glass, you can do some serious sampling during the course of a leisurely meal.
Open Tues–Fri noon–late,
Sat 6pm–late
Cost Lunch $35–45, dinner $45–55, twilight dinner (6pm–8pm) $25
Payment AmEx, Bankcard, Diners, MasterCard, Visa

Tilley's Divine Cafe

Cnr Brigalow and Wattle streets
Lyneham ACT 2602
Phone 02/6249 1543
Fax 02/6248 6021
Licensed bar and sidewalk café that's also the best place in town to catch major overseas and local acts (tickets for shows can be booked in advance). *Tilley's* has a choice of indoor and outdoor seating. The opulent decor is in the tradition of old-world European theatre with booths and plush red velvet.
Open Daily 8am–midnight
Cost Breakfast $5–15, lunch $10–15, dinner $15–20
Payment AmEx, Bankcard, EFTPOS, MasterCard, Visa

BARS AND CLUBS

Heaven

Upstairs, Garema Place, Civic
Canberra ACT 2600
Phone 02/6257 6189
Gender Mixed
Heaven holds speciality nights to cover a range of tastes: Goth Night, Hi NRG, Retro and House, with Saturday and Sunday traditionally being the gay nights. It regularly has shows, competitions and giveaways to keep everyone entertained.
Open Wed–Thurs 10.30pm–4am, Fri–Sun 9pm–9am
Admission Varies, depending on night
Payment Cash only

Liquid Lounge

33 Petrie Plaza
Canberra ACT 2600
Phone 02/6257 1110
Fax 02/6257 6541
Email office@liquidlounge.com.au
Web www.office@liquidlounge.com.au
Gender Mixed
Canberra's young and hip crowd gather here Wednesday to Saturday to dance and let their hair down. There's Latino night on Wednesday, Thursday is 'Mambo Fiesta', Friday is 'Flashbacks', Saturday night is good ol' handbag. This is not an exclusively queer place, but is very gay/lesbian-friendly.
Open Wed–Thurs 8pm–2am, Fri–Sat 8pm–5am
Admission $6 Fri–Sat
Payment AmEx, Bankcard, MasterCard, Visa

Meridian Club

34 Mort St
Braddon ACT 2612
Phone 02/6248 9966
Email meridian@webone.com.au
Web www.meridian@webone.com.au
Gender Mixed; women only on Wednesday
This community-owned and -run club, known as 'Club Med' to the locals, is a friendly, relaxed place where you can drop in to meet people and pick up gay/lesbian information, including the *Canberra Queer Directory*. Wednesday night is women's pool night. This is also the home of Olga Gorgonzola, Canberra's (and possibly the Southern Hemisphere's) only Russian Drag Tzarina whose occasional 'Olgaflot' guided bus tours

of beats and saunas in Canberra have become legendary. There are DJs on Friday and Saturday nights; Friday evenings have a relaxed, laid-back after-work-cocktails ambience. Bears meet here the first and third Sunday of the month at 3pm. The *Meridian*

carries a range of gay/lesbian newspapers. The club's profits go to AIDS charities.
Open Tues–Thurs & Sun 6pm–late, Fri 5pm–late, Sat 8pm–late
Admission $5 for special events
Payment Cash only

SEX CLUBS AND SAUNAS

Adam & Eve

125 Gladstone St
Fyshwick ACT 2609
Phone 02/6239 1121
Gender Men
Here you'll find the latest all-male videos running continuously. There's cruise space – and lube and condoms are provided.
Open Daily 9am–midnight
Admission $5
Payment AmEx, Bankcard, Diners, EFTPOS, MasterCard, Visa

Canberra City Steam

153 Newcastle St
Fyshwick Canberra ACT 2602
Phone 02/6280 6980
Email citysteam@citysteam.com.au
Web www.citysteam.com.au
Gender Men
At *City Steam* you'll find an Internet café, dry sauna, spa, gym equipment, snack bar, licensed bar, video lounge, cubicles, cruise space and an adult shop. There are discounts for Long Yang Club members and Bears, plus

'Buddies Night' on Tuesday (two for the price of one).
Open Fri–Sat noon–3am, Sun–Thurs noon–1am
Admission $15 Fri–Sat, $13 Sun–Thurs
Payment AmEx, Bankcard, Diners, EFTPOS, MasterCard, Visa

Champions Headquarters for Men

Unit 14, Molongolo Mall
Fyshwick ACT 2609
Phone 02/6280 6969
Fax 02/6280 5656
Gender Men
This is a large dry venue offering all sorts of cruise spaces and theme rooms with the latest videos, a coffee lounge, as well as magazines and videos for purchase. Showers and lockers are also available.
Open Fri–Sat 9am–2am, Sun–Thurs 9am–midnight
Admission $11 Fri–Sat, $9 Sun–Thurs
Payment AmEx, Bankcard, Diners, EFTPOS, MasterCard, Visa

COMMUNITY

AIDS Action Council
16 Gorden St
Acton ACT 2601
Phone 02/6257 2855
Fax 02/6257 4838
Email aidsaction@aidsaction.org.au
Web www.aidsaction.org.au
Gender Mixed
Community-based organization
providing information, referrals and
support for people affected by HIV
and/or AIDS. Action provides
condoms, needle exchange and
distributes the *Sydney Star*, *Quirk*,
Brother Sister and *ACT Queer
Directory*. An in-house counsellor is
available for those wanting to discuss
sexuality issues.
Open Mon–Fri 9am–5pm

Gay Information and Counselling Service
ACT
Phone 02/6247 2726
Gender Men
Confidential and anonymous phone
counselling and support for gay and
bisexual men.

Gender Outreach
PO Box 4707
Kingston ACT 2604
Gender Mixed
This small friendly group of cross-
dressers and transsexuals meets
monthly and organizes occasional
outings which cater especially to
those still 'in the closet'.

Lesbian Line
GPO Box 1645
Canberra ACT 2601
Phone 02/6247 8882
Gender Women
This volunteer collective provides a
lesbian What's On and referral service.

Long Yang Club
GPO Box 263
Canberra ACT 2601
Phone Sam 02/6231 8037 or
Keith on 02/6286 5739
Email canberra@longyangclub.org
Web www.longyangclub.org
Gender Men
Long Yang is an informal social group
of gay men that aims to foster
friendship between gay Asians and
non-Asians in a friendly, non-
threatening atmosphere. The *Long
Yang Club* takes its name from the
classic Chinese novel, *A Dream of Red
Mansions*, in which Long Yang Jun
was a minister and favourite of Wei
Wang, the Prince of Wei. The group
meets monthly for social evenings. All
enquiries are handled in strictest
confidence.
Cost Membership $10

Queensland

Queensland is Australia's second-largest state and, some might say, it's another country. Those seeking justification of such a stance need look no further than the fact that **homosexuality** was not **legalized** in Queensland until the early 1990s.

Brisbane (or 'Brissie' to its friends), in the south-east corner, is the state's capital, and there are plenty of exciting day-trips to be taken from the city. Some 75km to the south is its more vulgar sister-city of Surfers Paradise, on the **Gold Coast** – Australia's answer to Honolulu. The glitz and kitsch are quite a sight to behold, but the 70km of beach are kept immaculate and there are plenty of amusements to keep you entertained. About 90 minutes' drive **north** of Brisbane are the unspoiled beaches and national parks of Noosa and the **Sunshine Coast**. At the far end of the Queensland coast, 1000km from Brisbane, Cairns is the gateway to **Far North Queensland**. FNQ, as it is affectionately known, holds many of Australia's most famous attractions: the World Heritage-listed Daintree rainforest, the Great Barrier Reef and a string of coral-fringed offshore islands.

Queensland's **climate** ranges from subtropical in the south to tropical in the north. The southern centres experience a mild winter from May through until August, whereas Far North Queensland enjoys warm to hot weather all year round.

Queensland politics: from peanut farmer to fish shop owner

During the 1970s and 1980s, under the premiership of the notorious **Sir Joh Bjelke-Petersen**, Queensland gradually became over-run with casinos, tourist developments, family values and plenty of religious fundamentalists. While Sir Joh (a peanut farmer from South Africa) presided over the state with a firm hand and an increasingly unintelligible hyperbole, his wife Flo made pumpkin scones that were the envy of the neighbours.

Since those crazy days Queensland had become somewhat more moderate – at least until 1996, when the state gave rise to yet another political phenomenon, **Pauline Hanson** (the owner of a fish and chip shop) and the **One Nation Party**. As a spokesperson, Pauline wasn't much more eloquent than Sir Joh, but she had a knack for charming those who felt themselves to be dispossessed by mainstream politics – gun lobbyists, neofascists, homophobes and racists. Fortunately her party seems to have all but vanished into the mire of its own corruption, but along the way her singular approach to politics spawned some great comic spoofs, including the drag queen Pauline Pantsdown. With such a chequered political history, it's perhaps unsurprising that Queensland is a curious combination of **easygoing** and **reactionary**. The further north you go, the tougher you'll find the drag queens and the more discreet you'll find lesbians and gays when it comes to being 'out' about their sexuality.

Brisbane

With a population of 1.4 million, Brisbane is Australia's third-largest city and a very handsome one, boasting a tropical lifestyle and a relaxed pace to its daily rhythms. Brisbane owes much of its character to the languid **Brisbane River**, which is plied by ferries carrying commuters and sightseers. Right in the heart of the city, the **South Bank** development incorporates a huge swimming pool with a fake beach and sand, on the banks of the river.

For information on Brisbane's **bus, train and ferry services**, call 13 1230.

The inner-city areas of **Fortitude Valley**, **Spring Hill** and **New Farm** are the focus of gay and lesbian activity, although there are other venues scattered around the city and its suburbs.

BRISBANE PRIDE

Peter Cox

Peter Cox

Brisbane Pride Collective is a voluntary non-profit group which runs and co-ordinates the Brisbane Pride Festival, a thriving event for more than 12 years. Brisbane Pride runs from June through July each year, and the program includes cultural, arts, sporting and community events, as well as the famous Queen's Ball.

The culmination of the festival is the rally, march and fair day, followed by a big dance party. Highlights include the Pedigree Paws pet parade and the goings on at the Queer Beer tent . . .

Brisbane Pride Festival
Brisbane Pride Collective,
PO Box 5159
West End QLD 4101
Phone mobile 0418 152 801
Fax 07/3392 8695
Email cnspride@hotmail.com
Web www.pridebrisbane.org.au

Peter Cox

A **cultural renaissance** has recently swept through Brisbane, in the shape of the *Powerhouse Centre for the Live Arts* (see p.127), an initiative that has involved plenty of queer participation. Located in New Farm, on the banks of the Brisbane River, the centre hosts some very popular queer events, such as the **Queer Film Festival** and special **Brisbane Pride** events throughout the months of June and July. This strikingly designed building has risen phoenix-like from the ashes of a derelict power station, with graffiti-ed walls retained to create vibrant and edgy performance spaces, a visual arts area, a riverside restaurant and a very hip bar called the Spark Bar.

Brisbane highlights and hot-spots

- First gay/lesbian stop in Brisbane would have to be the **Wickham** Hotel, **Alliance** Tavern or **Sportsman** Hotel, where you can arm yourself with the essential listings newspaper and meet a few of the locals.

- **South Bank** is very touristy, but don't let that stop you taking the plunge at its amazing fake beach. This was the site of the World's Fair in 1988 and attractions such as the Butterfly House and the Maritime Museum still remain. On hot summer nights, outdoor jazz recitals entice Brisbane's more bohemian citizens to step out for a cooling dip.

- Brisbane's **Botanical Gardens** contain some wonderful natural flora, including a rainforest area and some huge bunya pines. Open-air concerts are held here on balmy summer evenings.

- A range of **ferry** services ply the river and **cruises** can also be arranged. To see some old 'Queenslander' houses (which stand proudly on stilts to help keep them cool and safe from white ants), catch a ferry to Bulimba, a riverside suburb full of beautifully restored homes, cafes and shops.

- There are also daily ferry services to Brisbane's Lone Pine wildlife sanctuary where there are hundreds of **koalas** and all sorts of other wildlife you can see up close and personal (call 07/3221 0300 for bookings).

- Brisbane has dveloped a reputation for **cutting-edge bistros**. One of the most-lauded is *E'cco Bistro* (see p.122) but if you can't squeeze in, the highly recommended Jameson's is just opposite. Other places worth a look are ARC in Brunswick Street, New Farm, and the Press Club, also in Brunswick Street, for cool drinks and food with a funky vibe.

ACCOMMODATION

Algoori Accommodation
92 Junction Rd
Morningside QLD 4170
Phone 07/3899 2626 or 0411 420 712
Fax 07/3399 6680
Gender Mixed
Basic double and twin rooms with
shared bathroom, kitchen and
common area with TV. There's
also a 25m pool and gym onsite.
Gay-owned and -operated.
Cost From $60 per room
Payment Bankcard, MasterCard, Visa

Allender Apartments
3 Moreton St
New Farm QLD 4005
Phone 07/3358 5832
Fax 07/3254 0799
Email allenderapartm@aussiemail.
com.au
Gender Mixed
Set in tropical gardens, these well-
appointed serviced apartments are
close to the city centre and have
plenty of cafés no more than a block
away. Apartments are fully self-
contained with air-conditioning and
polished wooden floors. Smoking
outside only.
Cost $72–94 per apartment; discounts
for weekly stays
Payment AmEx, Bankcard, Diners,
EFTPOS, MasterCard, Visa

Bridgewater Quest Apartments
55 Baildon St
Kangaroo Point QLD 4169
Phone 07/3391 5300

Fax 07/3392 1513
Email questbridgewater@
questaprtments.com.au
Web www.seqrents.com.au
Gender Mixed
Located on the banks of the river, just
5 minutes from the city by ferry, these
luxury apartments offer a choice of
studio and one-, two- or three-
bedroom units with private balconies
and city views. Apartments are air-
conditioned and self-contained, with
TVs in all rooms and VCRs available
for hire. The complex also contains a
pool, spa, sauna and gym. Breakfast
packs are available.
Cost $132–212 per apartment;
discounts for longer stays
Payment AmEx, Bankcard, Diners,
MasterCard, Visa

Central Brunswick Apartments
455 Brunswick St
Fortitude Valley QLD 4006
Phone freecall 1800/622 686
Fax 07/3852 1015
Email brunswick@strand.com.au
Web www.strand.com.au
Gender Mixed
This ultra-comfortable, very modern
establishment is close to all venues and
has a spa, sauna, gym and barbecue
area. Rooms are air-conditioned and
handy to some of Brisbane's best
restaurants.
Cost $100 per room,
$109 per apartment
Payment AmEx, Bankcard, Diners,
MasterCard, Visa

Sportsman Hotel

130 Leichhardt St
Spring Hill QLD 4000
Phone 07/3831 2892
Fax 07/3839 2106
Email sporties@sportsmanhotel.com.au
Web www.sportsmanhotel.com.au
Gender Mixed

Gay-owned and -operated, the
Sportsman Hotel provides budget
accommodation exclusively for gays
and lesbians. The hotel has its own
restaurant and three bars. All rooms
have air-conditioning and shared
facilities. A light breakfast is included
in the tariff, and a sundeck, lounge
and TV are all available for guests' use.
Cost $35 single, $45 double (plus $11
key deposit)

Payment AmEx, Bankcard, Diners,
EFTPOS, MasterCard, Visa

Thornbury House

1 Thornbury St
Spring Hill QLD 4000
Phone 07/3832 5985
Fax 07/3832 7255
Web babs.com.au/qld/thornbury.htm
Gender Mixed

Restored colonial residence situated in
a quiet leafy street within easy walking
distance of the city and Fortitude
Valley, and with an airport bus stop at
the door. Full breakfast is included in
tariff. Smoking outside only.
Cost $77 single, $100–111 double
Payment AmEx, Bankcard,
MasterCard, Visa

CAFÉS AND RESTAURANTS

2 Faces of Eve

Cnr Dudley St East and Ipswich Rd
Annerley QLD 4103
Phone 07/3848 4044
Fax 07/3848 1163

This kitsch and funky BYO café with
more fish tanks than a dentist's
waiting room is open all day every
day. Breakfast favourites include eggs
benedict or lumberjack pancakes –
served with sausages bacon, eggs
with maple syrup. Vegetarian dishes
are also provided. For lunch or
dinner try Whitlam's Last Stand –
fettucine with a wicked combination
of chicken, avocado and sun-dried
tomatoes in a pesto cream sauce.
Pauline's Revenge is fish of the day,
served with fries, citrus salad and
mango mayo. Everything is made on
the premises, and there are plenty of

vegetarian choices; bookings are
preferred. Lesbian-owned and
-operated.
Open Daily 7.30am–10.30pm
Cost Breakfast $10 per person,
lunch & dinner $10–16
Payment Bankcard, EFTPOS,
MasterCard, Visa

Chow Bistro and Bar

55 Railway Terrace
Milton QLD 4064
Phone 07/3368 1969
Fax 07/3369 6271
Email chow@powerup.com.au

Stylish bistro dining with Santa
Fe-style decor. The menu changes
seasonally, but favourites include duck
cottage pie served with lentils de puy,
fillet of beef with tomato *tarte tatin*
served with caramelized onions and

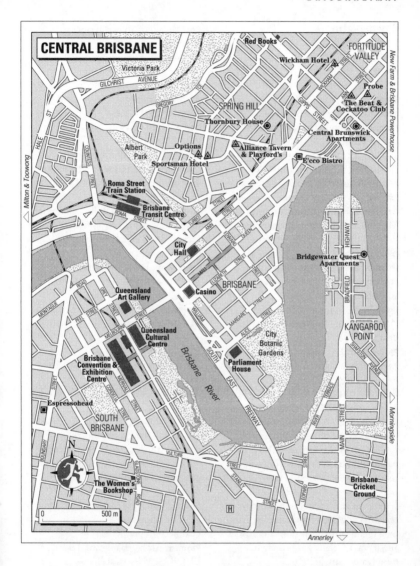

red wine jus. And if you still have room for dessert, try baked vanilla custard with praline crunch in pastry drizzled with caramel sauce.
Open Tues–Fri noon–10pm,

Sat 6pm–10pm
Cost Lunch $25 per person, dinner $35–40
Payment AmEx, Bankcard, Diners, EFTPOS, MasterCard, Visa

E'cco Bistro

100 Boundary St
Brisbane QLD 4000
Phone 07/3831 8344
Fax 07/3831 8460
Email ian@ecco.com.au
Web www.eccorestaurant.com.au
Award-winning, licensed and BYO
restaurant that is an absolute must for
any serious foodies passing through
Brisbane – in fact, for some it's
reason enough for a visit in itself.
Modern Australian cuisine is served
in sleek, minimalist surroundings.
Mouth-watering specialties include
field mushrooms on olive toast with
truffle oil, rocket and lemon; and
steamed mussels with saffron,
coriander and ginger. Bookings
advisable.
Open Tues–Fri noon–2pm &
Tues–Sat 6pm–10.30pm
Cost $45–50 per person
Payment AmEx, Bankcard, Diners,
MasterCard, Visa

Espressohead

169 Boundary St
West End QLD 4101
Phone 07/3844 8324
Lesbians on the Loose reckon this place
has 'undoubtedly the best coffee in
town'. And to soak-up all that
caffeine, there's a wide selection of
vegetarian and vegan dishes, all-day
breakfast and great lunchtime specials
on a menu that ranges from rice dishes
and pastas to salads and bruschetta.
Open Daily 7am–5.30pm

Cost Breakfast $6 per person,
lunch $10
Payment Cash only

Mariosarti

41 Sherwood Rd
Toowong QLD 4066
Phone 07/3870 4933
Fax 07/3870 9236
Email mariosarti@hotmail.com
Creative Italian cuisine with an
extended specials board and a wide
variety of gourmet pizzas, as well as
pasta and traditional dishes, all served
in friendly, rustic surroundings.
Licensed and BYO; smoking at
outdoor tables only.
Open Mon–Fri 11am–10pm,
Sat–Sun 6pm–10.30pm
Cost $20 per person
Payment AmEx, Bankcard, Diners,
MasterCard, Visa

Playford's

Alliance Tavern, 320 Boundary St
(cnr Leichhardt St)
Spring Hill QLD 2800
Phone 07/3832 7355
Fax 07/3236 5133
Located in the *Alliance Tavern*, a
popular gay/lesbian drinking venue,
Playford's serves hearty, no-nonsense
counter meals.
Open Mon–Fri noon–2pm;
Mon–Thurs 6pm–8pm &
Fri–Sun 6pm–late
Cost $10–15 per person
Payment AmEx, Bankcard, Diners,
EFTPOS, MasterCard, Visa

BARS AND CLUBS

Alliance Tavern
320 Boundary St (cnr Leichhardt St)
Spring Hill QLD 4000
Phone 07/3832 7355
Fax 07/3236 5133
Gender Mixed
The *Alliance Tavern* offers three floors to
play in, including a large bar that stages
drag shows on Friday and Saturday
nights, male strippers on Saturday and
jazz on Sunday afternoons. There is
also a cosy corner bar that's a popular
spot for putting away a few pre-
clubbing drinks, a restaurant (see
opposite) and a nightclub. The pub
itself is over 100 years old and is one of
Brisbane's oldest gay haunts.
Open Daily 10am–2am; nightclub
Wed–Sun until 3am
Admission Free
Payment AmEx, Bankcard, Diners,
EFTPOS, MasterCard, Visa

The Beat
677 Ann St
Fortitude Valley QLD 4006
Phone 07/3852 2661
Email throb@globalfreeway.com.au
Gender Mixed
Shows nightly, including occasional
karaoke sessions, and DJs on Friday
and Saturday night. 'Sunday Funday
for Boys' includes champers to kick
off with, $1 drinks and barbecue.
Trixie Lamont is your host(ess).
Open Wed–Sat 8pm–5am,
Sun 5pm–5am
Admission Cover charge may apply
after 10pm; Sunday Funday $10
Payment Cash only

Cockatoo Club
upstairs, 667 Ann St
Fortitude Valley QLD 4006
Phone 07/3852 2661
Email throb@globalfreeway.com.au
Gender Mixed
Mainly gay dance club with lots of
handbag and retro grooves.
Open Wed–Sat 8pm–late, Sun 5pm–late
Admission Cover charge on Sunday
Payment Cash only

Queensland Drags

Tamara
Of 'Tamara Tonight' fame (a show on local TV station Briz 31), Tamara also ran
in Brisbane's 2000 mayoral elections, coming in third. A vocal supporter of the
gay and lesbian community, she has to be one of Brisbane's most political
drags. She has her own show at *Options* in Spring Hill every Saturday night.

Simone Simons
Originally from Sydney, Simone is now vying heavily for Bris-Vegas's 'Super-
Bitch' title. With her dancing background, glamour has to be this one's middle
name. If you're sick of ballad drag, this girl's a must-see on Tuesday, Thursday,

Friday and Sunday, at her watering hole, the *Wickham Hotel* in Fortitude Valley. If her big entrance doesn't turn your head, her show certainly will!

Miss Synthetique

Miss Synthetique holds court at the *Wickham Hotel* several nights a week. 'Synth' has quite a reputation and when you see her show, you'll soon find out how she got it and why she can't get rid of it. When you're in the mood for a 'grand' number and a gutter mouth, she's your girl.

Trixie Lamont

Trixie has been a leading light in Brisbane for more years than even she would like to admit. Her mouth, long heard from Sydney to Townsville, came to rest in Brisbane. Trixie still treads the boards at the *Alliance Tavern* in Spring Hill every Friday and Saturday night.

Yana Michelle

This queen does more costume changes in one number than most would attempt in a twenty-minute show. She's been around, but she's still spitting out fiery new numbers at the *Cockatoo Club*, usually on Thursday nights. Get down with Yana – she's a good-value, good-time gal.

Lolinda Rear

Camp as tits is our Lolinda! A regular barfly at the *Sportsman Hotel*, she also performs a couple of nights a week if she can be bothered.

Patti-O

This high priestess of camp does really great shows at Spring Hill's *Sportsman Hotel* on Thursday, Friday and Saturday nights. Otherwise you'll probably catch her hanging out at the poker machine in the main bar. The way to this gin-lovin' lush's heart is to buy her a drink or keep her slot filled with loose change!

Wanda D' Park

The only live drag act in all of Bris-Vegas who really sings! Meet the karaoke queen who warbles up a storm, and in tune as well! The *Sportsman Hotel* is in quite a spin on Friday, Saturday and Sunday, when this queen hosts karaoke and Super Quiz.

Elle S D

The Beach Babe of the Gold Coast and Brisbane, Elle whirls out the best cossies in Queensland by day and then trades in the overlocker for a pair of

Fredericks at night. Catch an eyeful of Elle at the Gold Coast's *Meeting Place* every Tuesday and Friday, or at the *Wickham* in Fortitude Valley on Thursday.

Toye de Wilde is the mother of Bris-Vegas Drag – and a gorgeous mum she is too. Toye is a regular option at *Options* (see below) and *The Beat* (p.123).

Simone Simons and John Sadlier

Options
18 Little Edward St
Spring Hill QLD 4000
Phone 07/3831 4214
Email throb@globalfreeway.com.au
Gender Mostly women
Downstairs, the *Bird Cage* is a women-only bar, attracting a good crowd. And then there are two floors of dance: the 'Peacock Club' is mixed gay (mostly men), and 'Camp Cabaret' is girls only. 'Sunday Funday' is a megaparty for women, including free barbecue, champers and $1 beers.
Open Mon–Thurs 10am–3am, Sat–Sun 5pm–5am (nightly shows at 11.30pm & 1.30am)
Admission Free downstairs, upstairs $6 cover may apply
Payment Cash only

Probe
29 McLachlan St
Fortitude Valley QLD 4006
Phone 07/3852 2969
Fax 07/3852 1002
Web www.probeclub.com.au
Gender Men
Private, cruisy club and chill-out bar for men. Set over three levels, *Probe* has a dancefloor and DJs.
Open Daily 5pm–late
Admission Membership charge

Sportsman Hotel
130 Leichhardt St
Spring Hill QLD 4004
Phone 07/3831 2892
Fax 07/3839 2106
Email sporties@sportsmanhotel.com.au
Web www.sportshotel.com.au
Gender Mostly men
Gay-owned and -operated, this hotel has three floors, three bars and a bistro serving lunch and dinner. Gay men and lesbians of all ages and interests come here to engage in non-stop activities and entertainment, including pool comps, karaoke and quizzes, as well as drag shows on Friday and Saturday. The *Sportsman* is a meeting place for Boot Company and leather club Brisbears. Drag shows Friday and Saturday. Also the home of the men-only 'Mineshaft Gentlemans Club' on Friday and Saturday nights.
Open Daily noon–5am
Admission Free
Payment AmEx, Bankcard, Diners, EFTPOS, MasterCard, Visa

Wickham Hotel
308 Wickham St
Fortitude Valley QLD 4006
Phone 07/3852 1301
Fax 07/3852 1470
Web www.valleyweb.com.au

Gender Mixed

The *Wickham* is the most popular gay and lesbian venue in town and a great place to get your bearings when you arrive in Brisbane. In addition to a casual lunchtime café, a big courtyard and three pool tables, this pub settles into a dance party atmosphere every weekend, with a massive dancefloor, great lights and laser show. Upstairs is the *Departure Lounge*, an airport-themed cocktail lounge pumping with deep house.

Open Sun–Thurs 8am–3am,
Fri–Sat 8am–5am

Admission Free; cover charge may apply for special events

Payment EFTPOS

SEX CLUBS AND SAUNAS

Bodyline Sauna

43 Ipswich Rd
Woolloongabba QLD 4102

Phone 07/3391 4285

Gender Men

Steam room, dry sauna, spa and maze. Wednesday is buddies day – two for the price of one.

Open Sun–Thurs 11am–2am,
Fri–Sat 11am–5am

Admission $10–16

Payment Bankcard, MasterCard, Visa

The Den

181 Brunswick St
Fortitude Valley QLD 4006

Phone 07/3854 1981

Email den@deninternationl.com

Web www.deninternational.com

Gender Men

Dry cruise club for men, with lockers, showers, sling rooms, maze area and coffee lounge; *The Den* bookshop also offers a wide range of fantasy wear, toys, videos etc.

Open Sun–Thurs 11am–2am,
Fri–Sat 11am–6am

Admission $5.50–11

Payment AmEx, Bankcard, EFTPOS, MasterCard, Visa

WET

22 Jeays St
Bowen Hills QLD 4006

Phone 07/3854 1383

Email wetspa@hotmail.com.

Web www.wet.com.au

Gender Men

This complex includes an ozone spa, steam room, sauna, coffee shop, movie lounges, private rooms and heated pool, as well as showers, hairdryers, free razors, deodorants and hair products.

Open Sun–Thurs 11am–1am,
Fri–Sat 11am–3am

Admission $14–17

Payment Bankcard, EFTPOS, MasterCard, Visa

ARTS

Brisbane Powerhouse Centre for the Live Arts
119 Lamington St
New Farm QLD 4005
Phone 07/3254 4000
Fax 07/3358 2086
Email info@brisbanepowerhouse.org
Web www.brisbanepowerhouse.org
The *Brisbane Powerhouse* is Brisbane's
newest arts extravaganza offering a
range of performance and art spaces.
The Queer Film and Video Festival is
held in late March and gay/lesbian
events are held during Brisbane's
Pride Festival in late June and early
July. The *Spark Bar* has already
become a popular spot, and is open
until midnight most nights, while the
café makes a beautiful location to dine
alongside the Brisbane River.
Open Mon–Fri 9am–5pm,
Sat–Sun noon–4pm
Cost Free admission to centre; charge
for special exhibitions and events
Payment AmEx, Bankcard, EFTPOS,
MasterCard, Visa

BOOKSHOPS

Red Books
350A Brunswick St
Fortitude Valley QLD 4006
Phone 07/3216 0747
Fax 07/3216 0965
Email redbooks@powerup.com.au
A selection of gay and lesbian
fiction and non-fiction plus news-
papers and magazines, along with
travel, food, architecture and
lifestyle books. Mail-order service
available.
Open Mon–Sat 10am–6pm
Payment AmEx, Bankcard, EFTPOS,
MasterCard, Visa

The Women's Bookshop
15 Gladstone Rd
Highgate Hill QLD 4101
Phone 07/3844 6650
Email winbooks@ribbon.net.au
Web www.thewomensbookshop.
com.au
Specialists in books by and about
women, lesbian fiction and non-
fiction. Literary events are held
in the courtyard.
Open Tues–Fri 11am–6pm,
Sat–Sun 10am–4pm
Payment AmEx, Bankcard, EFTPOS,
MasterCard, Visa

NEWSPAPERS AND MAGAZINES

Brother/Sister Queensland
PO Box 2239
Fortitude Valley QLD 4006
Phone 07/3852 2155
Fax 07/3852 2822
Email brosisqld_reception@
satellitemedia.com.au
Gender Mixed
Free gay/lesbian newspaper issued
fortnightly and covering a wide range
of community issues. It also carries a
listing of venues and events. *Brother/
Sister Queensland* is available at gay and
lesbian businesses throughout the state.
Cost Free street distribution,
$50 annual subcription

Dykewise
PO Box 825
Mount Gravatt QLD 4122
Phone mobile 0412 728 173
Email dykewise@rainbow.net.au
Web www.rainbow.net.au/~dykewise
Gender Women
Dykewise offers all the latest on local
community events and politics. This
chatty community-based mag will
keep you up to date with health,
nutrition, parenting, cyberspace,
community listings and, of course,
horoscopes.
Cost Free street distribution,
$20 annual subscription

Queensland Pride
PO Box 8151
Woolloongabba QLD 4102
Phone 07/3392 2922
Fax 07/3392 2923
Email qldpride@powerup.com.au
Gender Mixed
Queensland Pride is a free monthly
publication, which is circulated
throughout the entire state of
Queensland and is also available at
some interstate locations. It offers lots
of regional and national news stories
as well as arts features, women's issues,
sport, health, personals and
community listings. It comes out on
the last Friday of the month.
Cost $35 annual subscription

BODY STUFF

Morningside Fitness
92 Junction Rd
Morningside QLD 4170
Phone 07/3899 2626
Fax 07/3399 6680
Gender Mixed
Seperate men's and women's gyms,
squash, aerobics, 25m pool and
cardio room. Gay-owned and
-operated.
Open Mon–Thurs 5.30am–9.15pm,
Fri 5.30am–8.30pm, Sat
8.30am–6.30pm, Sun 2pm–6.30am
Cost Casual visit $9, memberships
from $40 per month
Payment Bankcard, MasterCard, Visa

Team Brisbane
PO Box 428
Spring Hill QLD 4004
Phone Heather 07/3207 1746 or

Matthew 07/3847 4246
Gender Mixed
Main contact point for lesbian and
gay sports activities in Brisbane.

MEDICAL

Brunswick Street Medical Centre
665 Brunswick St
New Farm QLD 4005
Phone 07/3358 1977
Fax 07/3358 1966
Email brunswick@powerup.com.au
Gender Mostly men
Specialists in gay men's health,
offering bulk billing, HIV experts,
sexuality counselling, coming-out
support, sex-worker care and body
piercing. Bulk billing is available to
Medicare card holders.
Open Daily 9am–6pm
Cost $30 per consultation
Payment Bankcard, MasterCard, Visa

Gay and Lesbian Health Service
Gladstone Rd Medical Centre,
38 Gladstone Rd
Highgate Hill QLD 4101
Phone 07/3844 9599
Fax 07/3846 2957
Email grmcl@powerup.com.au
Gender Mixed
Lesbian and gay doctors available,
HIV drug prescriptions, HIV
management and home care,
acupuncture and massage plus all
general practitioner services. Bulk
billing is available to Medicare
card holders.
Open Mon–Thurs 8am–8pm,

Fri 8am–6pm, Sat 8am–5pm
Cost $30 per consultation
Payment Bankcard, MasterCard, Visa

Logan Women's Health Centre
21 Station Rd
Woodridge QLD 4114
Phone 07/3808 9233
Fax 07/3808 9657
Email lwhc@lrvnet.org.au
Gender Women
Counselling, referrals, information and
health promotion. All women's health
needs can be seen to or referred to
appropriate professionals. Bulk billing
is available to Medicare card holders.
Open Mon–Tues & Thurs–Fri
9am–5pm, Wed 1pm–5pm

Stonewall Medical Centre
52 Newmarket Rd
Windsor QLD 4030
Phone 07/3857 1222
Fax 07/3857 2333
Email smc1@powerup.com.au
Gender Mixed
Gay and lesbian health service staffed
by gay and lesbian doctors. Bulk
billing is available to Medicare card
holders. Male and female counsellors
also available by appointment only.
Open Mon–Thurs 8am–8pm,
Fri 8am–6pm, Sat 8am–noon
Cost $30 per consultation
Payment Bankcard, MasterCard, Visa

Australian Bisexual Network

PO Box 490
Lutwyche QLD 4030
Phone 07/3857 2500 or freecall
1800/653 223
Email ausbinet@rainbow.net.au
Web www.rainbow.net.au/~ausbinet
Gender Mixed
Support and social network for bisexuals.

BGLBN (Brisbane Gay and Lesbian Business Network)

PO Box 18
Paddington QLD 4064
Phone Lindon 07/3004 7144 or Chris
07/3856 2455
Gender Mixed
Brisbane's gay and lesbian business network offers opportunities for business and social networking, political lobbying and charity fundraising. Meets monthly.
Cost Membership $45

BLYSS (Brisbane Lesbian Youth in Social Support)

Brisbane QLD 4000
Phone mobile 0412 036 736
Gender Women
One-to-one support for young women contemplating sexuality and issues surrounding coming out.

Brisbears

PO Box 6
Nundah QLD 4012
Email brisbears@geocities.com
Gender Men
Brisbane branch of bears who like it

hairy. Social gatherings are held on the third Sunday of every month in the downstairs bar at the *Sportsman Hotel* (p.125).
Cost Membership $12; cover charge $3 non-members, $2 members

Gay and Lesbian Welfare Association (GLWA)

PO Box 1078
Fortitude Valley QLD 4006
Phone 07/3891 7377
Web glwa.queer.org.au
Gender Mixed
Support networks and advocacy for Queensland's gay, lesbian, bisexual and transgender population as well as co-ordination of youth suicide prevention programs.

Gayline

Brisbane QLD 4000
Phone 07/3891 7377 or freecall
1800/249 377
Gender Mostly men
Counselling and information service.

GLITF (Gay and Lesbian Immigration Task Force)

Brisbane QLD 4000
Phone Trevor 07/3367 0731
Email info@glitf.powerup.com.au
Web www.glitf.org.au
Gender Mixed
Support and information for overseas partners of Australian gays and lesbians. *GLITF* publishes a guidebook ($20) for couples seeking to stay together in Australia.

Inala GLBT

Inala QLD 4077
Phone Penny 07/3372 1711
Gender Mixed
Social/support group for gays, lesbians, bisexuals and transgenders in Inala and surrounding areas.

Lesbianline

Brisbane QLD 4000
Phone 07/3891 7388 or freecall 1800/249 377
Gender Women
Telephone counselling and information.
Open Daily 7pm–10pm

M.A.M (Mature Age Men)

PO Box 2011
Windsor QLD 4030
Gender Men
Mature age men's social group.

Maybe Baby

PO Box 2028
Windsor QLD 2028
Gender Mixed
For lesbians and gay men contemplating parenthood. Socials and bi-monthly newsletter.

M.E.N. (Males Enjoying Nudism)

PO Box 368
Mt Gravatt QLD 4122
Gender Men
Organizes weekends away for men who enjoy nudism.

Metropolitan Community Church

PO Box 317
Fortitude Valley QLD 4006

Phone 07/3891 1388 or 07/3891 2164
Fax 07/3891 2134
Email pastor@mccbrisacn.au
Web www.mccbris.asn.au
Gender Mixed
A church for everyone but with special outreach to the gay/lesbian/bisexual/transgender community: Reverend Ivor Holmans conducts two special services on Sunday at 10am and 7pm. Women's dialogue is held on the second Friday of each month, and bible study group on Wednesday at 7pm. Services held at the Rainbow Centre, 719A Stanley Street, Woolloongabba.

New Way Community Chapel

Swara Complex, Toc H Room,
61 College Rd
Spring Hill QLD 4000
Phone 07/3366 5412
Gender Mixed
Services every Sunday at 7pm preceded by dinner and fellowship from 6pm. Enjoy a totally inclusive worship environment and regular social get-togethers.

OWLS

PO Box 10106 Adelaide St
Brisbane QLD 4000
Gender Women
Group for lesbians over 35, providing socials, dances and newsletter.

Police Gay/Lesbian Liaison Officers

PO Box 500
Brisbane QLD 4003
Phone 07/3364 4800
Gender Mixed
Police liaison offices are strategically

placed officers who are trained to deal specifically with gay/lesbian issues. There are 34 officers in the south-east of the state and representatives in Rockhampton, Cairns, Townsville and Toowoomba.

Prospect House
Brisbane QLD 4000
Phone Peter 07/3277 2171 or Roger 07/3398 4222
Gender Mixed
Long-term accommodation for gay/lesbian/bisexual/transgender youth (16–24).

Queensland AIDS Council (QuAC)
32 Peel St or PO Box 3142
South Brisbane Business Centre
South Brisbane QLD 4101
Phone 07/3844 1990 or freecall 1800/177 434
Fax 07/3844 4206
Email info@quac.org.au
Gender Mixed
Information and support for those living with HIV/AIDS, lovers, family and friends. Plus safe-sex information, guidance and supplies. Also runs two medical centres.
Open Mon–Fri 9am–5pm

Rainbow Community Centre
719A Stanley St
Woolloongabba QLD 4102
Phone 07/3891 6322 or 0417 765 733
Gender Mixed
A meeting house which keeps a wide range of gay and lesbian magazines, videos, safe sex supplies and resource material. This volunteer-run project also offers referrals and counselling for people in need.
Open Wed 10am–4pm

Seahorse Society of Queensland
PO Box 574
Annerley QLD 4103
Email seahorse_soc@geocities.com
Web www.geocities.com/ WestHollywood/8009
Gender Mixed
Support and social group for cross-dressers and their partners: monthly meetings and social events.

Silver Wheat Society
PO Box 7485 MC
Toowoomba QLD 4350
Phone Bill Rutkin 07/4638 9098 or Steve Single 07/4634 5095
Gender Mixed
A social group for gays and lesbians which organizes dances and holds weekly men's pub nights.

Succulent Wild Women's Group
PO Box 2028
Windsor QLD 4030
Email swwg@ribbon.net.au
Gender Women
Women's social group open to all who identify as women. Meetings and a regular newsletter.
Cost Membership $20

Waves
PO Box 7069
Toowoomba QLD 4350
Gender Mixed
Social group for gays and lesbians.

TRAVEL SERVICES

Algoori Adventures
92 Junction Rd
Morningside QLD 4170
Phone 07/3899 2626 or 0411 420 712
Fax 07/3399 6680
Tailor-made trips to Brisbane's beaches and hinterland. *Algoori* specialize in horseriding, 4WD trips, rock climbing and abseiling. Gay-owned and -operated. (They also offer backpacker accommodation – see p.119.)
Open Mon–Fri 9am–5pm
Payment Bankcard, MasterCard, Visa

Global Gossip
288 Edward St
Brisbane QLD 4000
Phone 07/3229 4033
Fax 07/3229 4533
Gay-owned chain of communication centres, offering email, Internet access, chat, cheap phone calls, employment services, copying, faxing and mailbox rental.
Open Daily 8am–midnight
Payment Bankcard, EFTPOS, MasterCard, Visa; cheque

New Farm Flight Centre
880 Brunswick St
New Farm QLD 4005
Phone Vanessa 07/3358 6747
Fax 07/3358 6767
Email jonathan_souvlis.7cd3@ flightcentre.com
Custom packages in and around Australia as well as overseas, plus cheap flights.
Open Mon–Fri 9am–5pm, Sat 9am–4pm, Sun 10am–2pm
Payment AmEx, Bankcard, Diners, EFTPOS, MasterCard, Visa; cheque

Surfers Paradise and the Gold Coast

The **Gold Coast** has been memorably described as 'a sunny place for shady people', but one thing it does have going for it is that it is a relatively cheap holiday destination. Hotels and apartments offer fantastic rates during **off-peak seasons** and there are plenty of gay-owned places to choose from. Just be warned that in November/December Surfers Paradise is over-run with high-school graduates who descend on the place for '**Schoolies Week**', at which many of Australia's worst alcoholics have done their apprenticeships on beer and Southern Comfort – to be avoided at all costs!

There's a 'world' on the Gold Coast for everyone and, while this may be the family holiday capital of Australia, there are plenty of gays and lesbians who also get a kick out of these joints. Spot them as you walk around – they stick out like sore thumbs.

So, if you wanna talk **theme parks**, here's the lowdown. **Sea World** has spectacular rides, water slides and close encounters with sea creatures. **Dreamworld** for loop-the-loop roller coasters, splash rides and gravity-defying mechanisms on which to impress your friends and have your photo taken, as well as lots of shabby imitation Disney rides. **Wet 'n' Wild** (calm down – it's a waterslide theme park, not a lesbian sex-club) offers the chance to have a go at every sort of swimming pool feat. And, of course, Warner Brothers' **Movie World** is where you can be Batman, or finally get to see up Marilyn Monroe's skirt as she stands over the grate.

ACCOMMODATION

Narrowneck Court

204 Ferny Ave
Surfers Paradise QLD 4217
Phone 07/5592 2455
Fax 07/5538 4153
Email monet@joynet.com.au
Web www.about-australia.com/narrowneck
Gender Mixed
Fully equipped-self contained two-bedroom units with ensuite and bathroom, laundry, cable TV. There are ocean views from every room, barbecue, pool and gazebo, and the complex is walking distance to the main beach.
Cost From $94 per unit
Payment Bankcard, EFTPOS, MasterCard, Visa

Paradise Retreats

Admiralty Drive
Surfers Paradise QLD 4217
Phone 07/5571 1414 or freecall 1800/060 069
Fax 07/5531 0614
Email staygay@ion.com.au
Web www.ion.com.au/staygay
Gender Men
Gay-owned and -operated guest house on the Nerang River in the heart of the Gold Coast. There is a pool, spa, private sundeck, TV lounge, full use of kitchen and laundry facilities and continental breakfast is included in tariff. Smoking in outside areas only; clothing is optional. Drop-off service to nearby gay beach and bus stops is available.
Cost $65–90 per room
Payment Cheque

Quarterdeck

3263 Gold Coast Highway
Surfers Paradise QLD 4217
Phone Ivor or Peter 07/5592 2200 or freecall 1800/635 235
Email units@bigpond.com
Web www.quarterdeck.com.au
Gender Mixed
A gay-owned high rise block of units just 80m from the beach. The

complex includes two pools and saunas, secure underground parking and tour desk.

Cost $70–138 per unit
Payment Bankcard, EFTPOS, MasterCard, Visa

Sleeping Inn

26 Whelan St
Surfers Paradise QLD 4217
Phone 07/5592 4455 or freecall 1800/817 832
Fax 07/5592 5266
Email sleepinginn@hotmail.com
Gender Mixed

Sleeping Inn offers modern Santa Fe-style decor, backpacker and hotel accommodation within a very friendly complex five minutes' walk to gay venues. There is a games room, pool table, Internet access, saltwater pool, fully equipped kitchens, disabled facilities, movies

and book exchange. Gay-owned and -operated.

Cost $18.50 dorms, $60–120 per room
Payment AmEx, Bankcard, EFTPOS, MasterCard, Visa

Stay Gay Hi-Rise Apartments

Paradise Towers
Surfers Paradise QLD 4217
Phone 07/5592 3336
Fax 07/5592 3337
Email ptaaa@fan.net.au
Web www.paradise-aaa.fan.net.au
Gender Mixed

Quality one-bedroom, self-contained apartments with balconies offering great views right in the heart of Surfers only a minute's walk to the beach, shops, and gay venues. Gay-owned and -operated.

Cost From $65 per unit
Payment AmEx, Bankcard, Diners, EFTPOS, MasterCard, Visa

BARS AND CLUBS

Jaycees

Commercial Hotel, Cnr Price Rd and Ferry St
Nerang QLD 4211
Phone 07/5532 3016
Gender Mixed

Mixed gay and lesbian disco night with supper provided, and special shows some months. Dinner is available in the dining room downstairs.

Open Sat 8pm–1am (second Saturday of the month only)
Admission $10
Payment EFTPOS

The Meeting Place

Forum Arcade, 26 Orchid Ave (between Orchid Ave and Gold Coast Highway)
Surfers Paradise QLD 4217
Phone 07/5526 2337
Fax 07/5526 2335
Gender Mixed

Extremely friendly gay and lesbian club. Cheap drinks and strippers on Tuesday. Karaoke on Wednesday and drag and talent shows on Thursday, Friday and Sunday.

Open Tues–Thurs 5pm–late, Fri–Sat 5pm–5am, Sun 5pm–late
Admission $5 Fri, Sat & Sun
Payment Cash only

SEX CLUBS AND SAUNAS

Club R
Basement Carpark, Parkrise Building,
1/3 Alison St
Surfers Paradise QLD 4217
(Enter via circular drive at the end of
Alison Street – through the white door
painted with big black no 1)
Phone 07/5539 0955
Fax 07/5592 2209
Email clubr@clubr.com.au
Web www.clubr.aunz.com
Gender Men
Cruise club with members lounge,
two video lounges and play pen.
Club R stocks adult supplies and vibes
as well as Queensland and interstate
magazines. Gay-owned and
-operated.

Open Daily noon–midnight (later on
Fri & Sat)
Admission $7 before 7pm, $9.50 after
Payment AmEx, Bankcard, Diners,
EFTPOS, MasterCard, Visa

The Den
2557 Gold Coast Highway
Mermaid Beach QLD 4218
Phone 07/5575 4054
Web www.deninternational.com
Gender Men
Dry cruise club and adult shop with video
lounge, sling room and cruise space.
Open Daily 11am–midnight
Admission $7.70
Payment AmEx, Bankcard, EFTPOS,
MasterCard, Visa

ADULT SHOPS

Love Heart Adult Shop
2546 Gold Coast Highway
Mermaid Beach QLD 4218
Phone 07/5526 6666
Web www.loveheart.com.au
Carries free Queensland gay

newspapers and contact magazines.
Also stocks a wide range of adult
products and vibes.
Open Mon–Sat 10am–6pm
Payment AmEx, Bankcard, Diners,
EFTPOS, MasterCard, Visa

COMMUNITY

Gold Coast Mature Men's Group
PO Box 402
Mermaid Beach QLD 4218
Phone Kerry or Peter 07/5527 7675

Gender Men
Social and support group for mature
age and mature-minded gay men.
Barbecue and picnic on the first
Sunday of the month.

Queensland AIDS Council Gold Coast (QuAC)
3070 Gold Coast Highway or
PO Box 273
Surfers Paradise QLD 4217
Phone 07/5538 8922
Fax 07/5538 8142
Email info@quac.org.au

Gender Mixed
Information and support for those living with HIV/AIDS, lovers, family and friends. Transgender support group, contacts for young people coming out, gay/lesbian newspapers, and safe-sex information and supplies.
Open Mon–Fri 9am–5pm

Noosa and the Sunshine Coast

Travel agents offer **gay/lesbian packages** to the aptly named Sunshine Coast throughout the year. Frequented by the jetset, the upmarket resort town of **Noosa** boasts plenty of smart bars and restaurants – a very civilised little spot, so long as you avoid school holidays. Weekend gatherings are held at the *Discovery Beach Resort* in Marcoola, which attracts a friendly mix of gays and lesbians. There are several gay-owned apartments and resorts, as well as a gay-owned restaurant and bar. Twenty minutes' drive to the south of Noosa is **Peregian Beach**, with several other gay accommodation options, and further south is the more down-to-earth **Maroochydore**.

Heading inland to the Sunshine Coast **hinterland**, you'll chance upon country towns like Nambour and Maleny, surrounded by beautiful montane rainforests with rock-pools and waterfalls to bathe in – pure heaven at the end of a bushwalk.

ACCOMMODATION

Beachcomber Noosa/Peregian
384 David Low Way
Peregian Beach QLD 4573
Phone Gary or Patrick 07/5448 1306
Fax 07/5448 1331
Email info@beachcomber-peregian.com.au
Web www.beachcomber-peregian.com.au

Gender Mixed
Located close to a gay beach, these spacious self-contained gay-owned and -operated apartments with balconies. No children or pets are allowed.
Cost $88 per room ($386 weekly)
Payment Bankcard, MasterCard, Visa; cheque

Discovery Beach Resort

923 David Low Way
Marcoola QLD 4564
Phone 07/5448 8900
Fax 07/5448 8966
Email discoverybeach@bigpond.com
Web www.discoverybeach.com.au
Gender Mixed

This beachfront resort is 25 minutes'
drive from Noosa, 10 minutes from
Maroochydore. The bar at *Discovery
Beach Resort* is also a meeting place for
the local gay and lesbian community,
with 'Buddies' on second and fourth
Saturdays (see p.141) and 'Sunbears'
gatherings on the first Saturday of
each month.

Cost From $75 per room
Payment AmEx, Bankcard, Diners,
EFTPOS, MasterCard, Visa

Falcons at Peregian

PO Box 254
Peregian Beach QLD 4573
Phone Mark or John 07/5448 3710
Fax 07/5448 3712
Email falconsap@hotmail.com
Web www.linstar.com.au/falcons
Gender Men

This gay men's resort is 5 minutes'
walk from the gay nude beach and 10
minutes' drive from Noosa. Tariff
includes breakfast and pick-ups from
Maroochydore airport or Nambour
station. Facilities include a secluded
pool and terrace, and use of gym,
bikes and barbecue. Clothing
optional.

Cost From $50 single, $70 double
Payment Bankcard, MasterCard, Visa;
cheque

Hideaway Holiday Apartments

386 David Low Way
North Peregian Beach QLD 4573
Phone 07/5448 1006 or mobile 0409
068 738
Fax 07/5448 3891
Web www.qbeds.cjb.com
Gender Mixed

Located just outside Noosa, these
one-bedroom apartments are set in
subtropical gardens right next to a
quiet beach, and there's a gay beach
3km further south. The apartments
share a secluded saltwater pool and
barbecue area; clothing is optional.
Pets allowed. Gay-owned and
-operated.

Cost $72–135 per apartment
Payment AmEx, Bankcard,
MasterCard, Visa

Horizons at Peregian

45 Lorikeet Drive
Peregian Beach, QLD 4573
Phone 07/5448 3444
Fax 07/5448 3711
Email rods@ozemail.com.au
Web www.horizons-peregian.com
Gender Mixed

Located on 14km of beach frontage
and national park between Noosa and
Coolum, *Horizons* offers luxury two-
or three-bedroom self-contained
apartments. Amenities include a
heated saltwater pool, spa, barbecue,
secure parking, tour desk, voicemail
and modem access. GALTA-
approved; gay-owned and -operated.

Cost From $111 per apartment
Payment AmEx, Bankcard,
MasterCard, Visa

Lorikeet Lodge

31 Lorikeet Drive
Peregian Beach QLD 4573
Phone 07/5448 1315
Fax 07/5448 3006
Email sandune@ozemail.com.au
Web lorikeet.tripod.com
Gender Mixed
Gay-owned and -operated complex
of seven self-contained one-bedroom
units, each sleeping 4–5 people.
Lorikeet Lodge is situated right on the
beach, close to cafés and only a 10-
minute drive from Noosa. There is a
pool and barbecue in the tropical
gardens and the rooms are decorated
with cane furniture. Pets allowed.
Cost $72 per unit for two people, $11
each extra person
Payment Bankcard, EFTPOS,
MasterCard, Visa

Manyana Apartments

51 Kestral Cresent
Peregian Beach QLD 4573
Phone 07/5448 3355 or mobile 0418
747 088
Email manyana@bigpond.com
Web www.inthepink.com.au/manyana
Gender Men
Manyana Apartments comprises studios
and two-bedroom units with
bathrooms and kitchens (shared
laundry). The private guest lounge
opens onto a tiled pool, where
clothing is optional. Peregian Beach is
just 200m away, and there's also a gay
beach nearby.
Cost $66–88 per unit (discounted
weekly rates)
Payment Bankcard, MasterCard, Visa

Mikado Motor Inn

105 Cooloola Drive
Rainbow Beach QLD 4581
Phone 07/5486 3211 or freecall
1800/243 211
Fax 07/5486 3283
Email mikado@tpgi.com.au
Web www.rainbow-beach.org
Gender Mixed
Quiet, modern accommodation
with private balconies and views
across to Fraser Island. This largely
adult resort caters to couples of all
types, with breakfast and full room
service available, as well as a fully
licensed restaurant and bar. All
rooms have air-conditioning or
ceiling fans and TVs. Smoking is
allowed outside only.
Cost From $72 per room
Payment AmEx, Bankcard, EFTPOS,
MasterCard, Visa; cheque

Noosa Cove Holiday Apartments

82 Upper Hastings St
Noosa Heads QLD 4567
Phone 07/5449 2668
Fax 07/5447 5373
Email reservations@noosacove.com.au
Web www.noosacove.com.au
Gender Mostly men
Right in the heart of Noosa Heads,
near Noosa National Park, these
gay-owned and -managed
apartments offer luxury
accommodation. Studio, one- and
two-bedroom apartments are
available. Member of GALTA.
Cost $88–132 per room
Payment Bankcard, MasterCard, Visa

Noosa International
Edgar Bennet Ave
Noosa Heads QLD 4567
Phone 07/5447 4822
Fax 07/5447 2025
Email noosaintresort.com.au
Gender Mixed
Self-contained one- or two-bedroom apartments. Not especially gay, but centrally located, the resort has two pools, a sauna and spa, and an island bar.
Cost From $143 per apartment
Payment AmEx, Bankcard, Diners, EFTPOS, MasterCard, Visa

Sails Lifestyle Resort
43 Oriole Ave
Peregian Beach QLD 4573
Phone 07/5448 1011
Fax 07/5448 2882
Web www.sailslifestyleresort.com.au
Gender Mixed
Individual fully self-contained beach houses in a rainforest setting, with heated spa, pebble pool and undercover barbecue area. Very quiet environment,

but just 150m from the beach.
Cost From $110 per unit, $365 weekly
Payment Bankcard, EFTPOS, MasterCard, Visa; cheque

Villa Alba
191 Duke Rd
Noosa Valley QLD 4562
Phone 07/5449 1900
Fax 07/5449 1300
Email villaalba@houseofsunshine.com
Web www.houseofsunshine.com
Gender Mixed
Villa Alba has four private villas set around an ampitheatre and sandstone-lined pool, and is within 15 minutes of both Noosa and Peregian Beach. The villas are fully self-contained, linked by walkways, have sunken baths overlooking the forest, private decks and entertainment systems. Smoking outside only. Gay-owned and -operated.
Cost From $185 per villa
Payment AmEx, Bankcard, MasterCard, Visa

CAFÉS AND RESTAURANTS

Berardo's Restaurant and Bar
50 Hastings St
Noosa QLD 4567
Phone 07/5447 5666
Fax 07/5448 0707
Email info@berardos.com.au
Web www.berardos.com.au
Fine contemporary Australian cuisine served in elegant surroundings. Mediterranean- and Asian-influenced dishes include asparagus pannacotta or

Moreton Bay bug and pumpkin curry. There is also a piano bar most nights, with lots of impromptu guest performances. *Berardo's* offer indoor and al fresco dining, and guests are also welcome to enjoy casual drinks and tapas. Gay-owned and -operated.
Open Daily 6pm–late
Cost $25–40 per person
Payment AmEx, Bankcard, Diners, EFTPOS, MasterCard, Visa

BARS AND CLUBS

Buddies
Discovery Beach Resort
923 David Low Way
Marcoola Beach QLD 4564
Phone 0402 428 293
Email buddiesbar@hotmail.com
Web www.roads.to/buddies/
Gender Mixed

Buddies is a popular gay/lesbian get-together on the second and fourth Saturday of the month. Join in for dinner and dancing with $10 meals and a resident DJ.
Open Sat 6pm–midnight
Admission Cover charge may apply
Payment EFTPOS

BEACHES AND POOLS

Alexandria Naturist Beach
Alexandria Bay Noosa National Park
Noosa Heads QLD 4567
Gender Mixed
This nudist beach, surrounded by the beautiful Noosa National Park, offers everyone the opportunity to shed their gear. Typically with beaches such as this, you'll find plenty of guys lolling in the sun at one end.

MEDICAL

Blackall Terrace
87 Blackall Terrace
Nambour QLD 4560
Phone 07/5476 2489
Fax 07/5476 2491
Email blackall@m140.aone.net.au
Gender Mixed
Based in the outpatient department of the Nambour Hospital, *Blackall Terrace* offers support and monitoring pre- and post antibody tests. Also up-to-date therapy information, screening for hepatitis A, B and C; specialist referrals; needle exchange and a range of other services available.
Appointment preferred.

Open Mon–Fri 8am–4.30pm
Cost Free

Maroochydore Sexual Health Clinic
15 Maud St
Maroochydore QLD 4558
Phone 07/5479 2670
Fax 07/5479 2573
Email maudst@bigpond.com
Gender Mixed
Free and confidential screening and treatment for sexually transmitted diseases; no Medicare card required. Appointment essential.
Cost Free

**Queensland AIDS Council
Sunshine Coast (QuAC)**
4 Carrol St
Nambour QLD 4560
Phone 07/5441 1222
Fax 07/5441 1566
Email sunshinecoast@quac.com.au
Gender Mixed

Information and support for those living with HIV/AIDS, lovers, family and friends. Plus safe-sex information and guidance. Condoms, lube, needle exchange, information pamphlets and gay/lesbian newspapers.
Open Mon–Fri 9am–5am

Palm Tree Tours
Bay Village, Hastings St
(next to Sheraton)
Noosa Heads QLD 4567
Phone 07/5474 9166
Fax 07/5474 9686
Email noosaptt@ozemail.com.au
Web www.ozemail.com.au/~noosaptt

GALTA-approved travel agency, offering tailor-made tours and speciality accommodation, as well as day-trips to local sights and lower Barrier Reef trips.
Open Daily 9am–5pm
Payment AmEx, Bankcard, Diners, EFTPOS, MasterCard, Visa; cheque

Bundaberg to Bowen

This stretch of the Queensland coast takes in the **workaday towns** of Bundaberg and Rockhampton, as well as the **Capricorn Islands**, which are the equal of any further north on the reef but less-touristed, and the sailing playground of the **Whitsundays**.

Inland, the region becomes lusher the further north you go – a tangle of rainforests and screeching rainbow-coloured birds.

Mengyuan Country House
Lot 24 Woodswallow Drive
Gin Gin QLD 4671
Phone 07/4157 3024
Fax 07/4157 3025
Email fod@ozemail.com.au

Web www.ozemail.com.au/~fod
Gender Mostly men
Guesthouse, backpacker,camping and farmstay accommodation, as well as comfortable guesthouse facilities, hydro massage and library, are all

available at this tropical rural retreat. *Mengyuan* is located in spectacular bushland, 10 minutes off the Bruce Highway, just inland from the city of Bundaberg and the Wide Bay Coast. Pets are welcome.

Cost $60–70 per room
Payment Cheque

Rocky Rose Homestay
6 Pandanus St
Bowen QLD 4805
Phone 07/4786 2430

Gender Mixed

Homestay-style accommodation 5km from Bowen, with beach frontage, views to the islands and coral reef 20m offshore, as well as a turtle rookery. *Rocky Rose* has rooms with shared and private facilities; continental breakfast is included in the tariff, evening meals by arrangement (all vegetarian). Smoking outside only. Gay-owned and -operated.

Cost $50–100 per room
Payment Cheque

CAFÉS AND RESTAURANTS

Gnomes
106 William St
Rockhampton QLD 4700
Phone 07/4927 4713
Fax 07/4922 5321

Vegetarian/vegan BYO restaurant. Dishes include vegetarian sausage rolls, Swiss cheese and asparagus quiche or coconut steamed vegetables. *Gnomes* also has a wide range of cakes and good espresso. Smoking outside only. Gay-owned and -operated.

Open Mon–Sat 10am–10pm
Cost Lunch $12, dinner $15
Payment Bankcard, EFTPOS, MasterCard, Visa

Le Bistro on Quay
Quay St
Rockhampton QLD 4700
Phone 07/4922 2019
Fax 07/4927 0418

Located right on the waterfront, *Le Bistro* offers innovative Australian cuisine with a menu that changes monthly. It is fully licensed, with a separate bar. Smoking permitted in the bar and garden areas only. Gay-owned. Bookings advisable.

Open Mon–Fri noon–3pm & daily 6.30pm–late
Cost Lunch $25, dinner $45
Payment AmEx, Bankcard, Diners, MasterCard, Visa

BARS AND CLUBS

Pandora's
Heritage Tavern, Quay Lane
Rockhampton QLD 4700
Phone Heritage Tavern 07/4927 6996 or Bill 0417 191 627
Gender Mixed

Community-run nightclub with DJs, shows and dancefloor. Good mixed crowd of gays, lesbians and friends.

Open Sat 10pm–late
Admission $5
Payment EFTPOS

ADULT SHOPS

Love Heart Adult Shop

1/270 Bourberg St
Bundaberg QLD 4670
Phone 07/4152 5440

with branches at:

Shop 1/1 Mangrove Rd
Mackay QLD 4740
Phone 07/4953 4949;

245C Musgrave St
North Rockhampton QLD 4701
Phone 07/4927 7954

Web www.loveheart.com.au
Gender Mixed
Carries Queensland gay newspapers
and contact magazines; also stocks a
wide range of adult products and
vibes.
Open Mon–Sat 10am–6pm (North
Rockhampton branch Mon–Fri
9am–6pm & Sat 9am–1pm)
Payment AmEx, Bankcard, Diners,
EFTPOS, MasterCard, Visa

COMMUNITY

Mackay Genders

PO Box 1523
Mackay QLD 4740
Gender Mixed
Gay and lesbian social support group
that organizes regular meetings.

Metropolitan Community Church

CCDA Hall, Cnr Haigh and Cavell streets
Wandal QLD 4700
Phone Rev Ann James 07/4921 0799
Email rackhampton@mccbris.asn.au
Gender Mixed
Services are held at 6pm on the first
Sunday of each month. The church
also organizes a wide range of
activities and pastoral projects.

Rocky Road Society

PO Box 414
Rockhampton QLD 4700
Phone Bill Fernhill 0417 191 627
Email rockyroadglbt@hotmail.com
Gender Mixed
Gay and lesbian social group that
meets on Saturdays at *Pandora's*
(p.143). Regular newsletter.

Safe Harbour

PO Box 7074
Gladstone QLD 4680
Phone Ross 07/4972 1331
Gender Mixed
Gay and lesbian social group for
people in the Gladstone area.
Monthly functions and get-togethers.

TRAVEL SERVICES

Global Gossip
257 Shute Harbour Rd
Airlie Beach QLD 4802
Phone 07/4946 6488
Gay-owned chain of communication
centres, offering email, Internet
access, chat, cheap phone calls,
employment services, copying, faxing
and mailbox rental.
Open Daily 8am–midnight
Payment Bankcard, EFTPOS,
MasterCard, Visa; cheque

Townsville and Magnetic Island

Townsville is the gateway to some of the best islands on the
Great Barrier Reef, including Orpheus, which boasts spectacular
snorkelling spots. It also tends to have a drier, less humid, tropical
climate than places further north, and is the departure point for
Magnetic Island (ferries run hourly).

The *Sovereign Hotel* is the main gay and lesbian pub, and conveniently offers good-value accommodation. While the town's
gay population has some very good historical reasons for not
wearing its sexuality on its sleeve, it has clung onto a strange gay
male subculture, not least because of the military presence –
everyone loves a man in uniform, it seems! The city also boasts a
fine aquarium on the foreshore, and there are a number of queer-
operated businesses both in town and on Magnetic Island.

ACCOMMODATION

Island House
Nelly Bay
Magnetic Island QLD 4819
Phone Ray 0419 782 847
Email islandhouse@hotmail.com
Web www.islandhouseb_b.homestead.
com
Gender Men
Exclusively gay tropical resort where
clothing is optional. Facilities include
pool, spa and barbecue. All rooms
have air-conditioning as well as
ceiling fans, and continental
breakfast is included. Transport on
the doorstep, 100m from beach and
restaurants.
Cost From $59 single, $69 double
Payment AmEx, Bankcard,
MasterCard, Visa

Magnetic International Resort
Mandalay Ave, Nelly Bay
Magnetic Island QLD 4819
Phone Freecall 1800/079 902

Fax 07/4778 5806
Gender Mixed
Magnetic International Resort is a
member of GALTA, so you're assured
of a gay-friendly welcome. Facilities
include a pool, gym, games room,
tennis court, activities desk, restaurant
and bar. The resort is a ten-minute
walk from beach, and transfers from
Townsville can be arranged.
Cost From $109 per room
Payment AmEx, Bankcard, Diners,
EFTPOS, MasterCard, Visa

The Rocks Guest House

20 Cleveland Terrace
Townsville QLD 4810
Phone 07/4771 5700 or 0416 044 409
Fax 07/4771 5711
Email therocks@ultra.net.au
Gender Mixed
Historic Townsville home with wide
verandahs and stunning views of
Magnetic Island. Billiard room and
spa for guests' use; close to restaurants
and beach.
Cost $86 single, $97 double
Payment AmEx, Bankcard, Diners,
MasterCard, Visa

Sandy's on the Strand

PO Box 193
Townsville QLD 4810
Phone 07/4772 1193
Fax 07/4772 1193
Gender Mixed
Private B&B accommodation with
air-conditioning, queen size beds,
ensuites and private balconies. Close
to city and casino, pools and beach.
Smoking outside only.
Cost $61 single, $72 double
Payment Cheque

Sovereign Hotel

807 Flinders St
Townsville QLD 4810
Phone 07/4771 2909
Fax 07/4771 4300
Gender Mixed
Budget hotel accommodation which
includes tea, toast and coffee. All
rooms have shared facilities and
access to a TV lounge. Gay-owned
and -operated
Cost $33 single, $44 double,
$56 twin
Payment Bankcard, EFTPOS,
MasterCard, Visa; cheque

CAFÉS AND RESTAURANTS

Boiling Billy

18 Stokes St
Townsville QLD 4810
Phone 07/4771 4184
Fax 07/4771 4184
Email lounrat@yahoo.com
Boiling Billy is a lesbian-owned café
offering great value meals to suit all
tastes, including plenty of
vegetarian, vegan, gluten-free and

lactose-free dishes, as well as meat
dishes – including their fabulous
lamb curry. There's also a wide
range of salads and desserts, as well
as 30 types of coffee and loose tea
from all around the world to buy
and take home.
Open Mon–Fri 7am–3pm
Cost Breakfast $6–8, lunch $10–12
Payment Bankcard, MasterCard, Visa

Sticky Fingers

Cnr Palmer and Plume streets
South Townsville QLD 4810
Phone 07/4721 1033
Fax 07/4721 1049
Email macwood@beyond.net.au
Smart restaurant and wine bar with a
separate lunch and dinner menu.
Specialties include sushi and sashimi
platters, gazpacho, and baked ricotta
with field mushrooms, beans and
roasted capsicum sauce. All desserts
and cakes are made on the premises.
Smoking outside only. *Sticky Fingers*
is often open for drinks on weekends
until 2am, and you're welcome to
pop in for a drink only. Gay-owned
and -operated.
Open Lunch Tues–Fri noon–2pm &
Sun noon–3pm, dinner Mon–Sat
6pm–11pm
Cost $20–30 per person
Payment AmEx, Bankcard, Diners,
MasterCard, Visa

BARS AND CLUBS

Sovereign Hotel

807 Flinders St
Townsville QLD 4810
Phone James Muir 07/4771 2909
Fax 07/4771 4300
Gender Mixed
There are drag shows, pool tables,
bistro and beer garden in this
centrally located, gay-owned and
-operated hotel.
Open Sun–Thurs 4pm–late,
Fri–Sat 4pm–3am

Admission Cover charge Fri & Sat
Payment Bankcard, EFTPOS,
MasterCard, Visa

Townsville Women's Dances

Bellevue Hotel
Railway Estate QLD 4810
Phone Sue 07/4771 3824
Gender Mixed
Women's dances are held on the first
Saturday of the month at the *Bellevue
Hotel*. Tickets are available at the door.

ADULT SHOPS

Sweethearts

206A Charters Towers Rd
Hermit Park QLD 4812
Phone Colin 07/4725 1431
Fax 07/4725 1431
Gender Mixed
Wide range of adult products as well
as most major gay/lesbian
newspapers. They also have a contact
board for the Townsville area.
Open Daily 10am–1am,
Sat 8am–1am
Payment AmEx, Bankcard, EFTPOS,
MasterCard, Visa

Mary Who Bookshop
155 Stanley St
Townsville QLD 4810
Phone 07/4771 3832
Fax 07/4721 2761
Email marywhobooks@ultra.net.au
Lesbian and gay fiction and
non-fiction, as well as a good
range of travel books and second-
hand books, Internet access and
tickets for dances. Lesbian-owned
and -operated.
Open Mon–Thurs 9am–5pm,
Fri 9am–6pm, Sat 9am–1pm,
Sun 10am–1pm

Payment AmEx, Bankcard, Diners,
EFTPOS, MasterCard, Visa

QBD
305 Flinders Mall
Townsville QLD 4810
Phone 07/4771 6091
Fax 07/4721 4662
Email qbd@ozemail.com.au
This gay-owned and -operated
bookshop specializes in Australian
militaria and travel, but also has a
good selection of gay and lesbian titles.
Open Mon–Fri 9am–6pm,
Sat 9am–5pm

Queensland AIDS Council (QuAC)
3rd floor, Shaw's Arcade
Flinders St Mall Townsville QLD 4810
Phone 07/4721 1384
Fax 07/4721 3434
Gender Mixed

Information and support for those
living with HIV/AIDS, their lovers,
family and friends. Plus safe-sex
information and supplies; needle
exchange. Youth support, education
and referral.
Open Mon–Fri 9am–5pm

Cairns and Far North Queensland

While this part of Australia may be considered a tropical paradise,
booming **tourism** over the last 15 years has certainly taken its
toll – and the result is not always pretty. Cairns and the mountain
town of Kuranda nearby have been over-run by T-shirt shops,
malls and craft markets. Souvenir hunters will have a field day
buying up big – from change purses made out of kangaroo scro-
tums to personalised beer-can holders and mobiles made from
coral. But, for a more lasting impact, seek out the natural attractions: the magnificent **Daintree**, with its old-growth rainforests,
and the underwater splendour of the **Great Barrier Reef**.

One of the first things you need to know about **Cairns** itself is that there is no beach in the town. If you want a palm-fringed tropical beach on your doorstep, you'll need to make for one of the little coves north of town, such as Palm Cove, Clifton Beach or Yorkeys Knob (yes, you read that right). Further north still, about 60km or an hour's drive on beautiful winding coast road, **Port Douglas** makes a more tranquil, low-key base-camp, with plenty of stylish hotels and resorts strung out along beautiful Five Mile Beach, as well as cheaper backpacker-style accommodation in the centre of town.

Finally, remember that there are **natural dangers** here that exceed any rural bigotry you might encounter, so if you want to avoid meeting the same fate as Captain Hook, take advice from locals about where and when you should swim or walk.

ACCOMMODATION

18–24 James Street

18–24 James St
Cairns QLD 4870
Phone freecall 1800/621 824 or
07/4051 4644
Fax 07/4051 0103
Email 18_24james@internetnorth.
com.au
Web www.eagles.bbs.net.au/james
Gender Mixed

Gay-owned and -operated, this is 'Melrose Place' right in the heart of Cairns, with all the rooms overlooking the central courtyard and pool. There's also a gym, spa, sauna, restaurant and bar – which make it a great place to drop by for a drink or meal even if you're not staying.

Cost $98 single, $125 double
Payment AmEx, Bankcard, Diners, EFTPOS, MasterCard, Visa

Cleo's

PO Box 233
Yorkeys Knob QLD 4878
Phone 07/4055 7974
Fax 07/4055 7974
Email cleos@ozemail.com.au
Web www.ozemail.com.au/~cleos/
Gender Women

B&B-style accommodation for women only, in a private tranquil setting with tropical gardens and pool, just a short walk from the beach. *Cleo's* is about 15 minutes by car and 30 minutes by local bus from Cairns; airport pick-ups can usually be arranged, and there's a tour-booking service for trips to the reef and rainforest. English, French, Spanish, Portuguese and Italian are all spoken here.

Cost $60–110 single, $70–120 double
Payment Cheque

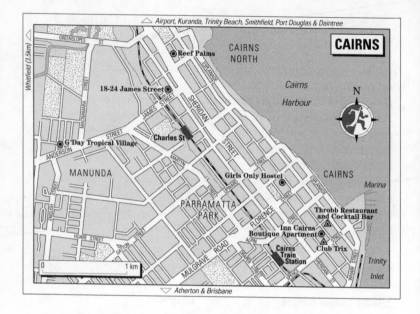

Airport, Kuranda, Trinity Beach, Smithfield, Port Douglas & Daintree

CAIRNS

GREENSLOPES ST
Whitfield (3.5km)
MACNAMARA STREET
Reef Palms
CAIRNS NORTH
Cairns Harbour
N
18-24 James Street
JAMES STREET
SHERIDAN STREET
ESPLANADE
ANDERSON STREET
G'Day Tropical Village
Charles St
MARLYN STREET
MANUNDA
Girls Only Hostel
CAIRNS
Marina
ENGLISH STREET
PARRAMATTA PARK
FLORENCE STREET
ESPLANADE
Throbb Restaurant and Cocktail Bar
HOARE STREET
GATTON STREET
ALPIN
Inn Cairns Boutique Apartment
Club Trix
MULGRAVE ROAD
Cairns Train Station
WHARF STREET
SHERIDAN STREET
Trinity Inlet
0   1 km

Atherton & Brisbane

Club Daintree

Cape Kimberley Rd
Daintree QLD 4873
Phone 07/4055 1338 or 07 458 1511
Fax 07 40907 500 or 07 40581 659
Gender Mixed
Club Daintree is a rare and secluded
island in the middle of World
Heritage-listed national park with 4km
of private beach. Bushwalking, river
cruises, Snapper Island tours and reef
tours are available through the tour
desk. Accommodation ranges from
camping to backpacker rooms and
cabins sleeping up to four. Meals are
available and there is a barbecue area
for guests' use. The bar is open all day.
Cost $132 per cabin, $28 backpacker
dorms, $11 campsites
Payment AmEx, Bankcard, Diners,
EFTPOS, MasterCard, Visa

G'Day Tropical Village

7–27 McLachlan St
Cairns QLD 4870
Phone 07/4053 7555
Fax 07/4032 1101
Email gday@gdaytropical.com.au
Web www.gdaytropical.com.au
Gender Mixed
All rooms are fully air-conditioned
with views over lush tropical
gardens. The resort complex includes
a tour booking office and resort
shop, as well as a lagoon-style
swimming pool, restaurant and bar.
Located 4km from the centre of
Cairns (free city shuttle service),
this place has plenty of helpful gay
and gay-friendly staff.
Cost From $15 in a dorm, $70 per room
Payment AmEx, Bankcard, Diners,
EFTPOS, MasterCard, Visa

Girls Only Hostel

147 Lake St
Cairns QLD 4870
Phone 07/4051 2016
Email mudcake_au@yahoo.com
Web www.girlshostel.webprovider.com
Gender Women

A range of rooms (sleeping 1–5) in a very clean hostel environment; dorms can be locked and a there is a security entrance to the property. There are communal kitchens and bathrooms, free use of washing machine and TV lounges.
Cost $17 per night, $88 per week
Payment Cash only

Inn Cairns Boutique Apartments

71 Lake St
Cairns QLD 4870
Phone 07/4041 2350
Fax 07/4041 2420
Email bookings@inncairns.com.au
Web www.inncairns.com.au
Gender Mixed

These fully equipped apartments in the heart of Cairns are surrounded by restaurants, shops and entertainment.
Cost From $120 per apartment
Payment AmEx, Bankcard, Diners, EFTPOS, MasterCard, Visa

Marlin Cove Resort

2 Keem St
Trinity Beach QLD 4879
Phone 07/4057 8299
Fax 07/4057 8909
Email marlincove@quest-inns.com.au
Web www.quest-inns.com.au
Gender Mixed

Award-winning, architect-designed apartments with full-size kitchens and air-conditioning. Complex has three pools on the premises (including a sandy lagoon pool) and restaurant. The beach and shops are only one block away.
Cost $138–199 per apartment
Payment AmEx, Bankcard, Diners, MasterCard, Visa; cheque

Penny Ford Center

13 Sommerville Cresent
Whitfield QLD 4870
Phone Stuart 07/4032 2955 or 0414 696 969
Email penny@pennyfordcenter.com.au
Web www.pennyfordcenter.com.au
Gender Mixed

Located 5km from the centre of Cairns, the *Penny Ford Center* is a rather different sort of place to the Betty Ford Center, offering bed and (all-day) brekkie in a lovely home setting with shared kitchen, tropical courtyard, pool and spa. The decor is the full troppo business, clothing is optional and transfers are available for international guests and famous drag queens. There is a barbecue for guests' use and cheap car hire is available.
Cost From $56 per room
Payment Cheque

Reef Palms

41–47 Digger St
Cairns QLD 4870
Phone 07/4051 2599
Fax 07/4051 7676
Email info@reefpalms.com.au
Web www.reefpalms.com.au
Gender Mixed

Traditional Queensland living in self-contained studio apartments. Rooms have air-conditioning, balconies, safes and phones. Guest facilities include a tour desk, Internet café, landscaped pool, spa and barbecue area.

Cost $83–143 per room
Payment AmEx, Bankcard, Diners, EFTPOS, MasterCard, Visa; cheque

Top Trop B&B

PO Box 405
Trinity Beach QLD, 4879
Phone 07/4057 8722
Fax 07/4057 8722
Email ggandtoptrop@hotkey.net.au
Web www.lithium.net.au/toptrop
Gender Mixed

Situated between the Daintree and the Great Barrier Reef, 20 minutes' drive from Cairns (aiport transfers available), *Top Trop* is an exclusively gay and lesbian resort. Overlooking the ocean and set among banana palms and mango trees, its architecturally designed polehouse and rock pool provide cool comfort in the hot tropics. Lesbian-owned and -operated.

Cost $95–115 single, $115–140 double
Payment Cheque

Turtle Cove Resort

Captain Cook Highway or PO Box 158
Smithfield QLD 4878
Phone 07/4059 1800
Fax 07/4059 1969
Email gay@turtlecove.com.au
Web www.turtlecove.com.au
Gender Mixed

Australia's premier gay/lesbian resort, this private gay-owned and -operated coastal resort is nothing short of idyllic. Located 45 minutes' drive north of Cairns, it has its own private beach, large pool and spa. The bar, restaurant and beach are open to visitors just passing by. Giant turtles often come ashore here and the surrounding bushland boasts lots of Australian fauna (especially kangaroos). The resort offers gay/lesbian tours of the Barrier Reef and trips to other local attractions. All rooms have balconies, ensuites and TV with free movie channels. Whether you are travelling alone or with others you'll be sure to meet lots of people at this resort and everyone is actively encouraged to mingle at dinner time. Nudism is allowed on the resort's beach and in the pool and the staff are the soul of discretion!

Cost $138–243 per room
Payment AmEx, Bankcard, Diners, EFTPOS, MasterCard, Visa

Witchencroft Women's Guest House

PO Box 685
Atherton QLD 4883
Phone 07/4091 2683
Fax 07/4091 2683
Email jenny.maclean@iig.com.au
Gender Women

Australia's longest-running women's guesthouse, *Witchencroft* is a lesbian-owned and -operated business, established in 1986. Comfortable rooms are set in peaceful gardens on the tropical Atherton Tablelands, an hour's drive from Cairns. Other amenities include 4WD tours, bushwalks, vegetarian meals and on-site bat hospital.

Cost $66 single, $88 double (discounted rates for longer stays)
Payment Cash only

CAFÉS AND RESTAURANTS

Throbb Restaurant and Cocktail Bar

Upstairs 10A Shield St
Cairns QLD 4870
Phone 07/4051 6887

This cosy and friendly cocktail lounge offers drag shows on Friday and Saturday nights. The food is modern Australian with specialties such as grilled barramundi on crispy potato scallops with tabasco tomato salsa or a wide range of pastas; a favourite is smoked salmon with wilted spinach. Their homemade ice creams are also popular. There is a pool table and you are welcome to drop in for drinks or coffee.

Open Wed–Sun 6pm–2am
Payment AmEx, Bankcard, MasterCard, Visa

BARS AND CLUBS

Club Danny

Upstairs, 32 Macrossan St
Port Douglas QLD 4871
Phone 07/4099 6266
Gender Mixed

Late night retro groove club, which is gay-owned and very gay-friendly. Drag shows, Latin American jazz bands and guest DJs. Neat tropical attire required.

Open Wed–Sun 10pm–4am (7 nights a week in peak season)
Admission Cover charge for special events only
Payment Bankcard, MasterCard, Visa

Club Trix

53 Spence St
Cairns QLD 4870
Phone 07/4051 8223
Gender Mixed

When you've had all the natural splendour you can take, come into the famous and friendly *Club Trix*. There's a bar and dancefloor with plenty of handbag, a friendly atmosphere . . . and a pool table.

Open Wed 9pm–2am, Thurs 9pm–3am, Fri–Sat 9pm–5am, Sun 9pm–1am
Admission Cover charge some weekends
Payment Cash only

Drag Queens of the Far North

Ms Rose Leaf

Diva Queen of Sydney, now relocated to tropical Cairns and the Barrier Reef. Star of Rose Leaf's Far North Queens, a talented drag team seen at *Throbb* or *Club Trix* (see listings above) and anywhere else game enough to have them.

Donna Peringon

More beautiful than Doris Day and as butch as Rock Hudson, this talented queen teams up with Delvine, a beached whale who is the star of the Pig-Pen strip joint.

Philipa Crevase

Known to marines in every port, Philipa left Melbourne in a hurry (don't they all) and now entertains the navy when the boys are in town. She is strikingly beautiful and available in all the major malls in Cairns.

Cherry Blossom

The tits-and-feather goddess of Rose Leaf's Far North Queens, Cherry is another Mexican (a south-of-the-border Sydneysider) who has brought her talented wares to share with the locals – and share she does.

Kara Van Park

An irresistible tramp and slut, this whore with more is one of the few drag queens in Australia who has successfully produced her own CD. She is booked out most of the year. Nice work if you can get it.

Pencil Vania is a licensed image consultant, international supermodel and heiress performing by appointment or occasionally impromptu. She is very generous and community-spirited, having initiated and trained many drags who have now become little starlets, and is also the proud owner of *The Penny Ford Center* in Cairns (see p.151).

Hugh Monroe has been working in Cairns for a couple of years at the Reef Casino. An hour's worth of singing, dancing and doing high-wire acts in drag with a very professional group.

Pencil Vania

ADULT SHOPS, PARTY AND FETISH WEAR

Erotica

10a Shields St
Cairns QLD 4870
Phone 07/4041 4069
Gender Mixed
Adult bookshop providing magazines and a selection of gay titles, with a special order service available. Stockists of *Queensland Pride*, *Brother/Sister* and all the usual vibes, magazines, sex toys and party wear.
Open Daily 2pm–10pm
Payment Bankcard, EFTPOS, MasterCard, Visa

BOOKSHOPS

Collins Booksellers
PO Box 20, Smithfield Centre,
Captain Cook Highway
Smithfield QLD 4878
Phone 07/4038 1786
Fax 07/4038 1035
Email collinsb@internetnorth.com.au
Offers a good range of literary fiction,
a special order service and has a small
gay and lesbian section.
Open Mon–Wed 9am–5.30pm,
Thurs 9am–8pm, Fri 9am–5.30pm,
Sat 9am–4pm, Sun 1pm–5pm
Payment AmEx, Bankcard, Diners,
EFTPOS, MasterCard, Visa; cheque

Walkers Bookshop
96 Lake St
Cairns QLD 4870
Phone 07/4051 2410
Fax 07/4031 6175
Email info@walkersbookshop.com.au
Web www.walkersbookshop.com.au
Walkers offers a gay and lesbian section,
as well as stocking all Queensland's free
gay/lesbian newspapers.
Open Mon–Thurs 9am–6pm,
Fri 9am–7pm, Sat 9am–3pm,
Sun 10am–2pm
Payment AmEx, Bankcard, Diners,
EFTPOS, MasterCard, Visa

BEACHES AND POOLS

Buchan Point
Captain Cook Highway
Palm Cove QLD 4879
Gender Mixed
Buchan Point is a popular nudist and
gay beach 30km north of Cairns. The
easiest way to find it is to drive north
from Cairns on the Captain Cook
Highway. Just past the Palm Cove
turn-off, where the highway first hits
the coast, there is a car park on your
right. Park there and walk along the
beach in a southerly direction for
about 200m and you'll soon notice a
distinct lack of bathing attire; the rest
of the beach as far as the rocks is
pretty much gay. Be warned, the
rocks are slippery and lethal – one slip
and your legs could be in shreds (as

the author knows only too well).
Note: police patrol this beach from
time to time.

Turtle Cove Beach
Tutle Cove Resort, Captain Cook
Highway PO Box 158
Smithfield QLD 4878
Gender Mixed
Turtle Cove Resort (p.152) owns a
private beach and welcomes gay and
lesbian visitors. Swimsuits are
optional and there is also a bar,
restaurant, pool and jacuzzi. The
beach is located two thirds of the
way to Port Douglas and nestled to
the right of the road; keep your eyes
open – the Turtle Cove sign is easy
to pass.

STD Clinic
Cairns Base Hospital Esplanade
Cairns QLD 4870
Phone 07/4050 6205
Gender Mixed

By appointment only; clinic times vary. Safe-sex information and supplies, counselling, testing and treatment.
Open Mon–Fri 8am–4pm

Boys Out
PO Box 234
Westcourt QLD 4870
Phone Chuck 07/4033 5380 or David 07/4057 8604
Gender Men
A men's social group that meets regularly and offers both indoor and outdoor activities.

Community Information Service
1st floor, Tropical Arcade
Cairns QLD 4870
Phone Clements 07/4051 4953
Email secretary@cisci.org.au
Web www.cisci.org.au
Gender Mixed
Community information provided without prejudice or cost. Contacts for over 2000 special-interest clubs and organizations in the Cairns region.
Open Mon–Fri 9am–5pm

Lesbian Support Group
Women's Centre Mulgrave Rd
Cairns QLD 4870
Phone 07/4051 4927
Gender Women
Lesbian support group meeting every Wednesday at 6pm.

Queensland AIDS Council (QuAC)
1st floor, Andrejic Arcade 55 Lake St
Cairns QLD 4870
Phone 07/4051 1028
Gender Mixed
Information and support for those living with HIV/AIDS, their lovers, family and friends. Plus safe-sex information and supplies; needle exchange. Youth support, education and referral.
Open Mon–Fri 9am–5pm

Tropical Gay FM
4CCR, 89.1 on the FM dial
Cairns QLD
Phone 07/4053 5866
Gender Mixed
Gay and lesbian news and grooves.
Open Sun 8pm–11pm

TRAVEL SERVICES

Boyz Brick Road

PO Box 795N
North Cairns QLD 4870
Phone 07/4031 5011
Fax 07/4051 1463
Email michael@boyz-brick-road.com.au
Web www.boyz-brick-road.com.au
Tailor-made tropical holidays and tours for gay men.

Gay Cairns Travel

28 Spence St
Cairns QLD 4870
Phone 07/4041 1969
Web www.gaycairns.com.au
Accommodation and tours for domestic and international travellers, with online booking service.

Global Gossip

125 Abbott St
Cairns QLD 4870
Phone 07/4031 6411
Fax 07/4031 6711
Gay-owned chain of Internet and communication centres, offering email, chat, cheap phone calls, employment services, copying, faxing and mailbox rental.
Open Daily 8am–midnight
Payment Bankcard, EFTPOS, MasterCard, Visa; cheque

Northern Territory

'The Territory' covers 20 per cent of the continent, but is **sparsely populated** – if you don't count the crocodiles, feral water buffalo, Jabiru storks, brolgas and dingoes. It is home to some of Australia's most magnificent **national parks** as well as significant Aboriginal sites and land.

Vast tracts of red-sand desert (the Simpson and Tanami) occupy the heart of the oldest landmass on the planet – its '**Red Centre**'. This ancient land is peppered with striking rock formations: Katherine Gorge, the Devil's Marbles, the MacDonnell Ranges, Kings Canyon, and, most memorable of all, that icon of outback Australia, Uluru (also known as Ayers Rock). The '**Top End**', as the farthest nothern tip of Australia is colloquially known, still represents the last redneck frontier in the minds of many Australians, but apparently the territory has always had a swinging under-belly; Dino Hodge's *Did you meet any Malagas?: A Homosexual History of the Northern Territory* (Little Gem Publications) is a useful anecdotal resource.

With its **tropical climate**, the Northern Territory has two seasons: the Dry (April–October) and the Wet (November–March). The soporific weather during the latter seems to contribute to the locals' laid-back nature.

Darwin

Despite having a population of only 84,000, Darwin occupies a special place in the Australian psyche. Dramatically situated atop the **Never–Never**, as the sparsely inhabited desert country has been dubbed, this pioneer town has been associated with lawlessness, cyclones, crocodiles, beer, heat and isolation. Much of that has changed over the past couple of decades. Suddenly discovering its prime position on the Asian–Australian cusp, Darwin has busily remodelled itself as a modern, bustling, colourful, cosmopolitan (and air-conditioned) capital. Late last century the Chinese outnumbered Europeans in the Territory by as many as eight to one, and this historical connection with Asia has been reclaimed and forms a vital part of the city's identity, as evidenced by Darwin's thriving **Asian–style markets**.

Darwin highlights and hot-spots

- For a slice of Darwin life, it's hard to beat the **markets**. During the dry season (April through to October), there is a night market on Thursday and Sunday at Mindil Beach; Parap Markets run on Saturday mornings all year round; and Rapid Creek and Nightcliff Markets on Sunday all year round.

- The **Territory Wildlife Park**, a 40-minute drive from Darwin (and on the way to Litchfield National Park), features striking biospheres of native fauna in their natural habitats.

- **Litchfield National Park** is closer to Darwin than the famous Kakadu National Park, and more compact in its beauty and accessibility. It has great swimming holes, waterfalls, bushwalking trails and camping sites. The park can be closed during the wet season (November to March).

- Darwin boasts some of the most extreme tides and magnificent **sunsets** on the planet. Check them out, champagne glass in hand, from the deck of one of the sunset harbour cruise boats.

- And, if you just can't resist smiling at a crocodile, make for **Crocodylus Park** (daily 9am–5pm; bus #5).

The city is a **mix of cultures** and contradictions: more than one in ten Darwinites identify as Aboriginal and the Territory is rich in Aboriginal art and cultural heritage – yet, come election time, politicians decry Native title and what they term 'the Aboriginal problem' (itinerancy and 'anti-social behaviour'). The balance between tolerance and diversity on the one hand and trenchant conservatism on the other is a tricky one in the Territory.

Gays and lesbians may well ask what this means for them. Well, Darwin does tend to pride itself on its anything-goes, **laissez-faire attitude** to just about everything really – except of course Native title. And with the advent of the backpacker market over the past five to ten years, Darwin tends to find itself regularly inundated with all sorts of bodies, faces and images which, for the gay and lesbian traveller, means you're not gonna stick out like a sore thumb, basically. So come up, kick back, and soak up the lazy northern tropics.

ACCOMMODATION

Moil on the Park
22 Pott St, Moil
Darwin NT 0810
Phone Bob and Tony 08/8927 5421
Fax 08/8927 5421
Gender Mixed
Surrounded by tropical gardens with a pool and spa, *Moil on the Park* offers homestay-style accommodation and is a few minutes' drive from the airport (free transfers are available), 15 minutes from the city (a bus stop is nearby) and walking distance to Casuarina shopping centre (Darwin's largest) and Casuarina nude beach. Breakfast is included and evening meals can be arranged. Complimentary tickets are available for current theatre productions.
Cost $77 single, $88 double
Payment Cheque

CAFÉS AND RESTAURANTS

All Sorts Café
130 Smith St
Darwin NT 0800
Phone 08/8941 2126
All Sorts is BYO and licensed and serves reliable café-style food.
Open Mon–Sat 6pm–late
Cost $10–20 per person
Payment Cash only

The Lost Arc
89 Mitchell St
Darwin NT 0800
Phone 08/8942 3300
Fax 08/8942 3311
Web www.discoverdarwin.com.au
This popular recovery spot serves snacks, lunch and dinner, and is licensed for drinks. The menu charts a

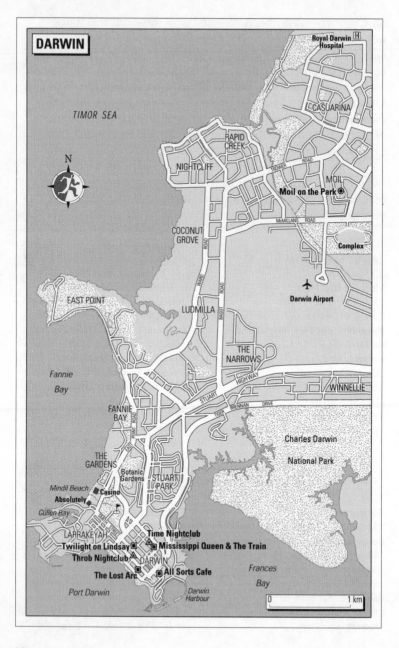

DARWIN

Royal Darwin Hospital 🏥

TIMOR SEA

CASUARINA

RAPID CREEK

NIGHTCLIFF

MOIL

Moil on the Park ◉

COCONUT GROVE

TROWER ROAD

McMILLANS ROAD

Complex

EAST POINT

LUDMILLA

DICK WARD DRIVE

BAGOT ROAD

✈ Darwin Airport

THE NARROWS

Fannie Bay

FANNIE BAY

WINNELLIE

HIGHWAY

STUART

TIGER BRENNAN DRIVE

Charles Darwin National Park

THE GARDENS

Botanic Gardens

STUART PARK

PINE ROAD

Mindil Beach ■ Casino

Absolutely ◆

Cullen Bay

LARRAKEYAH

Time Nightclub

Twilight on Lindsay ◨ ◨ Mississippi Queen & The Train

Throb Nightclub △

The Lost Arc ◧ DARWIN

◨ ■ All Sorts Cafe

Frances Bay

Port Darwin

Darwin Harbour

0   1 km

course through comfort-food stalwarts, such as garlic bread, laksa, burgers, fish dishes and bowls of pasta. Monday night is popular for its cheap drinks, and there is entertainment most nights.
Open Daily noon–4am
Cost $15–20 per person
Payment AmEx, Bankcard, EFTPOS, MasterCard, Visa

Mississippi Queen
4 Gardiner St
Darwin NT 0800
Phone 08/8981 3358
Darwin's oldest and most famous dining venue is set in tropical gardens and offers the taste sensations of kangaroo, buffalo, crocodile or barramundi. Bookings essential.
Open Daily 7pm–2am
Cost From $35 per person
Payment AmEx, Bankcard, Diners, MasterCard, Visa

Twilight on Lindsay
2 Lindsay St
Darwin NT 0800
Phone 08/8981 8631
This gay-owned and -operated establishment offers fine al fresco dining in tropical style. It is fully licensed, and bookings are essential.
Open Mon–Sat 6.30pm–midnight
Cost $30–40 per person
Payment AmEx, Bankcard, Diners, MasterCard, Visa

BARS AND CLUBS

Time Nightclub
3 Edmunds St
Darwin NT 0800
Phone 08/8981 9761
Gender Mixed
Though not a gay nightclub as such, *Time* is considered by locals in the know to be gay-friendly. It has special guest DJs.
Open Fri–Sat 10pm–late
Admission Cover charge after midnight
Payment Cash only

The Train (Mississippi Queen)
6 Gardiner St
Darwin NT 0800
Phone 08/8981 3358
Gender Mixed
This famous gay-owned establishment is a must to visit. Set in a lush tropical garden, its old railcar bar is simply amazing. There's a pool table, juke box and Sunday-afternoon entertainment. Bar meals are available – and the bar really comes to life after 10pm.
Open Daily 7pm–2am
Admission Free
Payment AmEx, Bankcard, Diners, MasterCard, Visa

Throb Nightclub
Level 1, 64 Smith St
Darwin NT 0800
Phone 08/8942 3435
Gender Mixed
This gay and lesbian nightclub offers the best queer club scene in town. There are pool tables, guest DJs, a dancefloor and drag shows.
Open Thurs–Sat 9pm–late
Admission Cover charge for shows
Payment Cash only

Northern Territory Drag Queens

Although the scene is more discreet than in Sydney or Melbourne, there are still a few names worth looking out for. **Catherine Gorge** (if her dresses were any shorter you could just about fall in!) is a premier entertainer and nightclub operator throughout the state, while **Laura Gravity** has her feet planted anywhere

but firmly on the ground. **Naomi Canbolt** is even leaner than her namesake and a truly gorgeous sight to behold. And you should never say 'Never-Never' near **Julie Jabiru** – a modern vision of the Dreamtime.

Neal Drinnan

ADULT SHOPS

Fantasy Lane Lounge
4 Charles St
Stuart Park NT 0820
Phone 08/8941 2441
Fax 09 8941 2778
Web www.risque.com.au
Gender Men

This lounge offers a wide range of adult toys and free local newspapers, as well as a contact board.
Open Daily 9am–midnight
Payment Amex, Bankcard, Diners, EFTPOS, MasterCard, Visa

BOOKSHOPS

Absolutely
6/48 Marina Boulevard
Cullen Bay NT 0820
Phone 08/8941 1363
Fax 08/8941 1375
Email absolutelybooks@bigpond.com
Gay-owned and -operated, this shop
stocks gay and lesbian fiction and
non-fiction, as well as cards and gifts.
Also carries gay/lesbian newspapers
and magazines.
Open Daily 10am–10pm
Payment AmEx, Bankcard, EFTPOS,
MasterCard, Visa

Dymocks Casuarina
256 Casuarina Square
Casuarina NT 0810
Phone 08/8927 2080
Fax 08/8927 2082
Email dymocks@topend.com.au
A general bookshop housing small
sections on gay and lesbian issues and
gender studies.
Open Mon–Thurs 9am–5.30pm,
Fri 9am–9pm, Sat 9am–5pm,
Sun 10am–3pm
Payment AmEx, Bankcard, Diners,
EFTPOS, MasterCard, Visa

NEWSPAPERS AND MAGAZINES

Gay NT
PO Box 39
Darwin NT 0801
Phone Cliff Anderson (editor)
0409 611 028
Email gayntmagazine@hotmail.com
Gender Mixed

This monthly magazine covers gay and
lesbian issues and offers up-to-date
information on the Territory scene.
Outlets include *Absolutely* (above) and
Northern Territory AIDS Council (p.166).
Cost $3.50 per issue
Payment Cheque

BEACHES AND POOLS

Casuarina Beach
Casuarina NT 0810
Gender Mostly men
Casuarina Free Beach (so-called for
its tolerance of nudity) is at the north
end of Casuarina Beach. At the end
of Trower Road, turn off at the
beach sign following Daribah Road

to the car park. Then follow the
track at the north end of the car
park. It's 450m to the section of
beach most popular with gays –
identifying and otherwise.
Remember there are deadly stingers
(box jellyfish) in Darwin's waters
from October to May.

MEDICAL

Clinic 34
Block 4, Royal Darwin Hospital
Darwin NT 0800
Phone 08/8922 8007
Gender Mixed

This confidential sexual health service offers free condoms, lube and safe-sex packs.
Open Mon–Thurs 8.30am–4pm (appointment preferred)

COMMUNITY

Emergency Accommodation
Darwin NT 0800
Phone 08/8948 0216 or 08/8941 1711
Gender Mixed
Offers emergency short-term accommodation for those in crisis situations and genuine need; also attempts to secure a safe haven for those in abusive or difficult situations while a resolution is sought.

Gay North Incorporated
Darwin NT 0800
Phone Michael 08/8948 0216
Gender Mixed
A social group for gay, lesbian, bisexual and transgender people of the Top End that organizes regular dances, pool parties, video nights and special events. It also provides information to travellers and new arrivals.

Men's Line
Darwin NT 0800
Phone Freecall 1800/181 888
Gender Men
Provides confidential counselling and support for men.
Open Sun–Tues 5.30pm–10pm

Northern Territory AIDS Council (NTAC)
6 Manton St
Darwin NT 0800
Phone 08/8941 1711
Fax 08/8941 2590
Email ntac@octa4.net.au
Web www.octa4.net.au/ntac
Gender Mixed
NTAC offers a range of health and social services to the territory's gay, lesbian, bisexual and transgender communities and organizes monthly dances, a young indigenous support program, needle exchange and sex worker outreach project, as well as stocking all national gay and lesbian newspapers.
Open Mon–Fri 9am–5pm

Sexual Reality 104.1 FM
Darwin NT 0800
Phone 08/8946 6266
Fax 08/8945 1788
Gender Mixed
This weekly radio program (Wed 10.30pm–12.30am) covers gay and lesbian issues, as well as music and gossip for all.

UNITY
Nightcliff NT 0810
Phone 08/8985 2658
Gender Mixed

A network for lesbians, gays, bisexuals, their friends and family based in the Uniting Church. *UNITY* gathers to eat, talk and share Holy Communion.

TRAVEL SERVICES

Global Gossip
44 Mitchell St
Darwin NT 0800
Phone 08/8942 3044
Fax 08/8942 3055
Gay-owned chain of communication

centres offers email, Internet, cheap phone calls, employment services, copying, faxing and mailbox rental.
Open Daily 8am–midnight
Payment Bankcard, EFTPOS, MasterCard, Visa; cheque

Alice Springs

Home to 25,000 people, 'The Alice' has a diverse, welcoming **gay and lesbian community** (largely the latter – three lesbians to every gay man, it's rumoured locally) spanning a broad range of ages, races, backgrounds and professions. Many and varied events feature in the gay/lesbian calendar.

On the third Friday of each month, a gay and lesbian dance is held to celebrate sexual freedom and the spirit. Friday evenings are spent lazing around the **Alice Springs Resort** (see p.169) – by the pool when it's warm, or around a log fire when it's not. The culmination of the Friday dances is the **SPIN-FX dance party** and a gay and lesbian festival called 'Alice's Wonderland', both of which take place in March, the weekend after the Mardi Gras parade in Sydney. SPIN-FX is an ideal adjunct for inter-

national travellers wishing to experience the outback, get a taste of a new kind of gay and lesbian Dreaming, and party on in an entirely different setting. Tickets are available on the night and further information on this (and most other gay/lesbian happenings in the area) is available from the *Rainbow Connection* or the *AIDS Council of Central Australia* (see p.170). Visiting lesbians might like to contact Desert Rose (phone and fax 08/8952 7639) – a leading light within the lesbian community in Central Australia, its entertainment director and general fun-and-frolics organizer.

Heading out of town, you can check-out the local flora and fauna (and the inspiration for all those *Priscilla*-style drag outfits) at the **Desert Park**, a couple of kilometres out of Alice. A number of sensational drives lead to beautiful **gorges and waterholes** to swim in, or you can join biologist Matthew Fowler in a group tour of the Todd River and surrounding regions (see p.171).

ACCOMMODATION

Alice Springs Resort Hotel
34 Stott Terrace
Alice Springs NT 0870
Phone Jane 08/8951 4545
Fax 08/8953 0995
Email janeoakley-lohm@aliceresort.mtx.net.au
Web www.alicespringsresort.com.au
Gender Mixed
Facilities at this resort-style hotel include a restaurant, lounge, pool and pool bar. Room service is available.
Cost From $188 per room
Payment AmEx, Bankcard, Diners, MasterCard, Visa

Annie's Place
4 Traeger Ave
Alice Springs NT 0870
Phone Annie or Mulga 08/8952 1545
Gender Mixed
This friendly, budget motel and hostel with a swimming pool is ten minutes' walk from the centre of Alice. It provides dormitory accommodation or double rooms with ensuites, and has a licensed café which is open for all meals (dinner from $5).
Cost $22 dorm beds, $50 double
Payment Bankcard, EFTPOS, MasterCard, Visa; cheque

The Rainbow Connection
22 Raggatt St
Alice Springs NT 0870
Phone Phil Walcott 08/8952 6441 or mobile 0407 526 441
Fax 08/8952 6441
Email rainbow@dove.net.au
Gender Mixed
The Rainbow Connection offers bed and breakfast accommodation in two adjoining properties just over a kilometre from the town centre. Rooms have ensuite facilities, use of a pool and the tariff includes full

breakfast. Phil Walcott, a keen gay promoter of the 'outback experience', also organizes a 'homestay brokerage' system whereby visitors can stay in someone's home from within the gay and lesbian community, and he can also help you find a tour guide.
Cost $88 single, $110 double
Payment Cheque

CAFÉS AND RESTAURANTS

Bar Doppio
2/3 Fan Arcade (off the Todd Mall)
Alice Springs NT 0870
Phone 08/9852 6525
This Mediterranean-style café in the centre of Alice is popular with local gays and lesbians.
Open Mon–Sat 7am–10pm, Sun 10am–5pm
Cost Breakfast $5–10, lunch $10–15, dinner $15–25
Payment Cash only

Didee's
2 Reg Harris Lane (just off Todd Mall)
Alice Springs NT 0870
Phone 08/8952 1966
Lesbian-owned *Didee's* serves breakfast and lunch, specializing in vegetarian food with an Asian influence. *Didee's* also offers homemade cakes and muffins, great coffee and fresh juices.
Open Daily 8am–5pm
Cost Breakfast from $5, lunch $8–12
Payment Cash only

BARS AND CLUBS

Alice Springs Resort Hotel
34 Stott Terrace
Alice Springs NT 0870
Phone Jane 08/8951 4545
Fax 08/8953 0995
Email janeoakley-lohm@aliceresort. mtx.net.au
Web www.alicespringsresort.com.au

Gender Mixed
Friday evenings at 5.30pm is when the lesbian and gay citizens of Alice Springs get together for Happy Hour (until 6.30pm) in the hotel bar.
Payment AmEx, Bankcard, Diners, MasterCard, Visa

ARTS

Gallery Gondwana
43 Todd Mall
Alice Springs NT 0870
Phone 08/8953 1577
Fax 08/8953 2441
Email fineart@gallerygondwana. com.au

Gallery Gondwana exhibits and sells a wide range of local artists' work as well as traditional Aboriginal crafts.
Open Mon–Sat 10am–5pm
Payment AmEx, Bankcard, Diners, MasterCard, Visa

The Breathing Space
22 Raggatt St
Alice Springs NT 0870
Phone 08/8952 3638
Gender Mixed
Sigrid, Kalika and Phil offer massage, yoga, breathing techniques, counselling, educational and psychological services. *The Breathing Space* also provides a range of other health services for lesbians and gays.

Clinic 34
Alice Springs Hospital
Public Health Services,
Gap Rd, Alice Springs NT 0870
Phone 08/8951 7549
Email population.health@health.nt. gov.au
Gender Mixed
This free and confidential sexual health service (no Medicare card required) provides needle exchange, safe-sex information and supplies, testing, counselling and treatment.
Open Mon–Fri 8am–5pm

AIDS Council of Central Australia
119 Todd St
Alice Springs NT 0870
Phone 08/8953 1118
Email acoca@dove.net.au
Gender Mixed
This service offers a range of health and social services to gay, lesbian, bisexual and transgender communities, as well as indigenous outreach work. Needle exchange, sex-worker information, free safe-sex packs and gay and lesbian newspapers from around the country are also available.
Open Mon–Fri 9am–5pm

Gayline
Centre Network, PO Box 1567
Alice Springs NT 0871
Phone 08/8953 2844
Gender Mostly men
Gayline hosts gay dances on the first Friday of every month, Happy Hour gatherings at *Alice Springs Resort* (see p.169), and is a good point of contact for local happenings.
Open Daily 6pm–10pm

Mulga's Adventures
PO Box 3531
Alice Springs NT 0871
Phone 08/8952 1545 or
freecall 1800/359 089
Fax 08/8952 8280
Email info@mulgas.com.au
Web www.mulgas.com.au
Gender Mixed
Camping experiences to Uluru (3 days from $325) or the Kimberley in Western Australia, via Darwin and Broome (10 days from $985).

Todd River Tours
PO Box 3779
Alice Springs NT 0871
Phone 0412 887 243
Fax 08/8953 4448
Email ozytours@ozemail.com.au
Web www.ozemail.com.au/~ozytours
Gender Mixed
Biologist guide Matthew Fowler offers tailor-made, special-interest (wildlife, Aboriginal culture, walking and cycling, bush food and medicine) tours in and around Alice Springs.

Into the outback

A wander in the outback is well worth a few days of anybody's time. Most visitors to Darwin take at least a brief spin into Kakadu National Park, on the western edge of **Arnhem Land**, to see the rock art and wildlife, but an overnight trip further onto the Arnhem Land plateau is a truly unforgettable experience. South of Darwin, on the road to Alice Springs, worthwhile stopovers include remote and peaceful **Daly River**, about 100km west of the Stuart Highway; **Katherine**, with its gorgeous gorge; and the classic outback town of Tennant Creek, with the weird and wonderful Devil's Marbles (relatively) nearby. Off the highway south-west of Alice Springs lies the dramatic **Kings Canyon** in Watarrka National Park, and **Uluru**.

When you go walkabout, be sure to notify a responsible person of your plans, carry plenty of **water** and **sunscreen** – and maybe a mobile phone, if you have one.

Kings Canyon Resort

Watarrka National Park, RMB 136
Alice Springs NT 0870
Phone 08/8956 7442
Fax 08/8956 7410
Gender Mixed

Not a gay and lesbian resort, but you won't get much else in these parts. All standard and deluxe rooms have private bathrooms, but there are also budget family rooms and campsites. The resort has a restaurant, bar, mini supermarket, tour desk, petrol pump, laundry, two swimming pools, tennis court and room service.

Cost From $255 per room, campsites from $25
Payment AmEx, Bankcard, Diners, MasterCard, Visa

Walkabout Lodge

PO Box 221
(12 Westal St, Nhulunbuy Cove)
Arnhem Land NT 0881
Phone 08/8987 1777
Fax 08/8987 2322
Email info@walkaboutlodge.com.au
Web www.walkaboutlodge.com.au
Gender Mixed

Set on a remote beach in Arnhem Land, *Walkabout Lodge* has a pool, restaurant, gardens and bar, with disco nights on Thursday and Saturday. The lodge can also arrange eco tours, diving, fishing charters, Aboriginal culture experiences, birdwatching and 4WD hire.

Cost From $188 per room (up to four people)
Payment AmEx, Bankcard, Diners, EFTPOS, MasterCard, Visa

Mango Farm

PMB 120, Winnellie Port, Keats Rd
Daly River NT 0822
Phone 08/8978 2464 or
freecall 1800/000 576
Fax 08/8978 2331
Email mangofarm@mangofarm.com.au
Web www.mangofarm.com.au
Gender Mixed

Located some 230km south-west of Darwin, the *Mango Farm* was the first mango plantation in Australia, and it now offers a range of accommodation for those wishing to experience the real outback. A stone cabin sleeps up to six, and smaller cabins sleep up to five, all sharing communal bathroom blocks. There is also a unit with private bathroom sleeping up to nine. Both powered and unpowered camp sites are available, as is tent hire (with beds and linen included, though not towels). There is a communal camp kitchen and barbecue, and the Settlers Bistro and bar, which caters for vegetarians as well as meat-eaters. For recreation there is a pool, bushwalks, boat hire, and guided fishing tours. Other local attractions include the Jesuit ruins and historic settlers' graveyard, and the indigenous arts and crafts produced by the Daly River Aboriginal Community.

Cost Cabins $80 per couple ($9 per extra person), family units $138 for up to four ($11 per extra person), powered campsites $22 per couple ($6 per extra person), tent hire $33 per couple
Payment Bankcard, EFTPOS, MasterCard, Visa

MEDICAL

Tennant Creek Hospital
Schmidt
Tennant Creek NT 0860
Phone 08/8962 4218
Fax 08/8962 4311
Gender Mixed

Appointments are advisable for this free and confidential sexual health service. The hospital also provides a needle exchange and safe-sex supplies.

Western Australia

Western Australia is the **largest state**, taking up roughly a third of the continent. So remote is it from the rest of the nation that a hard core of West Australians would like to see it secede.

On a socio-political level Western Australia has never exactly been a trailblazer when it comes to enlightened policy-making and, while it may have produced some of Australia's more crooked mega-millionaires, it remains reluctant to reduce the age of consent for gay men below 21 (it's 18 for lesbians). With the exception of inner-city **Perth and Fremantle**, gays and lesbians would be advised to behave with a certain amount of discretion in WA. In a state this huge and sparsely populated, no one can hear you scream . . .

The **Southwest** offers plenty of lush countryside and tall trees, produces some of Australia's best wines and has a few fine guesthouses that make fine bases for your explorations of this region. Heading **north**, you'll meet few fellow travellers – especially once you've passed Monkey Mia and its visiting dolphins. Those who travel the lonely stretch of road beyond here will be rewarded by the pristine reef at Coral Bay and the magnificent expanse of Broome's famed Cable Beach.

Perth and Fremantle

Perth is among the world's most **isolated** cities, with a population of only 1.3 million people. Situated on the sprawling Swan River, which flows into the sea at Perth's port of **Fremantle**, 15km to the west, the city enjoys a **Mediterranean climate**. This means lots of sunshine and informal living, so don't forget the sunscreen and a hat during summer, when it can get *very* hot.

If you are heading to the beach in the warmer months, remember that a sea breeze (known as the Fremantle Doctor, for its beneficial cooling effect) usually kicks in around lunchtime. So you might want to time your beach visit for the morning if you don't like wind-blown sand on your towel or in your eyes.

> Perth's **public transport** is run by Transperth, which has information centres at the City Busport, Wellington Street Bus Station, Plaza Arcade and Perth Train Station; or you can call 13 6213.
>
> Buses are **free** in the central zone, as are the red and blue 'cat' loop services, which run every 10 minutes around the city.

Perth's central business district, south of the railway line, is populated mainly during daylight hours, though the trend towards inner-city living has spawned a few early morning/late-night cafés along King Street. Perth has a vibrant **arts** scene, especially during the months of January and February, when the Perth International Arts Festival is held. The main **theatres** are in the CBD, including the historic His Majesty's Theatre, on the corner of Hay and King Streets – take a peek inside during the day to see if archivist Ivan King has a display of theatrical memorabilia on show.

For nightlife, head to **Northbridge**, on the north side of the railway line, which stays busy and buzzy after dark, and offers plenty of options for casual dining, pubbing and clubbing. Also in Northbridge, just outside the train station, is the Perth Cultural Centre. Here you will find the Western Australian Art Gallery, Museum and State Library, as well as the avant-garde PICA (Perth Institute of Contemporary Art) and Arts House, containing the Blue Room Theatre and the Photography Gallery.

PRIDE

Don't forget Lesbian and Gay Pride month, which starts with **Fair Day** in Hyde Park on the Queen's Birthday long weekend at the end of September and runs for a month. The community-run festival showcases lesbian and gay art, culture, theatre, music, performance and educational forums. Local gay press provide listings of events or you can pick up a program from one of the gay/lesbian venues or *Arcane Bookshop* (p.183–184). The festival culminates in an annual **Great Debate**, **parade** and **party**. Subscriptions allow you to stay up to date with events year-round.

Lesbian and Gay Pride WA
PO Box 30, North Perth WA 6906
Phone 08/9227 1767 **Fax** 08/9227 6811
Email pride@pridewa.asn.au
Web www.pridewa.asn.au
Gender Mixed
Cost Membership $25 individual, $15 concession
Payment AmEx, Bankcard, MasterCard, Visa; cheque

Southwest of the CBD, the green swathe of **Kings Park** offers stunning views over the city and the river – as well as beautiful gardens and magnificent bushland criss-crossed by walking and bike tracks (bikes are available for rent at the park). You can get to Kings Park by walking up the 'hill of hell', via Mount Street or Malcolm Street (great for the legs!), or you can catch any bus going up the hill.

Fremantle, which is served by both bus and train, features the oldest public building in Western Australia, the Round House, perched in a commanding position at the end of High Street. Built by convicts in 1830 as a gaol, its earliest inhabitants probably drew little consolation from the sweeping views over the Indian Ocean. Walking south along Marine Terrace will take you past the Western Australian Maritime Museum, which charts the exploration of the state's lengthy coastline, to the Fishing Boat Harbour. Clustered around the harbour are seafood restaurants (and flocks of gulls primed to steal the odd chip) where you can satisfy your sea–air hunger. Alternatively, take a stroll up the cappuccino strip of South Terrace for a caffeine hit and an al fresco meal.

Perth highlights and hot-spots

- First gay/lesbian stop in Perth should be the **Court Hotel** (see p.182). This huge pub and beer garden is Queer Central – whether you're gay, lesbian or transgender. With a nice cold drink in one hand and a copy of the *West Side Observer* in the other, you'll quickly find out how laid back Perth is, and you may find yourself here all night.

- Perth has many fine **restaurants**: recommended are *Jackson's* in Highgate, just north of the city, and *Star Anise* in Shenton Park (see listings on p.181). Other hotspots include *Friends*, at the Hyatt in East Perth, for fine dining overlooking the river, *Frasers* for the view from the top of Kings Park and *Jones'* in trendy Subiaco.

- A drive to Fremantle, via the **ritzy riverside suburbs** of Dalkeith and Peppermint Grove, is an absolute must if you like perving at the mansions of media magnates or the extraordinarily ostentatious *Prix d'Amour,* home of Australia's most (in)famous dowager and **camp icon**, Rose Hancock. On your way back, stop off at one of the beaches for a refreshing dip in the Indian Ocean.

- Take a ferry trip to **Rottnest Island** to see quokkas (cute little marsupial things) and to walk barefoot on gorgeous beaches or dive in unbelievably clear, turquoise waters. No cars are allowed, so rent a bike and circumnavigate the island. Accommodation is available, but you'll need to book well ahead, especially during school holidays. The old gaol has been converted into a luxury hotel, and rumour has it that the restless souls of former prisoners still linger in some of the rooms – and the staff won't let on which ones . . .

- Take a boat trip on the spectacular **Swan River**. It's the widest river in any Australian city and now has an extremely phallic bell tower.

ACCOMMODATION

Abaca Palms

34 Whatley Crescent
Mount Lawley WA 6050
Phone 08/9271 2117
Email abapalm@multiline.com.au
Gender Men
This is a gay, male-only guesthouse in a comfortable Art Deco house. There's a spa, sun deck and large subtropical garden. Rooms are upstairs and shared bathroom facilities are downstairs. A hearty cooked breakfast is included in the tariff and airport transfers are available on request.
Cost From $55 per room
Payment Bankcard, MasterCard, Visa

Court Hotel

50 Beaufort St
Northbridge WA 6003
Phone 08/9328 5292
Fax 08/9227 1570
Clean, centrally located, basic accommodation: most rooms share bathrooms, but there are also some ensuite rooms.
Cost $25 single, $35–80 double
Payment AmEx, Bankcard, Diners, EFTPOS, MasterCard, Visa

Sullivans Hotel

166 Mount St
Perth WA 6000
Phone 08/9321 8022

Fax 08/9481 6762
Email perth@sullivans.com.au
Web www.sullivans.com.au
Gender Mixed
Sullivans is a family-owned and -operated boutique hotel in central Perth, with a free shuttle bus to the city centre. There's a small, intimate cocktail bar, a swimming pool and a garden, as well as free parking, in-house movies and bicycles for guests' use.
Cost $110–130 per room
Payment AmEx, Bankcard, Diners, EFTPOS, MasterCard, Visa

Swanbourne Guesthouse

5 Myera St
Swanbourne WA 6010
Phone 08/9383 1981
Fax 08/9385 4595
Email ralphh@wantree.com.au
Web www.wantree.com.au/~ralphh
Gender Mixed
Gay-owned and -operated. This private residence set in a verdant garden has large rooms and a rear patio for sunbathing. As well as four guest rooms with ensuites, there's a separate villa that sleeps four people. Close to a gay beach, and near bus and train stops. Smoking outside only.
Cost $95 per room
Payment Bankcard, MasterCard, Visa

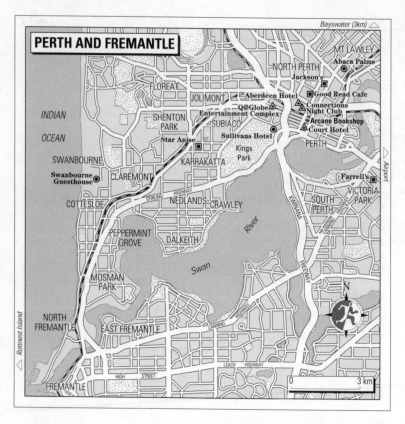

PERTH AND FREMANTLE

Bayswater (3km)

MT LAWLEY
Abaca Palms
NORTH PERTH
Jackson's
FLOREAT
JOLIMONT
Aberdeen Hotel
Good Read Cafe
Q@Globe
Connections
Night Club
Entertainment Complex
SHENTON
PARK
SUBIACO
Arcane Bookshop
Court Hotel
Star Anise
Sullivans Hotel
PERTH
Kings
Park
SWANBOURNE
KARRAKATTA
INDIAN
OCEAN
Swanbourne
Guesthouse
CLAREMONT
Farrell's
VICTORIA
PARK
COTTESLOE
NEDLANDS
CRAWLEY
SOUTH
PERTH
STIRLING
Highway
River
PEPPERMINT
GROVE
DALKEITH
Swan
MOSMAN
PARK
NORTH
FREMANTLE
EAST FREMANTLE
CANNING
HIGHWAY
FREMANTLE
HIGH
STREET
LEACH
HIGHWAY
N
Airport
KWINANA
FREEWAY
Rottnest Island
0
3 km

CAFÉS AND RESTAURANTS

Farrell's

Cnr McMaster St and Albany Highway
Victoria Park WA 6100
Phone 08/9472 7227
Fax 08/9472 5501

This establishment not only offers
good food but the owner is a true
music lover and the musical themes
change from day to day. The menu is
Mediterranean with a twist and the
surroundings are eclectic. *Farrell's*
offers indoor or al fresco dining.

Open Daily 7am–11pm
Cost Breakfast $10, lunch $18,
dinner $25
Payment AmEx, Bankcard, Diners,
EFTPOS, MasterCard, Visa

Good Read Cafe

Cnr Brisbane and William streets
Northbridge WA 6000
Phone 08/9227 0540
Fax 08/9227 0541

Enjoy fine coffee, browse through a

few books, indulge in one of their great cakes and sit for a while in the idyllic garden courtyard. Wide range of sandwiches, focaccias, bruschettas, curries and daily specials as well as a special backpackers' breakfast deal from $5. Good range of gay and lesbian titles available, in addition to a comprehensive fiction section.
Open Daily 8.30am–6pm
Cost Breakfast from $5, lunch from $8
Payment Bankcard, EFTPOS, MasterCard, Visa

Jackson's
483 Beaufort St
Perth WA 6000
Phone 08/9328 1177
Fax 08/9228 1144
Contemporary, minimalist decor and fine food. Duck and soufflés are among the specialties, accompanied by a selection of Australian wines.
Open Tues–Sat 6.30pm–late, Fri lunch from noon
Cost $40–60 per person
Payment AmEx, Bankcard, Diners, MasterCard, Visa

Star Anise
225 Onslow Rd
Shenton Park WA 6008
Phone 08/9381 9811
Serving modern Australian food and fully licensed, *Star Anise* is perfect for casual fine dining. Bookings are essential.
Open Tues–Sat 6.30pm–late; also Fri lunch (summer only) from noon
Cost $35–50 per person
Payment Bankcard, EFTPOS, MasterCard, Visa

That Food Company
11 Kingwilliam St
Bayswater WA 6000
Phone 08/9272 1422
Deli and BYO café offering a wide range of gourmet food and groceries, including specialty teas and mustards. All-day breakfasts are served, as well as snacks, bagels and full meals – the chicken and corn pie is hard to go past.
Open Mon–Thurs 8.30am–4.30pm, Fri–Sat 7.30am–10.30pm, Sun 7.30am–4pm
Cost Breakfast $10, lunch $10–15
Payment EFTPOS, MasterCard, Visa

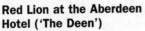

BARS AND CLUBS

Red Lion at the Aberdeen Hotel ('The Deen')
84 Aberdeen St
Northbridge WA 6003
Phone 08/9227 9361
Gender Mixed
Great Sunday afternoon session with guest DJs and drag shows.
Open Sun 6pm–1am

Admission Free
Payment Cash only

Connections Night Club (Connie's or CNC)
81 James St
Northbridge WA 6003
Phone 08/9328 1870
Fax 08/9328 5357

Gender Mixed

Perth's premiere gay nightclub is now in its 27th year. Open six nights a week, with some truly spectacular drag shows on weekends, or gogo boys and strippers on Tuesdays. Friday and Saturday are the really big nights for gays, lesbians and friends, with spot shows and lots of dancing.

Open Tues–Wed 10pm–6am (men only on Tues), Fri–Sat 9pm–6am, Sun 9pm–1am

Admission $5–10 cover charge may apply after 10pm

Payment Cash only

Court Hotel

50 Beaufort St
Northbridge WA 6003
Phone 08/9328 5292
Fax 08/9227 1570
Gender Mixed

Friendly local pub with pool tables, counter meals, a few drag and other shows scattered through the evenings. There's a large beer garden for al fresco imbibing and a bar menu is

available. The *Court Hotel* is the central meeting place for both gays and lesbians in Perth – and visitors to Perth will quickly discover how friendly locals are in this hotel.

Open Mon–Thurs 11am–midnight, Fri & Sat 11am–1am, Sun 3pm–10pm

Admission Free

Payment AmEx, Bankcard, Diners, EFTPOS, MasterCard, Visa

Club Fiesta @ Globe Entertainment Complex

393 Murray St
West End WA 6000
Phone 08/9481 2521
Fax 08/9481 5520
Email globe@omen.net.au
Gender Mixed

Club Fiesta Latino night is a fun event for all sexualities. Come early for the beginners' dance class (7pm–9pm).

Open Fri 9pm–late (licensed until 6am)

Admission $8

Payment Bankcard, EFTPOS, MasterCard, Visa

SEX CLUBS AND SAUNAS

Beaufort 565

565 Beaufort St
Mount Lawley WA 6050
Phone 08/9328 7703
Gender Men

Perth's original gay sauna, with special bear and leather nights each month. They offer dry and wet sauna, spa, cruise maze, cubicles, private rooms and sling rooms, video lounge and Internet access. Refreshments available from snack

bar. Condoms and lube provided.

Open Mon–Thurs noon–1am, Fri–Sat noon–3am, Sun noon–midnight

Admission $10–17

Payment AmEx, Bankcard, EFTPOS, MasterCard, Visa

Club X

114 Barrack St
Perth WA 6000
Phone 08/9325 3815

also at:
50A High St
Fremantle WA 2795
Phone 08/9336 2993

Gender Men
Adult bookshop with 'Ram Lounge'
offering adult movies and back-room
activities.
Open Daily 9am–late
Payment AmEx, Bankard, EFTPOS,
MasterCard, Visa

Perth Steam Works
369 William St (entrance in Forbes Rd)
Northbridge WA 6865
Phone 08/9328 2930

Fax 08/9328 2271
Gender Men
Located within walking distance of
the nightclubs, *Perth Steam Works*
offers wet and dry saunas, spa, fantasy
rooms, sling rooms, cruising maze and
TV lounge. They also have a fully
licensed bar. Very clean safe-sex venue
providing condoms and lube in all
cubicles. On Monday nights, the
Western Australian AIDS Council offers
counselling and testing.
Open Mon–Thurs noon–1am,
Fri–Sat noon–3am
Admission $10 Mon, $16 Tues–Sat
Payment Bankard, MasterCard, Visa

ARTS

ASP House
PO Box 284
Leederville WA 6903
Phone 08/9444 2989
Email asphouse@hotmail.com
Gender Women
ASP House is a lesbian arts space
project in Western Australia, which
began as a talking circle at the Perth
lesbian confest in 1993. Every year
the group stages an art exhibition, as
well as publishing poetry and staging
musical performances.

Gay and Lesbian Singers (GALS)
North Perth Town Hall – Lesser Hall,
24 View St
North Perth WA 6006
Phone Jackie 08/9227 9375 or Gerri
08/9227 0609
Web www.geocities.com/
Broadway/Wing/3783/index.html
Gender Mixed
Gay and lesbian singing group which
meets weekly on Thursdays at
7.30pm in North Perth Town Hall.
No auditions required.

BOOKSHOPS

Arcane Bookshop
212 William St
Northbridge WA 6000
Phone 08/9328 5073
Fax 08/9228 0410

Email arcbooks@highway1.com.au
Arcane stocks the best range of gay and
lesbian titles in Perth, with lots of
literary fiction, theatre, philosophy
and gender studies. They also have all

the local and national gay/lesbian
magazines, as well as handling ticket
sales for Pride and gay/lesbian events.
Open Mon–Wed 10am–6pm,
Thurs–Sat 10am–9pm,
Sun noon–5pm
Payment AmEx, Bankcard, Diners,
EFTPOS, MasterCard, Visa

NEWSPAPERS AND MAGAZINES

West Side Observer
PO Box 131
North Perth WA 6006
Phone 08/9228 3277
Fax 08/9228 1055
Email editorial@wso.com.au
Web www.wso.com.au
Gender Mixed
Perth's own local gay and lesbian
publication is published fortnightly,
providing up-to-date listings of all the
latest events and venues as well as lots
of local and national gay and lesbian
news, events and gossip. Available
from all gay/lesbian venues.
Cost $35 annual subscription

WOW (Women Out West)
PO Box 1121
West Leederville WA 6901
Phone Ruth White 08/9371 1049
Fax 08/9371 1049
Email wow@vianet.net.au
Web www.womenoutwest.com.au
Gender Women
For all the news, blues and hues of
lesbian life in Western Australia,
WOW gives you the goods.
Includes a calendar of events and
comprehensive list of contacts
and organizations.
Cost $3.50 per issue, $42 annual
subscription

BEACHES AND POOLS

City Beach
Floreat WA 6014
Gender Mixed
A popular spot, with lots of dunes for
sunbathers. City Beach is just off the
West Coast Highway, between
Cottesloe and Scarborough.

Floreat Beach
Floreat WA 6014
Gender Mixed
South of City Beach, Floreat Beach is
popular with gay men, but is not nude.
To get here, turn off the West Coast
Highway onto Challenger Parade;
there's plenty of beachside parking.

Swanbourne Beach
Swanbourne WA 6010
Gender Mixed
The northern end of this beach is
designated a free (nude) beach and
the dunes are popular sunbaking
haunts for gay men but beware, the
nearby Campbell Barracks and rifle
range often do army training in these
dunes and some of the soldiers may
not be at all sympathetic to indecent
behaviour. To get to Swanbourne
Beach, turn left onto North Street
from the West Coast Highway,
then park at the northern end of
Marine Parade.

MEDICAL

AIDSline
West Perth WA 6005
Phone 08/9429 9944
Web www.waaids.asn.au
Gender Mixed
Telephone information and referral
service on HIV, AIDS, hepatitis C and
sexually transmitted infections.
Open Mon–Fri 9am–5pm

Hepatitis C Council of WA
85 Stirling St
Perth WA 6000
Phone 08/9328 8216, 08/9328 8538
or freecall 1800/800 070
Email hepccwa@highway1.com.au
Gender Mixed
For information on hepatitis C, as
well as counselling and support.
Open Mon–Thurs 9am–8pm,
Fri 9am–5pm

Sexual Assault Referral Centre
PO Box 842
Subiaco WA 6008
Phone 08/9340 1828 or freecall
1800/199 888
Gender Mixed
Duty counsellors are available as first
point of contact. A team of female and
male doctors is available to offer medical
attention and take forensic evidence.

Women's Health Care House
100 Aberdeen St
Northbridge WA 6003
Phone 08/9227 8122
Fax 08/9227 6615
Email whch@iinet.net.au
Web www.womenshealthwa.
iinet.net.au

Gender Women
This centre offers a range of medical
services provided according to
need and charged on an ability-
to-pay basis: sympathetic doctors,
nurses, counsellors, mental health
outreach, education and information
service, ethnic outreach program
and domestic violence support,
older women's network. Also
serves as a drop-in women's space
with heaps of information, and
tea and coffee available. Bulk
billing is available to Medicare
card holders.
Open Mon 8.30am–7pm, Tues–Thurs
8.30am–4.30pm, Wed 8.30am–5pm,
Fri 8.30am–1.30am
Cost Donation may be requested

Women's Healthworks
Suite 6, 70 Davidson Terrace
Joondalup WA 6027
Phone 08/9300 1566
Fax 08/9300 1699
Email healthwk@iinet.net.au
Gender Women
General practitioner and nurse
available. Other services include
counselling, courses, workshops,
forums, information, referrals,
massage, naturopathy and reflexology.
Library and newsletter available for
members ($10 per year). Bulk billing
is available to Medicare card holders,
and every effort is made to keep all
fees reasonable; counselling fees are
negotiable.
Open Mon 9am–5pm,
Tues 9am–6.30pm, Wed 9am–6pm,
Thurs 9am–5pm, Fri 9am–4.30pm

10% Plus Business Association of Western Australia

PO Box 242
Northbridge WA 6865
Email tenplus@equitech.net
Gender Mixed
This gay and lesbian business association welcomes overseas visitors and holds dinner meetings on the last Tuesday of each month with guest speakers.
Cost Dinner & drinks $35, membership from $75
Payment AmEx, Bankcard, Diners, MasterCard, Visa; cheque

Breakaway

City West Lotteries House, 2 Delhi St
West Perth WA 6005
Phone 08/9420 7201
Gender Men
Young (15–25) gay male support group which meets every second weekend.

Chameleon Society of WA

PO Box 367
Victoria Park WA 6100
Phone 0412 771 753
Email chameleonswa@xoomail.com
Web members.xoom.com/chameleonswa
Gender Mixed
Social support group for cross-dressers of all types (and their partners). Meetings are held twice monthly, often with guest speakers. They also hold outings and occasional parties.
Cost Membership $40

Club West

PO Box 283
North Perth WA 6906
Phone 08/9227 0757
Fax 08/9328 1470
Gender Mixed
Perth's biggest party organizers *Club West* are 10 years strong and are prominent fundraisers for HIV. They regularly organize drag shows and parties on a grand scale. They also organize theatre outings and other fun get-togethers.

Dykes on Bikes

Perth, WA
Phone Louise 08/9328 9271, Val 08/9420 3076, Gill 08/9319 1727
Gender Women
Organizers of bike rides and occasional social events. Also a great contact for riders visiting Western Australia and wanting details on some great country or metro rides to take.

Freedom Centre

Address – enquire at *WAAC* (p.188)
Phone Midge Turnbull 08/9228 0354
Fax 08/9429 9901
Email freedom@q-net.net.au
Web www.q-net.net.au/~freedom
Gender Mixed
A drop-in centre for young people who are gay, lesbian, bisexual, transgender or questioning their sexuality. Courses and retreats are available, as is information, support and referral.
Open Wed & Fri 3pm–10pm, Sat noon–9pm

Gay and Lesbian Equality (GALE)

PO Box 420
Northbridge WA 6865
Phone 08/9388 6626
Email galewa@galewa.queer.org.au
Web www.galewa.queer.org.au
Gender Mixed

GALE is working to give gays and lesbians legal protection from discrimination, and to overturn discriminatory age of consent laws. In WA, it is still legal to refuse jobs, accommodation and services to people because of sexuality, and gay men under 21 and their partners are theoretically criminals. The group's activities include parliamentary lobbying, media liaison, community education and direct action and it has a commitment to the politics of visibility and community empowerment.

Gay and Lesbian Immigration Task Force

PO Box 23
Applecross WA 6953
Phone 08/9364 1797
Web www.glitf.org.au
Gender Mixed
Support group for mixed-nationality couples seeking to remain together in Australia.
Cost Membership $30

Gay and Lesbian Community Services (GLCS)

City West Lotteries House, 2 Delhi St
West Perth WA 6005
Phone 08/9420 7201, counselling 08/9486 9855
Fax 08/9486 9855

Gender Mixed
Counselling and information service.
Open Mon & Thurs 1pm–4pm & 7.30pm–10.30pm, Tues–Wed & Fri–Sun 7.30pm–10.30pm

Groovy Girls

c/- GLCS, City West Lotteries House
2 Delhi St
West Perth WA 6005
Phone 08/9420 7201
Gender Women
Social group for young lesbians, bisexual or questioning women aged between 15 and 30. Meets last Tuesday of the month at 7pm.

Muff Divers

Perth, WA
Phone Sue 08/9349 1693
Gender Women
Lesbian social snorkelling group which meets every Sunday from October to May at Mettams Pool off North Beach. Occasional more distant dives. Call Sue for meeting times.

Perth Men's Line

Perth WA 6000
Phone 08/9322 8401 or freecall 1800/671 130
Gender Men
Support, information and referral service.

Perth Metropolitan Community Church

PO Box 513
Mirrabooka WA 6941
Phone 08/9443 6550
Email coma@networx.net.au
Gender Mixed

A church welcoming all members of the gay/lesbian/bisexual/transgender community. Services at 7.30pm every Sunday at Banks Reserve Hall, East Perth.

Perth Outdoors Group

PO Box 47
Northbridge WA 6865
Phone Ian 08/9472 5947
Gender Mixed
Indoor and outdoor activities for gays and lesbians of all ages and creeds. Picnics, barbecues, camping, dinners and lots of fun.
Cost Membership $20

Q Pages Directory

Web www.qpages.com.au
Online directory of queer-friendly businesses in Perth.

PFLAG Perth (Parents, Families and Friends of Lesbians and Gays)

PO Box 354
Northbridge WA 6865
Phone 08/9228 1005
Email pflagperth@telstra.easymail. com.au
Gender Mixed
Support group for families and friends of gays and lesbians.

Rainbow Connections

c/- Freedom Centre PO Box 1510
West Perth WA 6005
Phone 08/9429 9900
Email freedom@q-net.net.au
Gender Mixed
Penpal connection service for young (under 30), isolated gay men, lesbians, bisexuals and those questioning their sexuality.

Team Perth

PO Box 3234, Stirling St
Perth WA 6000
Phone Ray 0412 599 577
Gender Mixed
Information on gay and lesbian sporting activities.

WA Bisexual Network

Perth WA 6000
Phone Ian 08/9472 5947
Gender Men
Offers counselling, support and information to bisexual men. Call between 9am and 9pm.

West Australian Police Service Gay and Lesbian Liason Unit

8 Burton St
Cannington WA 6107
Phone Sgt Michelle Fyfe 08/9356 0555 or 0407 477 834
Email michelle.fyfe@police.wa.gov.au
Gender Mixed
Ensures an equitable service is provided to the gay/lesbian community and enables a direct line of contact with the community.

Western Australia AIDS Council (WAAC)

664 Murray St
West Perth WA 6005
Phone 08/9429 9900
Fax 08/9429 9901
Email waac@waaids.asn.au
Web www.waaids.asn.au
Gender Mixed
Support for people living with HIV/ AIDS, their partners and carers: safe-sex supplies, peer education programs, referral services and welfare assistance. Also carries gay/lesbian newspapers.
Open Mon–Fri 9am–5pm

TRAVEL SERVICES

Directions
7 Rokeby Rd
Subiaco WA 6008
Phone 08/9381 7855
Fax 08/9388 2916
Email directions@directionstravel.com.au
Travel agency offering corporate, individual and group travel.
Open Mon–Fri 9am–5.30pm, Sat 9am–noon
Payment AmEx, Bankcard, Diners, MasterCard, Visa

Rainbow Worldwide Tours and Travel
Suite 11, 336 Churchill Ave
Subiaco WA 6008
Phone 08/9382 4023
Fax 08/9388 2864
Email rbowtour@opera.iinet.net.au
Web www.iinet.net.au/~rbowtour
Specifically gay and lesbian travel arrangements, with Western Australia a speciality. Tailor-made itineraries for all gay and lesbian travellers.
Open Mon–Fri 9am–5pm
Payment AmEx, Bankcard, Diners, EFTPOS, MasterCard, Visa; cheque

The Southwest

The southwestern corner of Western Australia thrives on a gentle climate, stunning scenery, towering **forests**, surf **beaches** and award-winning **wineries**. And all within 4–5 hours' drive from Perth. What more could you want?

ACCOMMODATION

Caves House Hotel
Caves Rd
Yallingup WA 6282
Phone 08/9755 2131 or freecall 1800/632 131
Fax 08/9755 2041
Email reservations@caveshouse.com.au
Web www.caveshouse.com.au
Gender Mixed
Close to the Margaret River wine region, *Caves House* has kept its deco character of the 1930s, with a formal dining/function room, bistro, cosy bar and a beer garden. Tranquil gardens provide access to beautiful Yallingup beach, or take a leisurely stroll to the Ngilgi Caves. Croquet and tennis also available. Bookings are essential for accommodation.
Cost $88–188 per room
Payment AmEx, Bankcard, Diners, EFTPOS, MasterCard, Visa; cheque

Peacehaven Mountain Escape
Lot 4 Millinup Rd
Porongurup WA 6324
Phone 08/9853 2141 or freecall 1800/445 577

Fax 08/9853 2141
Email peace@omninet.net.au
Gender Mixed
This B&B is set in wooded countryside at the foot of the Porongurup Ranges, 50km north of Albany. All rooms have ensuites, a full breakfast is included and evening meals (BYO wine) are available by prior arrangement. A barbecue is available for guests' use. Smoking outside only. Wheelchair access.
Cost From $88 per room
Payment Bankcard, MasterCard, Visa; cheque

BEACHES AND POOLS

Bunbury Nudist Beach
Bunbury WA 6230
Gender Mixed
Bunbury is situated about 200km south of Perth and is a popular beach with gay men, as well as with naturists generally.

The Avon Valley

Heading east of Perth, the Avon River wends its way through agricultural country to **York**, a pioneering settlement with many well-preserved buildings, riverside walks and picnic areas.

Asparagus Patch B&B
1555 Doconing Rd
Chidlow WA 6556
Phone 08/9572 6006
Fax 08/9572 6007
Email jlingard@opra.iinet.net.au
Gender Mixed
Quiet, cosy retreat less than an hour east of Perth. Pool, forest reserve and bushwalks on the doorstep – and yes, they do grow their own asparagus. Smoking is permitted outside only.
Cost $100 single, $132 double (discounted rates for longer stays)
Payment Bankcard, EFTPOS, MasterCard, Visa

Greenhills Inn
Greenhills Rd
Greenhills WA 6302
Phone John and Ashley 08/9641 4095
Fax 08/9641 4095
Gender Mixed
This splendid country homestead 120km from Perth offers old-world charm with all the modern luxuries, including an outdoor spa. Choose from a range of different theme rooms. There is also a bar and restaurant. Handy to the town of York. Gay-owned and -operated.
Cost From $105 per room
Payment Bankcard, EFTPOS, MasterCard, Visa

Out of Town Inn
58 Newcastle St
York WA 6302
Phone Chris or Steve 08/9641 2214
Fax 08/9641 2214
Gender Mixed
A large historic colonial style 1870s home offering B&B accommodation, with big rooms, open fire and shared bathrooms.

Full breakfast is included, other meals by arrangement. A courtesy car is available, and there are complimentary chocolates, port, sherry and afternoon teas. Guests are free to use the kitchen. Gay-owned and -operated.
Cost From $100 per room (discounts for longer stays)
Payment Cheque

South Australia

South Australia has been a pioneer of **civil liberties** for over a century. In the 1890s the South Australian parliament was the first in Australia to grant women the vote and in the 1970s South Australia was the first to enact homosexual law reform.

South Australia is a **gateway to the Outback**. It is the driest state in the country and, while the southern half of the state is well-populated and thoroughly tamed, the northern half is not. Australia's largest salt lake, **Lake Eyre,** is 600km north of Adelaide and it only ever fills with water every few years, so you may be happy just to view it from the plane. (After all, gays and lesbians do tend to have a morbid fear of pillars of salt.)

The capital city, **Adelaide**, is surrounded to the north, east and south by the historical and picturesque **wine-making regions** of the Clare and Barossa valleys, the Adelaide Hills, McLaren Vale and Coonawarra – each ideally suited for full- or half-day jaunts. Closest to the city is the Southern Vales wine region, which includes McLaren Vale, a town popular with Adelaide's weekend wine-tasters. In South Australia, it's never too long between drinks!

Adelaide

As luck would have it, the city of Adelaide is named after a queen. In 1836 King William IV named the city after his wife Queen Adelaide, making this the only Australian capital to be named after a woman.

The city, which has a population of 1.1 million, has been shaped by the state's forward-looking leadership. During the 1970s, under the premiership of Australia's most famous queer politician, Don Dunstan, Adelaide underwent a cultural boom, becoming a national focus for the arts – and was renowned for its **relaxed attitudes** to sexuality, nudity and hedonism in general. Don Dunstan's social vision and cultural influence remain close to the heart of many Adelaideans, particularly those in the gay and lesbian community.

The city of Adelaide boasts the best **sandstone architecture** in the country. There is a strong colonial influence in the city's plan, which was drawn up by Colonel William Light, who also planned Christchurch in New Zealand. The Torrens River winds its way through the immaculate **parks and gardens** that stretch north from the city. This green swathe is perfect for long walks – and, when it's not too hot, joggers pound the riverside paths. The less active can while away a blissful few hours just messing about on the river. Wide streets give an impression of space and ease, which is reinforced by sturdy old hotels with huge balconies – most welcome in the midst of a hot, dry South Australian summer when you'll be grateful for a Cooper's ale, the local brew, or a chilled wine from the nearby wine districts. Adelaide is a relaxed, civilized and sociable city, where drinking and eating are a real and very affordable pleasure.

Adelaide highlights and hot-spots

- The mainstay of Adelaide's gay and lesbian community and its most popular meeting place is the handsome **Edinburgh Castle Hotel** (see p.202).
- The oldest gay club of all is the **Mars Bar**, where disco and drag have reigned supreme for decades (see p.203).
- Fans of the great Australian TV soap of the 1970s, 'No. 96', will want to pay homage to Chantal Contouri (aka the panty-hose murderer), who now

runs a fine Greek restaurant, **The Original Barbecue Inn** (see p.201).

- **Eat streets** worth checking out are Gouger Street and Moonta Street, where Chinatown offers everything from a cheap and cheerful bowl of noodles to a Peking duck banquet. The eastern end of Rundle Street also has plenty of upmarket pubs, cafés and restaurants to choose from.

- The **Indigenous Cultures Gallery** at the South Australian Museum on North Terrace has the largest permanent collection of Aboriginal art and artefacts anywhere in the world.

The famous **Adelaide Festival** of Arts is one of the largest and oldest arts festivals in Australia. Held every two years in March during even-numbered years, the main festival and the concurrent Fringe Festival attract artists, performers, musicians, dancers and authors from all around the world. The gay and lesbian festival, **FEAST** is held annually in October–November.

The main **shopping** area is Rundle Mall, where 'Bert's Balls' make a popular meeting place. Sculpted by Bert Flugelman, these two giant metallic balls provide a brief diversion while you're waiting for that hot date. On the east side of the mall, Rundle Street is the city's prime café and restaurant strip. For **nightlife**, wander down Hindley Street, the western extension of Rundle Mall, where you'll find plenty of flashing lights and nocturnal happenings.

Adelaide has witnessed the odd nasty homophobic **crime** – the gardens near the Torrens River to the north of the city and the parklands at the south are areas to avoid at night.

Adelaide **public transport** is predominantly buses, but there are suburban trains that will take you as far as the Adelaide Hills and a tram runs to the beachside suburb of Glenelg from Victoria Square every 15 to 20 minutes. The transport **infoline** is on 08/8210 1000, or click on www.adelaidemetro.com.au.

To the west of the city lies the Gulf St Vincent, fringed by some of the finest **beaches** in South Australia – among them the (nude) summer mecca of **Maslin Beach**, which is very popular with the boys. Much closer in, to the north-west of the city, the beachside suburb of **Semaphore** has become a hot-spot for dykes and boasts a number of sister-owned cafés. The **Fleurieu Peninsula** to Adelaide's south also offers plenty of beach options.

FEAST: Adelaide Lesbian and Gay Cultural Festival

Adelaide Lesbian and Gay Cultural Festival takes place in late **October** and early **November** and encapsulates the best of South Australia's gay, lesbian, indigenous, queer and transgender creativity, as well as featuring guests from all over the country. The first FEAST was in 1997, so this is a young festival that has already been hailed as Australia's third major lesbian and gay festival. The festival includes visual arts, performing arts, literature, forums, food, drink, pool parties, party parties, picnics, cabaret, garden tours, a women's sauna night, community and sporting events, radio specials, drag, a film event and even shopping. A comprehensive **guide to events** is available from gay/lesbian-friendly businesses and AIDS Councils around the country.

FEAST

Rosey Boehm

Mij Tanith

Tickets are available through the BASS agency (phone 13 1246 or book online at www.bass.sa.com.au), or at these outlets: the Adelaide Festival Centre, King William Rd; Centre Pharmacy, 19 Central Market Arcade; Myers Department Store, 5th floor, Rundle Mall. It is possible to get tickets at the door for many

For specific FEAST information, call 08/8231 2155 between 9.30am and 5.30pm, fax 08/8231 8793, or email feast@bigpond.com. Visit the Web site at www.feast.org.au and find out how to become a volunteer or a Sugar Daddy or Mummy (by taking out a FEAST membership).

Rosey Boehm

Hotel Adelaide International

62 Brougham Place (cnr O'Connell St)
North Adelaide SA 5006
Phone 08/8267 3444
Fax 08/8239 0189
Email info@hoteladelaide.com.au
Web www.hoteladelaide.com.au
Gender Mixed
This tourist-class hotel is situated a
15-minute walk from the city.
Boasting spectacular views of the city
and hills, *Hotel Adelaide* offers
friendly service and fabulous
breakfasts served in the rooftop
restaurant, as well as a totally 70s
cocktail bar downstairs. The hotel is
close to some of North Adelaide's
best restaurants.
Cost From $105 per room
Payment AmEx, Bankcard, Diners,
EFTPOS, MasterCard, Visa

East End Astoria Serviced Apartments

33 Vardon Ave
Adelaide SA 5000
Phone 08/8224 2400
Fax 08/8224 0820
Email stay@eastendastoria.com.au
Web www.eastendastoria.com.au
Gender Mixed
Central, brand-new spacious
accommodation situated in the thriving
cosmopolitan East End. Apartments are
serviced daily, and there is undercover
car parking available.
Cost $164–179 per apartment
Payment AmEx, Bankcard, Diners,
EFTPOS, MasterCard, Visa

Greenways Apartments

45 King William Rd
North Adelaide SA 5006
Phone 08/8267 5903
Fax 08/8267 1790
Email bpsgways@camtech.net.au
Gender Mixed
Gay-owned and -operated,
Greenways is near restaurants,
theatres, parklands, department stores
and tourist attractions. It provides
clean, comfortable and private
accommodation in fully furnished
one-, two- and three-bedroom
apartments.
Cost From $100 per apartment
Payment AmEx, Bankcard, Diners,
EFTPOS, MasterCard, Visa

Princes Arcade Motel

262 Hindley St
Adelaide SA 5000
Phone 08/8231 9524
Fax 08/8231 2671
Gender Mixed
This budget accommodation is
centrally located, and there are
plenty of cafés on the doorstep. (*Kiwi
Lodge*, situated next door, is part of
the same business and offers dorm
accommodation.)
Cost $15 dorm beds, $72 per room
Payment AmEx, Bankcard, Diners,
EFTPOS, MasterCard, Visa

Rochdale B&B

349 Glen Osmond Rd
Glen Osmond SA 5064
Phone 08/8379 7498

Fax 08/8379 2483
Email rochdale@camtech.net.au
Web www.adelaide.net.au/~rochdale
Gender Mixed
The only exclusively gay and lesbian B&B in Adelaide, offering a wonderfully relaxed Art Deco environment close to the city. There is an indoor pool, open fires, gourmet breakfast, ensuites in all rooms, a reading room, formal lounge and dining room.
Cost $115 single, $165 double
Payment AmEx, Bankcard, Diners, MasterCard, Visa

Ruahine Homestay Bed and Breakfast

38 Chelmsford Ave
Millswood SA 5034
Phone 08/8371 0707
Fax 08/8371 3113
Email gavan@senet.com.au
Web www.senet.com.au/~gavan
Gender Mixed
A gay-owned and -operated luxury oasis in suburban Adelaide, *Ruahine* is a renovated 1920s bungalow 10 minutes from the city and airport. It offers cooked breakfasts, a spa, garden, pool and tennis court.
Cost $90 single, $120 double
Payment AmEx, Bankcard, Diners, MasterCard, Visa

CAFÉS AND RESTAURANTS

CAOS

188 Hindley St West End
Adelaide SA 5000
Phone 08/8231 8300
Fax 08/8231 8313
Popular meeting place with the gay and lesbian 'in crowd' (plus a few loudmouthed drag queens thrown in for good measure). Queer-owned and -operated, *CAOS* offers special deals during the FEAST festival and even hosts some events.This up-to-date, fully licensed venue is lively, noisy and has big-screen TVs, so you won't miss any of the action. It serves everything from a great cup of coffee to inspiring three-course dinners, and breakfast is available all day. On the first Friday of the month, the lesbian social group 'Out for Tea' meets at *CAOS* from 7pm

onwards to chat, catch up on the gossip and find out what's happening (phone Dee 08/8346 8577 or email on dneagle@picknowl.com.au for details).
Open Mon–Sat 8am–late (kitchen closes 9pm)
Cost Breakfast $6–9, lunch & dinner $10–20
Payment AmEx, Bankcard, Diners, EFTPOS, MasterCard, Visa

Charlick's Restaurant and Wine Bar

27–29 Ebenezer Place
Adelaide SA 5000
Phone 08/8223 7566
Fax 08/8223 7065
Email charlicks@adelaide.on.net
Web www.maggiebeer.mtx.net
Fresh produce is the main thrust of Maggie Beer's famous restaurant,

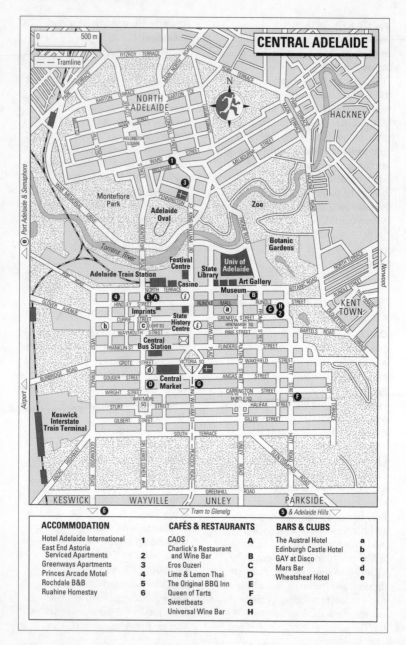

CENTRAL ADELAIDE

0 — 500 m

- - - Tramline

ACCOMMODATION

Hotel Adelaide International	1
East End Astoria Serviced Apartments	2
Greenways Apartments	3
Princes Arcade Motel	4
Rochdale B&B	5
Ruahine Homestay	6

CAFÉS & RESTAURANTS

CAOS	A
Charlick's Restaurant and Wine Bar	B
Eros Ouzeri	C
Lime & Lemon Thai	D
The Original BBQ Inn	E
Queen of Tarts	F
Sweetbeats	G
Universal Wine Bar	H

BARS & CLUBS

The Austral Hotel	a
Edinburgh Castle Hotel	b
GAY at Disco	c
Mars Bar	d
Wheatsheaf Hotel	e

which also includes a wine bar and function room. Maggie Beer signature dishes are pâté with wood-fired bread and cornichons and Pheasant Farm gum-smoked kangaroo pasta with sundried tomatoes, flaked almonds and Reggiano. There is an awesome wine list, many available by the glass. Desserts include shared platters or homemade ice-creams, pavlova and baked vanilla custard with a shot of espresso.

Open Tues–Fri & Sun noon–3pm, Tues–Sun 6pm–10pm (bar open daily from noon)
Cost Lunch from $20, dinner from $25
Payment AmEx, Bankcard, Diners, MasterCard, Visa

Eros Ouzeri

275–277 Rundle St
Adelaide SA 5000
Phone 08/8223 4022
Fax 08/8359 2474
Email erosouzeri@bigpond.com.au
This fully licensed establishment serves authentic Greek cuisine; reservations are required, but bookings for more than 12 people are not accepted on weekends.

Open Mon–Fri noon–3pm, Sat–Sun noon–4pm; daily 5.30pm–11pm
Cost $20–30 per person
Payment AmEx, Bankcard, Diners, MasterCard, Visa

Lime & Lemon Thai

89 Gouger St
Adelaide SA 5000
Phone 08/8231 8876
Fax 08/8231 9985
Open for lunch (Mon–Fri) and dinner daily, this neat little noodle

bar and fully licensed restaurant offers Thai with a distinctly Australian influence. Great stir-fries, curries and noodle dishes. A perfect quick cheap eat right in the heart of things.

Open Mon–Fri noon–11pm, Sat–Sun 6pm–11pm
Cost Lunch from $6, dinner from $15
Payment AmEx, Bankcard, Diners, MasterCard, Visa

The Original Barbecue Inn

196 Hindley St
Adelaide SA 5000
Phone 08/8231 3033
Fax 08/8212 8267
Owned by actress Chantal Contouri, this popular traditional barbecue establishment has been going strong for over 40 years. It offers great Greek food and is fully licensed.

Open Daily 11.30am–late
Cost From $10 per person
Payment AmEx, Bankcard, Diners, MasterCard, Visa

Queen of Tarts

178 Hutt St
North Adelaide SA 5006
Phone 08/8223 1529
Fax 08/8232 5634
Gay-owned and -operated and serving food fit for a queen, these finger-food and gourmet-lunch specialists offer tarts, cheesecakes, quiches and cakes, as well as healthy wholesome food to eat in or take away.

Open Mon–Fri 9am–5pm
Cost $5–10 per person
Payment AmEx, Bankcard, Diners, EFTPOS, MasterCard, Visa

Sweetbeats

Crown and Sceptre Hotel
308–312 King William St,
Adelaide SA 5000
Phone 08/8212 4159
Fax 08/8231 9169
An American-influenced menu offers
bagels, wraps, vegan fare, Cajun
dishes, Southern-fried chicken and
a great selection of salsas.
Open Mon 8am–5pm,
Tues–Sat 8am–11pm (or later)
Cost Breakfast $9, lunch $15,
dinner $25
Payment AmEx, Bankcard, Diners,
EFTPOS, MasterCard, Visa

Universal Wine Bar

285 Rundell St
Adelaide SA 5000

Phone 08/8232 5000
Fax 08/8232 5757
Email universal@senet.com.au
This very popular restaurant and
bar offers a wide range of meals
(from beef rib eye with confit of
beetroot and horseradish sauce to
chargrilled quail with pickled figs
and celery salad) – or you might
prefer a bar-plate that includes a
selection of hot and cold morsels,
octopus, bread for dipping,
marinated mozzarella and tomato,
caramelized onion and potato
frittata, and rocket and prosciutto
salad.
Open Mon–Sat noon–midnight
Cost Lunch from $20, dinner from $30
Payment AmEx, Bankcard, Diners,
MasterCard, Visa

BARS AND CLUBS

The Austral Hotel

205 Rundle St
Adelaide SA 5000
Phone 08/8223 4660
Gender Mixed
The *Austral* is not a gay or lesbian
pub, but, as one of Adelaide's oldest
and artiest pubs, it does attract a very
mixed crowd. Music, live bands and
meals are all on offer here.
Open Daily noon–late
Admission Free
Payment Cash only

Edinburgh Castle Hotel

233 Currie St
Adelaide SA 5000
Phone 08/8410 1211
Fax 08/8231 2477
Gender Mixed

This charming old Victorian pub is
the central venue for the local gay
and lesbian community. The 'Ed' or
'Eddie' has several rooms to explore,
where something is always
happening. There are pool tables, a
beer garden and a friendly, relaxed
crowd. Lunch and dinner is available
at counter-meal prices every day
but Sunday. There's dance floor
with DJs on Friday and Saturday,
and Sunday is drag night (showtime
is at 10pm).
Open Sun 2pm–2am, Mon–Tues
11am–2am, Wed–Sat 11am–3am
(may close earlier some nights, but
always open until midnight)
Admission Free
Payment Bankcard, Diners, EFTPOS,
MasterCard, Visa

GAY at Disco

69 Light Square
Adelaide SA 5000
Phone 08/8212 6969
Gender Mixed
Very popular with the party-hard
crowd and lovers of drag shows, this
club serves half-price West End
Draught and champagne before
midnight. Lots of shows and special
guest DJs.
Open Wed 9pm–5am (mixed retro),
Fri 9pm–5am (mixed night),
Sat 10pm–4am (gay night),
Sun 4am–noon (rise recovery)
Admission $5
Payment AmEx, Bankcard, EFTPOS,
MasterCard, Visa

Mars Bar

120 Gouger St
Adelaide SA 5000
Phone 08/8231 9639
Fax 08/8212 8881
Gender Mixed
One of the longest-standing gay and
lesbian venues in Adelaide (20 years
plus) makes everyone welcome and is
the place to go for some serious

dancing. Fridays and Saturdays
feature dance shows, while the Drag
Ball (usually held in June) is an
institution that has Adelaide's sewing
machines running hot for months.
Open Wed–Sun 10.30pm–5am (may
close earlier some nights)
Admission Wed gold coin, Thurs–Sun
$5 (more on special nights)
Payment Bankcard, EFTPOS,
MasterCard, Visa

Wheatsheaf Hotel

39 George St
Thebarton SA 5031
Phone 08/8443 4546
Gender Mixed
Two kilometres west of the city,
this wacky, friendly local pub with
beer garden attracts the full '360
degrees of love and peace',
according to the owner. Popular
with both gays and lesbians, the
Wheatsheaf is home to the *Cougar
Leather Club* (see p.209).
Open Mon–Sat 10am–midnight,
Sun noon–midnight
Admission Free
Payment Cash only

Adelaide's Drag Queens (and King)

Every year during the FEAST Festival, the night of nights on the drag calendar
rolls round, with over forty kings and queens and three hours of non-stop drag
shows: it's got to be the **Mega Drag Cabaret** – legendary, historic, histrionic
and hysterical, big, bold and brash! Drag performances are held throughout
the week at both *Mars Bar* (above) and the *Edinburgh Castle Hotel* (opposite).

Rouge Shepherd is an original member of the Gay Deceivers, Australia's
longest-running drag troupe. Much loved, Rouge is a real professional, with
the best legs in the business.

The leader of the Adelaide Drag Kings, **Ben Dover**, known for renditions of everything from Dean Martin to Ricky Martin, has gained many adoring fans since leading the Kings at the opening of the 1998 FEAST Festival to a capacity crowd of 3000.

A real sweetie, always on the scene selling lollipops to raise funds for charity, **Crystal Brook (aka Miss Chuppa Chups)** is frequently seen on the Adelaide Float at the Sydney Gay & Lesbian Mardi Gras.

Larger than life at six foot six and weighing in at twenty stones, **Penny Traitor** is Adelaide's answer to Courtney Love. A high-energy performer with real momentum – when she gets going.

Gayel Warning is the proprietor of the Gayel Warning Frock Salon, the exclusive supplier of all things pretty to the larger-boned girl (appointments essential). Rare performances at gala events are much anticipated. Never seen with her plain-Jane sister, Storm Drain.

Rochelle and Fifi can be found most nights leading the floorshows at the *Mars Bar*, Australia's longest-running gay nightclub, with big production numbers and special guests. Rochelle is the acid-tongued hostess, while Fifi is a gender illusionist with an extraordinary talent – two gals who make sure the show does go on in the tradition of vaudeville.

As her name suggests, **Malt Biscuit** is melt-in-your-mouth smooth and dark. 'Who's black trash now?' she asked as winner of the Tosca Award for Drag Queen of the Year. This girl has come a long way in a very short time and looks like having a glamorous future.

Vonni is the host of 'Sunday Night Shows' at the *Edinburgh Castle Hotel*. An ex Les Girl with a heart of gold, she has years of professional experience – and it shows.

Luke Cutler

SEX CLUBS AND SAUNAS

Club X Adelaide
71 Hindley St
Adelaide SA 5000
Phone 08/8410 0444
Gender Men
This adult bookshop with 'ram

lounge' offers adult movies and backroom activities. Lube and condoms are provided.
Open Daily 9am–late
Payment AmEx, Bankcard, EFTPOS, MasterCard, Visa

Phoenix

1st floor, 147 Waymouth St
Adelaide SA 5000
Phone 08/8221 7002
Fax 08/8221 7002
Gender Men
Phoenix has a spa, steam room,
private cubicles, movie lounge, B&D
area, sling room, fantasy rooms and
adult movies.
Open Mon–Thurs noon–3am,
Fri noon–6am, Sat noon–8am,
Sun 2pm–3am
Admission $15
Payment Cash only

Pulteney 431

431 Pulteney St
Adelaide SA 5000
Phone 08/8223 7506
Fax 08/8232 9444
Email pultney431@hotmail.com
Gender Men
Adelaide's original male sauna has a
heated pool, wet sauna, dry sauna,
spa, private rooms and coffee lounge.
Open Mon–Tues 7pm–1am,
Wed–Thurs noon–1am,
Fri–Sat noon–3am, Sun noon–3am
Admission $15
Payment Cash only

BOOKSHOPS

Imprints

107 Hindley St
Adelaide SA 5000
Phone 08/8231 4454
Fax 08/8410 1025
Email imprints@camtech.net.au
Imprints is a gay-operated bookshop
with a diverse range of titles and a
good range of local and national gay
and lesbian newspapers, as well as
information on the latest arts events.
Open Mon–Thurs 9am–6pm,
Fri 9am–9pm, Sat 9am–5pm,
Sun 11am–5pm
Payment AmEx, Bankcard, Diners,
EFTPOS, MasterCard, Visa; cheque

Murphy Sisters

240 The Parade
Norwood SA 5067
Phone 08/8332 7508
Fax 08/8331 3559

Email enquiry@murphysisters.com.au
Web www.murphysisters.com.au
This friendly gay-owned and
-operated business specialises in gay,
lesbian and indigenous literature.
Open Wed and Fri 11am–6pm,
Thurs 11am-8pm, Sat 10am–5pm
Payment Bankcard, EFTPOS,
MasterCard, Visa

Sisters by the Sea

14 Semaphore Rd
Semaphore SA 5019
Phone Lorraine 08/8341 7088
Fax 08/8242 4100
This bookshop caters to sisters of all
kinds, with a fantastic selection of
lesbian books, music, children's
literature and Aboriginal studies.
Open Daily 11am–6pm
Payment AmEx, Bankcard,
MasterCard, Visa

NEWSPAPERS AND MAGAZINES

Adelaide GT

18 Freemasons Lane (PO Box 10141),
Gouger St
Adelaide SA 5000
Phone 08/8232 1544
Fax 08/8232 1560
Email adelaidegt_reception@
satellitemedia.com.au
Web www.adelaidegt.com.au
Gender Mixed

Published fortnightly, *GT* (*Gay Times*)
offers essential listings of gay and
lesbian venues and services, local and
national news and is available free from
gay/lesbian-friendly venues and shops.
It can also be picked up at *Bookshop
Darlinghurst* in Sydney and *Hares &
Hyenas* bookshop in Melbourne.
Cost Free street distribution,
$54 annual subscription

BEACHES AND POOLS

Adelaide Aquatic Centre

Jeffcott Rd
North Adelaide SA 5006
Phone 08/8344 4411
Gender Mixed
Adelaide's premier health and fitness
centre is very popular with the boys
and has a fully equipped gymnasium
and Olympic-sized pool.
Open Daily 5am–10pm
Cost $4.40 swim, spa, sauna;
$7.50 gym, swim, spa, sauna
Payment Bankcard, MasterCard, Visa

Maslin Beach

Maslin Beach Rd
McLaren Vale SA 5171
Gender Mixed
Maslin Beach is about 25km south-
east of Adelaide. Head toward
McLaren Vale on the Main South
Road and turn right on Maslin Beach
Road. In 1975 this became Australia's
first unclad beach. The most popular
section of the beach for gay men is
the southern end near the rocks – but
watch out for undercover cops.

BODY STUFF

City Gym and Fitness Centre

Level 1, 63 Light Square
Adelaide SA 5000
Phone 08/8212 4866
Fax 08/8212 4866
Gender Mixed
Weights, aerobics, cardio-kickboxing,
squash, sauna, yoga, massage

solarium, this air-conditioned gym
has it all – whether you want to
punish your body or soothe it.
Open Mon–Thurs 6.30am–11pm,
Fri 6.30am–7pm, Sat noon–7pm,
Sun 5pm–9pm
Cost $5–8
Payment Bankcard, MasterCard, Visa

Team Adelaide

GPO Box 271
Adelaide SA 5000
Phone Brian Thalbourne 08/8232
4231 or Julie Mitchell 08/8332 2842
Email mang01@senet.com.au
Web members.xoom.com/
mang01/tapage.htm
Gender Mixed
Anybody interested in tennis,
squash, ten-pin bowling, volleyball,
golf, swimming, bushwalking,
cycling, netball, or triathlon? This
South Australian lesbian and gay
sporting body is involved in just
about every sport imaginable. It is
a non-profit organization and the
coordinating body organizes teams
for gay games both nationally and
internationally.
Cost Membership $10
Payment Cheque

MEDICAL

Clinic 275

First Floor, 275 North Terrace
Adelaide SA 5000
Phone 08/8226 6025
Fax 08/8226 6560
Email stdservices@dhs.sa.gov.au
Web stdservices.on.net
Gender Mixed
Clinic 275 provides free and
confidential counselling and testing
for STDs (with both male and
female doctors), needle exchange,
free hepatitis B vaccinations, free
morning-after pill and condoms and
lube. No appointment or Medicare
card is necessary. Its Web site offers
more specific information on sexual
health issues.
Open Mon, Thurs & Fri 10am–4pm,
Tues & Wed noon–7pm

Gay Men's Health

64 Fullarton Rd
Norwood SA 5067
Phone Freecall 1800/671 582,
08/8362 1617 or 08/8362 1611
Fax 08/8363 1046
Email aidscouncilsa@bigpond.org.au
Web www.aidscouncil.org.au
Gender Men
This service provides education,
support, discussion groups, outreach
education, condom distribution and
telephone support for gay men in
city and rural South Australia.
Open Mon–Fri 9am–5pm

Lesbian Healthline

North Adelaide SA 5006
Phone 08/8267 4185 or freecall
1800/182 098 (ask for line 9)
Gender Women
A free health service operated by
lesbian nurses, *Healthline* is able to
answer general and specific health
questions and offer counselling
support and referrals.
Open Mon–Fri 9am–5pm

SHine (Sexual Health Information Networking Education)

17 Phillip St
Kensington SA 5068
Phone 08/8431 5177 (TTY available)
or freecall 1800/188 171
Fax 08/8364 2389

Web www.shinesa.org.au
Gender Mixed
SHine offers a range of services,
including clinical, medical, counselling,
education, information and resources.
Appointments are preferred.
Open Mon–Fri 9am–5pm
Cost A small fee may apply
Payment Bankcard, MasterCard, Visa;
cheque

Women's Health Statewide
64 Pennington Terrace
North Adelaide SA 5006

Phone 08/8267 5366
Fax 08/8267 5597
Email info@whs.sa.gov.au
Web www.whs.sa.gov.au
Gender Women
This entirely women-run group
offers a wide range of free
health and information services,
including printed resources,
counselling and referrals. No
Medicare card is required;
appointments are advised, but
are not essential.
Open Mon–Fri 9am–5pm

COMMUNITY

Adelaide Happy Wanderers
PO Box 997
Victor Harbor SA 5211
Phone Warren 08/8352 8383 or
Keith 08/8552 7581
Email herbig@granite.net.au
Gender Mixed
Adelaide's gay and lesbian walking
group organizes day walks the first
Sunday of the month. Walking group
meets at 9am outside Al Fresco, 260
Rundle Street East, Adelaide.
Cost $2 per walk

AIDS Council of South Australia (ACSA)
64 Fullarton Rd
Norwood SA 5067 (or PO Box 907,
Kent Town SA 5071)
Phone Freecall 1800/888 559 or
08/8362 1611, TTY 08/8362 0306
Fax 08/8363 1046
Email acsa@aidscouncil.org.au
Web www.aidscouncil.org.au

Gender Mixed
ACSA offers a range of services for
people living with HIV/AIDS, their
lovers, family, friends and carers. Also
available from *ACSA* are local and
national gay magazines, condoms,
lube and needle exchange.
Open Mon–Fri 9am–5pm

BFRIEND
Adelaide Central Mission, 10 Pitt St
Adelaide SA 5000
Phone Des 08/8202 5192
Fax 08/8202 5507
Email bfriend@acm.asn.au
Gender Mixed
Trained volunteers offer support and
free confidential service to people
questioning their sexuality. Sponsors
interesting group discussions on
issues relating to sexuality and
provides a great opportunity to meet
with others in similar situations.
Open Mon–Fri 9am–5pm

Chameleons Group

PO Box 907
Kent Town SA 5071
Phone 08/8293 3700 or 08/8346 2516
before 9pm
Gender Mixed
A support group for the transgender
community of South Australia,
especially for those newly emerging.

Coffee, Cake and Conversation

Fleet St Café, cnr Pultney St and
Hindmarsh Square
Adelaide SA 5000
Phone Kate 08/8271 3436
Gender Women
This group meets the first Saturday
of each month from 2pm to 4pm,
providing an opportunity for visiting
and resident lesbians to meet.

Cougar Leather Club

Wheatsheaf Hotel, 39 George St
Thebarton SA 5031
Phone Garry and Tony 08/8443 6852
Email cougar@bettanet.net.au
Gender Men
On the first and third Tuesday of
every month, from 9pm to midnight,
the men-only leather crowd (bears,
uniform and bikers, with a good
smattering of denim and body
piercings) meets at the *Wheatsheaf
Hotel* (p.203).
Admission Membership $15, door
charge for some functions

Darling House Community Library

64 Fullarton Rd
Norwood SA 5067
Phone 08/8362 3106
TTY 08/8362 0306

Fax 08/8363 1046
Email library@aidscouncil.org.au
Gender Mixed
This is a joint library of the *AIDS
Council of SA* and the *Gay and
Lesbian Counselling Service of SA*. It
collects and makes available resources
that increase awareness of HIV/AIDS
and related issues. It also aims to
affirm and promote gay and lesbian
identity and provide information on
homosexuality and related issues.
This library is one of the largest of
its kind and membership is free.
Darling House also keeps lots of
gay/lesbian magazines and offers
local information.
Open Mon–Fri 9.30am–5pm, Sat
2pm–5pm (enter from Gray St on
Saturdays)

Gay and Lesbian Counselling Service of SA

PO Box 459
North Adelaide SA 5006
Phone Freecall 1800/182 233 or
08/8362 3223
Web www.glcssa.org.au
Gender Mixed
A confidential support and counselling
service for gays and lesbians.
Open Mon–Fri 7pm–10pm,
Sat–Sun 2pm–5pm

Golden Club

PO Box 69
Seacliff Park SA 5049
Email blackham@camtech.net.au
Gender Women
Social club for lesbians, meeting
once a month for dances, quizz
nights and other activities.

Inside Out

The Second Story Youth Health
Service, 57 Hyde St
Adelaide SA 5000
Phone 08/8232 0233
Email ctss.insideout@saugov.sa.gov.au
Gender Mixed

This regular social and support group
for gays and lesbians under 26 years
old provides a safe and relaxed space
to have coffee, meet others and join
a range of fun activities in mixed and
single-sex groups.

LOFTY (Lesbians Over Forty)

North Adelaide SA 5006
Phone Kate 08/8271 3436
Gender Women

LOFTY meets for discussion on the
third Saturday of each month from
2pm to 4pm.

Long Yang Club Adelaide

PO Box 4
Park Holme SA 5043
Phone Thinh or Kerry 08/8387 1237
or John 08/8297 1925
Email aldous@rebel.net.au
Web www.longyangclub.org
Gender Mixed

This is the Adelaide branch of the
world-famous Asian friendship
network of Long Yang Clubs that
foster friendship between gay Asians
and non-Asians. They have
sister/brother organizations in many
parts of the world. Long Yang Clubs
are especially concerned with
helping Asian guys make contact
with others in a friendly, non-
threatening atmosphere. There are
monthly karaokes, weekly get-
togethers at gay friendly pubs,

regular activities, house parties,
dinners and East–West dance parties,
and the annual Australia Day Beach
Party, *songkran* festival and Chinese
New Year celebrations.

Metropolitan Community Church

GPO Box 1006
Adelaide SA 5001
Phone 08/8278 6622
Fax 08/8278 6622
Email mccadel@senet.com.au
Gender Mixed

An Ecumenical Christian church
serving the gay/lesbian/bisexual/
transgender and straight communities.
Meets Sundays at 7pm for service
and supper afterwards at the Society
of Friends Meeting House, 40A
Pennington Terrace, North Adelaide.

Mitrasasana

PO Box 39
Woodville SA 5011
Gender Mixed

This is a group for gay people
inspired by the teachings of Buddha.

OZBEARS of South Australia

PO Box 89
Lobethal SA 5241
Phone 08/8389 4292
Fax 08/8389 4292
Gender Mixed

This group for hirsute mature men
and their admirers meets monthly in
suburban and nearby country venues.

Positive Living Centre

16 Malwa St
Glandore SA 5037
Phone 08/8293 3700
Fax 08/8293 3900

Email plwhasa@camtech.net.au
Web www.adelaide.net.au/~plwhasa
Gender Mixed

This is a community drop-in and resource centre for people living with HIV. Its services include organizing transport service for medical appointments; general support service for liaison between clients, social security and housing; a Positive Speakers bureau; a clinic service offering massage and alternative therapies including reiki, yoga and meditation; a weekly peer-support luncheon program; a treatment officer; a women and family support officer; Internet access and skills-building classes and recreational learning programs.
Open Mon & Wed–Fri 9am–5pm, Tues 9am–9pm (social night with light meals)

Shangri-La

Youth Health Service,
2nd floor, 57 Hyde St
Adelaide SA 5000
Phone Phillip 08/8232 0233
Email shangri_la94@hotmail.com
Gender Mixed

This free and confidential social and support group for Asian gay men (and their Asian or non-Asian partners and friends) offers a range of ongoing social and support programs and access to medical clinics, health screenings and more.
Open Mon, Tues & Thurs 9am–5pm

South Australian Transexual Support (SATS)

PO Box 907
Kent Town SA 5071

Phone Jacqui mobile 0409 698 462
Email supportsa@geocities.com
Web host2.mbcomms.net.au/tg/satsg
Gender Mixed

SATS is a support group for transexuals who have changed or are about to permanently change their gender role, and their partners. It also offers information for people on transexualism, as well as support and information for those facing gender-identity difficulties.

Southern Region Motor Club

GPO Box 252
Adelaide SA 5000
Phone 08/8331 7451 or mobile 0412 213 785
Gender Men

This leather, uniform and boot club arranges regular private functions.

TAFS (Talking About Female Sexuality)

PO Box 2337
Regency Park SA 5942
Phone Belinda 08/8243 55679
Fax 08/8347 3632
Gender Women

This is a support/drop-in social group offering a safe place for young women aged under 26 who identify as non-heterosexual. They meet and discuss anything and everything and can arrange occasional outings and transport to meetings.
Open Wed 5.30pm–7.30pm

Unity

PO Box 3361, Rundle Mall
Adelaide SA 5001
Phone Paul 08/8341 6496

Email marshpaul@yahoo.com.au
Web www.adelaide.net.au/
~wmaster/index.html
Gender Mixed
This support and social group for
gay/lesbian/bisexual/transgender
people in the Uniting Church meets
on the fourth Friday of the month,
usually at Pilgrim Church. Meetings
start at 7pm with a shared meal,
followed by a speaker/Bible
study/activity and conclude with
Communion.

WEST (Women Exploring Sexuality Together)

Dale St Health Clinic
Port Adelaide SA 5015
Phone 08/8447 7033
Gender Women
A discussion and support group for
women.

Women in the Bush

PO Box 90
Little Hampton SA 5250
Phone Sue 08/8391 1805
Gender Women
A volunteer feminist lesbian group
which organizes monthly bushwalks
of varying lengths and fitness-level
requirements, as well as the occasional
overnight and weekend walk.

Women of the Wilderness

c/- YWCA 17 Hutt St
Adelaide SA 5000
Phone Heidi 08 822 70155
Fax 08/8227 0166
Gender Women
Wild women are welcome to join
this all-ages walking group for low-
stress day walks in the wilderness
surrounding Adelaide.
Cost Membership $10

TRAVEL SERVICES

Parkside Travel

70 Glen Osmond Rd
Parkside SA 5063
Phone Freecall 1800 88 85 01 or
08/8274 1222
Fax 08/8272 7371
Email parkside@harveyworld.com.au
This gay-owned and -operated

organizer of gay and lesbian travel
specializes in cruises, but can also
arrange national and international,
corporate and leisure travel.
Open Mon–Fri 8.30pm–5.30pm,
Sat 9am–noon
Payment AmEx, Bankcard, Diners,
EFTPOS, MasterCard, Visa; cheque

Barossa Valley

To the north-east of the city is the most touristy of the wine regions, the Barossa Valley, where you'll find many of the big wineries of international repute. The Barossa Valley begins just 50km to the north of Adelaide and takes in the towns of Gawler, Lyndoch, Tanunda, Nuriootpa and Angaston.

To avoid driving under the influence, you'd be well-advised to take a **tour** – or hire a bike. Pedal-off your last tasting and work up a thirst for the next brand-name vintage as you weave your way between well-known **wineries** such as Wolf Blass, Saltram, Penfolds, Yalumba, Krondorf, and Grant Burge. Best to ask them to mail your case purchases, unless you have a very big basket attached to your bike and a steady hand on the handlebars!

The Lodge Country House

Seppeltsfield Rd
Seppeltsfield SA 5355
Phone 08/8562 8277
Fax 08/8562 8344
Email thelodge@dove.net.au
Web www.thelodge.mtx.net
Gender Mixed

Gay-owned and -operated, stylish accommodation at the Seppelt Family Homestead in the Barossa Valley. The lodge is set in gardens with a swimming pool and tennis court. All rooms have private bathrooms and the dining room serves gourmet meals as well as fine wines. Smoking permitted outside only. Bookings are essential for both accommodation and meals.
Cost From $254 single, $314 double
Payment AmEx, Bankcard, Diners, MasterCard, Visa

Rural Lesbian Network – Barossa

c/- Plum Farm Women's Land
PO Box 254
Angaston SA 5353
Phone 08/8565 3284 (6pm–9pm)
Email owlspurr@dove.net.au
Gender Women

Plum Farm Women's Land is a co-operative drug-free community for rural lesbians and their female children (phone or email for map and suitable times for visiting). The amenities are basic and include outdoor fireplaces, two cabins and caravan without electricity, though rainwater and a pot-belly stove are available. Electricity, shower and telephone are available at the main house. Camp sites with gum tree shelter are also available on the farm. The location is one and a half hour's drive from Adelaide, and is served by country buses. Some work exchange is available, and baby sons and dogs are sometimes allowed by negotiation. Friendship network links to other lesbians and feminists in other states of Australia and in New Zealand.
Cost Donation to cover gas, electricity, etc.
Payment Cash only

Clare Valley

Some 160km to the north of the city is the less touristy Clare Valley and many wonderful wineries, including the **Sevenhill winery**, where the Jesuit Brothers have been making wine since 1851. Movie buffs should look out for **Martindale Hall**, the setting for the girls' school in the famous Australian film *Picnic at Hanging Rock*.

Thorn Park Country House

College Rd, Clare Valley
Sevenhill SA 5453
Phone David 08/8843 4304
Fax 08/8843 4296
Email thornpk@capri.net.au
Web www.thornpark.com.au
Gender Mixed

Thorn Park is a 150-year-old homestead in a secluded setting surrounded by extensive gardens. This wine country gourmet retreat offers fine dining (with a choice of dining rooms) and frequent residential cooking schools. There is an elegant sitting room and library, and walking trails. Gay-owned and -run. Smoking is permitted outside only.

Cost From $195 single, $290 double (two-night minimum stay at weekends)

Payment AmEx, Bankcard, Diners, EFTPOS, MasterCard, Visa; cheque

The Adelaide Hills

In the Adelaide Hills (or Lofty Ranges), south-east of the city, you'll find quaint touristy towns such as **Hahndorf**, its Bavarian-style shops and eateries a legacy of its first German settlers. At **Bridgewater**, on the way back to Adelaide, you can visit the Bridgewater Mill winery and the Petaluma winery, source of Croser, one of Australia's premier champagnes.

Chatsworth Manor

3 Eton Rd
Aldgate SA 5154
Phone 08/8339 1455
Fax 08/8339 1655
Gender Mixed

Enjoy luxurious three-roomed suites (Victorian or Elizabethan and furnished in antiques) in an elegant Adelaide Hills manor house set in a large garden. You can dine in your own suite from the à la carte menu or relax in the spa. *Chatsworth Manor* is 5 minutes' drive from Stirling, 20 minutes from Adelaide.

Cost From $154 per room midweek, $199-243 weekends (prices include full breakfast)

Payment AmEx, Bankcard, Diners, EFTPOS, MasterCard, Visa

Fleurieu Peninsula

This triangular chunk of land to the south of Adelaide is renowned for its **beaches**, which stretch along both coasts, historic towns – and, inland, the **wineries** of the Southern Vales.

ACCOMMODATION

Sleepy Hollow Farm Cottage
PO Box 451 Woodvale Rd
Yankalilla SA 5203
Phone Cilla and George 08/8558 3190
Fax 08/8558 3770
Email adler@yankalilla.net.au
Gender Mixed
Just an hour's drive from Adelaide, this chalet-style self-contained cottage near Normanville Beach sleeps up to six people. The tariff includes breakfast. Pets are allowed by prior arrangement; smoking outside only.
Cost From $111 per couple ($22 each extra person)
Payment AmEx, Bankcard, Diners, MasterCard, Visa

Sunnyside Grange
Adelaide Rd
Strathalbyn SA 5255
Phone 08/8536 4470
Email sunnyside@olis.net.au
Web olis.net.au/~sunnyside/
Gender Mixed
Lesbian-owned and -operated, *Sunnyside Grange* is an exclusively gay and lesbian bed and breakfast. It is located near to wineries, galleries and antique shops, just outside Strathalbyn. Bookings are essential for rooms at this handsome Art Deco home set on gum-studded farmland.
Cost From $85 single, $105 double
Payment Bankcard, MasterCard, Visa; cheque

COMMUNITY

South Coast Gay and Lesbian Social Group
PO Box 997
Victor Harbor SA 5211
Phone Keith 08/8552 7581 or Fran and Janis 08/8554 2826

Email herbig@granite.net.au
Gender Mixed
This group arranges monthly social activities and regular dances for gays and lesbians living on the South Coast.

Kangaroo Island

A trip to Kangaroo Island is highly recommended. The island is a great location to experience unspoilt wilderness and see plenty of wildlife. You can drive down the Fleurieu Peninsula to Cape Jervis and put your car on the **ferry** (note that most of the roads are unsealed) or catch a short **flight** from Adelaide airport. Peak season is December and January, when bookings are essential.

The Lookout

PO Box 566
Penneshaw SA 5222
Phone Peter and Malcolm
08/8553 1048
Fax 08/8553 1048
Gender Mixed

Gay-owned and -operated, this adults-only bed and breakfast has superb views of the Fleurieu Peninsula and is set in a wonderfully maintained garden. The two-bedroom self-contained apartment sleeps up to four. Smoking is permitted outdoors only. Breakfast is included, and other meals are available at extra cost.
Cost $132 per room
Payment Bankcard, MasterCard, Visa

Matthew Flinders Terraces

PO Box 42, American River
Kangaroo Island SA 5221
Phone 08/8553 7100
Fax 08/8553 7250
Web www.falconweb.net.au/ ~matthewflinders
Gender Mixed

Located by American River, this small gay/lesbian-friendly boutique retreat has spectacular sea views from all suites. There's also a pool and spa. Packages available, including ferry and two nights' accommodation.
Cost $108 per room
Payment AmEx, Bankcard, Diners, MasterCard, Visa

The South-East

Robe, over 300km south-east of Adelaide, on a stretch of rugged coastline, was one of South Australia's earliest settlements. It is now a popular resort and crayfishing centre, with well-preserved streetscapes.

Ketiga Mata (the Third Eye)

9 Denning St
Robe SA 5276
Phone Erik 08/8768 2376
Fax 08/8768 2990
Email info@ketigamata.com
Web www.ketigamata.com
Gender Mixed

This exclusively gay and lesbian retreat on South Australia's historic shipwreck coast is gay-owned and -operated. There are self-contained one-bedroom and studio apartments.
Cost From $88 single, $105 double (discounts for longer stays)
Payment Bankcard, MasterCard, Visa

Victoria

Victoria is named after the most famous queen of them all. Victoria's temperate climate means it has some of the best farming land in Australia, and it has always been one of the most moderate states politically. In the last few years gay and lesbian social networks have strengthened – for links, check out the ALSO Foundation at www.also.org.au.

While the focus of Victoria's gay life is the state's capital city of Melbourne, there is plenty of queer life elsewhere. Because Victoria is relatively densely populated, gays and lesbians seem to feel more at ease with rural living. The most popular location for the gay/lesbian diaspora is **Daylesford** and its sister spa town of **Hepburn Springs**, which offer the perfect romantic getaway. But all Victoria's regions seem to offer something gay/lesbian-friendly and are teeming with eminently suitable accommodation. The **Mornington Peninsula**, southeast of Melbourne, has many wineries and lovely beaches. Further east, but still just an hour and a half's drive from Melbourne is **Phillip Island**, famous for its **fairy penguin parade** at dusk. To the southwest of Melbourne, the **Great Ocean Road** winds its way along a truly spectacular coastline, making this one of the most dramatic and beautiful drives in the country.

Melbourne

With a population of 3.3 million, Melbourne is Australia's second-largest city. It is famous for its unreliable weather, Aussie Rules football enthusiasts, beautiful gardens with avenues of deciduous trees, and its distinctive green-and-yellow trams.

Melbourne highlights and hot-spots

- The small bar at the front of the **Prince of Wales Hotel** (see p.241) is popular with both gays and lesbians (you might also want to try some of the classier bars in this rambling hotel while you're there).

- **Shopping** on **Chapel Street** is a must. It's the one place in Australia where you can see all the international and Australian fashion designers displaying their wares. Have lunch at *Globe* (see p.230), *Red Orange* (see pp.230–31) or any of the excellent cafés along this strip, and make a day of it.

- **St Kilda** (a mere 25 minutes from the city by tram) and Elwood (just a bit further south) are very popular, grand old seaside suburbs boasting a true carnival atmosphere – from the spooky laughing clown of St Kilda's Luna Park to the calorific nightmare of the smart bars and Acland Street's Eastern European cake shops.

- The **Botanical Gardens**, on the south bank of the Yarra River east of Princes Bridge, are a magnificent place to commune with nature, or to see movies and Shakespeare productions throughout the summer months.

- Also on the south bank of the Yarra River, across from the Flinders Street railway station, is the **Victorian Arts Centre**, where culture vultures could easily lose days at a time in the National Gallery of Victoria, Concert Hall, Theatres Building and Performing Arts Museum.

- From this celebration of creativity, it is only a short walk along Southbank to the **Crown Casino** – a monument to mammon, if ever there was one. If your wallet isn't up to a stint on the tables, just take a peek at the Las Vegas-style water-and-light show in the main lobby.

Lesbians will find the highest **dyke population** in the northern inner-city suburbs of Fitzroy, Collingwood and Brunswick – as well as in Richmond, Prahran and East St Kilda, southeast of the city centre. For **gay men**, the entire inner belt of suburbs offers suitable abodes, as well as specific services. (The film *Head On*, based on gay writer Christos Tsiolkas's novel *Loaded*, was filmed on location in these stomping grounds.) **Commercial Road, South Yarra**, is as close as you'll get to a gay precinct, offering a number of bars, clubs, restaurants and Melbourne's gay/lesbian bookshop, *Hares & Hyenas* (see pp.245–246). It is adjacent to **Chapel Street,** which provides the longest, most glamorous and interest-packed shopping strip in Australia. Look out for the **Chapel Street Bazaar** (between Commercial Road and High Street), which features amazing collectibles from every decade of the twentieth century – it's a veritable cornucopia of kitsch and camp.

To the north of the CBD, **Brunswick Street**, **Fitzroy**, and, running parallel to it, **Smith Street**, **Collingwood**, offer a bohemian dose of cafés and restaurants among some of the most amazing concept shops you'll ever see. Take a look at *LURE* hairdressing on Smith Street or the windows of *Gluttony* café. Wherever you look in Fitzroy and Collingwood you'll see art – from the in-your-face shop signs to the mosaic benches on street corners. Be a little cautious along Smith Street, though – this is also a heroin hot-spot, so hang onto your family jewels.

Melbourne's efficient **public transport** system is called the Met; its information line is 13 1638.

Probably the most fantastic thing about Melbourne is its vibrant **bar and café culture**, which is made possible by Victoria's progressive licensing laws. The plethora of small bars and cafés provide intimate and comfortable environments for people to meet, drink, eat and socialise. You'll find many of the bars have a mixed clientele, making for a relaxed ambience, regardless of your sexual preferences.

Melbourne, like Sydney, has bouts of **anti-gay violence**. Caution should be taken at night around the Russell Street and Lonsdale Street areas in the city, as these have become notorious areas for heroin trafficking. And although the Commercial Road and Chapel Street area is usually busy with people at night, attacks are not infrequent, especially in the back streets.

Midsumma Festival

MIDSUMMA FESTIVAL

Angela Bailey

The **Midsumma Festival** is a community festival, mainly volunteer-run and staffed, with a mission to present an arts and cultural festival to the gay, lesbian, queer and allied communities. The festival takes place each year in mid-January to early February, at the height of summer, with three weeks of cabaret, theatre, parties, community events, and arts and cultural events.

This gay and lesbian festival of arts and culture has steadily built a reputation over the past 12 years for the quality and diversity of its many registered events showcasing theatre, dance, visual arts, literature and sport. In addition, each of the four weekends during the Festival is marked by a major public event:

- **Midsumma Street Party** (in Commercial Road, at the heart of Melbourne's gay precinct) sets the scene. As the sun sets on a hot summer's night, 40,000 come to dance, disco, boogie, bootscoot, rock 'n' roll or rap their way through the night. The traditional Mass Debate between community icons takes place at the Athenaeum.

- The *ALSO Foundation* (p.251) hosts its annual **Red Raw dance party**. This legendary rave is the hottest event on the *Midsumma* calendar and is followed by an array of 'recovery' parties, including the official *Midsumma* one.

Angela Bailey

- The festival also includes the annual **Pride March**, in which 30,000 people march, mince or meander their way down Fitzroy Street, St Kilda, to express their pride and solidarity. Following the march, the St Kilda foreshore acts as the backdrop for *Midsumma*'s version of the great Aussie beach party – with a twist (of course).

- The closing event is the **Midsumma Carnival** and picnic in the park (with over 80,000 of your closest friends) at Alexandra Gardens, on the banks of Melbourne's Yarra River. A day for all 'our family' with dog shows, amateur drag competitions, lube wrestling, amusement rides, and over a hundred businesses and community groups exhibiting their wares.

While Midsumma is committed to conducting participative, free events, many registered events are ticketed. For ticket enquiries, phone 03/9415 9819, and for the latest on this year's festival happenings, point your mouse at www.midsumma.org.au.

Most of the places to stay listed in **Inner Melbourne** are within walking distance of the city centre – though you might choose to hop on a tram or train if you've been pounding the streets all day (or night). Hotels and B&Bs south of the centre have the advantage of proximity to great shopping in Chapel Street and **Prahran**. Further south again takes you into the crazy-clown territory of **St Kilda** with its funky bars and the Esplanade lined with palm trees and weekend craft stalls.

INNER MELBOURNE

163 Drummond

163 Drummond St
Carlton VIC 3053
Phone 03/9663 3081
Fax 03/9663 6500
Email drummond163@bigpond.com
Gender Mixed
Ensuite rooms or shared facilities are available in this Victorian B&B, just 10 minutes' walk from city. Bookings are recommended and airport pick-up is available.
Cost From $56 single, $88 double
Payment AmEx, Bankcard, Diners, MasterCard, Visa

Adelphi Hotel

187 Flinders Lane
Melbourne VIC 3000
Phone 03/9650 7555
Fax 03/9650 2710
Email info@adelphi.com.au
Web www.adelphi.com.au
Gender Mixed
For lovers of post-modernism and Memphis design, the *Adelphi* offers a chic alternative to the major hotels. Featuring a restaurant (Mon–Fri lunch & dinner, Sat dinner only), rooftop bar and gravity-defying heated swimming pool, the *Adelphi* is popular with the arts crowd. There is also a fitness room and sauna, as well as a function space catering for up to 80 people. Continental breakfast is included in tariff.
Cost $275–496 per room
Payment AmEx, Bankcard, Diners, MasterCard, Visa

California Motel

138 Barkers Rd
Hawthorn VIC 3122
Phone 03/9818 0281 or freecall 1800/331 166
Fax 03/9818 6845
Email california_motel@bigpond.com
Web www.californiamotel.com.au
Gender Mixed
This motel could have just been beamed over from LA. Consisting of 80 rooms and plenty of parking in one of Melbourne's more charming suburbs, it also has a restaurant and bar.
Cost $110 single, $130 double
Payment AmEx, Bankcard, MasterCard, Visa

Fitzroy Stables

124 Victoria St
Fitzroy VIC 3065
Phone Judith and Rose 03/9415 1507
Gender Mixed
Lesbian-owned and –operated, self-contained converted stables in the heart of Fitzroy offer private bathroom, lounge, dining room, kitchen and loft bedroom.
Cost $83 single, $100 double
Payment Cash only

Gatehouse

10 Peel St (enter via Club 80)
Collingwood VIC 3066
Phone 03/9417 2182
Fax 03/9416 0474
Email club80@qmail.com.au
Gender Men
The *Gatehouse* offers a truly unique form of accommodation ideal for leather men and B&D lovers, geared as it is to gay male sexual pleasure. Each room has a sleeping loft upstairs with individual private playrooms below. Slings and bondage equipment come with each room. Bathroom facilities are shared, as is guest lounge and kitchen. Off-street parking is available and a secluded courtyard to relax in. Music in rooms, entry to *Club 80* (p.242) and a light breakfast is included in tariff.
Cost $80 per room
Payment AmEx, Bankcard, EFTPOS, MasterCard, Visa

Gay Trade Backpackers

9 Peel St
Collingwood VIC 3066
Phone 03/9417 6700
Fax 03/9417 2170
Email opsmanager@rabbit.com.au

Gender Mostly men
This bunkhouse accommodation also houses a popular bar (see p.233).
Cost From $22 per night
Payment EFTPOS, Visa

Laird Hotel

149 Gipps St
Abbotsford VIC 3067
Phone 03/9417 2832
Fax 03/9417 2109
Email hotel@laird.com.au
Web www.lairdhotel.com
Gender Men
The *Laird*, Melbourne's favourite leather bar, offers guesthouse-style accommodation with shared bathroom; continental breakfast is included, as is admission to *Club 80* (see p.242). Airport transfers can be arranged.
Cost $72 single, $83 double, $122 apartment
Payment AmEx, Bankcard, Diners, EFTPOS, MasterCard, Visa

Palm Court B&B

22 Grattan Place
Richmond VIC 3121
Phone 03/9427 7365
Fax 03/9427 7365
Email palmc@ozemail.com.au
Gender Mostly men
This magnificently restored row of Victorian houses, opposite the Melbourne Cricket Ground and a pleasant walk from the city centre, is gay-owned and -operated. There is a large guest lounge, and breakfast is included in the tariff. Smoking is permitted outside only.
Cost From $66 single, $100 double
Payment AmEx, Bankcard, MasterCard, Visa

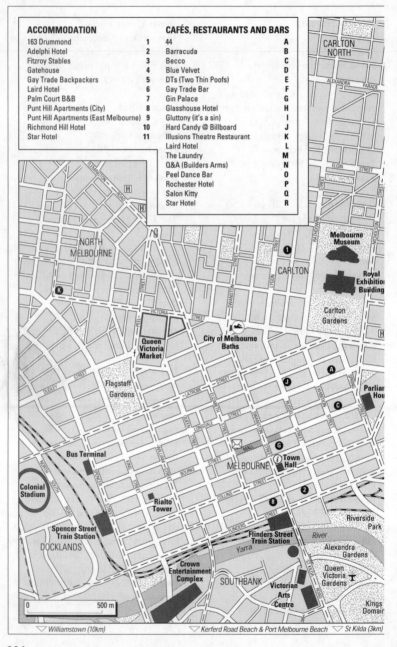

ACCOMMODATION	
163 Drummond	1
Adelphi Hotel	2
Fitzroy Stables	3
Gatehouse	4
Gay Trade Backpackers	5
Laird Hotel	6
Palm Court B&B	7
Punt Hill Apartments (City)	8
Punt Hill Apartments (East Melbourne)	9
Richmond Hill Hotel	10
Star Hotel	11

CAFÉS, RESTAURANTS AND BARS	
44	A
Barracuda	B
Becco	C
Blue Velvet	D
DTs (Two Thin Poofs)	E
Gay Trade Bar	F
Gin Palace	G
Glasshouse Hotel	H
Gluttony (it's a sin)	I
Hard Candy @ Billboard	J
Illusions Theatre Restaurant	K
Laird Hotel	L
The Laundry	M
Q&A (Builders Arms)	N
Peel Dance Bar	O
Rochester Hotel	P
Salon Kitty	Q
Star Hotel	R

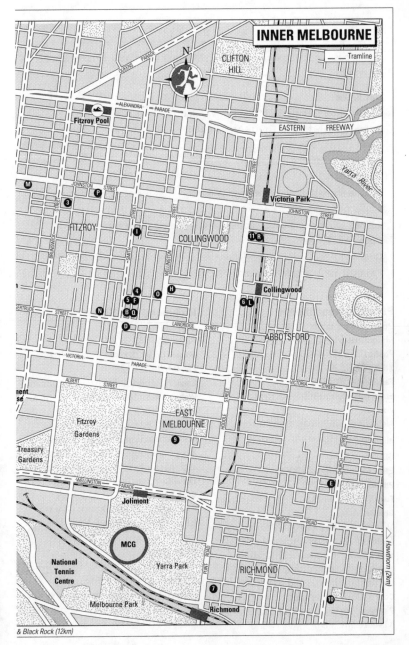

Flatshare

Just in case you get *too* comfortable in Melbourne and want to hang your hat for a while . . .

Gay Share
Level 4, 501 Latrobe St, Melbourne VIC 3000
Phone 03/9691 2290 Fax 03/9602 4484
Email mckenzie@wire.net.au
Web www.safehome.com.au
Gender Mixed
A home-share service for gay men and lesbians: a fee is payable by both the household searching for a new tenant and the seekers themselves. The fee entitles you to two months' access to *Gay Share*'s database.
Open Mon–Fri 9am–5pm
Cost $77
Payment Bankcard, MasterCard, Visa; cheque

Punt Hill Apartments
267 Flinders Lane
Melbourne VIC 3000
Phone 03/9650 4409 or freecall
1800/331 529
Fax 03/9650 4409
Email info@punthill-apartments.
com.au
Web www.punthill-apartments.com.au
also at:
60 Gipps St
East Melbourne VIC 3002
Phone 03/9650 1299
Fax 03/9650 4409
Gender Mixed
With several branches in Melbourne, *Punt Hill Apartments* provide a relaxed atmosphere in convenient locations close to gay venues, shopping, cafés, restaurants, theatres and attractions.
Cost $125–226 per unit
Payment AmEx, Bankcard, Diners, MasterCard, Visa

Richmond Hill Hotel
353 Church St
Richmond VIC 3121
Phone 03/9428 6501
Fax 03/9427 0128
Email richmondhill@ozemail.com.au
Web www.richmondhillhotel.com.au
Gender Mixed
This gay/lesbian-friendly boutique hotel situated in an historic mansion has a tram route outside the front door and there is free off-street parking. Breakfast is included in the tariff.
Cost $95 single, $110 double
Payment AmEx, Bankcard, Diners, EFTPOS, MasterCard, Visa

Star Hotel
176 Hoddle St
Collingwood VIC 3066
Phone 03/9417 2696 or 0416 068 572
Fax 03/9417 2696
Gender Mixed

This popular gay and lesbian hotel offers comfortable rooms close to northside venues and just 3km from the city centre. The bathrooms are shared, but there is a TV in every room and the tariff includes breakfast.
Cost $56–77 per room
Payment AmEx, Bankcard, EFTPOS, MasterCard, Visa

PRAHRAN, ST KILDA AND WILLIAMSTOWN

Cosmopolitan
2–8 Carlisle St
St Kilda VIC 3182
Phone 03/9534 0781
Fax 03/9534 8262
Email info@cosmopolitan-motor-inn. com.au
Gender Mixed
This clean, modern motel's main advantage is its location – the absolute heart of St Kilda, with cafés and the tram right on your doorstep. There is a café for breakfast, room service and off-street parking.
Cost $120–182 per room
Payment AmEx, Bankcard, Diners, EFTPOS, MasterCard, Visa

Heathville House
171 Aitken St
Williamstown VIC 3016
Phone Stuart and Philip 03/9397 5959
Fax 03/9397 5959
Email heath@jeack.com.au
Web melbournebest.com.au/ heathville.html
Gender Mixed
This beautiful Victorian home in Melbourne's charming Williamstown is close to shops, restaurants and public transport (including ferries to Southgate and St Kilda).
Cost From $88 single, $126 double
Payment AmEx, Bankcard, Diners, MasterCard, Visa; cheque

Prince of Wales
2 Acland St
St Kilda VIC 3182
Phone 03/9536 1111
Fax 03/9536 1100
Email thedesk@theprince.com.au
Web www.theprince.com.au
Gender Mixed
An innovative, elegant, 40-room hotel combining classic Deco architecture and furniture with contemporary design and *objets*. If you've the budget you probably can't go past this hotel for location and style. The *Prince* has some of the top bars and restaurants in the city downstairs, the beach is across the road, and the hotel can arrange passes to nearby sports facilities. There is a laundry service, security valet parking, 24-hour room service, safes in rooms, Internet access, and state-of-the-art entertainment systems. The *Prince*'s restaurants may be a little on the pricey side, but there is plenty of choice nearby and the city is only 20 minutes' away by tram.
Cost $275–$496 per room
Payment AmEx, Bankcard, Diners, MasterCard, Visa

Punt Hill Apartments
The Stanton, 622 St Kilda Rd
Melbourne VIC 3000
Phone 03/9650 1299

Fax 03/9650 4409
Email info@punthill-apartments.com.au
Web www.punthill-apartments.com.au

also at:
470 Punt Rd
South Yarra VIC 3141
Phone 03/9650 1299
Fax 03/9650 4409;

44 Davis Ave
South Yarra VIC 3141
Phone 03/9650 1299
Fax 03/9650 4409
Gender Mixed
With several branches in Melbourne, *Punt Hill Apartments* provide a relaxed atmosphere in convenient locations close to gay venues, shopping, cafés, restaurants, theatres and attractions.
Cost $127–303 per unit
Payment AmEx, Bankcard, Diners, MasterCard, Visa

Hotel Saville
5 Commercial Rd
South Yarra VIC 3141
Phone freecall 1800/651 081

Email info@saville.com.au
Web www.saville.com.au
Gender Mixed
One of the handiest hotels for those who love the Melbourne nightlife, this comfortable, basic motel-style accommodation is on the doorstep of Commercial Road's gay venues.
Cost $98 per room
Payment AmEx, Bankcard, Diners, EFTPOS, MasterCard, Visa

Tolarno
42 Fitzroy St
St Kilda VIC 3182
Phone 03/9537 0200
Fax 03/9534 7800
Email mail@htltolarno.com.au
Web www.htltolarno.com.au
Gender Mixed
This cosy but cool, retro hotel is popular with the arts crowd and perfectly situated for easy access to the city, gay venues and lively St Kilda. The rooms are comfortable and well appointed, and there is a fine bar and restaurant downstairs.
Cost From $110 per room
Payment AmEx, Bankcard, Diners, EFTPOS, MasterCard, Visa

 CAFÉS AND RESTAURANTS

Melbourne prides itself on being the **foodie capital** of Australia. In addition to the queer-friendly places listed here, check out its claims for yourself at some of the city's temples of gastronomy, such as *Stella* and *Flower Drum* in the city, *Circa* in St Kilda, or the *Richmond Hill Café and Larder*, at the city end of Bridge Road in Richmond.

INNER MELBOURNE

Becco

11–25 Crossley St
Melbourne VIC 3000
Phone 03/9663 3000
Fax 03/9663 3949
Email becco@ozemail.com.au
Web www.becco.com.au
This excellent restaurant/deli/bar
serves modern cuisine with an Italian
influence: popular dishes include the
sensational Fiorina's stuffed olives with
ravioli, and roast duck with a muscatel
and grappa sauce. The deli sells all the
ingredients used in the restaurant, as
well as books, bread, gourmet food
and roses; and the bar is a popular
hangout with the artsy city set.
Open Restaurant Mon–Sat noon–late;
deli Mon–Sat 9am–late; bar Mon–Fri
10am–late
Cost $30–40 lunch, $50–60 dinner
Payment AmEx, Bankcard, Diners,
MasterCard, Visa

Gluttony (it's a sin)

278 Smith St
Collingwood VIC 3066
Phone 03/9416 0336
Fax 03/9416 0336

This gay-owned and -operated fully
licensed restaurant offers wicked
excesses of home-cooked fare to the
gays, lesbians, intellectuals, bohemians,
ferals and their mums who patronize it.
Everything is made on the premises
and the servings are generous.
Specialties include all-day breakfasts
and a self-serve breakfast bar offering
their delicious home-made muesli.
The wood interior is charming with
old-fashioned dining tables.
Open Daily 7am–11pm
Cost Breakfast $7–15, lunch &
dinner $10–20
Payment Bankcard, MasterCard, Visa

Two Thin Poofs

164 Church St
Richmond VIC 3121
Phone 03/9428 5724
Fax 03/9428 5724
Inside *DTs* hotel (p.232), this
excellent and inexpensive bistro
serves 'real honest pub grub'.
Open Tues–Sun 6pm–10pm
Cost $10–15 per person
Payment Bankcard, EFTPOS,
MasterCard, Visa

PRAHRAN AND ST KILDA

Circ

2 Acland St (cnr Fitzroy St)
St Kilda VIC 3182
Phone 03/9536 1122
Fax 03/9536 1183
Email thedesk@theprince.com.au
Web www.theprince.com.au
The glamorous baby sister of *Circa*
(see below), *Circ* has an inspirational

menu and a dazzling interior.
Open Daily 8am–3pm
Cost Breakfast $15–20, lunch $30–40
Payment AmEx, Bankcard, Diners,
MasterCard, Visa

Circa

2 Acland St (cnr Fitzroy St)
St Kilda VIC 3182

Phone 03/9536 1122
Fax 03/9536 1183
Email thedesk@theprince.com.au
Web www.theprince.com.au
This truly divine interior will amaze
you. It's a vision of smoked glass and
banquettes and the ultimate in chic
dining – fortunately, the food is
inspirational too. After dinner, pop
downstairs and sample the vodka at
Mink (see p. 240).
Open Daily 6pm–late
Cost $80–165 per person
Payment AmEx, Bankcard, Diners,
MasterCard, Visa

Globe Cafe

218 Chapel St
Prahran VIC 3181
Phone 03/9510 8693
Fax 03/9529 1288
Email globe@vicnet.net.au
Web www.citysearch.com.au/mel/
globecafe
This popular gay mecca has been
offering flavours from around the
world for nearly 10 years. Their all-
day breakfast menu can include
Laotian omelettes, Indian rice
breakfasts and Spanish eggs. The
lunch and dinner menu continues the
international theme with jerked
chicken marinated in Jamaican spices
or a traditional Indian thali plate with
five different dishes and condiments.
Among their sensational cakes are
chocolate ripple and coffee pistachio.
Open Mon–Fri 8.30am–midnight, Sat
9am–midnight, Sun 10am–11pm
Cost Breakfast $10, lunch &
dinner $15–20
Payment AmEx, Bankcard, Diners,
MasterCard, Visa

Jackie O

204 Barkly St
St Kilda VIC 3182
Phone 03/9537 0377
Fax 03/9537 0890
This smart and modern, fully licensed
bar and restaurant has funky music to
accompany your eggs benedict
breakfast, or warm chicken salad for
lunch, or hearty chicken parmigiana
for dinner. Cocktails are $5 on
Sunday nights, when everyone
crowds in for Long Island Iced Teas
and Margaritas.
Open Daily 7.30am–1am
Cost Breakfast $10–15, lunch &
dinner $10–20
Payment AmEx, Bankcard, Diners,
EFTPOS, MasterCard, Visa

The OutLook

196 Commercial Rd
Prahran VIC 3181
Phone 03/9521 4227
Email theoutlook@hotmail.com
Web www.theoutlook.com.au
The OutLook is your all-in-one travel
stop in Melbourne's gay precinct
where you can get cheap meals in the
café, Internet access, cards, gadgets
and even cheap haircuts.
Open Daily 10am–9pm
Payment AmEx, Bankcard, Diners,
EFTPOS, MasterCard, Visa

Red Orange

194 Commercial Rd
Prahran VIC 3181
Phone 03/9510 3654
Fax 03/9521 3370
Web www.redorange.com.au
This stylish establishment is a great
place to refuel as you enjoy a

Commercial Road bender. It provides a good vantage point from which to watch the passing scene. A reliable eatery specializing in modern Australian food with Asian influences, it is licensed as a bar and restaurant, and also has a function room.

Open Tues–Fri 11.30am–late, Sat–Sun 10.30am–late
Cost Breakfast $8–10, lunch $15–20, dinner $20–25
Payment AmEx, Bankcard, Diners, EFTPOS, MasterCard, Visa

The Stokehouse

30 Jacka Boulevard
St Kilda VIC 3182
Phone 03/9525 5555
Fax 03/9525 5291

The Stokehouse enjoys pride of place on St Kilda's foreshore. The downstairs restaurant offers fresh pasta, seafood and grills in an airy casual environment. Upstairs (bookings are advisable) offers a more stylish à-la-carte menu. Both are fully licensed.

Open Daily noon–late
Cost Downstairs $20–30, upstairs $60–80
Payment AmEx, Bankcard, Diners, MasterCard, Visa

Wall Two 80

rear 280 Carlisle St
Balaclava VIC 3183
Phone 03/9593 8280
Fax 03/9593 8280

In the heart of Melbourne's Jewish district, this gay-owned space-age lunch and breakfast spot rubs shoulders with bagelries, Russian cake shops and kosher butchers. Voted 'best eating venue for under $15' by *Mietta's Eating and Drinking in Melbourne*, *Wall* offers innovative *pides*, soups, homemade baked beans and European cakes and pastries served with the finest Genoese coffee.

Open Daily 7.30am–6pm
Cost $7–15
Payment MasterCard, Bankcard, Visa

BARS AND CLUBS

There are far worse ways to spend a few hours in Melbourne than indulging in a **bar crawl**, taking in some of the city's ritziest hotel bars. Start with the piano bar at the *Windsor*, on Spring Street, opposite Parliament House – where you can also take afternoon tea in splendid surroundings. The bar at the *Sofitel*, in Collins Place, at the top end of Collins Street, is perched on the 35th floor (make sure you use the toilets – the **views** are phenomenal, you'll feel like you've walked onto the set of *Towering Inferno*).

Assuming you're still standing, *Hotel Australia*, in Collins Street, is worth a visit just because it was the first bar in Melbourne where 'people like us' used to meet. From the 1940s until more enlightened times, this bar provided a precarious sanctuary to nervous men in raincoats. It has been completely revamped, rebuilt and remodelled now, but its homo-history can still be sensed if the winds of time are blowing in the right direction!

INNER MELBOURNE

44

44 Lonsdale St
Melbourne VIC 3000
Phone 03/9654 9144
Fax 03/9654 9155
Email melb44@vicnet.net.au
Gender Mixed
This popular and hip bar is great for after-work drinks, but really goes off after 1am. There is house and garage music on weekends, while week nights are more mellow with lots of rare grooves played by popular local DJs.
Open Mon–Tues 4pm–1am,
Wed 4pm–3am, Thurs noon–3am,
Fri noon–5am, Sat 6pm–5am
Admission Free
Payment AmEx, Bankcard, EFTPOS, MasterCard, Visa

Barracuda

64 Smith St
Collingwood VIC 3066
Phone 03/9415 7123
Gender Mixed
Barracuda has a dance bar, pool room, gaming room and cocktail lounge. Friday is 'Grasshopper Night', offering a fun and friendly environment for Asian gay men, lesbians and their friends.
Open Daily 6pm–late
Admission Free
Payment Cash only

Blue Velvet

60 Smith St
Collingwood VIC 3066
Phone 03/9415 9800
Fax 03/9853 1990
Email bluevelvet@gothic.net.au
Web www.bluevelvet.com.au
Gender Mixed
This bar and nightclub attracts an eclectic, unconventional and theatrical crowd. There are three rooms, two bars, dancefloor and DJs. 'Software' (on Thursdays) offers a hip way to computer network and a great way to mix technology and entertainment. Friday's is 'Belfry', with industrial, gothic and alternative-music imports only. Saturday night is party night. Poetry readings are also held each month. Check out the Web site for specific events and contemporary art exhibits.
Open Thurs–Sat 8pm–late
Admission Free
Payment Bankcard, MasterCard, Visa

DTs

164 Church St
Richmond VIC 3121
Phone 03/9428 5724
Fax 03/9428 5724
Gender Mixed
DTs is an unpretentious watering hole for poofs and dykes, featuring occasional drag shows, pool music

and videos. On Sunday afternoon relax with friends (old or new) and a few beers.
Open Mon–Fri 4pm–1am, Sat 2pm–1am, Sun 2pm–11pm
Admission Free
Payment Bankcard, EFTPOS, MasterCard, Visa

Gay Trade Bar
9 Peel St
Collingwood VIC 3066
Phone 03/9417 6700
Fax 03/9417 7155
Email opsmanager@rabbit.com.au
Gender Mixed
At the *Gay Trade Bar* you'll find an Internet café, DJ and dancefloor, pool table, music videos and gay backpackers' accommodation.
Open Mon 5pm–noon, Tues 5pm–1am, Sat–Sun noon–1am
Admission Free
Payment EFTPOS

Gin Palace
190 Little Collins St
(enter via Russell Place)
Melbourne VIC 3000
Phone 03/9654 0533
Fax 03/9654 0522
Gender Mixed
This sophisticated martini bar has a cosy lounge ambience, eclectic 20th-century modern gothic furniture and friendly table service. A great place to enjoy kitschy and mellow music in a playful and relaxed atmosphere and what a place to stop in after dinner – with 24 types of gin, 20 scotches, 12 cognacs, 12 vodkas, local and imported beers, a wide range of champagne, and cigars. Friday night gets very busy.

Open Daily 4pm–3am
Admission Free
Payment AmEx, Bankcard, Diners, EFTPOS, MasterCard, Visa

Glasshouse Hotel
51–55 Gipps St
Collingwood VIC 3066
Phone 03/9419 4748
Gender Mostly women
There's a bar and pool table and food from Wednesday to Sunday (when there is entertainment all day and Sunday roast). Karaoke is on Thursday and DJs on Friday.
Open Mon–Thurs 5pm–1am, Fri–Sun 24 hours
Admission Free
Payment Cash only

Hard Candy @ Billboard
162 Little Bourke St
Melbourne VIC 3000
Phone 0418 377 227 or 0412 331 065
Gender Mixed
This club features progressive to hard house, nu NRG, power trance, rare grooves and club classics and is patronized by a really uplifting (though not specifically gay) dance-dedicated crowd.
Open Fri 11pm–10am
Admission $10
Payment Cash only

Illusions Theatre Restaurant
26 Errol St
North Melbourne VIC 3051
Phone 03/9348 9488
Gender Mixed
Drag shows and four-course dinners feature at this theatre-restaurant on Friday and Saturday. Bookings advised.

Open Fri & Sat from 7pm
Cost $38 Fri, $44 Sat
Payment Cash only

Laird Hotel

149 Gipps St
Abbotsford VIC 3067
Phone 03/9417 2832
Fax 03/9417 2109
Email hotel@laird.com.au
Web www.lairdhotel.com
Gender Men
Men in leather, denim and uniforms
frequent this headquarters of
Melbourne's leather community, but
it remains a friendly venue. Buzz cuts
are available on Saturday night, if you
feel in need of a trim.
Open Sun–Thurs 5pm–1am;
Fri & Sat 5pm–3am
Admission Free
Payment AmEx, Bankcard, Diners,
EFTPOS, MasterCard, Visa

The Laundry

50 Johnston St
Fitzroy VIC 3065
Phone 03/9419 6115
Fax 03/9419 7111
Gender Mixed
In the heart of the lesbian district,
this groovy lounge bar has a 70s
feel with regular DJs playing a range
of rare grooves and techno. Upstairs
there is a dance floor, while
downstairs is more of a chill-out
space. *The Laundry* also hosts
theatrical productions and live
bands. Snack foods are available.
Open Daily 3pm–3am
Admission Cover charge Fri & Sat
Payment Cash only

Peel Dance Bar

113 Wellington St (cnr Peel St)
Collingwood VIC 3066
Phone 03/9419 4762
Fax 03/9416 0474
Gender Mostly men
The last stop in Melbourne for many
disco fans, this is the place to go late
for good long all-night boogie,
especially if you like handbags or
taking to the podium. The shows on
Friday and Saturday feature drag or
exotic male dancers. You haven't
experienced gay Melbourne until
you've wound up at the *Peel*.
Open Wed–Sun 10pm–dawn
Admission $5 after 11pm Fri & Sat
Payment EFTPOS

Q&A (Builders Arms)

Builders Arms, 211 Gertrude St
Fitzroy VIC 3065
Phone 03/9419 0818
Gender Mixed
Funky Thursday night at the *Builders
Arms* isn't called 'Q&A' (Queer &
Alternative) for nothing. If you want
to meet political radical poofs or
dykes, this is probably the place. Lots
of piercings and dreadlocks and heaps
of queer fun.
Open Thurs 8pm–1am
Admission Free
Payment Bankcard, EFTPOS,
MasterCard, Visa

Rochester Hotel

202 Johnston St
Fitzroy VIC 3065
Phone 03/9416 3133
Gender Mixed
This is a popular bar for gays, lesbians
and their friends with special events

throughout the week (student night is Thursday, karaoke is Friday, drag shows and guest DJs on Saturday). Check the gay newspapers for up-to-date listings.
Open Wed–Thurs 3pm–1am, Fri–Sat 3pm–3am
Admission Free
Payment Cash only

Salon Kitty

Upstairs, 64 Smith St
Collingwood VIC 3066
Phone 0416 243 195
Email lawhite@optusnet.com.au
Gender Mostly women
A funky lounge for women of all ages to meet and groove.
Open Fri–Sat 9pm–3am
Admission Free
Payment Cash only

Star Hotel

176 Hoddle St
Collingwood VIC 3066
Phone 03/9417 2696
Fax 03/9417 2696
Gender Mixed
This friendly northside venue has the real feel of a gay/lesbian local with theme nights ('Lotus Night' for Asians and friends on Wednesday, Thursday is mixed bootscoot, Friday is 'Bear Night', Sunday is a 60s 'Retro Night'), but everyone is welcome every night.
Open Wed–Thurs & Sun 7pm–1am, Fri–Sat 7pm–3am
Admission $5 after 9pm Wed, cover charge may apply on specific nights
Payment AmEx, Bankcard, EFTPOS, MasterCard, Visa

Melbourne's Drag Queens

Miss Candee

Queen mother of the clubs, Miss Candee holds court from Thursday night through till Monday night at just about all (or so it seems) of Melbourne's bars. Jump onto her roller-coaster and travel the highs and lows of a weekend. Those with heart conditions should exercise extreme caution under the influence of this Damsel of Drag.

Paris

Paris must have shares in Frederick's of Hollywood. This gal has got it goin' on. From Geisha to Gidget, Paris is the one with 'The Look'. Never without a witticism or a kind word of encouragement, Paris, like her namesake, is an experience you'll remember forever.

Rita LeCoqueta

This girl just screams supermodel! If she wears feathers around her neck, betcha Naomi will be draped in them the week after. If she throws a star turn one week, Linda will follow. If she collapses on a dancefloor, you can bet your bottom dollar Kate will hit the deck a day or two later! Rita, with Paris, rules the roost at the *Market* (p.240), where all of Melbourne's beauties perch themselves for a view of the action.

Zoe Knox

Mistress of the Dark, Zoe Knox's Goth-meets-New-Romantic style would be comfortable in the company of Pete Burns, Boy George or Marianne Faithful. Zoe is a late, late, late-night girl. At her best just before dawn.

Millie Minogue

The party princess of Melbourne is a great mate of Molly Meldrum, Australia's most famous music guru. The Millie and Molly travelling sideshow can be seen on a regular basis at the more ritzy nightspots around town. Known as 'The Unsinkable Millie Minogue', this little diva just doesn't stop. Find her on the bar-top Friday nights at *DIVA* (p.238).

Doreen Manganine

Having perfected lip-synch, Doreen has now moved on to live vocals. Her simmering style has earned her a place at the top of the heap performing regularly all around town.

Miss Jane

Miss Jane presides over her own bar at *Dome* (p.238) on Saturday nights. With almost militant charisma, she plays mother to a bevy of young, emerging starlets whom she parades like pussy cats up and down her bar, while Jane herself commands attention like no other.

Tootsie

Certifiably the oldest drag queen in the southern hemisphere and with the wooden false teeth to prove it, Tootsie took a stage dive to stardom from the bar at *Virgin Mary's* (now *Chihuahua's*) and landed downstream at the *Greyhound Hotel* (affectionately known as 'The Hound'– one look at the Saturday night show and you'll see why). She can't sing, she can't dance, she can't even see, but one thing's for sure – she can drink!

Dulcie Du Jour

Still the Grande Dame of Drag, Dulcie's booming style has the sophistication of a slops bucket, and a stage presence akin to a herd of buffaloes. Don't miss!

Feral Beral

As her name suggests, she's out there! The newest, brightest, kookiest kid on the block, she's trailer-park trash and knows how to sell it. Beral and her mates, Debbie Dole Bludger and Miss Shitty, can be caught in action at 'Homosexuelle', on Sunday nights, at the *Prince of Wales* (p.241).

Sara Pax
A gender-bender-stupenda! With a look of steel, but a heart of warm apple pie, Sara Pax pushes the envelope – just far enough. Her vamp-drag Barbarella features and post-punk fixtures will take your breath away. A whore with so much more.

Tony 2000
Tony 2000 assaults Melbourne clubland with her tricks of the turntable – mixin' it and movin' through the DJ scene like a Peter Pan on acid (or should that be Wendy?). She's got gigs goin' on all over town causing a stiletto-stompin' stampede on dancefloors, or wherever she casts her spell.

Brenton Geyer

PRAHRAN AND ST KILDA

161
Upstairs, 161 High St (cnr Chapel and High streets)
Prahran VIC 3181
Phone 03/9533 8433
Gender Mixed
161's cool scene is popular with the over 25s. It has groovy 70s furniture, fish tanks, dance floor and DJs.
Open Thurs–Sun 4pm–6am
Admission Free
Payment Cash only

AM: PM
138 Commercial Rd
Prahran VIC 3181
Phone 03/9629 3872
Gender Mixed
This is an all-day disco–dancing recovery spot for folks who just don't know when to go home.
Open Sun 6am–6pm

Admission Free
Payment Cash only

Chihuahua's
199 Commercial Rd
South Yarra VIC 3141
Phone 03/9829 6611
Gender Mixed
This dance bar has become quite an icon. It first became famous through the courts as it tried to keep its original name (*Virgin Mary's*) and then there was a mysterious fire-bombing which gutted the original interior. Still, it has risen from the ashes to provide more hours of glamorous pumping disco fun and Sunday recoveries and it is a great place to watch Melbourne's young, buff and beautiful strut their stuff.
Open Thurs–Sun 6pm–late
Admission Free
Payment Cash only

DIVA

153 Commercial Rd
South Yarra VIC 3141
Phone 03/9824 2800
Gender Mixed
A mixed gay and straight crowd of
fun-loving people looking gorgeous
frequents this intimate little cocktail
bar. When this place goes off, we're
talking barmen and drag queens
dancing on the bar, while everyone
else sings along. Excellent fun.
Open Tues–Sat 6pm–3am,
Sun 6pm–1am
Admission Free
Payment Cash only

Dome

19 Commercial Rd
South Yarra VIC 3141
Phone 03/9529 8966
Fax 03/9529 8977
Email thedome@bigpond.com.au
Gender Mixed
Hard and fast dance music runs right
through the weekend at the *Dome*,
starting with 'Skin and Queer Night'
on Saturday at Jane's Bar – a venue
within a venue.
Open Sat 10pm–Sun 2pm
Admission $15
Payment EFTPOS

Freakazoid

Chevron Hotel, cnr Commercial and
St Kilda roads (enter from rear of 519
St Kilda Rd)
Melbourne VIC 3000
Phone 03/9510 1281
Gender Mixed
Definitely a must for all-night ravers,
this groovy scene has guest DJs and

comfy lounge chairs. You may have to
queue to get in.
Open Sat midnight–Sun noon
Admission Free
Payment Cash only

Globe Back Bar

218 Chapel St (enter from back of
Globe Café)
Prahran VIC 3181
Phone 03/9510 8693
Fax 03/9529 1288
Email globe@vicnet.net.au
Web www.citysearch.com.au/
mel/globecafe
Gender Mixed
This funky laid-back bar offers a
casual dinner menu and a hip and
cosy spot to have a quiet drink
with friends.
Open Wed–Sat 7.30pm–1am
Admission Free
Payment AmEx, Bankcard, Diners,
MasterCard, Visa

Greyhound Hotel

1 Brighton Rd (cnr Carlisle St)
St Kilda VIC 3182
Phone 03/9534 4189
Fax 03/9534 4274
Gender Mixed
The *Greyhound* or 'Hound'
(sometimes even affectionately called
the 'Dirty Hound' or 'Filthy Hound')
is a neighbourhood pub which is
pretty straight throughout the week,
but has a big drag show on Saturday
nights when it gets packed.
Open Mon–Fri noon–1am,
Sat noon–3am, Sun noon–11am
Admission $5 Sat
Payment EFTPOS

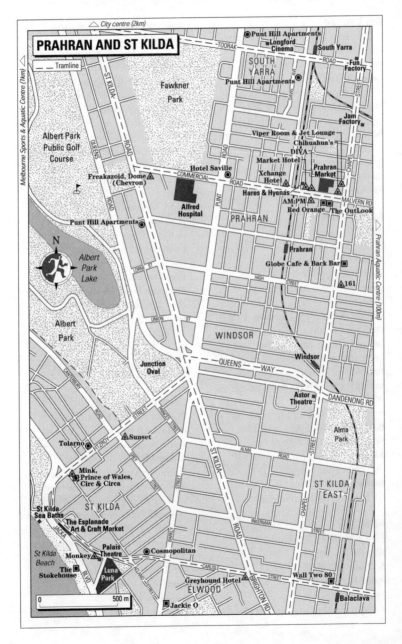

△ City centre (2km)

PRAHRAN AND ST KILDA

— Tramline

Melbourne Sports & Aquatic Centre (1km)

TOORAK

◉ Punt Hill Apartments
■ Longford Cinema
■ South Yarra

SOUTH YARRA

ROAD

Fun Factory

Fawkner Park

Punt Hill Apartments

DAVIS AVE

STREET

Jam Factory

Viper Room & Jet Lounge
Chihuahua's
DIVA
Market Hotel
Hotel Saville ◉
Xchange Hotel
Prahran Market

CHAPEL

Freakazoid, Dome (Chevron) △

COMMERCIAL   ROAD

PUNT   ROAD

Hares & Hyenas △
AM:PM △   □■
Red Orange △ The OutLook

MALVERN RD

Albert Park Public Golf Course

QUEENS   ROAD

Alfred Hospital

PRAHRAN

Punt Hill Apartments ◉

■ Prahran
Globe Cafe & Back Bar ■

N

Albert Park Lake

LORNE ST

HIGH   STREET

△161

UNION   ST

Albert Park

WINDSOR

Junction Oval

QUEENS   WAY

Windsor

Astor Theatre

DANDENONG RD

Alma Park

CANTERBURY   ROAD

HIGH   STREET

PRINCES STREET

ALMA   ROAD

CHAPEL   STREET

ST KILDA EAST

Tolarno ◉   △Sunset

FITZROY   STREET

ST   KILDA   ROAD

Mink, ■
Prince of Wales, Circ & Circa

ST KILDA

St Kilda Sea Baths ■
The Esplanade Art & Craft Market

BARKLY   STREET

INKERMAN   STREET

JACKA

Palais Theatre
St Kilda Beach   Monkey △
Cosmopolitan ◉

BLVD

The Stokehouse ■
Luna Park △

Greyhound Hotel △
ELWOOD

CARLISLE   STREET

ROAD   STREET

BRIGHTON RD

Wall Two 80 ■

Balaclava

■ Jackie O

0   500 m

△ Prahran Aquatic Centre (100m)

Jet Lounge

373 Chapel St (at the Viper Room)
Prahran VIC 3141
Phone 0417 267 553 or 0411 187 755
Gender Mixed

This funky transit lounge or all-night
stopover is home to the self-appointed
cool and groovy. The door policy can
be selective, but once you're in – fasten
seatbelts, disarm doors and cross-check.
Open Fri 9pm–late
Admission $5
Payment EFTPOS

Market Hotel

143 Commercial Rd
South Yarra VIC 3141
Phone 03/9826 0933
Fax 03/9826 8827
Email sdrummond@jade.net
Gender Mixed

The *Market Hotel* has the best drag
shows (especially on Thursday) and
lots of dancing, great lighting and
lasers on a multi-level moving dance
floor with a viewing balcony and
multiple bars. The cocktail lounge
offers patrons the option of renting
their own private liquor cabinets.
Open Mon–Wed 5pm–1am, Thurs
5pm–3am, Fri–Sun 5pm–6am
Admission Cover charge (up to $10,
depending on the night)
Payment AmEx, Bankcard, Diners,
EFTPOS, MasterCard, Visa

Mink

Prince of Wales, 2B Acland St
(Cnr Fitzroy St)
St Kilda VIC 3182
Phone 03/9536 1199
Fax 03/9536 1175
Email thedesk@theprince.com.au
Web www.theprince.com.au
Gender Mixed

Mink is tucked away behind the main
bar of the *Prince of Wales*. Descend
into a candle-lit tavern that's like
being in a chamber of linked caves.
Historically, in the days of 6pm
closing, this bar used to serve sly grog
after hours. *Mink* now shelters
Melbourne's bohemians and black-
clad intelligentsia. The vodka bar is
legendary, offering every brand
you've ever heard of – and a few
more besides. Be waited on, call
over the cigar person and see who's
in the VIP booths. Pure class this
joint and it has a fabulous
dinner/supper menu as well.
Open Daily 6pm–3am
Admission Free, but when it's crowded
there are door bitches
Payment AmEx, Bankcard, Diners,
MasterCard, Visa

Monkey

The Palace (rear of Palace Hotel,
next to the Palais Theatre)
Lower Esplanade
St Kilda VIC 3182
Phone 0419 897 809 or 03/9534 0655
Web www.monkey.com.au
Gender Mixed

Come here for groovy sounds and a
hip cool crowd. There is serious
dancing from midnight until dawn.
One-off dance events sometimes take
over the whole Palace Complex and
their groove is so popular that they
often hit the road with it and do
special interstate nights.
Open Sun 11pm–dawn
Admission $12
Payment Cash only

Prince of Wales ('The Prince')

2 Acland St (cnr Fitzroy St)
St Kilda VIC 3182
Phone 03/9536 1177
Email thedesk@theprince.com.au
Web www.theprince.com.au
Gender Mixed

The *Prince of Wales* has been a part of queer life in Melbourne forever. In addition to housing *Circa* (p.229) and *Mink* (see opposite), the *Prince* hosts 'Homosexuelle' upstairs on Sunday (8pm–late). And then there's the grungy public bar on the corner and the pooftah bar downstairs at the back, where some of Melbourne's most famous drag divas could give you some haircurling history of the place. And now that it has the last word in designer accommodation upstairs, you could easily spend a most enjoyable weekend without leaving the building!
Open Daily: main bar 10am–late; hours for other bars vary
Admission Free
Payment EFTPOS

Sunset

16 Grey St
St Kilda VIC 3182
Phone 03/9534 9205
Fax 03/9534 9205
Gender Mixed

DJs and live bands are to be found at this queer-friendly bar. Bent TV run a gay night on Monday with beers for a dollar. Wednesday is 'Comedy Night' and the bar offers a cosy retro ambience.
Open Daily 5pm–5am
Admission $5 after midnight Fri–Sat
Payment AmEx, Bankcard, Diners, EFTPOS, MasterCard, Visa

Viper Room

373 Chapel St
Prahran VIC 3141
Phone 03/9827 1771
Fax 03/9804 8540
Email info@viperoom.com.au
Gender Mixed

This mixed dance club is for serious party people who like to dance the night away to progressive trance and dance or uplifting house with vocals. The *Viper Room* specializes in the most popular DJs. The ambience is relaxed, but up-tempo with plenty of space to chill-out.
Open Fri–Sat 11pm–8am
Admission $15 Fri, $8 Sat
Payment Cash only

Xchange Hotel

119 Commercial Rd
South Yarra VIC 3141
Phone 03/9867 5144
Fax 03/9820 9603
Email xchange@xchange.com.au
Web www.xchange.com.au
Gender Mostly men

There is top drag entertainment from Wednesday to Sunday at the 'SexChange', as it's often called. *Xchange* hosts Mr Gay Melbourne and occasional talent contests. It has a huge video screen with unedited video clips not seen elsewhere. There is a dancefloor, pool table and comfortable chill-out lounge area. This is a popular after-work drinking hole, as well as a cruisy dance bar later on.
Open Sun–Thurs 2pm–1am (or later), Fri–Sat 2pm–3am
Admission Free
Payment AmEx, Bankcard, Diners, EFTPOS, MasterCard, Visa

55 Porter Street

55 Porter St
Prahran VIC 3181
Phone 03/9529 5166
Gender Men

This popular sauna is close to all the Commercial Road venues. It offers two floors of cruising with dry and wet saunas, solarium, spa, gymnasium, sling rooms, in-house masseurs, coffee bar and video lounge.
Open Mon–Thurs 6pm–7am,
Fri 2pm–Mon 7am
Admission $12 before 9pm, $15 after
Payment AmEx, Bankcard, Diners, EFTPOS, MasterCard, Visa

Bay City Caulfield

482D Glenhuntly Rd (upstairs)
Elsternwick VIC 3185
Phone 03/9528 2381
Gender Men

This cosy sauna offers dry and wet rooms, spa, video lounge, coffee bar and cruise space. *Melbourne Wankers* (www.home.aone.net.au/melbournewankers) meet here at 7pm for 8pm on the second and fourth Monday of each month: join dozens of friendly guys for massage, caressing and conversation in a non-discriminatory, totally nude environment (full nudity is mandatory). Guys mingle and participate in this totally safe-sex activity based on the worldwide jack-off group policy of 'No Lips Below the Hips'. Because of the extravagant use of oil, any other sexual activity is totally out – oil and condoms do not

mix. The atmosphere at *Wankers* meetings is vastly different to the bath-houses and bar mentality, with low background music and dimmed lighting.
Open Sun–Thurs noon–1am,
Fri–Sat noon–4am
Admission $10 before 2pm, $12 after
Payment Bankcard, MasterCard, Visa

Bay City Club Seaford

2/16 Cumberland Drive
Seaford VIC 3198
Phone 03/9776 9279
Gender Men

This bayside sauna operates every day of the year. It offers a dry and wet sauna, spa, gymnasium, masseur, two TV lounges (one with in-house movies), cubicles, sling rooms, solarium, orgy room, outside lawn area and coffee shop.
Open Daily noon–2am
Admission $12
Payment Amex, Bankcard, MasterCard, Visa

Club 80

10 Peel St
Collingwood VIC 3066
Phone 03/9417 2182
Fax 03/9416 0474
Email club80@qmail.com.au
Web www.club80.net
Gender Men

Club 80 has become Australia's largest and most famous dry venue. It offers almost unimaginable acres to cruise in over several floors. The movie lounge shows latest release videos on a huge screen, there's a free coffee bar, cyber lounge with 12 stations to play on and plenty of private rooms to play in. The loft offers special heavy-duty rooms.

Open Mon–Fri 5pm–8am; Sat, Sun & public holidays 2pm–8am
Admission $15
Payment Bankcard, EFTPOS, MasterCard, Visa

Club X

216 Swanston St
Melbourne VIC 3000
Phone 03/9663 8094

with branches at:

74 Acland St
St Kilda VIC 3182
Phone 03/9534 5835;

172 Nicholson St
Footscray VIC 3011
Phone 03/9687 4421
Gender Men
Adult bookshop with 'ram lounge' offering adult movies and back-room activities.
Open Daily 9am–late
Payment AmEx, Bankcard, EFTPOS, MasterCard, Visa

Spa Guy

551B and 553 Victoria St
Abbotsford VIC 3067
Phone 03/9428 5494
Gender Men
Besides the spa, there are wet and dry saunas, cubicles, two TV lounges and an outdoor area.
Open Mon–Thurs 5pm–1am, Fri–Sun 4pm–1am
Admission $12
Payment Cash only

Steamworks

279 LaTrobe St
Melbourne VIC 3000
Phone 03/9602 4493
Fax 03/9640 0652
Web www.steamworks.com.au
Gender Men
Australia's largest sauna boasts a heated pool, dry and wet sauna, spa, gym, video lounge and coffee bar. It also provides an Internet lounge, video porn lounge, fully licensed bar and restaurant serving full meals, four levels of cruising, sling rooms, private rooms with video monitors, water sports and heavy-duty areas. In-house masseurs are available. On Wednesday, by appointment, there are free blood tests and counselling. 'Leather and Fetish Night' is held on the first Friday of the month.
Open Mon–Thurs noon–5am, Fri–Sun & public holidays 24 hours
Admission $17.60
Payment Bankcard, EFTPOS, MasterCard, Visa

Subway Sauna

Vault 13, Banana Alley, Flinders St
Melbourne VIC 3000
Phone 03/9620 7766
Gender Men
Melbourne's newest sauna is located in the old riverside storage vaults right by the Yarra River, opposite the casino. It offers wet sauna, dry sauna, spa, two mazes with cubicles, sling room, in-house video lounge and snack bar.
Open Daily (24 hours)
Admission $10–15
Payment AmEx, Bankcard, EFTPOS, MasterCard, Visa

Ten Plus
59 Porter St
Prahran VIC 3181
Phone 03/9525 0469
Fax 03/9777 0299
Gender Men
Close to the Commercial Road
venues, this clean dry venue offers
indoor and outdoor cruising, private
rooms, latest-release Champion
videos, popular movies, coffee bar,
Internet and free chat lines.
Open Mon–Thurs 5pm–4am, Fri
5pm–8am; Sat 2pm–Mon 4pm
Admission $5 Mon, $10 Tues (two for
the price of one) & Wed–Sun
Payment Bankcard, EFTPOS,
MasterCard, Visa

ADULT SHOPS, PARTY AND FETISH WEAR

The Beat Bookshop
157 Commercial Rd
South Yarra VIC 3141
Phone 03/9827 8748
Gender Mixed
Melbourne's original gay adult
bookshop carries a huge range of
adult toys, international magazines
and videos. There's a video lounge
and upstairs cruise area.
Open Sun–Thurs 10am–8pm,
Fri–Sat 9am–2am
Payment AmEx, Bankcard, EFTPOS,
MasterCard, Visa

Bliss
1st Floor, 245 Lonsdale St
Melbourne VIC 3000
Phone 03/9639 1522
Fax 03/9639 1544
Email bliss@netspace.net.au
Web www.bliss4women.com
Gender Women
Owned and staffed by women, *Bliss*
offers a comfortable, safe environment
for women to shop for products
which both inform and enhance
sexual pleasure: books, aromatherapy,
lingerie, sex-toys, videos and safe-sex
products. There is also a mail order
service and catalogue.

Open Mon–Fri 11am–7pm,
Sat 11am–5pm
Payment AmEx, Bankcard, EFTPOS,
MasterCard, Visa; cheque

Eagle Leather
58 Hoddle St or PO Box 202
Abbotsford VIC 3067
Phone 03/9417 2100
Fax 03/9416 4235
Email admin@eagleleather.com.au
Web www.eagleleather.com.au
Gender Mostly men
This is the place to get your leather
and latex, adult toys, bondage and
SM gear, accessories, books and
videos. Secondhand leather and
latex clothing, toys and accessories
are available, as well as a repair and
cleaning service. Gay-owned and
-operated, *Eagle Leather* also gives
seminars and workshops on
bondage, discipline, electric sex and
sexual health and safety. It handles
ticketing and information for
selected leather, fetish and BDSM
events throughout Australia.
Open Sun–Thurs noon–6pm, Fri–Sat
noon–9pm
Payment AmEx, Bankcard, Diners,
EFTPOS, MasterCard, Visa

ARTS

Alsounds
PO Box 142
Coburg VIC 3058
Phone 03/9380 5538
Gender Mixed
This gay and lesbian choir meets each
Wednesday for practice.

Film Buffs Society
PO Box 308
Essendon VIC 3040
Phone Geoff 03/9578 5504 or David
03/9827 7353
Gender Mixed
This group offers monthly video
evenings, outings, musical afternoons
and a periodic newsletter for lovers
of movies made between 1930
and 1960.

Melbourne Gay and Lesbian Chorus
GPO Box 813F
Melbourne VIC 3001
Phone 03/9532 9066
Fax 03/9572 4948
Email mglc@ozemail.com.au
Web www.ozemail.com.au/~mglc/
Gender Mixed
Australia's longest-running gay and
lesbian choir is now over 10 years old.
With two CDs (*Kaleidoscope* and *In
Flight*), the MGLC welcomes those
interested in singing, as well as public
relations, sponsorship, administration
and production assistance. Auditions
take place two or three times per year,
with two major events annually and
loads of community events.

BOOKSHOPS

Chronicles
91 Fitzroy St
St Kilda VIC 3182
Phone 03/9537 2677
Fax 03/9537 2733
Email chronicles@pacific.net.au
This stylish shop stocks a great range
of gay and lesbian material, as well as
imported cards, CDs and mags.
Open Daily 10am–10pm
Payment AmEx, Bankcard, Diners,
EFTPOS, MasterCard, Visa; cheque

Come-by-Chance Bookshop
81 Gamon St
Yarraville VIC 3013
Phone 03/9396 1121
Fax 03/9396 1121
This new and secondhand gay and

lesbian book specialist offers a mail-
order service.
Open Mon–Sat 9am–6pm, Sun
10am–5pm
Payment Cash only

Hares & Hyenas
135 Commercial Rd
South Yarra VIC 3141
Phone 03/9824 0110
Fax 03/9824 2839
Email hares@interdomain.net.au
Web www.hares-hyenas.com.au
This much-cherished gay and lesbian
bookstore is located in the heart of
Melbourne's gay mile. It stocks the
city's best range of gay and lesbian
titles, including newspapers, as well as
cards and lesbian/gay merchandise

and videos. It hosts readings, book signings, and sells tickets for many of the dance parties and gay and lesbian events. Check out their Web site for reviews and events. *Hares & Hyenas* is a great first stop for information and leaflets when visiting Melbourne. It also provides mail order.
Open Mon–Sat 10am–8pm, Sun noon–6pm
Payment AmEx, Bankcard, Diners, EFTPOS, MasterCard, Visa

Spellbound Books
460 Lygon St
Brunswick East VIC 3057
Phone 03/9386 5044
Fax 03/9386 8392
The bookshop has a strong leaning towards feminism and lesbian fiction, but also stocks some gay fiction.
Open Mon–Sat 10am–5.30am, Sun 11am–4pm
Payment AmEx, Bankcard, Diners, EFTPOS, MasterCard, Visa

NEWSPAPERS AND MAGAZINES

Brother/Sister (Victoria)
PO Box 2934
Fitzroy VIC 3065
Phone 03/9429 8844
Fax 03/9429 8966
Email brosisvic_satellitemedia.com.au
Web www.brothersister.com.au
Gender Mixed
Published fortnightly and available free from gay/lesbian-friendly venues and shops, this newspaper offers the latest in gay, lesbian, bi and transgender news, entertainment, culture and clubbing, with plenty of gossip and personals too.
Cost Free street distribution, $50 annual subscription

Lesbiana
PO Box 260
Northcote VIC 3070
Phone 03/9489 9474 or 0407 347 403
Fax 03/9489 9474
Email lesbiana@werple.net.au
Gender Women
Lesbiana is published at the beginning of each month and is read by 2,500

lesbians throughout Victoria. The magazine is packed with insightful news and views on current lesbian affairs. It offers articles on love, life and all the other wonders of 'lesbiana' and has a thorough listing of community events, as well as a social calendar for each month.
Cost $4.95 per issue, $54.80 annual subscription

Melbourne Community Voice
PO Box 2849
Fitzroy MDC VIC 3065
Phone 0413 706 462
Email momo99@bigpond.com
Web www.egroups.com/group/qmelb
Gender Mixed
Published weekly, available free from gay/lesbian-friendly venues and shops or by subscription, *Melbourne Community Voice* is filled with news, politics and a round-up of current gay and lesbian affairs.
Cost Free street distribution, annual subscriptions available
Payment Cheque

OUT Magazine Australia

73 Gertrude St
Fitzroy VIC 3065
Phone 03/9415 6585
Fax 03/9419 1644
Email outartwork@rabbit.com.au
Web www.gaynet.com.au/out

Gender Mixed
This monthly lifestyle magazine with
community listings and gossip is
available at most gay-friendly
businesses.
Cost Free street distribution,
$55 annual subscription

BEACHES AND POOLS

City of Melbourne Baths

420 Swanston St
Melbourne VIC 3000
Phone 03/9663 5888
Fax 03/9639 2048
Gender Mixed
This was the first public baths in
Melbourne. It is considered very cool
and hip and is right in the heart of the
city. Housed in a heritage-listed
building, it offers a wide range of
facilities, including water aerobics,
work out, swimming, spa, sauna,
gym, sundeck, aerobics and massage.
Open Mon–Fri 6am–10pm,
Sat–Sun 8am–6pm
Cost $3 swim, $13 casual gym (includes
spa & sauna), $10 casual aerobics
Payment Bankcard, EFTPOS,
MasterCard, Visa

Fitzroy Pool

Alexander Parade
Fitzroy VIC 3065
Phone 03/9417 6493
Gender Mixed
This 50m heated pool has eight lanes
for lap swimming and a baby pool
with a water slide. Yoga classes are
held here and this is Victoria's major
triathlon training centre.
Open Nov–March: Mon–Fri

6am–8pm, Sat–Sun 8am–6pm
Cost $3.10
Payment Bankcard, MasterCard, Visa

Half Moon Bay (Black Rock)

Beach Rd
Black Rock VIC 3193
Gender Mixed
This popular gay beach is about 12km
south of the city, on the eastern shore
of Port Phillip Bay. There are plenty
of winding tracks to lose yourself in;
the paths to the left of the car park
offer the best route to the beach.

Harold Holt Swim Centre

Cnr High & Edgar streets
Malvern VIC 3144
Phone 03/9824 8800
Fax 03/9824 8356
Email hhsc@rans.com.au
Gender Mixed
Possibly the only swimming pool in
the world to be named after a prime
minister who drowned, this pool
offers lovely lawns for sunbathers and
a very high diving tower, if you're
game enough. There is a 50m heated
outdoor pool, a 25m indoor pool, a
diving pool, spa, sauna and a range of
exercise classes.
Open Mon–Thurs 5.45am–8.45pm,

Fri 7.45am–7.45pm, Sat
6am–6.45pm, Sun 7am–6.45pm
Cost $3 swim; $5.50 swim, spa &
sauna; $7.50 casual aerobics
Payment Bankcard, EFTPOS,
MasterCard, Visa

Kerferd Road Beach
Beach Rd
South Melbourne VIC 3205
Gender Mixed
This popular section of gay beach is
located at the end of Kerferd Road,
South Melbourne, and is famous for
its nickname 'Screech Beach' – a name
not undeserved! You'll find the area to
the west of the pier the most popular
area for boys sunning themselves.

Melbourne Sports and Aquatic Centre
Albert Rd
Albert Park VIC 3206
Phone 03/9926 1555
Fax 03/9926 1666
Email msac@msac.com.au
Gender Mixed
High, state-of-the-art body
enhancement facility with everything
for the modern athlete, as well as the
aquatic dilettante, from spa to sauna
and wave pool.

Open Mon–Fri 5.30am–8pm,
Sat–Sun 7am–8pm
Cost $4 swim, $7 sauna & spa
Payment Bankcard, EFTPOS,
MasterCard, Visa

Port Melbourne Beach
Beach Rd
Port Melbourne VIC 3207
Gender Mixed
The western end of Port Melbourne
beach offers plenty of opportunities
for male bathers and bike riders to
meet each other.

Prahran Aquatic Centre
41 Essex St
Prahran VIC 3181
Phone 03/9522 3248
Gender Mixed
This outdoor heated pool, spa and
sauna (with a view of the pool) is
where the Melbourne gay boys hang
out in summer, idling the time away
in the area known as the 'Pansy Patch'
– the grassy bit at the deep end of
the pool.
Open Oct–April only: Mon–Fri
6am–7.30pm (later on hot nights),
Sat–Sun 8am–6pm
Cost $3 swim; $5.50 swim, sauna & spa
Payment Cash only

BODY STUFF

Colts
33–35 Cato St
Prahran VIC 3181
Phone 03/9529 1900
Fax 03/9510 3800
Gender Mixed
This black and chrome body factory
will get you into shape. The chic

muscle set can be seen polishing up
their biceps here. There are weights
and warm-up machines, an outdoor
training area, steam room, spa,
aerobics classes, martial arts, yoga and
solarium. A naturopath is available by
appointment.
Open 24 hours

Cost $10 casual visit
Payment AmEx, Bankcard, Diners, EFTPOS, MasterCard, Visa

Gym & Tonic
180 Victoria Rd
Northcote VIC 3070
Phone 03/9510 4476
Gender Women
It's not an excuse to hang round the bar sipping martinis, but the first women-only gym in Melbourne offers personal trainers, a fully equipped weights room, sauna, nutritional advice, massage and cardio facilities.
Open Mon–Thurs 9am–8.30pm, Fri 9am–7.30pm, Sat 9am–3pm,

Sun noon–5pm
Cost $10 casual visit
Payment Bankcard, MasterCard, Visa

Piercing Urge
1st floor, 206 Commercial Rd
Prahran VIC 3181
Phone 03/9530 2244
Fax 03/9530 2427
Web www.thepiercingurge.com.au
Gender Mixed
Male and female piercers and a wide range of jewellery are available.
Open Mon–Wed 11am–7pm, Thurs–Fri 11am–8pm, Sat 10am–6pm
Payment AmEx, Bankcard, Diners, EFTPOS, MasterCard, Visa

MEDICAL

Carlton Clinic
88 Rathdowne St (near Elgin St)
Carlton VIC 3053
Phone 03/9347 9422
Fax 03/9349 2991
Email carclin@corplink.com.au
Web www.thecarltonclinic.com.au
Gender Mixed
This gay and lesbian medical practice offers acupuncture and counselling among its many services. There are male and female doctors available and appointments are preferred. Bulk billing for concession card holders.
Open Mon–Fri 8.30am–7pm, Sat–Sun 9.30am–12.30pm
Cost $30 per consultation
Payment Bankcard, EFTPOS, MasterCard, Visa; cheque

Melbourne Sexual Health Centre
580 Swanston St
Carlton VIC 3053
Phone 03/9347 0244
Gender Mixed
This free and confidential medical service is for people concerned about their sexual health or needing treatment for sexually transmitted diseases. No Medicare card is required. Phone for an appointment to avoid long waits.
Open Mon–Wed & Fri 9am–5pm, Thurs 10am–7pm

Middle Park Clinic
41 Armstrong St
Middle Park VIC 3206
Phone 03/9699 3758

Gender Mixed

This general medical practice offers a range of health services, including HIV, dietitian, podiatrist, counsellor and psychiatrist. Male and female practitioners are available.

Open Mon–Thurs 8.30am–6.30pm, Fri 8.30am–5.30pm, Sat–Sun 9am–noon
Cost $35 per consultation
Payment Bankcard, EFTPOS, MasterCard, Visa

COMMUNITY

18 and Under

6 Claremont St
South Yarra VIC 3141
Phone 03/9865 6700 or freecall 1800/134 840
Fax 03/9826 2700
Email jim_sotiropoulos@vicaids.asn.au
Web www.vicaids.asn.au
Gender Men

This support group for gay and bisexual guys 18 years and under meets monthly on Saturday afternoons in the city.
Open Mon–Fri 9am–5pm

Acceptance

PO Box 4214
Hoppers Crossing VIC 3029
Phone Bernie 03/9748 5688
Fax 03/9748 5688
Email accept@alphalink.com.au
Web www.alphalink.com.au/~accept
Gender Mixed

A gay and lesbian Catholic group which holds monthly masses at a central city location.

Alcoholics Anonymous

St Joseph's Hall (opposite the Jam Factory), Fitzgerald Street
South Yarra VIC 3141
Phone 03/9429 1833
Gender Mixed

This gay and lesbian *AA* group meets every Friday.

Aleph Melbourne

PO Box 696
South Yarra VIC 3141
Phone Michael 0417 595 541
Email alephmelb@geocities.com
Web www.alephmelb.welcome.to
Gender Men

Aleph Melbourne offers guidance, support and companionship for Jewish gay and bisexual men through social activities, confidential telephone and personal support. The group was formed in 1995 and currently has around 50 members from all walks of life. All members identify as gay and Jewish.

ALSO Canasta Pack

125 Raglan St
South Melbourne VIC 3205
Phone Michael 03/9690 5397
Email micgib@alphalink.com.au
Gender Mixed

Canasta players meet the last Wednesday of every month at the *Cricketers Arms Hotel*, Port Melbourne. Drinks, supper and partners are supplied, and learners are welcome.
Cost $15

ALSO Foundation

Community Centre, 1st floor, 35 Cato St
Prahran VIC 3181
Phone 03/9510 5569
Fax 03/9510 5699
Email also@also.org.au
Web www.also.org.au
Gender Mixed
This foundation presents
Melbourne's biggest dance parties
(New Year's Eve, Red Raw,
Resurrection and Winterdaze). The
funds raised go to supporting other
community groups through office
space, facilities, equipment and
financial assistance. It produces the
annual *ALSO Directory* – a complete
business and community directory for
gays and lesbians througout Victoria
(available from the *ALSO* office,
AIDS Council offices and *Hares &
Hyenas* bookshop). Its Web site
carries a comprehensive updated
guide to community groups around
the state.
Open Mon–Fri 9am–5pm
Cost Membership $25
Payment Cheque

AMBER (South Asian Gay Group)

Melbourne VIC 3000
Phone David Voon 03/9865 6700
Email david_voon@vicaids.asn.au
Gender Mixed
This group is for gays, lesbians and
bisexuals of South Asian origin.

Australian Lesbian and Gay Archives

PO Box 124
Parkville VIC 3052
Gender Mixed

This group collects a wide range
of material from groups and
individuals in order to preserve
our history. It welcomes donations
of relevent letters, magazines,
photos and so on.

Bound Men

PO Box 202
Abbotsford VIC 3067
Gender Men
This group is for men who enjoy
bondage.

Boyant

6 Claremont St
South Yarra VIC 3141
Phone 03/9865 6700 or freecall
1800/134 840
Fax 03/9826 2700
Email jim_sotiropoulos@vicaids.asn.au
Web www.vicaids.asn.au
Gender Men
Boyant is a *Victorian AIDS
Council/Gay Men's Health Centre*
youth project offering free and
confidential support for gay and
bisexual guys under 27 years of age.
Twice monthly meetings (Sunday
2pm–4.30pm) are organized, which
offer an opportunity to meet other
guys and stay up to date on safe-sex
information.
Open Mon–Fri 9am–5pm

Dare

PO Box 13
Prahran VIC 3181
Email daremelb@mailcity.com
Gender Women
This support and social group is for
women from minority racial, cultural
and ethnic backgrounds.

Dinner for Singles

Blackburn VIC 3130
Phone Christine 03/9893 3429 or
0409 258 096
Gender Women
Wine and dine with women, friendly
and romantic ambience; private
dinners held weekly.
Cost $25 for dinner, BYO drinks

Footy Poofs

Northcote VIC 3070
Email footypoofs@gray-lee.com
Web www.gray-lee.com
Gender Mostly men
Footy Poofs is a social organization for
gay members and fans of all AFL
clubs. Go to the Web site to subscribe
to their newsletter.

GAMMA (Gay and Married Men's Association)

Positive Living Centre, 46 Acland St
St Kilda VIC 3182
Phone 03/9376 8171
Gender Men
This support group for married and
previously married gay men holds a
meeting at 8pm on the last Monday of
each month.

Gay Asian Proud

6 Claremont St
South Yarra VIC 3141
Phone David Voon 03/9865 6700
Fax 03/9826 2700
Email david_voon@vicaids.asn.au
Web www.vicaids.asn.au
Gender Men
This fun and exciting workshop
group for gay Asian men will soon
prove you have plenty of friends and
are not alone. This is a *Victorian Aids*

Council/Gay Men's Health Centre
initiative. The free program runs on
evenings and weekends over several
weeks and involves workshops and
social events.
Open Mon–Fri 9am–5pm

Gay and Lesbian Entertainment Info

Phone freecall 1900 912 504
Gender Mixed
Give them a call to find out what's
happening around Melbourne.

Gay and Lesbian Immigration Task Force (GLITF)

PO Box 2387
Richmond South VIC 3121
Phone 03/9523 7864
Web www.glitf.org.au
Gender Mixed
Support and information for overseas
partners of Australian gays and
lesbians who are trying to stay in
Australia. A *GLITF* guide book for
couples is available for $20.

Gay and Lesbian Switchboard

35 Cato St
Prahran VIC 3181
Phone 03/9510 5488 or freecall
1800/631 493
Gender Mixed
The *Switchboard* welcomes calls from
lesbians, gays, bisexuals or transgender
people. Whether you're coming to terms
with your sexuality or having problems
with a health or discrimination issue,
Switchboard is there for a friendly chat. All
calls are anonymous and treated with the
strictest confidentiality.
Open Wed 2pm–10pm, Thurs–Tues
6pm–10pm

Gay Saints
Northcote VIC 3070
Email gaysaints@gray-lee.com
Web www.gray-lee.com
Gender Mostly men
This is a social organization for gay members (and fans) of the mighty St Kilda Saints Football Club.

GLOBE (Gay and Lesbian Organisation of Business and Enterprise)
PO Box 2063
Albert Park VIC 3206
Phone 03/9529 3020
Fax 03/9529 3020
Email globe@gaybusiness.com.au
Web www.gaybusiness.com.au/globe
Gender Mixed
This organization welcomes gay and lesbian businesspeople from all walks of life and holds dinner functions, featuring guest speakers, on the first Monday of the month. *GLOBE*'s 'Fruits in Suits' functions are held on the third Thursday of each month (6pm–8pm). The women's function 'Puss 'n' Boots' is held on the fourth Thursday of the month (6pm–8pm).
Cost Membership $66
Payment AmEx, Bankcard, Diners, MasterCard, Visa; cheque

Greek and Gay
6 Claremont St
South Yarra VIC 3141
Phone David Voon 03/9865 6700
Email greek_gay@hotmail.com
Gender Men
This discussion group and social network meets on the first and third Monday of the month.

HIV Community Support
Victorian AIDS Council, 6 Claremont St
South Yarra VIC 3141
Phone 03/9865 6700
Email plwhavic@netspace.net.au
Web www.gaynet.com.au/PLWHA/main.htm
Gender Mixed
Community support offers services to people living with HIV/AIDS. The services include personal and practical assistance at home, transport to medical appointments, as well as social and emotional support. Confidentiality is assured.

HIV Positive Peer Support
46 Acland St
St Kilda VIC 3182
Phone 03/9525 4455, 03/9865 6723 or freecall 1800/134 840
Email vic_perri@vicaids.asn.au
Web www.vicaids.asn.au
Gender Men
This service gives one-to-one support and referrals for HIV-positive men, as well as the chance to meet other men and share experiences in a supportive environment. Social activities, discussion groups and workshops are held regularly.

Jewish Lesbian Group of Victoria (JLGVIC)
PO Box 99
Fairfield VIC 3078
Phone Karen 03/9489 1130
Email jlgvic@hotmail.com
Gender Women
This women's social and support group meets monthly. Membership is open to all who identify as Jewish lesbians (it includes both secular and

religious members). It has a regular newsletter, holds social events, celebrates some Jewish holidays together and maintains a presence at Gay Pride, Sydney Mardi Gras and the Jewish Community Festival in Melbourne. Most of all *JLGVIC* hangs out together and has fun!
Cost Membership $10, plus $20 joining fee (first year only)

Koorie and Gay

6 Claremont St
South Yarra VIC 3141
Phone 03/9865 6700 or freecall 1800/134 840
Email enquiries@vicaids.asn.au
Web www.vicaids.asn.au
Gender Men

This *Victorian AIDS Council / Gay Men's Health Centre* initiative gives friendly and confidential support for indigenous gays, bisexuals and transgendered men in the form of monthly discussion groups and regular social gatherings.

Leather Action

PO Box 2125
Brighton North VIC 3186
Gender Men

Get on the leather gang's list and come to their next function.

Lesbian Open House

Collingwood VIC 3066
Web www.ozemail.com.au/~mcnosh/
Gender Women

This discussion group gets together twice monthly (visit the Web site for dates) upstairs at 18 Smith Street, Fitzroy from 8pm–9.30pm. Great for those coming out or women keen to broaden their group of friends.

Long Yang Club

PO Box 2016
Richmond South VIC 3121
Phone 03/9857 4696 or 03/9510 2222
Email lycmelb@hotmail.com
Web www.longyangclub.org/melbourne
Gender Men

The Melbourne chapter of this worldwide organization was established in 1998 to promote friendship, anti-racism, cooperation and understanding between gay Asians and Caucasian friends, partners and supporters. This is achieved by monthly 'drop in' nights (normally the second Friday of each month), and a monthly major event (normally the fourth weekend of each month). A schedule of upcoming events can be found on the club's Web site. Send an email to request further information.
Cost Membership $25

The Melbourne Buddhist Centre

1 Pitt St
Brunswick VIC 3056
Phone 03/9380 4303
Email melbourne@fwbo.org.au
Web www.melbourne@fwbo.org.au
Gender Mixed

This Buddhist centre offers a friends' night on Wednesday for meditation and guest speakers or for Puja ceremonies (held every other Wednesday); beginners are welcome. The centre draws its religious influences from a broad range of Buddhist traditions and has a bookshop with an extensive range of texts, both traditional and modern.
Cost $10

Melbourne Leather Pride Association

PO Box 359
Abbotsford VIC 3067
Gender Mixed
This pansexual group organizes events and promotes educational programs for those interested in leather/fetish/bondage/discipline/sado-masochism.

Melbourne Motorcycle Tourers

PO Box 11
Highpoint City VIC 3032
Phone Pete 03/9808 4398
Email twowheel@netspace.net.au
Web www.netspace.net.au/~twowheel/mtweb/
Gender Mixed
This club for gays and lesbians who enjoy motorbike riding invites you to join in the fun of informal monthly meetings, day rides, weekend rides and other social activities. Guest riders are welcome.
Cost Membership $20

Metropolitan Community Church

271 Burnley St
Richmond VIC 3121
Phone 03/9421 4219
Gender Mixed
This Christian church extends a special welcome to the gay/lesbian/bisexual/transgender communities with services every Sunday at 7pm.

Minus 18

PO Box 741
Glen Waverley VIC 3150
Phone 03/9511 4083 (P/FLAG) or 03/9510 5569 (ALSO Foundation)
Fax 03/9752 2081
Email minus18@mailcity.com
Web also.org.au-18
Gender Mixed
Affiliated with *P/FLAG* (*Parents and Friends of Lesbians and Gays*; p.256), *Minus 18* offers under-age nightclub events every school holidays for gay, lesbian, transgender youth. Events are fully supervised and no one over 18 years will be admitted. No pass-outs are given and these are strictly alcohol- and drug-free events.
Cost $10, includes soft drink

Momentum

6 Claremont St
South Yarra VIC 3141
Phone Kenton 03/9865 6700 or freecall 1800/134 840
Fax 03/9826 2700
Email kenton_miller@vicaids.asn.au
Web www.vicaids.asn.au
Gender Men
This *Victorian AIDS Council/Gay Men's Health Centre* initiative is a free workshop conducted over six weeks which aims to coach gay men about a range of gay-related issues – such as coming out, safe sex, identity, discrimination and finding and maintaining relationships.
Open Mon–Fri 9am–5pm

Motafrenz Car Club

PO Box 351
Blackburn VIC 3130
Phone Ross 03/9557 9635
Email motafrenz@hotmail.com
Web www.geocities.com/motafrenz
Gender Men
This gay motoring enthusiasts' social group for those into classic cars, four-

VICTORIA

wheel drives and sports cars right up to
the modern-day vehicle runs a number
of events throughout the year (many
do not even involve cars!). Those
without 'special' cars can easily and
fully participate in the life of the club.
Cost Membership $30

Multicultural Gay Group

PO Box 2057
St Kilda West VIC 3182
Phone Peter 03/9537 1053 or Orlando
03/9387 5367
Email multigg@hotmail.com
Web members.tripod.co.uk/
MGG/index.html
Gender Men
This support group for men from
diverse cultures provides
opportunities to make friends and
network through regular social
functions. Visitors should make
contact by post, phone or email to see
what organized or informal events are
coming up.

New Frontier Dance
Association (NFDA)

PO Box 29
North Melbourne VIC 3051
Email nfda@vicnet.net
Web www.vicnet.net.au/~nfda
Gender Mixed
New Frontier Dance Association
promotes country and western music
and dancing and offers special nights
for clogging and line dancing lessons
and weekly social events at the *Star
Hotel* (p.235). Everyone is welcome,
including straight participants.
Cost $5

New Wave Christian Fellowship
Church

PO Box 331
Heidelberg VIC 3084
Phone Carol 03/9801 9405 or
Fred 03/9879 1704 or
Duane 03/9459 6686
Email newave@eisa.net.au
Gender Mixed
This supportive interdenominational
church has a special outreach to the
lesbian and gay community.
Services are held on Sunday at 11am,
2 Napier Street (near Victoria
Parade), Fitzroy.

Nomads

PO Box 56, Flinders Lane
Melbourne VIC 8009
Phone Paul 03/9484 2449
Email nomads@bigfoot.com
Web www.bigfoot.com/~thenomads
Gender Mixed
This vibrant gay outdoor group
enjoys activities such as day walks,
car camping, bushwalking, cycling,
skiing and organizes regular social
events.

P/FLAG (Parents and Friends
of Lesbians and Gays)

PO Box 741
Glen Waverley VIC 3150
Phone 03/9511 4083
Email pflagvic@hotmail.com
Gender Mixed
This support group for families and
friends of gays and lesbians meets the
fourth Tuesday of each month at
7.30pm, Toorak Bowling Club,
Mandeville Cresent, Toorak.

People Living with HIV/AIDS

6 Claremont St
South Yarra VIC 3141
Phone 03/9865 6772
Fax 03/9804 7978
Email plwhavic@netspace.net.au
Web www.gaynet.com.au/
PLWHA/main.htm
Gender Mixed

This group assists people with
HIV/AIDS to improve their quality of
life through information, advice,
advocacy, support and representation.
It organizes the *PLWHA* speakers'
bureau (people living with HIV/AIDS
who are prepared to speak publicly
about their experiences). A treatments
action group meets monthly to discuss
latest treatment access and updates and
to maintain and improve the delivery
of health services.
Open Mon–Fri 9am–5pm

Positive Living Centre

46 Acland St
St Kilda VIC 3182
Phone 03/9525 4455
Fax 03/9534 2708
Email plc@vicaids.asn.au
Web www.vicaids.asn.au
Gender Mixed

This neighbourhood centre is a
friendly drop-in spot for people
living with HIV/AIDS. The centre
offers referrals to HIV-competent
natural therapists and further
information on using complementary
therapies for reducing side-effects
of HIV drugs. It gives information
on treating symptoms which
aren't responding to medication and
suggests new ways to increase
immune function. Massage is

available to people living with
HIV/AIDS at minimal cost (BYO
towel) and yoga classes are free.
There are also exercise classes on
offer to build up muscle tone; phone
for an appointment.
Open Mon–Thurs 10am–9pm, Fri
10am–5pm

Prospective Lesbian Parents Support Group

35 Bennett St
Richmond VIC 3121
Phone 0414 422 877
Fax 03/9897 1753
Email plp@qmail.com.au
Web www.geocities.com/plpsg
Gender Women

This group provides support and
information for lesbians considering
pregnancy for themselves, partners or
friends. The group meets the third
Thursday of each month at 7pm at
the *Victorian AIDS Council*, 6
Claremont Street, South Yarra, and
regularly includes guest speakers.
Cost Membership $10

QUID (Queer Users of Illicit Drugs)

293 Punt Rd
Richmond VIC 3121
Phone 03/9429 3322
Fax 03/9428 3655
Email info@buoyancy.org.au
Web www.buoyancy.org.au
Gender Mixed

This is a confidential support group
for gay, lesbian, bisexual and
transgender people who wish to
change their drug use. Members are
free to come and go from the group as
they wish and the meetings are

conducted in a non-judgemental, non-threatening environment offering peer support and harm-minimization education.
Open Mon–Fri 9am–5pm

Quilt Project
Room 19, 6 Claremont St
South Yarra VIC 3141
Phone 03/9865 6700
Gender Mixed
The *Quilt Project* commemorates the lives of those who have died from AIDS. It is a volunteer-based organization. Quilt panel workshops are held on the first Saturday of each month.

QYC (Queer Young Christians)
Melbourne VIC 3000
Phone Tim 03/9529 3226
Caitlin 03/9416 6638
Matthew 03/9380 9161
Web www.come.to/qyc
Gender Mixed
This group of queer young Christians (not all of whom attend traditional churches) meets regularly for worship and social functions.

Seahorse Club
PO Box 86
St Kilda VIC 3182
Phone 03/9513 8222
Email seahorse.victoria@iname.com
Web www.vicnet.net.au/~seahorse
Gender Mixed
A fun and accepting self-funded community social group for transgenders, their partners and friends meets twice monthly, produces a monthly magazine, holds restaurant nights and shopping trips throughout the year.
Cost Membership $40

Spaced Out Inc
Prahran VIC 3181
Phone Alan or Stephen 03/9528 2457
Email spaceout@vicnet.net.au
Web www.vicnet.net.au/~spaceout
Gender Mixed
These science-fiction lovers from gay/lesbian/bisexual/transgender communities enjoy regular movie outings and social activities. This fun group is keen to give a queer edge to sci fi.
Cost Membership $20, plus $5 joining fee (first year only)

St Agnes' Anglican Parish
114 Booran Rd
Glenhuntly VIC
Gender Mixed
All are welcome to celebrate the Eucharist at 6pm on Saturday and 8am and 10am Sunday at this church offering music, inclusive liturgy and affirming pastoral care.

Victorian AIDS Council (VAC) Peter Knight Centre
6 Claremont St
South Yarra VIC 3141
Phone 03/9865 6700,
TTY 03/9827 3733
Fax 03/9826 2700
Email enquiries@vicaids.asn.au
Web www.vicaids.asn.au
Gender Mixed
This is the main HIV/AIDS support organization in Victoria. Contact *VAC* for information on treatments, support services, suitable doctors and any other HIV/AIDS information, or visit to peruse its wide range of resource leaflets. It also carries a wide range of gay/lesbian newspapers and safe-sex supplies, and has a needle exchange.
Open Mon–Fri 9am–5pm

Victorian Gay and Lesbian Rights Lobby

PO Box 2156
Fitzroy VIC 3065
Phone Katy 0417 484 427 or Kenton 0417 484 438
Email vglr_lobby@hotmail.com
Web www.vicnet.net.au/~vglrl
Gender Mixed

This group of political lobbyists aims to achieve social justice and legal equality for lesbians and gays. Their work involves research, education, law reform, monitoring and responding to parliamentary policy makers.

Vintage Men

Phone Bruce 03/9773 2570
Gender Men

This discreet social and support group for mature gay and bisexual men has weekly activities and meetings.

Wayward Women Walkers Incorporated

Burwood VIC 3125
Phone Gudrun 03/9888 8306 or 03/9754 7320
Email wwwalkers@today.com.au
Gender Women

This group organizes a six-monthly program which includes walking, birdwatching, cycling, weekends away, day-hikes and weekend walks. It sometimes does walks with the *Nomads* (see p.256) as well as friends and family walks. So come along for a healthy stress-free way to make new friends.
Cost Membership $15, then $5 per walk

Young and Gay

6 Claremont St
South Yarra VIC 3141
Phone 03/9865 6700 or freecall 1800/134 840
Fax 03/9804 7978
Email youthproject@vicaids.asn.au
Web www.vicaids.asn.au
Gender Men

This *Victorian AIDS Council/Gay Men's Health Centre* health initiative offers a confidential, free six-week course for guys under 27 years. The course builds self-esteem, covers issues such as safe sex and relationships and is an ideal way to make new friends.
Open Mon–Fri 9am–5pm

Young Bucks

7 Giselle Court
Frankston VIC 3199
Phone Michael 03/9750 6080 or 0411 111 572
Email mykaljay@optusnet.com.au
Gender Men

Young Bucks caters for gay and bisexual men aged 18 to 35 with a heavy weekly social program, as well as discussion nights every two weeks.

Global Gossip

440 Elizabeth St
Melbourne VIC 3000
Phone 03/9663 0511
Fax 03/9633 0522
Gay-owned chain of Internet and
communication centres, offering
email, Internet, chat, cheap phone
calls, employment services, copying,
faxing and mailbox rental.
Open Daily 8am–midnight
Payment Bankcard, EFTPOS,
MasterCard, Visa; cheque

Go Travel-Jetset Prahran

188 Commercial Rd
Prahran VIC 3181
Phone 03/9533 6166
Fax 03/9529 5541
Email jetset@bluep.com
Web www.jetset.com.au/
agents/prahran
This upmarket travel specialist offers
exclusive gay and lesbian destinations
and boutique hotels around the world.
Open Mon–Fri 9am–5pm,
Sat 10am–2.30pm
Payment AmEx, Bankcard, Diners,
EFTPOS, MasterCard, Visa; cheque

Pride Travel Tours

254 Bay St
Brighton VIC 3186
Phone 03/9596 7100
Fax 03/9596 7761
Email jetbay@ergo.com.au
A gay-friendly, efficient and
knowledgeable travel service.
Open Mon 9am–5.30am,
Sat 10am–1pm
Payment AmEx, Bankcard, Diners,
MasterCard, Visa; cheque

Rainbow Tours Australia

PO Box 726
Belmont VIC 3216
Phone 03/9397 0023
Fax 03/5241 6370
Email paul@rainbowtours.com.au
Web www.rainbowtours.com.au
This travel service offers day tours to
the Great Ocean Road, Phillip Island,
Daylesford, Yarra Valley wineries,
Mornington Peninsula and
Queenscliff, as well as overnight tours.
Open Mon–Fri 8am–6pm
Payment Amex, Bankcard, Diners,
EFTPOS, MasterCard, Visa

Strathmore Travel Centre

12 Lloyd St
Strathmore VIC 3041
Phone Marlene 03/9379 3886
Fax 03/9374 2463
Email strathtrav@bigpond.com
This is a discreet travel centre with
advice for all travelling needs.
Payment Amex, Bankcard, Diners,
EFTPOS, MasterCard, Visa

Tearaway Travel

52 Porter St
Prahran VIC 3181
Phone Jonathan and Greg 03/9510 6644
Fax 03/8660 2021
Email tearaway@bigpond.com
Web www.tearaway.com
Located near the gay strip, this specialist
travel service is for gay men and
lesbians. Among its local destinations
are Phillip Island penguin parade, the
Great Ocean Road and Daylesford.
Open Mon–Fri 10am–5pm
Payment AmEx, Bankcard, Diners,
EFTPOS, MasterCard, Visa; cheque

Yarra Valley and the Dandenongs

North-east of Melbourne, about 60km via the Maroondah Highway, lies the **Yarra Valley**, where you will find thriving wineries and **Healesville Sanctuary**, one of Australia's most famous native wildlife parks and a popular **day-trip** destination from Melbourne. The many free-range enclosures give you the opportunity to view Australia's fauna in their natural habitats. The mountains near Healesville make for an exceptional drive and the damp eucalyptus scents of the forests are invigorating. Autumn is the best time to be in the mountains, but they make glorious summer and winter escapes as well.

When you feel the need of a day's break from Melbourne, the **Dandenong Ranges** offer lush, picturesque scenery barely an hour from the city by car or train. Whatever your age, you're bound to enjoy travelling back in time on **Puffing Billy** (phone 03/9754 6800). This gorgeous, shiny red steam train charts a narrow-gauge course through the ferny rainforests.

While the Dandenongs are famed for their Devonshire teas, craft shops, mock Tudor houses and Teutonic restaurants, they also boast wonderful forests and lookouts. **Sherbrooke Forest** offers plenty of easy walks and is only a couple of kilometres from Belgrave. Most spectacular of all would have to be the **Rhododendron Gardens** in Olinda, which are truly a sight to behold from September through to November.

ACCOMMODATION

Aabedan B&B
12 Kallista-Emerald Rd
Kallista VIC 3791
Phone 03/9756 6163
Fax 03/9756 6163
Gender Mixed
Set in the heart of Sherbrooke Forest, 1km from Kallista village, *Aabedan* offers B&B accommodation with a pot-belly stove; ensuite and kitchenette available in one room. All rooms overlook bird-filled gardens.

Smoking is permitted outside only.
Cost From $83 single, $111 double
Payment Bankcard, MasterCard, Visa; cheque

Cathedral View B&B
482 South Cathedral Lane
Buxton VIC 3711
Phone Kay and Nora 03/5774 7545
Fax 03/5774 7545
Email cathedralview@mmtourism. com.au

Web mmtourism.com.au/
cathedralview/
Gender Mixed

There are magnificent views and sumptuous breakfasts to be had at this B&B, as well as outdoor activities nearby and, if you overdo it, massage and natural therapies are also available.

Cost $88–127 per room
Payment Amex, Bankcard, MasterCard, Visa

Delvin Country House

25 Monash Ave
Olinda VIC 3788
Phone Michael 03/9751 1800
Fax 03/9751 1829
Email michael@delvin.com.au
Web www.delvin.com.au
Gender Mixed

Gay-owned and -operated *Delvin* is located 150m from Olinda town centre. The spectacular Rhododendrom Gardens are right on the doorstep. All six bedrooms are decorated in the Art Deco style, and have queen-size beds and private bathrooms. Some rooms have balconies overlooking forest and gardens. Full breakfast is included and evening meals can be arranged. Massage, beauty therapy and spa are also available.

Cost From $83 single, $100 double
Payment AmEx, Bankcard, MasterCard, Visa; cheque

Echidna Earth Women

145 Ninks Rd
St Andrews VIC 3761
Phone 03/9710 1703
Fax 03/9710 1170
Gender Mixed

This lesbian-owned and -operated B&B offers a real break from urban life. The farm grows all its own organic produce and produces free-range eggs which guests may purchase. Glen Halcyon and Echidna Cottage offer the choice of a two-bedroom, self-contained cottage with cedar hot tub, air-conditioning and pot-belly stove heating; or a suite with private entry, ensuite, and private lounge with hot tub. Full breakfast is included in the tariff, and dinner is also available. Smoking is permitted outside only.

Cost From $165 per room
Payment Cheque

Fruit Salad Farm

30–32 Aubry-Cuzens Drive
Marysville VIC 3779
Phone 03/5963 3232 or freecall 1800/645 494
Fax 03/5963 4331
Email info@fruitsaladfarm.com.au
Web www.fruitsaladfarm.com.au
Gender Mixed

These gay-owned and -operated, self-contained cottages (all with open fires and some with spas) are located on four acres of natural bushland. Some cabins sleep up to 13. A breakfast hamper is included. Smoking is permitted outside only.

Cost From $122 per couple ($28 each extra person)
Payment Amex, Bankcard, Diners, EFTPOS, MasterCard, Visa

Grandma's Cottage

PO Box 733
Warburton VIC 3799
Phone David 0412 057 814 or 03/5966 2256

Gender Mixed

This 1920s traditional cottage is a short walk from town. The three-bedroom cottage sleeps up to six, has a wood fire and electric barbecue. Champagne, chocolates and ingredients for a full breakfast are provided.

Cost $132 per couple ($22 each extra person)

Payment Bankcard, MasterCard, Visa; cheque

Kingbilli

Cathedral Lane
Taggerty VIC 3714
Phone 03/5774 7302
Email kb@kingbilli.com.au
Web www.kingbilli.com.au
Gender Mixed

Located at the foot of Cathedral Mountain, these secluded bluestone cottages are located by a trout-filled stream. All cottages have open fires, private spas and are fully self-contained. Fishing, swimming, boating, tennis, cycling and llama trekking are available on the property, with horseriding, ballooning, golf and wineries nearby.

Cost From $390 per couple for two nights

Payment Bankcard, MasterCard, Visa; cheque

Marysville Scenic B&B

16 Darwin St
Marysville VIC 3779
Phone 03/5963 3247
Fax 03/5963 4232
Email scenic@mmtourism.com.au
Web www.mmtourism.com.au/scenic/
Gender Mixed

Set in beautiful gardens, these 10 cosy motel-style units come with fantastic mountain views and ensuites. Gay-owned and -operated, *Marysville Scenic B&B* offers a licensed and BYO dining room with guest lounge and a barbecue area outside.

Cost $69–99 per unit

Payment Bankcard, EFTPOS, MasterCard, Visa; cheque

St Lawrence Traditional B&B

13 Richard Rd
Warburton VIC 3799
Phone Alan 03/5966 5649 or 0419 102 825
Fax 03/5966 5007
Gender Mixed

This charming Federation-style homestay accommodation with magnificent gardens and traditional decor is an easy walk from the centre of town and close to restaurants. All rooms have private bathrooms, guest lounge with TV, video and open fire. Full breakfast is included, other meals are by arrangement. No smoking is permitted inside. Bike hire and eco-tours can be organized.

Cost From $132 per room

Payment Bankcard, MasterCard, Visa; cheque

Toolebewong Cottage

120 Toolebewong Rd
Healesville VIC 3777
Phone 03/5962 3437 or 0413 487 456
Gender Mixed

This secluded cottage sleeps up to five, and is within walking distance of Healesville Sanctuary. The cottage has an open fire and an extensive library of books, music and videos. Guest can also avail themselves of a spa, shiatsu massage, suppers and gourmet breakfasts. Pets are allowed and smoking is permitted outside only.

Cost From $143 per couple
Payment Bankcard, EFTPOS, MasterCard, Visa; cheque

Villa Toscana

13 Barbers Rd
Kalorama VIC 3766
Phone 03/9728 1298
Fax 03/9728 5484
Email villatos@uu.com.au
Web www.villatoscana.com.au
Gender Mixed

Less than an hour's drive from Melbourne, this boutique hotel has fantastic views of the Yarra Ranges. *Villa Toscana* has been built with Italian building materials and incorporates antique European architectural pieces found in the villas of Tuscany. The restaurant (which serves drinks and coffee throughout the day) specializes in Mediterranean and Tuscan food. The guest lounge has an open fireplace, rooms have balconies and some rooms have spas. Smoking is permitted outside only.

Cost From $115 per room
Payment Amex, Bankcard, Diners, MasterCard, Visa

CAFÉS AND RESTAURANTS

Gilberts Restaurant

30–32 Aubry-Cuzens Drive
Marysville VIC 3779
Phone 03/5963 3232
Fax 03/5963 4331
Email gilberts@fruitsaladfarm.com.au
Web gilberts.fruitsaladfarm.com.au

This rustic, intimate gay-owned and -operated, fully licensed restaurant showcases local fresh produce. Enjoy the tastes of the season during a cosy, candlelit dinner in a smoke-free environment.

Open Fri–Tues 6.30pm–10pm, Sat–Sun noon–3pm
Cost Lunch $20–25, dinner $30–40
Payment Amex, Bankcard, Diners, EFTPOS, MasterCard, Visa

Wild Thyme

3391 Warburton Highway
Warburton VIC 3799
Phone 03/5966 5050
Fax 03/5966 5055

This stylish gay-run café features local produce (including smoked trout, yabbies and venison, wines and beer), as well as a comprehensive vegetarian menu. Breakfast is available all day. Smoking is permitted outside in the beer garden. Bookings are advisable, especially at weekends.

Open Mon & Wed 5pm–10pm, Thurs–Fri noon–late, Sat–Sun 9am–midnight
Cost Breakfast $10, lunch & dinner $12–20
Payment Bankcard, EFTPOS, MasterCard, Visa

COMMUNITY

Feral Womyn: Anarchist Feminist Collective
PO Box 1102
Upwey VIC 3158
Phone Jude 0409 1644 36
Gender Women
Contact point for women and children interested in establishing a rural community in Victoria.

Gay Nudist Victoria
GNV PO Box 7471
Dandenong VIC 3175
Gender Mostly men
This nudist group for gay men holds frequent get-togethers in the raw.

Mornington Peninsula and Phillip Island

The boot-shaped Mornington Peninsula, just a short drive south-east of Melbourne, has many **wineries**, magnificent **beaches** and historic **homesteads**. Across Western Port Bay, Phillip Island is famous for its nightly **penguin parade**, but also has some attractive beachside towns.

ACCOMMODATION

Birdrock Breakaway
6 Birdrock Ave
Mount Martha VIC 3934
Phone Phil and Rob 03/5975 5536
Fax 03/5975 4175
Gender Mostly men
This small resort is situated 200m from Birdrock Beach. It has a spa, sauna, saltwater swimming pool and tennis court. Some rooms have ensuites, some have shared facilities, and one self-contained apartment is available; breakfast is included in the tariff. Smoking is permitted outside only.
Cost From $100 single, $132 double
Payment Bankcard, MasterCard, Visa

Botanica Farm Accommodation
55 Gwenmarlin Rd
Flinders VIC 3929
Phone 03/5989 0774
Email nhallam@hotmail.com
Web www.botanicalodge.8m.com
Gender Mixed
Botanica offers a private three-roomed suite overlooking Mornington Peninsula National Park, 5km from Flinders township. It has a hot tub under the stars, full breakfast is included, a barbecue is available and evening meals can be arranged. Smoking is allowed outside only.
Cost $143 per unit
Payment Cheque

Glynt by the Sea

16 Bay Rd
Mount Martha VIC 3934
Phone 03/5974 1216
Fax 03/5974 2546
Email glynt@smart.net.au
Web www.glynt.com.au
Gender Mixed

This grand historic house is close to the beach and wineries. All rooms have ensuites and are decorated with period art and furniture. There's a bar and dining room.
Cost From $150 single, $250 double
Payment Amex, Bankcard, Diners, MasterCard, Visa

BEACHES AND POOLS

Sunnyside Beach

Sunnyside Rd
Mount Eliza VIC 3930
Gender Mixed

This popular gay haunt is at the west end of the beach. Turn off the Nepean Highway onto Sunnyside Road and drive all the way to the end.

COMMUNITY

Mornington Peninsula Lesbian Network

Mount Martha VIC 3934
Phone Sue 03/9783 3211
Gender Women

This social group for lesbians living on the Mornington Peninsula meets the first Tuesday of the month.

Peninsula Guys Incorporated

PO Box 161
Frankston VIC 3199

Phone Graeme 03/9769 6331 or Ian 0411 228 142
Gender Men

This social and support group for gay and bisexual men in the Frankston area meets every Thursday (7.30pm–9.30pm). Activities on weekends include winery tours, barbecues and picnics. The group is in its fifth year and produces a six-month calendar of events.
Cost Membership $25

Geelong and the Bellarine Peninsula

Geelong is located 60km south-west of Melbourne on **Corio Bay**. Due to its proximity to Melbourne, it does not really have specific gay or lesbian bars, though there are several cafés, as well as a thriving community network. It has many fine historic buildings, and is the gateway to the **Bellarine Peninsula** – where grand clifftop guesthouses in Queenscliff and Portarlington have long been a place of retreat and repose for Melburnians – and to the Great Ocean Road.

ACCOMMODATION

Ebony Quill Cottage
620 Princes Highway
Waurn Ponds VIC 3216
Phone 03/5266 1394
Fax 03/5266 1580
Gender Mixed
There are panoramic views at this
modern, gay/lesbian-friendly fully
self-contained cottage, with spa, air-
conditioning and log fire. A breakfast
basket is provided. Waurn Ponds is
about 10km west of Geelong, on the
way to the Great Ocean Road.
Cost $143 per unit
Payment Cheque

Roses by the Sea
16 Evandale Ave
Portarlington VIC 3223
Phone Liz and Wendy 03/5259 3805
Gender Mixed
This lovely, lesbian-owned and
-operated seaside residence offers a
fully self-contained Japanese-style
cottage (breakfast provisions
included), sensational views and
Devonshire teas. Enjoy a private
courtyard and garden spa. Evening
meals are available by prior
arrangement. Dogs are welcome.
Cost From $88 per room
Payment Cheque

Ruby's B&B
2 Saint Andrews St
Queenscliff VIC 3225
Phone 03/5258 4838 or 0407 512 145
Email rubys@marine-ecology.com.au
Gender Mixed
This Cape Cod-style cottage, located
in a quiet street, is close to the beach
and shops. All rooms have ensuites
with spas and there is one suite with
wood fire and spa. Full breakfast is
included in the tariff.
Cost $88–132 per room
Payment Bankcard, MasterCard, Visa;
cheque

Sea View Retreat
167 Dare St
Ocean Grove VIC 3226
Phone 03/5255 1917
Email sabu@netlink.com.au
Gender Mixed
Lesbian-owned and -operated and
conveniently located 50m from beach
and a short walk to shops, these fully
self-contained apartments sleep two.
There's a microwave, TV, VCR, CD
player and stereo in each apartment.
Breakfast provisions can be provided.
Smoking is permitted outside only.
Cost $56–77 per apartment
Payment Cheque

CAFÉS AND RESTAURANTS

Cafe Botticelli
111 Pakington St
West Geelong VIC 3218
Phone 03/5229 8292
Fax 03/5229 7699

Email botticel@pipeline.com.au
This cosy, eclectic, gay-run café is
fully licensed. The cuisine is
influenced by Mediterranean, Middle
Eastern and Asian culinary traditions.

Favourites include the tapas platter, handmade ricotta gnocchi, pastas, risottos and vegetarian dishes.
Open Mon–Sat noon–late
Cost Lunch $15, dinner $20
Payment Amex, Bankcard, Diners, EFTPOS, MasterCard, Visa

Craig's Cafe

1 Harding St
Portarlington VIC 3223
Phone 03/5259 1311
Everything is made on the premises at this fully licensed café with ocean views. Bookings are preferred. Dishes include local seafood, bruschetta, pasta and steak dishes. Light meals, coffee and cakes are also available. Traditional breakfast is served on Sunday only. There is a separate bar area. Gay-owned and -operated, *Craig's* has set aside the first Friday of the month as a gay and lesbian evening (from 7pm).
Open Fri–Sat 11am–late, Sun 9am–late (extended hours during summer)
Cost Breakfast $12, lunch $20, dinner $35
Payment Bankcard, EFTPOS, MasterCard, Visa

GO Cafe

37 Bellarine St (cnr Little Malop St)
Geelong VIC 3220
Phone 03/5229 4752
Located in a nineteenth-century house, *GO* is fully licensed and offers a sophisticated, Melbourne-style dining experience. The food is Mediterranean-influenced and the decor is funky and kitsch. The second and fourth Monday of the month are gay and lesbian nights.
Open Sun–Fri 7.30am–late

Cost Breakfast & lunch $7–10, dinner $15–20
Payment Amex, Bankcard, EFTPOS, MasterCard, Visa

Cafe Q

79 Hesse St
Queenscliff VIC 3225
Phone 03/5258 3663
Located at the rear of a nineteenth-century church, lesbian/gay-operated *Cafe Q* serves breakfast, lunch and afternoon tea in a courtyard. Specialties include homemade bread and cakes, biscuits, chutneys, mayos and jams. Breakfast dishes include all the favourites and they'll even cook bacon for your dog! Dishes reflect a range of international influences and use plenty of fresh produce.
Open Mon, Wed–Fri 10am–5pm, Sat–Sun 8am–6pm (also open Tues 10am–5pm in summer)
Cost Breakfast $10, lunch $15
Payment Cash only

Two Faces

8 Malop St
Geelong VIC 3220
Phone 03/5229 4546
Fax 03/5224 1533
Email yarhamsfinefoods@telstra. easymail.com.au
This gay-owned and -operated, fully licensed, smoke-free restaurant specializes in contemporary Australian cuisine. There are daily specials with lots of fresh seafood and vegetarian dishes. Bookings preferred.
Open Lunch Wed–Fri for bookings only, dinner Tues–Sat 6pm–late
Cost Lunch $15–20, dinner $35–40
Payment Amex, Bankcard, Diners, EFTPOS, MasterCard, Visa

COMMUNITY

GASP (Gay Adolescent Support Program)

PO Box 104
Geelong VIC 3220
Phone Narelle 03/5227 0699
Fax 03/5222 5175
Email ngoodland@geelongcity.vic.gov.au
Gender Mixed

GASP is predominantly an information and referral service for young gay people. It provides one-to-one short-term counselling support to young people on a needs basis. In addition, it facilitates Activ8, a committee of community representatives whose primary role is to raise community awareness and identify service delivery gaps in the region for gay young people.

Geelong Lesbian Group (GLG)

PO Box 2050
Geelong VIC 3220
Phone Rose 03/5229 9548
Gender Mixed

This social support group for lesbians in the Geelong region meets monthly at lesbian-owned cafés and organizes a range of social events including dances, canoeing, bushwalks, pool games and barbecues. It also combines with other groups for special events. *GLG* produces a monthly newsletter and gives membership discounts at gay/lesbian businesses.
Cost Membership $15

Geelong's All Inclusive Network (GAIN)

PO Box 68
Geelong VIC 3220
Phone Louise 03/5248 6592 or Nick 0414 434 790
Email gaingeelong@yahoo.com
Gender Mixed

This group of representatives from greater Geelong supports gay/lesbian/bisexual/transgender communities and is an ideal first point of contact for people in the region seeking other groups. The group addresses issues such as social opportunities, support, access to facilities, health and equity. It holds get-togethers on the first and third Wednesday of each month at a gay-owned café.

The Great Ocean Road and the Otway Ranges

The Great Ocean Road is one of Victoria's most fantastic drives, taking in much of the state's most **rugged coastline** on precarious cliff-edge roads, backed by the **rolling hills** of the Otway Ranges. Along this winding route you'll pass lovely seaside resorts such as **Lorne** and **Apollo Bay.** Lorne is one of the state's most popular and smartest holiday resorts (it is usually booked solid in January) with plenty of good restaurants. Plan to stay away for at least one night if you want to take in spectacular sights such as the **Twelve Apostles**, **Loch Ard Gorge** and **Erskine Falls** and especially if you decide to go as far as **Warrnambool**, **Portland** or historic **Port Fairy** – all well worth a look.

ACCOMMODATION

Beachcomber Motel and Apartments

15 Diana St
Apollo Bay VIC 3233
Phone 03/5237 6290
Fax 03/5237 7474
Email beach@vicnet.net.au
Web www.tourvic.com.au/
accommodation/beachcomber.htm
Gender Mixed
Luxury and budget units are available at the *Beachcomber*, which is just minutes from the beach, shops, and restaurants. Some rooms have spas and open fires; the apartments have fully equipped kitchens. Continental breakfast is available on request. There is a barbecue area and guest laundry.
Cost $72–154 per room
Payment Amex, Bankcard, EFTPOS, MasterCard, Visa

Boomerang Cabins

Cnr Great Ocean Rd & Johanna Red Rd
Johanna VIC 3238
Phone 03/5237 4213
Fax 03/5237 4213
Email bookings@boomerangcabins.com
Web www.boomerangcabins.com
Gender Mixed
Situated in Victoria's Otway Ranges, this is the ideal location for a romantic retreat. The architect-designed cabins

have wood fires, spas, laundry facilities and spectacular views through panoramic windows and from large verandahs. Each cabin is fully self-contained, has two double bedrooms and open-plan living with polished floors. Gas barbecues are also available.
Cost From $140 per cabin
Payment AmEx, Bankcard, EFTPOS, MasterCard, Visa; cheque

Cimarron

105 Gilbert St
Aireys Inlet VIC 3231
Phone 03/5289 7044
Fax 03/5289 7044
Email cimarron@primus.com.au
Web cimarron.com.au
Gender Mixed
Cimarron is set in bushland at Aireys Inlet, 10km east of Lorne. There are panoramic ocean views from every room, as well as open fires, buffet breakfasts and an extensive video library.
Cost $70–138 per room
Payment Bankcard, MasterCard, Visa

Cumberland Lorne Resort

150 Mountjoy Parade
Lorne VIC 3232
Phone 03/5289 2400
Fax 03/5289 2256

Email info@cumberland.com.au
Web www.cumberland.com.au
Gender Mixed
The perfect gay/lesbian-friendly stopover if you are touring the Great Ocean Road. The resort has serviced apartments and a licensed restaurant, heated indoor pool, gymnasium, spa, sauna, tennis and squash courts.
Cost From $215 per room
Payment Amex, Bankcard, Diners, EFTPOS, MasterCard, Visa

King Parrot Holiday Cabins
Dunse Track
Pennyroyal VIC 3235
Phone 03/5236 3372
Fax 03/5236 3332
Email kingparrot@primus.com.au
Web www.kingparrot.com.au
Gender Mixed
This tranquil mountain retreat just 20 minutes' drive inland from Lorne offers total privacy in self-contained cabins with log fires. All cabins have ensuites and views, and breakfast baskets are available. There's also a mini-golf course and bushwalking tracks on the property.
Cost From $130 per cabin
Payment Bankcard, MasterCard, Visa; cheque

Seaviews B&B
150 Merri St
Warrnambool VIC 3280
Phone 0419 394 836
Fax 03/5560 5436
Email percyeccles11@telstra.easymail.com.au
Gender Mixed
This homestay-style accommodation

has ensuites, balconies and queen-size beds in a modern building close to town and not far from the beach. A spa room is also available.
Cost $122–143 per room
Payment Bankcard, MasterCard, Visa

Victoria House
5–7 Tyers St
Portland VIC 3305
Phone 03/5521 7577
Fax 03/5523 6300
Gender Mixed
An elegantly restored Georgian bluestone hotel with cottage gardens, queen-size beds and ensuites close to the beach, town and port.
Cost From $91 single, $108 double
Payment Amex, Bankcard, Diners, MasterCard, Visa

Waverley House
Cnr Waverley Ave and Great Ocean Rd
Lorne VIC 3232
Phone 03/5289 2044
Fax 03/5289 2508
Email waverleyhouse@iprimus.com.au
Web www.greatoceanrd.org.au
Gender Mixed
This historic stone residence has been fully restored and offers spacious, fully self-contained apartments, all with ensuites, queen-size beds, microwave, fridge and full breakfast provisions. *Waverley House* is within walking distance of the Erskine River, beaches, restaurants and a short drive from the magnificent Erskine Falls. Smoking is permitted outside only.
Cost From $110–185 per room
Payment AmEx, Bankcard, Diners, MasterCard, Visa; cheque

Lorne Beach Books
1088 Mountjoy Parade
Lorne VIC 3232
Phone 03/5289 2489
Fax 03/5289 2689
Lorne Beach Books offers a range of lesbian fiction and erotica, some gay titles, travel guides, general fiction and unusual postcards.
Open Daily 9am–5.30pm
Payment Amex, Bankcard, Diners, EFTPOS, MasterCard, Visa

Point Addis
Between Torquay & Anglesea
Anglesea VIC 3230
Gender Mixed
Follow the Anglesea Road from Geelong and take the beach turnoff 2km past the famous surfing spot of Bells Beach.

Point Impossible
Torquay VIC 3228
Gender Mixed
This gay beach (also a popular surf break) is about 10km east of Torquay; take the beach road from Torquay to Breamlea.

Warrnambool Gay and Lesbian Group
PO Box 2827
Allansford VIC 3277
Phone Mark or Geoffrey 03/5566 3346
Email pegasus1@tpg.com.au
Gender Mixed
This support and social group for gay/lesbian/bisexual/transgender communities in the Portland, Hamilton, Port Campbell, Port Fairy, Camperdown and Colac regions holds a gathering on the first Friday of the month and produces a newsletter.

Ballarat and the Grampians

When **gold** was discovered during the nineteenth century in central Victoria, many fortunes were made and quite a few were lost. Towns such as Ballarat and Bendigo are the largest surviving monuments to those fortunes and most of the ostentatious, 'I've-discovered-more-gold-than-you' architecture still remains. These towns are really very gracious and give a taste of what early

Australian Victorian cities were like. Ballarat even has a Gold Rush theme park, **Sovereign Hill** (phone 03/5331 1944), where you can take tours through the mine shafts and be photographed in period gear.

To the west of Ballarat is the majestic Grampians National Park, its rugged sandstone ridges best explored on foot from a base in nearby **Ararat**, or to the south of the park in **Dunkeld** or **Hamilton**.

ACCOMMODATION

Keebles of Clunes

114 Bailey St
Clunes VIC 3370
Phone 03/5345 3220
Fax 03/5345 3200
Email keeblesofclunes@bigpond.com.au
Web www.ballarat.com/keebles.htm
Gender Mixed
All rooms have ensuites in this elegant historic home (1863). The dining room is open to non-residential guests on Saturday or at other times by arrangement.
Cost $154–210 per room
Payment Bankcard, Diners, MasterCard, Visa

The Loft B&B

203 Doveton St
Ballarat South VIC 3350
Phone Edith and Anne 03/5331 6766
Gender Mixed
This loft-style accommodation in the heart of historic Ballarat features ensuite facilities, airconditioning and queen-size beds.
Cost $105 per room
Payment Cash only

Southern Grampians Log Cabins

35 Victoria Valley Rd
Dunkeld VIC 3294
Phone Steve 03/5577 2457
Fax 03/5577 2489
Email ward7sb@ansonic.com.au
Gender Mixed
These self-contained one- and two-bedroom cottages have log fires, barbecues and verandahs. Breakfast is available, as are picnic hampers and barbecue packs. The cabins are handy to town, mountains and bushwalks, wildlife, wineries and a golf course.
Cost $88–160 per cottage
Payment Bankcard, MasterCard, Visa; cheque

Turf Hotel

157 Barkly St
Ararat VIC 3377
Phone Andrew or Robert 03/5352 2393
Fax 03/5352 2893
Gender Mixed
This gay-owned and -operated Deco extravaganza offers traditional pub-style accommodation. All rooms have

hand basins with shared bathroom facilities. The owners organize day-tours of the nearby Grampians, including lunch, and they can arrange winery tours in surrounding regions. Counter meals in the pub are $5 and the restaurant has an Australian/

Chinese menu (mains $8–11).
Open Daily 10am–10pm (later on weekends)
Cost $14 dorm, $22 single, $33–50 double
Payment Bankcard, EFTPOS, MasterCard, Visa

CAFÉS AND RESTAURANTS

The Hamilton Strand
56 Thompson St
Hamilton VIC 3300
Phone 03/5571 9144
Fax 03/5571 9167
This fully licensed restaurant's modern cuisine influenced by European and Asian culinary traditions is highly rated.

The fish curry is very popular, as is the local Hopkins River beef, rabbit pie, seafood bisque and caramel pudding.
Open Daily 11am–10pm (sometimes later)
Cost Lunch $10, dinner $30
Payment Amex, Bankcard, Diners, EFTPOS, MasterCard, Visa

BOOKSHOPS

Belcourt Books
63 Gray St
Hamilton VIC 3300
Phone 03/5572 1310
Fax 03/5572 1310
Email belcourt@ansonic.com.au
A charming lesbian-owned and

-operated bookshop stocking literary and secondhand books, plus some gay/lesbian titles, videos and CDs.
Open Mon–Fri 9am–5.30pm, Sat 9.30am–12.30pm
Payment Bankcard, EFTPOS, MasterCard, Visa

COMMUNITY

BGLAD
PO Box 1156
Ballarat VIC 3352
Phone 03/5334 7849
Email bglad@qonline.com.au
Gender Mixed
Ballarat's gay and lesbian social group has a video library, organizes bus

trips to gay and lesbian events, holds regular meetings, a monthly drop-in night at a discreet location and several dances each year. It also produces a monthly newsletter and a radio show on 3BBB, 99.9FM (Mon 10pm).
Cost Membership $20

Daylesford and Spa Country

Daylesford and Hepburn Springs, in the heart of spa country, are fast becoming the **gay and lesbian relaxation centre** of Victoria with many of the accommodation venues, restaurants and businesses in the area being gay-owned or gay-friendly. Here you can experience the famous natural **mineral springs** and spa resort, scenic surroundings, eclectic arts community and galleries, historical and cultural attractions, bushwalking opportunities, sophisticated and award-winning restaurants, stylish accommodation, and gay **events and activities**. There is a wonderful energy to the area, which doubtless stems from its reputation as a place of healing and relaxation; there really seems to be something about those subterranean springs.

CHILL OUT

Alison Pouliot

Each year Daylesford hosts the **'Chill Out' Festival** – one of Australia's only bent country events. A celebration of gay and lesbian life and culture in the region, the festival just keeps on growing bigger, bolder and more outrageous (over 10,000 people attended the March 2000 festival).

Alison Pouliot

Avalon Mists
Mount Franklin VIC 3461
Phone 03/5476 4337 or 0427 051 361
Web www.bol.com.au/avalon/a.html
Gender Women
This women's rural escape is close to
Daylesford and provides farm-style
accommodation (with breakfast) at
the foot of Mount Franklin.
Cost $80–100 per room
Payment Cheque

The Balconies of Daylesford
35 Perrins St
Daylesford VIC 3460
Phone Geoff and Theo 03/5348 1322
Fax 03/5348 1322
Email balconys@netconnect.com.au
Web www.spacountry.net.au/balconys
Gender Mixed
Catering specifically to gay and
lesbian clientele, *The Balconies* offers
open fires, heated indoor pool and
spa, smoking and billiards room,
extensive gardens and in-house
massages can be arranged. It overlooks
Lake Daylesford and all rooms have
private facilities.
Cost From $95 single, $145 double
Payment Bankcard, MasterCard, Visa

Blackwood Retreats
25 Golden Point Road
Blackwood VIC 3458
Phone 03/5368 6607
Fax 03/5368 6798
Email holiday@blackwoodretreats.
com.au
Web www.blackwoodretreats.com.au
Gender Mixed
These clean and comfortable one-,

two- and three-bedroom cottages are
set in the bush close to Daylesford and
spa country. Pets are allowed.
Blackwood Retreats also manages other
self-catered cottages scattered around
the area.
Cost From $70 per unit
Payment Bankcard, EFTPOS,
MasterCard, Visa; cheque

Blue Mount Accommodation
276 Kearneys Rd
Newbury VIC 3458
Phone 03/5424 1296
Email blumnt@iaccess.com.au
Gender Mixed
This self-contained secluded cottage
and garden, with views of the forest
and farmland, is close to Trentham,
Daylesford and spa country attractions.
It has a lounge/dining area, wood
fire, kitchenette, microwave, queen-
size bed and room for one child.
Pets are allowed by arrangement;
smoking is permitted outside only.
Accommodation comes with full
breakfast provisions and real coffee.
Champagne, chocolates and home-
made cakes are served on arrival.
Picnic hampers can be arranged.
Cost $297 for a weekend package;
discounted midweek rates
Payment AmEx, Bankcard, Visa

Daylesford and Hepburn Villas
110 West St
Daylesford VIC 3460
Phone 03/5348 3722
Fax 03/5348 3777
Email dhv@dayget.com.au
Web www.urbanplaces.com.au

Gender Mixed

These beautiful, self-contained architect-designed villas are located close to the lake, town, restaurants and spas.

Cost From $175 per unit
Payment AmEx, Bankcard, Diners, EFTPOS, MasterCard, Visa

Double Nut of Switzerland

5 Howe St
Daylesford VIC 3460
Phone 03/5348 3981
Gender Mixed

These self-contained bungalows in a garden setting have private decks, spas and kitchenettes.

Cost $66 single, $88 double
Payment Amex, Bankcard, Diners, MasterCard, Visa

Alison Pouliot

Elaine Country Cottages

69 Parkinsons Lane
Elaine VIC 3334
Phone Karen or Jane 03/5341 5561
Fax 03/5341 5561
Web www.ballarat.com/elaine.htm
Gender Mixed

These self-contained cottages have spas, wood fires, tennis courts and walks and are just over half an hour's drive from Daylesford. They are set in extensive gardens and herbs are for sale.

Cost $132–165 per room
Payment Cheque

Green Gully Bush Retreat

Pyrenees Highway
Green Gully VIC 3462
Phone 03/5476 2557
Email nandvee@netcon.net.au
Gender Mixed

This retreat offers self-catering accommodation in cabins (sleeping up to four) with verandahs and barbecues in a bush setting. It is 13km to Castlemaine, handy to Maldon, spa country and historic towns. Assisted meditation and massage are available. Pets allowed by arrangement.

Cost From $66 single, $72 double (then $6 each extra person)
Payment Cheque

Hepburn Haven

5 Wynvale Rd
Hepburn Springs VIC 3461
Phone Christine 03/9893 3429 or 0409 258 096
Gender Mixed

This fully self-contained three-bedroom cottage has ducted heating, a barbecue area and is walking distance from the spa complex and cafés. Smoking is permitted outside only.

Cost $286–308 per weekend (two-night minimum stay); discounted midweek rates

Payment Cheque

Hesket House

1201 Romsey Rd
Romsey VIC 3434

Phone Peter or Shaun 03/5427 0608

Email trilogy@intermet.net.au

Gender Mixed

Gay-owned and -operated *Hesket House* is set in bushland with well-maintained walking tracks; the rustic, poured-mud house has a tropical conservatory and breakfast area. Accommodation ranges from bunkhouses to rooms with ensuites. Continental breakfast is included in the tariff; all meals and picnic hampers are available on request at extra cost. There is a spa, and a guest lounge with books and pianola sessions in the evening. The lake on the property is suitable for swimming and there is abundant wildlife in the surrounding forest.

Cost From $44 single, $132 double

Payment AmEx, Bankcard, Diners, MasterCard, Visa; cheque

Holly Lodge

19 Grenville St
Daylesford VIC 3460

Phone John 03/5348 3670

Fax 03/5348 3670

Email hollylodgings@hotmail.com

Gender Mixed

Relax in your own suite in this lovely gay-owned and -operated Victorian home set in a large garden. There are open fires, central heating, guest lounge with TV, VCR, stereo and library. All rooms have private ensuites and sunrooms, queen-size beds, and the tariff includes a scrumptious breakfast. *Holly Lodge* is close to the centre of Daylesford and there is transport to spas available. Smoking is permitted outside only.

Cost $308 per weekend (two-night minimum stay); discounted midweek rates

Payment Bankcard, MasterCard, Visa; cheque

Alison Pouliot

Kattemingga Lodge

PO Box 39
Newbury VIC 3458

Phone 03/5424 1415

Fax 03/5424 1609

Email enquiries@kattemingga.com.au

Web www.kattemingga.com.au

Gender Mixed

This garden oasis surrounded by forest is a great weekend getaway, but also caters for conferences, commitment ceremonies, parties and workshops. There is an outdoor spa, tennis courts, horse-riding. Smoking is permitted outside only.

Cost From $105 per room
Payment Cheque

Max Wellton B&B

107 Clarkes Lane
Woodend VIC 3442
Phone 03/5427 3128
Gender Mixed

Close to spa country, Mount Macedon and Hanging Rock, and set in extensive grounds with resident peacocks, this B&B offers all the comforts of home. Continental breakfast is included. Smoking is permitted outside only.

Cost From $160 per room
Payment Bankcard, MasterCard, Visa; cheque

Newlife Farm Retreat

PO Box 55
Newstead VIC 3462
Phone Margot and Jen 03/5476 2401
Gender Mixed

These solar- and wind-powered cottages with full kitchens, wood fires, TV and barbecue provide a bush escape close to Maldon and Daylesford.

Cost From $77 per couple
Payment Bankcard, MasterCard, Visa

Poolway Cottages

PO Box 18
Hepburn Springs VIC 3461
Phone 03/5348 1049
Fax 03/5348 1049
Web www.mineralsprings.net.au/poolway
Gender Mixed

These peaceful cottages with private balconies, queen-size beds and wood fires in a bush setting are just a short walk to the spa resort. Continental breakfast provisions are provided.

Cost From $150 per room midweek, $386 for two-night minimum stay at weekends
Payment Bankcard, EFTPOS, MasterCard, Visa; cheque

The Rose of Daylesford

58 Ragland St
Daylesford VIC 3460
Phone Tulka-Rose 03/5348 1482
Gender Mixed

This charming B&B is close to shops, galleries and restaurants. Rooms have open fires, and spas and massage are available.

Cost From $83 per room
Payment Cash only

Springs Hotel

124 Main Rd
Hepburn Springs VIC 3461
Phone 03/5348 2202
Fax 03/5348 2506
Email stay@thesprings.com.au
Web www.thesprings.com.au
Gender Mixed

This charming Deco hotel is a short walk from the spa resort and offers hotel or cabin accommodation with buffet breakfast. The hotel has a restaurant, counter meals are served at the bar and there's a pool table. During summer there is live jazz in the beer garden.

Cost $240–320 per weekend (two-night minimum stay); discounted midweek rates
Payment Amex, Bankcard, Diners, EFTPOS, MasterCard, Visa

Villa Parma

128 Main Rd
Hepburn Springs VIC 3461
Phone 03/5348 3512
Fax 03/5348 3158
Email vparma@netconnect.com.au
Web www.spacountry.net.au/
villaparma
Gender Mixed
This spectacularly restored Tuscan-style
mansion offers B&B accommodation
with shared bathrooms. There is a guest
lounge with TV, stereo, library and
open fire; gardens surround the
property. The self-contained Parma
studio comes complete with kitchen,
bathroom, lounge and bedroom
decorated in a contemporary
warehouse style. This gay-owned and
-operated establishment is a short walk
from the spa complex and cafés.
Cost From $280 per couple per
weekend (two-night minimum stay),
$130 per night midweek
Payment AmEx, Bankcard,
MasterCard, Visa; cheque

Villa Vita

Main Rd
Kingston VIC 3364
Phone 03/5345 6448
Gender Mixed
This historic site is set amidst lovely
gardens in the charming hamlet of
Kingston, only 15 minutes' drive from
Daylesford. *Villa Vita* offers full
breakfasts, dinner on request and
late checkouts. There is one room
with a spa.
Cost From $111 per room
Payment Amex, Bankcard,
MasterCard, Visa

Willowbank Farm and Cottage

199 Muckleford School Rd,
Muckleford via Tasmania
Castlemaine VIC 3450
Phone Jeremy 03/5472 2483
Fax 03/5472 2483
Email jemnic@hotmail.com
Gender Mixed
This gay-owned, 1860s stone
cottage with log fires set in an
award-winning garden is close to
spa country and the towns of
Maldon and Castlemaine. The
cottage, furnished in an eclectic mix
of old and new, sleeps up to four, is
fully self-contained and breakfast
is provided. Complimentary
champagne on arrival.
Cost $100 per person per night (two-
night minimum stay at weekends)
Payment Cheque

Woodbury Cottage

Jason Drive
Woodend VIC 3442
Phone 03/5427 1876
Email woodbury@netcon.net.au
Gender Mixed
Lesbian-owned and -operated
Woodbury Cottage caters for only one
or two guests at a time. Guests have
the exclusive use of their own private
wing, which includes a sitting room,
TV, library, and log fire or central
heating. Breakfast is included and
simple home-cooked suppers are
available by prior arrangement.
Young children and pets are not
catered for, and smoking is not
permitted.
Cost From $88 single, $111 double
Payment Cheque

CAFÉS AND RESTAURANTS

The Boathouse

Lake Daylesford, Foreshore Leggat St
Daylesford VIC 3460
Phone 03/5348 1387
Fax 03/5348 1387

Daylesford's most famous restaurant is built on the edge of a picturesque lake. *The Boathouse* offers a changing seasonal menu, but favourites include the bull-boar sausage (a local speciality, served here on a pizza) and chicken and mango salad with fresh raspberry dressing. All wines served come from local wineries. There is a bar, indoor and al fresco dining. Smoking is restricted to outside tables. Bookings are essential at weekends.

Open Mon–Thurs 9am–5pm, Fri–Sun 9am–late
Cost $20–30 lunch, $30–40 dinner
Payment Amex, Bankcard, Diners, MasterCard, Visa

BODY STUFF

Hepburn Spa Resort

Mineral Springs Reserve, PO Box 93
Hepburn Springs VIC 3461
Phone 03/5348 2034
Fax 03/5348 1167
Web www.hepburnspa.com.au
Gender Mixed

This historic temple of relaxation, set amid some of Victoria's most beautiful scenery, offers an extraordinary range of pampering options. Hydrotherapies include calcium, silica, magnesium, bicarbonate and iron treatments. There are communal spas, couch spas, private spas for singles or couples, flotation tanks, massage, sauna and a range of health and beauty services. Bookings are essential for treatments. The resort is fully equipped with disabled facilities and is a delightful place to while away an afternoon.

Open Mon–Fri 10am–8pm, Sat 9am–9.30pm, Sun 9am–8pm
Cost From $8.80 for public pool to $215 for packages including therapies and lunch
Payment Amex, Bankcard, Diners, EFTPOS, MasterCard, Visa

COMMUNITY

Castlemaine Gay

Castlemaine VIC 3450
Phone Anthony 03/5470 5966
Gender Mixed

This group organizes regular social functions and a bar night on the first Saturday of each month.

CVLN (Central Victorian Lesbian Network)

PO Box 773
Woodend VIC 3442
Phone Tina 03/5427 1876
Pam 03/5441 6771
Email woodburycottage@netcon.net.au

Gender Women

The *Central Victorian Lesbian Network* promotes a supportive and positive lesbian community and provides social contacts for lesbians in rural central Victoria. The group meets monthly on a rotating basis at women's homes throughout the region to share a light lunch and conduct discussions.

TRAVEL SERVICES

Daylesford Getaways
Shop 2, 123 Vincent St
Daylesford VIC 3460
Phone 03/5348 4422
Fax 03/5348 4333
Email bookings@dayget.com.au
Web www.dayget.com.au
The spa country's only gay-owned and -operated holiday booking service offers tailor-made spa country holiday packages to suit your budget. It has a selection of accommodation, from traditional miners' cottages to cutting-edge apartments.
Open Daily 9am–7pm
Payment Amex, Bankcard, Diners, EFTPOS, MasterCard, Visa

Bendigo and the Goulburn Valley

Like Ballarat, the gold town of **Bendigo** has retained some stunning architecture from the Gold Rush era, including the **Joss House**, which was built in the 1860s by Chinese miners who came to work the goldfields. As you head east, the land-scape softens into the rich farming country of the **Goulburn Valley** and historic riverports such as **Echuca**.

ACCOMMODATION

Cheviot Glen Cottages
Limestone Rd
Yea VIC 3717
Phone 03/5797 2617 or 0419 514 334
Email info@cheviotglencottages.com.au
Web www.cheviotglencottages.com.au
Gender Mixed
Enjoy magnificent views from these luxurious self-contained cottages on a Goulburn Valley grazing property. Cottages have ensuites and spas and wood fires. A full breakfast is provided, including plunger coffee and home-baked bread. There are scenic drives, bushwalking and trail rides in the area.
Cost $135 per unit
Payment Bankcard, MasterCard, Visa

Daisy Lodge Cabins

Baxters Rd
Goulburn Weir, Victoria 3608
Phone 03/5794 7271
Fax 03/5794 7394
Email buckjane@hotmail.com
Web www.qbeds.findhere.com
Gender Mostly women
This lakeside accommodation in the
Goulburn Valley is popular with gays
and lesbians. The self-contained
cabins are surrounded by vineyards,
and meals are available over the road
at *Daisy Lodge*. Dogs are welcome and
there is even an enclosed cat
playground.
Cost $100 per cabin midweek, $185 at
weekends; $485 weekly
Payment Cheque

Echuca Gardens

103 Mitchell St
Echuca VIC 3564
Phone Kym and Klavis 03/5480 6522
or 0419 881 054
Gender Mixed
This two-storey, gay-owned and
-operated, log cabin B&B is a must
for lovers of kitsch. Each room
features hand-painted Australian
wildflower themes, and there are
abundant murals and artefacts, as well
as a garden spa, landscaped water
garden and a resident pianist.
Smorgasbord breakfasts are served on
the balcony. Smoking is permitted
outside only.
Cost From $100 single, $132 double
(discounted midweek rates)
Payment Bankcard, MasterCard, Visa

Kirralea Lodge B&B

6 Wheelhouse St
Toolamba VIC 3614
Phone Warren 03/5826 5439
Fax 03/5826 5439
Gender Mixed
This modern gay-owned and
-operated homestay has cosy rooms
with old-world charm. A full country
breakfast is served daily in the main
dining room and dinner is available on
request. There is a smoking lounge
downstairs. *Kirralea Lodge* is close to
the Goulburn River and bushland,
and situated right in the village.
Cost From $44 single, $100 double
Payment AmEx, Bankcard, Diners,
MasterCard, Visa; cheque

Whispering Winds

Strathbogie VIC 3666
Phone 03/5798 1608
Gender Women
Fifteen minutes' off the Hume
Highway, situated between Euroa and
Violet Town, *Whispering Winds* is a
romantic women's retreat set in native
forest. The spacious hand-built earth
and stone cottage with loft bedroom
is fully self-contained and sleeps up to
four. A breakfast basket is included.
There is a large dam on the property
for swimming, there are camp fires in
the winter and plenty of wildlife to
see in the reserve. Massage and sauna
are available. Pets are welcome.
Smoking is permitted outside only.
Cost From $100 per couple
($17 each extra person)
Payment Cheque

Bendigo Gay Society

PO Box 1123
Bendigo VIC 3552
Country AIDS Network
Phone 03/5443 8355 or
03/5443 8187 (after hours)
Fax 03/5443 8198
Email bgs@can.org.au
Web www.can.org.au
Gender Mixed
This social support group for gays
and lesbians in the Bendigo area offers
weekly drop-in nights and monthly
social functions.

CAN Resource Centre

34 Myers St
Bendigo VIC 3550
Phone 03/5443 8355
Email www.can.org.au
Gender Mixed
CAN (Country AIDS Network) run
this community house and drop-in
centre. A volunteer-run project, it
aims to provide the community with
information about health (specifically
STDs, HIV/AIDS and other blood-
borne viruses) and social issues in the
Bendigo region.
Open Mon–Fri 10am–3pm

The High Country

Four hours' drive or 280kms to the north of Melbourne is the
breathtaking scenery of the High Country. Towns like
Myrtleford, Bright, Mount Beauty, Yackandandah and
Beechworth all offer charming attractions and accommodation.
Beechworth, in particular, has several queer-friendly establishments. During the warmer months (November–May), driving
through the High Country is an inspiring adventure, though it
does involve some unpaved roads. Snow chains need to be used
in the winter and some roads become impassable when it rains,
even in summer, so it pays to ask locals about driving conditions
before setting off. The **Ovens River**, which runs through Bright,
is a delightful spot to swim and nearby **Mount Buffalo** is great if
you're interested in exploring some Aussie mountain wilderness.

Braeview B&B

4 Stuart Rd
Mount Beauty VIC 3699
Phone 03/5754 4746
Fax 03/5754 4746
Email info@braeview.com.au
Web www.braeview.com.au

Gender Mixed
Choose between a self-contained
studio with ensuite, spa, full kitchen
and cable TV or rooms with ensuites
(some with spas) and breakfast. All
guests are welcome to use the hot tub
in the garden, and to indulge in

complimentary port and chocolates. Evening meals are available by prior arrangement.

Cost $110–132 per room, $148 for studio

Payment Bankcard, MasterCard, Visa

Buckland Valley B&B

PO Box 353, off Buckland Valley Rd
Bright VIC 3741

Phone 03/5756 2656

Fax 03/5756 2656

Gender Mixed

This farmstay-style accommodation is a unique construction of local eucalypt logs and riverstone, and is located 15km from Bright. It has a magnificent river frontage; massage and kinesiology are available. All rooms have ensuites, and are decorated with antiques and rustic memorabilia. Continental breakfast is included, and dinners can be arranged for groups of four or more. Smoking is permitted outside only.

Cost From $105 per room

Payment Amex, Bankcard, MasterCard, Visa

Dinner Plain Central Reservations

Big Muster Drive
Dinner Plain VIC 3898

Phone 03/5159 6451

Fax 03/5159 6515

Email dinnerplain@b150.aone.net.au

Web www.dinnerplain.com

Gender Mixed

This ski resort booking service offers a range of self-contained cabins and chalets for small or larger groups of guests.

Open Daily 9am–5pm

Cost From $339 per cabin per weekend

Payment Amex, Bankcard, Diners, EFTPOS, MasterCard, Visa

Nutwood House

Harris Lane Lot 12A
Porepunkah VIC 3740

Phone David and Peter
03/5756 2084 or freecall 1800/675 300

Gender Mixed

Each room has an ensuite and superb views of the alps; spas and massage are available.

Cost From $66 single, $100 double

Payment Amex, Bankcard, MasterCard, Visa

Rosewhite House Rural Retreat

RMB 2555 Carrolls Rd
Myrtleford VIC 3737

Phone Noel or Beverly Stone
03/5753 5300 or freecall 1800/675 300

Fax 03/5753 5239

Email rosewhitehouse@netc.net.au

Web www.rosewhitehouse.com.au

Gender Mixed

Enjoy peace and tranquillity at the heart of Victoria's High Country with a heated spa pool, guest kitchen and barbecue. Champagne and a cheese platter are served on your arrival, then there are gourmet breakfasts – and evening meals are available by prior arrangement. Smoking is permitted outside only.

Cost $160 per couple; discounts for longer stays

Payment Bankcard, MasterCard, Visa; cheque

Stanley Croft

PO Box 332
Beechworth VIC 3747

Phone Mark or Kim 03/5728 6626

Fax 03/5728 6626
Email scroft@netc.net.au
Web home.netc.net.au/~scroft
Gender Mostly men
Located just outside the historic township of Beechworth, *Stanley Croft* offers self-contained accommodation with continental breakfasts included. This gay-owned and -operated establishment offers a true escape with no phones or TVs, but sprawling gardens. Bookings are essential for Easter and long weekends.
Cost $65 single, $100 double
Payment Bankcard, MasterCard, Visa

Gippsland

Gippsland, southeast of Melbourne, is where you'll find the green **pastureland** of Victoria's dairy country cheek by jowl with **power stations**, vast deposits of coal in the Latrobe Valley, the Bass Strait oil fields and the hook-shaped projection of **Wilsons Promontory**, Victoria's most popular national park.

ACCOMMODATION

The Barn at Glenwood
Roberts Rd, Macks Creek
Tarra Valley VIC 3971
Phone 03/5186 1310
Web www.netspace.net.au/~glenwoodfarm
Gender Mixed
This secluded valley hideaway, close to Wilsons Promontory, Tarra-Bulga National Park, Ninety Mile Beach and Port Albert, has two bedrooms with loft, combustion stove and kitchen. Pets are welcome by arrangement, there's a barbecue area and breakfast is available. There are great views of the valley from the barn and plenty of walks to do and birdlife to see.
Cost From $85 per couple ($11 each extra person)
Payment Bankcard, MasterCard, Visa; cheque

Eilean Donan Gardens
Tarra Valley Rd
Yarram VIC 3971
Phone 03/5182 6165
Gender Mixed
Close to historic Port Albert and Tarra-Bulga National Park, this heritage property is ideal for groups of up to eight and has its own river frontage. All rooms have ensuites and balconies. Catering and breakfast baskets can be arranged.
Cost From $44 per room (two-night minimum stay at weekends)
Payment Cheque

Kookaburra Rise B&B
Lot 6 Raintree Court
Sarsfield VIC 3875
Phone 03/5156 8661
Fax 03/5156 8535

Email mscgmc@i-o.net.au
Web www.lakesandwilderness.com.au
Gender Mixed
Self-contained accommodation (one double and two singles) with breakfast provided, and dinner available on request. *Kookaburra Rise* is only 25 minutes' drive from Lakes Entrance and 13km from Bairnsdale.
Cost $55 single, $80 double
Payment Bankcard, MasterCard, Visa; cheque

Sundowner Lodge
128 Inlet View Rd
Venus Bay VIC 3956

Phone Fay and Di 03/5663 7099
Fax 03/5663 7099
Email sundown@tpg.com.au
Web interbed.com.au/sundowner.htm
Gender Mixed
Boutique accommodation with queen-sized beds, TV, ensuites, communal spa and licensed restaurant and cocktail bar. The lodge is within walking distance of a spectacular ocean beach which allows nude bathing. Pets are welcome.
Cost From $75 single, $100 double
Payment Bankcard, EFTPOS, MasterCard, Visa

COMMUNITY

Gippsland Gay and Lesbian Network
PO Box 848
Morwell VIC 3840
Phone Heather 03/5174 8106
Gender Mixed
This support group for gays and lesbians living in Gippsland holds meetings in Orbost, Bairnsdale, Warragul, Venus Bay and Morwell, as well as arranging social activities. It also hosts a youth group and 'The Gippy Gals', specifically for lesbians in Gippsland.

Tasmania

Tasmania, with a population of 1.3 million, is an island renowned for both its natural beauty and its grim convict past. Tasmania offers **wilderness** enthusiasts, bushwalkers, nature lovers and photographers an array of national parks of World Heritage standing.

The grandeur of **Cradle Mountain**, in the state's northwest, is mantled in snow during the winter and (if you're lucky), bathed in dazzling sunshine on a summer's day. The story of 'The Cradle' over the past two centuries is told on murals in the nearby town of Sheffield: it's a rollicking saga of the fur trappers who once roamed the western tiers and of the arduous construction of hydro-electric schemes. One of the more poignant incidents involved one Henry Hellyer, a colonial surveyor and the first white man to climb Cradle Mountain. Tragically, he committed suicide when rumours of his relationship with a male convict spread throughout Tasmania.

Wilderness aside, Tasmania's other hard currency is history and **quaintness** – as you'll soon discover in the myriad antique shops and home-made jam outlets – yet there is a real freshness to some of the less commercial centres.

The fight for rights

Salamanca Place, on Hobart's waterfront, was the birthplace of the modern Tasmanian **gay and lesbian rights movement**. It was here in 1988 that a small gay and lesbian stall was the focus of large-scale protests and arrests, following its banning by Hobart City Council. Over a decade later, much has changed in Tasmania due, in part, to the tireless campaigning of the Tasmanian Gay and Lesbian Rights Lobby sparked by their weekly presence at Salamanca Market.

Tasmania now has some of the most **progressive laws** and policies on sexual minorities in the world. There is an equal age of consent for everyone, regardless of sexual preference, and laws that provide heavy penalties for discrimination and vilification on the grounds of sexuality. Tasmania is now among the most proactive states in Australia in this regard: there are gay and lesbian police liaison officers in each area of the state; mandatory anti-homophobia programs in all state schools; mentoring services for young lesbian, gay, bisexual and transgender people; and workshops in sexual diversity for tourist-service providers.

Historically, it was a very different story. In the first half of the nineteenth century, when Tasmania was primarily a **penal colony**, the middle classes reacted with consternation to the sight of **same-sex** convict **couples** walking hand-in-hand through the streets of Hobart. Women who formed amorous relationships with other women at the Female Prison in South Hobart were labelled 'pseudo-males', separated from their companions and sent away to another part of the island. Men who fell in love with other men were consigned to the hated Model Prison at Port Arthur or, even worse, were sent to work the coal mines or banished to the remote Sarah Island, near Strahan on Tasmania's harsh west coast. When visiting Tasmania's **convict sites**, take a moment to recall the lives and the suffering, as well as the brave defiance, of our forebears who endured the convict system.

Hobart

Hobart offers a rare glimpse of early Australian heritage, especially in the city's National Trust-listed areas, such as **Battery Point,** with its maze of narrow streetscapes and historic buildings. Popular throughout the year and attracting some 10,000 people every Saturday, Hobart's weekly **Salamanca Market** is renowned for its quality arts and crafts and its fresh produce. Food and drink are taken very seriously in Hobart. There are many fine **restaurants** to choose from in the vicinity of Salamanca Place – and most of the **gay venues** are also within walking distance.

> For **public transport** timetables and fares in Hobart, call 13 2201.

After the bustle of the market and the dockside, take a pleasant stroll on the wooded slopes of **Mount Wellington**. Interpretation signs along the well-worn **Pipeline Track** include photos of people who enjoyed the mountain in years gone by. Among them are the oldest photos of gay couples in Australia, taken in Hobart's mountain suburb of Ferntree in the 1920s.

ACCOMMODATION

Bavarian Tavern

281 Liverpool St
Hobart TAS 7000
Phone 03/6234 7977
Fax 03/6236 9573
Gender Mixed
This popular gay/lesbian pub offers basic, clean accommodation with shared facilities and a TV lounge.
Cost $25 single, $39 double, $45 self-contained unit
Payment Bankcard, EFTPOS, MasterCard, Visa

Corinda's Cottages Heritage Accommodation

17 Glebe St
Glebe TAS 7000
Phone Wilmar and Matthew 03/6234 1590
Fax 03/6234 2744

Email info@corindascottages.com.au
Web www.corindascottages.com.au
Gender Mixed
Share in the splendour of a bygone era at this gay-owned and -operated stately mansion surrounded by beautifully tended gardens. The servants' quarters, coach house and gardener's cottage have all been refurbished – each is self-contained with a lounge, dining-room, laundry, fully equipped kitchen, antique furnishings, CD, TV, wood fires and fresh flowers. Breakfast is supplied. The city is 10 minutes' walk away. Smoking is permitted outside only.
Cost $170–190 per couple (discounts for longer stays)
Payment AmEx, Bankcard, Diners, EFTPOS, MasterCard, Visa

The Lodge on Elizabeth
249 Elizabeth St
Hobart TAS 7000
Phone 03/6231 3830
Fax 03/6234 2566
Email thelodgehobart@trump.net.au
Gender Mixed
This beautiful old mansion built by convicts in 1829 is conveniently located close to some of Hobart's best restaurants.
Cost $94–132 per room
Payment AmEx, MasterCard, Visa

Wellington Lodge
7 Scott St
Glebe TAS 7000
Phone 03/6231 0614
Fax 03/6234 1551
Gender Mixed
This classic residence (circa 1885) is located in historic Glebe, just 10 minutes' walk to the city. All rooms have Victorian-style decor and private facilities. A cooked breakfast is included. No smoking allowed.
Cost From $83 single, $105 double
Payment Bankcard, MasterCard, Visa; cheque

CAFÉS AND RESTAURANTS

Beaujangles
49 Elizabeth Mall
Hobart TAS 7000
Phone 03/6236 9980 David Seaben
Fax 03/6236 9101
Email dsiepen@h130.aone.net.au
Web www.home.aone.net.au
This gay-owned and -operated BYO establishment has been a part of Hobart gay life for 20 years – and things can get quite cruisy on the front tables. Everything is made on the premises – from the quiches to the muffins, focaccias and pies. There's an al fresco area and lots of artwork on display.
Open Mon–Sat 8am–6pm
Cost $8–15 per person
Payment AmEx, Bankcard, EFTPOS, MasterCard, Visa

Cumquat
10 Criterion St
Hobart TAS 7000
Phone 03/6234 5858
Email cumquat@southcom.com.au
Cumquat specializes in delicious breakfasts and lunches (bookings advisable for lunch). Their most popular breakfast dish is sweet risotto with banana and vanilla beans, while lunch includes their signature laksa. Vegan, vegetarian and gluten-free dishes are also available. The ambience of this lesbian-owned and -operated café is casual; the interior is hip and groovy with a glimmer of stainless steel. No smoking is permitted.
Open Mon–Fri 8am–6pm
Cost $10–15 per person
Payment Cash only

Kaos Cafe
237 Elizabeth St
North Hobart TAS 7000
Phone 03/6231 5699
Fax 03/62310 880

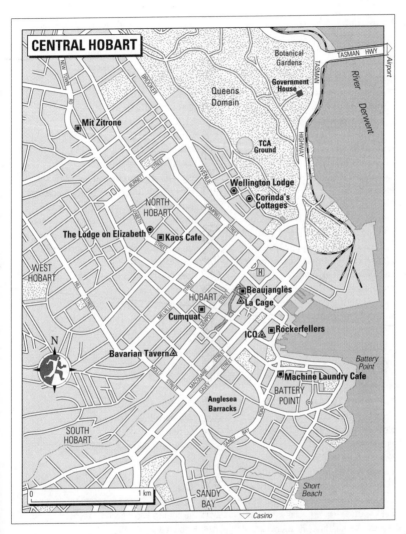

CENTRAL HOBART

Botanical Gardens

TASMAN HWY

Airport

Queens Domain

Government House

TCA Ground

Mit Zitrone

BURNET STREET

AVENUE

CAMPBELL STREET

HIGHWAY

River Derwent

TASMAN

BROOKER

NEW TOWN RD

Wellington Lodge

Corinda's Cottages

NORTH HOBART

ELIZABETH STREET

The Lodge on Elizabeth

Kaos Cafe

WEST HOBART

PARK STREET

HOBART

H

Beaujangles

La Cage

Cumquat

MELVILLE STREet

MURRAY STREET

HARRINGTON STREET

ICQ

Rockerfellers

Bavarian Tavern

N

MILL STREET

MACQUARIE STREET

DAVEY STREET

SANDY BAY ROAD

Battery Point

Machine Laundry Cafe

BATTERY POINT

Anglesea Barracks

SOUTH HOBART

0   1 km

SANDY BAY

Short Beach

Casino

This BYO café serves a great range of desserts and salads. Among their most popular dishes are the Kaos Cajun club sandwhich or Kaos steak sandwich.
Open Daily noon–midnight
Payment Cash only

Machine Laundry Cafe

12 Salamanca Square
Hobart TAS 7000
Phone 03/6224 9922
Fax 03/6224 9922
Email rbrake@optusnet.com.au

Enjoy contempory Australian cuisine, serious coffee, free-range eggs and a totally cool laundrette – all in one convenient location.
Open Daily 8am–6pm
Cost $10 per person
Payment AmEx, Bankcard, EFTPOS, MasterCard, Visa

Mit Zitrone

333 Elizabeth St
Hobart TAS 7000
Phone 03/6234 8113
Fax 03/6231 9150
This award-winning BYO restaurant combines fresh ingredients with global inspiration, to stunning effect. *Mit Zitrone*'s most popular dishes include twice-cooked eggs with chilli and palm sugar sauce and sea-urchin custard with warm oysters. The mood is casual and the style contemporary. Bookings are recommended for lunch

and dinner. Gay-owned and -operated.
Open Mon–Sat 10.30am–late
Cost Lunch $15–20, dinner $25–35
Payment AmEx, Bankcard, MasterCard, Visa

Rockerfellers

11 Morrison St
Hobart TAS 7000
Phone Gary and Ian 03/6234 3490
Fax 03/6224 4490
Web www.view.com.au/rockerfellers
This restored flour mill has an eclectic interior, combining displays on the historic waterfront area with modern art. The lunch menu is tapas and in the evening there are burgers, grills and seafood.
Open Mon–Fri noon–2.30pm, daily 6pm–late
Cost Lunch $14–18, dinner $30–35
Payment AmEx, Bankcard, Diners, EFTPOS, MasterCard, Visa

BARS AND CLUBS

Bavarian Tavern

281 Liverpool St
Hobart TAS 7000
Phone 03/6234 7977
Fax 03/6236 9573
Gender Mixed
If they're gay, lesbian, trannies or queer, they'll be found lolling around in the back lounge bar, especially on Sunday nights. At the 'Bav Tav' there's a dancefloor, darts, and two pool tables; look out for their dance parties, held on the first Saturday of the month. Dinner available Wednesday to Saturday.
Open Mon–Tues 2pm–midnight, Wed–Thurs 2pm–2am, Fri noon–3am,

Sat 4pm–3am, Sun 4pm–2am
Admission Free, cover charge for party nights
Payment Bankcard, EFTPOS, MasterCard, Visa

ICQ

7 Despard St (a lane off Murray St, parallel to Morrison & Davey)
Hobart TAS 7000
Phone 03/6224 4411
Gender Mixed
This cosy downstairs speakeasy-style bar also has a restaurant and dancefloor. *ICQ* offers casual meals, drinks and music on Wednesday and

Thursday, and on Friday night it pumps to a hot dance mix. Saturday nights specialize in high NRG and trance. Dinners and late suppers available ($6–15).
Open Wed–Fri 5pm–late, Sat 7pm–late
Admission Cover charge $6; more for special events
Payment AmEx, Bankcard, EFTPOS, MasterCard, Visa

La Cage
Ship Hotel (downstairs)
59 Collins St
Hobart TAS 7000
Phone 03/6231 5882
Gender Mixed
This is a cruisy, even legendary, disco bar where Saturday is the big night.
Open Thurs–Sat 11pm–5am
Payment Cash only

NEWSPAPERS AND MAGAZINES

Centrelines
PO Box 152
North Hobart TAS 7002
Phone 03/6228 7241
Email editor@gaytas.org
Web www.gaytas.org
Gender Mixed

This monthly newsletter of the *Gay and Lesbian Community Centre* (p.296) is bursting with personals, local news, events, contacts and articles of general interest.
Cost $2 per issue

BEACHES AND POOLS

Seven Mile Beach
TAS 7170
Gender Mixed
The eastern end of Seven Mile Beach is the most popular gay beach in

Tasmania. Take the A3 eastbound, follow the airport signs, and turn right into the suburb of Cambridge (just before you get to the airport). The beach is 15km east of Hobart.

MEDICAL

Women's Health Centre
326 Elizabeth St
North Hobart TAS 7002
Phone 03/6231 3212, freecall 1800/353 212
Fax 03/6236 9449
Email hwhc@trump.net.au
Web www.tased.edu.au/tasonline/hwhc/hwhc.htm
Gender Women

This free holistic health service offers women information, referrals, counselling, workshops, the services of a general practitioner and lesbian health workers, a library and community noticeboard. Childcare is available for groups.
Open Mon–Tues 9am–4pm, Wed 3pm–6.30pm, Thurs–Fri 9am–4pm

Criss Cross
GPO Box 595F
Hobart TAS 7001
Gender Mixed
A cross-dressers' support group.

Gay Information Line
Phone 03/6234 8179
Gender Mixed
This 24-hour recorded information service gives referral numbers and a full listing of clubs, bars, restaurants and events (from barbecues to car rallies and golf days) for gay and lesbians.

Gay and Lesbian Community Centre of Tasmania
PO Box 152
North Hobart TAS 7002
Phone mobile 0419 565 452
Email president@gaytas.org or ghornsey@southcom.com.au
Web www.gaytas.org
Gender Mixed
This community organization puts on functions and other activities (Queens' Ball, Halloween, monthly dance parties, Australia Day Picnic, car rallies). It also produces a monthly newsletter, *Centrelines* (see p.295), and a business and services directory.
Cost Membership $20

Lesbian Line
PO Box 637
North Hobart TAS 7002
Phone 03/6231 4228
Gender Women
Information, support and referrals for lesbians.
Open Thurs 6pm–10pm

Lesbian Space
c/- Women's Health Centre,
326 Elizabeth Street
North Hobart (PO Box 248) TAS 7002
Phone 03/6231 5991
Gender Women
A drop-in centre offering activities, discussions and entertainment.
Open Thurs 6pm–8pm

Lesbians in Space
c/- Hobart Women's Health Centre
326 Elizabeth St
North Hobart TAS 7002
Gender Women
A casual meeting place for women of all ages to share a coffee and a chat on Tuesdays. Children are welcome.
Open Tues 6pm–8pm

TasCard (Tasmanian Council on AIDS and Related Diseases)
319 Liverpool St
Hobart TAS 7000
Phone 03/6234 1242
Fax 03/6234 1630
Email mail@tascard.org.au
Web www.tascard.org.au
Gender Mixed
This group offers advocacy, education and support, as well as safe-sex supplies and a needle exchange.
Open Mon–Fri 9am–5pm

Tasmania Police Gay and Lesbian Community Liaison
GPO Box 308c
Hobart TAS 7001
Phone 03/6230 2111
Email lyn.jones@police.tas.gov.au
Gender Mixed

Inspectors Lyn Jones and Ken Saunders are contact officers who can put you in contact with other officers around the state.

Tasmanian Gay and Lesbian Rights Group

Room 201, 82 Hampden Rd
Battery Point TAS 7004
(GPO Box 1733, Hobart TAS 7001)
Phone 03/6224 3556 or 03/6224 3557
Email medico@tasgroup.wow.aus.com
Web www.tased.edu.au/tasonline/tasqueer/tasqueer.html
Gender Mixed

This group offers advocacy, lobbying and community education on behalf of gay, lesbian and queer communities, as well as operating a weekly stall at the Salamanca Market.
Open Mon–Fri 9am–5pm

Youthline

Phone Freecall 1800/633 900
Gender Mixed
This statewide toll-free support service is for those under 26 years of age seeking advice, assistance or peer support.

TRAVEL SERVICES

Cycling Adventures Tasmania

GPO Box 55
Hobart TAS 7001
Phone Rowan 0412 913 148
Email rowanburns@hotmail.com
Web www.tasadventures.com
Gender Mixed

This group offers a variety of half-day, one-day and multi-day tours, as well as bicycle-hire facilities ($15–30 per day), operating from Salamanca Square.
Open Daily 7.30am–6pm
Payment Bankcard, MasterCard, Visa

The Midlands

Straddled by the Midland Highway, which connects Hobart and Launceston, this district is distinguished by historic towns and a rich legacy of convict stonemasonry that has stood the test of time. It's worth taking a brief diversion from the highway in order to visit **Richmond,** 25km north of Hobart. **Richmond Gaol** (daily 9am–5pm) is a fine example of a convict prison and the town's bridge, constructed in 1823 by convict labour, is the oldest in Australia. Another convict-built bridge to stretch your legs on during the journey north or south is in **Ross**. The stonemason who executed the carvings on the arches of the bridge was granted a pardon for his fine work.

The Barracks

253 Midland Highway
Pontville TAS 7030
Phone 03/6268 1665
Fax 03/6268 1011
Email thebarracks@netspace.net.au
Gender Mixed
These self-contained cottages in a
heritage building are handy for sights
in central and southern Tasmania, Mt
Field National Park, and the historic
Midland towns. Breakfast is included.
Cost $111–143 per room
Payment Cheque

Colonial Cottages of Ross

Church St
Ross TAS 7209
Phone 03/6381 5354
Fax 03/6381 5408
Email tim@tasmania.com
Gender Mixed
These four colonial cottages in the
heart of the village are furnished
with antiques, but have modern
conveniences. Breakfast provisions are
supplied in all cottages, which sleep
up to six people.
Cost $132–180 per unit ($22–30 each
extra person)
Payment Bankcard, MasterCard, Visa;
cheque

Daisy Bank Cottages

Middle Tree Rd
Richmond TAS 7025
Phone 03/6260 2390
Fax 03/6260 2635
Gender Mixed
Enjoy farm accommodation, just 4km
from town, in sandstone Victorian
barns converted into self-contained
lofts which sleep up to four. Breakfast
is provided and both cottages have
wood fires; one also has a spa.
Cost From $143 per couple ($22 each
extra person)
Payment Bankcard, MasterCard, Visa;
cheque

Mrs Currie's B&B

4 Franklin St
Richmond TAS 7025
Phone Frank 03/6260 2766
Fax 03/6260 2110
Email curries@mpx.com.au
Web www.scu.edu.au/tasrural/curries
Gender Mixed
Set in a cottage garden, *Mrs Currie's*
was originally a public house in the
first half of the nineteenth century. A
cooked breakfast is included, and
bookings are essential.
Cost $128 per room
Payment AmEx, Bankcard, Diners,
MasterCard, Visa; cheque

Wilmot Arms Inn

120 Main Rd
Kempton TAS 7030
Phone 03/6259 1272
Fax 03/6259 1396
Email wilmotarms@trump.net.au
Gender Mixed
On the Midland Highway, this 1843
coaching inn is full of memorabilia
but has modern amenities. Some
rooms have ensuites and breakfast is
included.
Cost From $83 single, $105 double
Payment AmEx, Bankcard,
MasterCard, Visa

Launceston and the North Coast

Launceston is a tranquil city located in the dramatic Tamar Valley. **Cataract Gorge**, with its formal gardens patrolled by peacocks, chairlift rides and fantastic swimming in the summer, should not be missed. To either side of the mouth of the Tamar are the port towns of **Bridport** (to the east) and **Devonport** (on the west side); the latter is where the *Spirit of Tasmania* ferry from Melbourne docks.

ACCOMMODATION

Brickfields Terrace

64–68 Margaret St
Launceston TAS 7250
Phone 03/6331 0963 or 0417 100 578
Fax 03/6331 7778
Gender Mixed
Overlooking historic Brickfields Reserve, these 1889 terraces offer refined, stylish accommodation just a short walk from the city centre. There are two fully self-contained houses with log fires for guests' exclusive occupancy, and full breakfast provisions are provided.
Cost From $159 per room
Payment AmEx, Bankcard, Diners, MasterCard, Visa; cheque

Cottages on the Park

27 Lawrence St
Launceston TAS 7250
Phone 03/6334 2238 or 0417 540 721
Fax 03/6334 5061
Email edgington@microtech.com
Web www.focusontas.net.au
Gender Mixed
While retaining their authentic appeal and appearance, these two fully restored and centrally located cottages (catering for up to five guests each) have been fully equipped with modern conveniences, log fires and electric blankets. A hearty continental breakfast is included, and well-trained pets are allowed. Smoking outside only.
Cost From $122 single, $160 double
Payment AmEx, Bankcard, MasterCard, Visa

Gingerbread Cottage

52 William St
Westbury TAS 7303
Phone 03/6393 1140
Fax 03/6393 1140
Email clarkes@42south.com
Web www.clarkesantiques.com/colonial.htm
Gender Mixed
This self-contained 1850 cottage sleeps two, and is just 20 minutes' drive west of Launceston; it is furnished with antiques, and comes with breakfast provisions and a garden for guests' use. There are several museums and a pub in Westbury and a restaurant is close by, or evening meals can be organized by prior arrangement. Smoking is permitted outside only.
Cost $126 per cottage
Payment AmEx, Bankcard, MasterCard, Visa; cheque

Norfolk Reach B&B

84 Motor Rd
Exeter TAS 7275
Phone 03/6394 7681
Fax 03/6394 7681
Gender Mixed

This 1890 heritage homestead building is set in a bush and wildlife sanctuary, in the heart of vineyard country only 25 minutes' drive northwest of Launceston. All rooms have ensuites and breakfast is included in the tariff. There is a guest lounge with open fire, on-site bushwalks and a river for swimming. Evening meals can be arranged. Smoking is permitted outside on the covered verandah.

Cost From $88 per room
Payment Bankcard, MasterCard, Visa; cheque

Platypus Park Country Retreat

Ada St
Bridport TAS 7262
Phone 03/6356 1873
Fax 03/6356 0173
Email platypus@tasmail.com
Web www.bridport.tco.asn.au/platypus
Gender Mixed

Platypus Park, 2km from the centre of Bridport, offers ocean views, an outdoor spa and fishing in the retreat dam, with bushwalks on your doorstep. There are a range of one- and two-bedroom self-contained cottages and units, including a disabled-accessible unit and Lavender Cottage, with a double spa. Breakfast is included in the tariff, and there are barbecue and laundry facilities. Smoking is permitted outside only, and pets are allowed by prior arrangement.

Cost From $83–150 per unit
Payment AmEx, Bankcard, MasterCard, Visa; cheque

Rosalie Cottage

66 Wenvoe St
Devonport TAS 7310
Phone 03/6424 1560
Fax 03/6424 2090
Email dhc@tassie.net.au
Gender Mixed

This fully restored, self-contained historic house sleeps up to four and is just a short walk to town. It comes with a four-poster bed, TV, video, laundry, open fires, cottage garden, electric heating, full breakfast, and barbecue area. Pets are welcome by arrangement. Smoking is permitted outside only.

Cost From $154 per room
Payment Bankcard, MasterCard, Visa; cheque

Trelawney by the Sea

6 Chalmers Lane
Devonport TAS 7310
Phone 03/6424 3263
Fax 03/6424 3263
Email dickinson.services@bigpond.com
Gender Mixed

This large unit, 4km from Devonport, has a deck overlooking Coles Beach, with bikes and fishing gear available for guests' use, as are the barbecue, piano, and outdoor solar-heated spa. Full breakfast is provided, and evening meals can be served on request. Pets by prior arrangement.

Cost $100–122 per room
Payment Cheque

York Mansions

9–11 York St
Launceston TAS 7250
Phone 03/6334 2933
Fax 03/6334 2870
Email information@yorkmansions.com.au
Web www.yorkmansions.com.au
Gender Mixed
Chose between two- or three-bedroom self-contained apartments in this 1840 National Trust-listed mansion. All apartments have an open fire and a balcony, and breakfast provisions are included. Smoking is permitted outside only, and there is a large garden containing Launceston's oldest oak tree.
Cost $179–196 per apartment
Payment AmEx, Bankcard, Diners, MasterCard, Visa

BARS AND RESTAURANTS

Metz

119 St John St (cnr York St)
Launceston TAS 7250
Phone 03/6331 7277
Fax 03/6331 0223
Email themetz@bigpond.com
This friendly hotel attracts a diverse clientele, with a popular bar and a restaurant downstairs serving wood-fired pizzas and a wide range of dishes.
Open Daily 7.30am–late
Payment AmEx, Bankcard, MasterCard, Visa

The Venue

St James Hotel, York St
Launceston TAS 7250
Phone 03/6334 7231
A very mixed gay and lesbian get-together held weekly in the back room of the *St James Hotel*.
Open Fri 9.30pm–late
Admission $4
Payment Cash only

COMMUNITY

Women's Health Information Service (WHIS)

75 Cameron St, Civic Square
Launceston TAS 7250
Phone 03/6334 8335 or freecall 1800/675 028
Fax 03/6334 8331
Email whis@microtech.com.au
Gender Women
WHIS provides health information and medical referrals, organizes discussion groups, has a library and a meeting place.
Open Mon–Fri 9am–5pm

The East Coast

With its dazzling quartzite beach and deep blue water, **Wine-glass Bay** is a star attraction on Tasmania's east coast. Walk over the imposing granite humps that dominate the **Freycinet National Park** and be rewarded by Wineglass Bay's serenity and timelessness. If you're lucky, you may even glimpse some of the whales or dolphins that abound in Tasmania's pristine seas.

South of Freycinet is the **Tasman Peninsula** and **Port Arthur**, an infamous historical site and a place of significance for Australia's gay and lesbian community. Some of the male and female convicts sent to Tasmania from Britain were transported for 'crimes against nature' and, according to official reports and surviving love letters, some even formed long-term committed same-sex relationships.

Coombend Cottages

Coombend Estate
Swansea TAS 7190
Phone 03/6257 8256
Fax 03/6257 8484
Email coombendestate@vision.net.au
Gender Mixed

These two self-contained farm cottages sleep up to six and are located amid vineyards and olive groves, with Freycinet National Park just across Great Oyster Bay. Guests can enjoy wine tastings on the premises, and freshly baked bread, biscuits and fruit basket are provided. Breakfast is included and dinners are by arrangement. Smoking is permitted outside only.
Cost From $105 per couple ($28 each extra person)
Payment AmEx, Bankcard, MasterCard, Visa; cheque

Kabuki by the Sea

Tasman Highway (12km south of Swansea)
Swansea TAS 7190
Phone 03/6257 8588
Fax 03/6257 8588
Web www.view.com.au/kabuki
Gender Mixed

These gay-owned and -operated cottages afford spectacular views of Great Oyster Bay and the Freycinet Peninsula. Each one-bedroom suite has its own sitting room and kitchen, and there's a fully licensed Japanese restaurant on the premises. Continental breakfast is included in the tariff; there are also packages and special midweek deals.
Cost From $132 per couple; $193 dinner, B&B
Payment AmEx, Bankcard, Diners, EFTPOS, MasterCard, Visa

The West Coast

There are not too many choices to be made about where to stay on the west coast – there is only one town, **Strahan**. Situated on Macquarie Harbour, it is a relaxed place and a good springboard to the magical, World Heritage-listed **Franklin–Gordon Wild Rivers National Park**.

McIntosh Cottages

18 Harvey St
Strahan TAS 7468
Phone 03/6471 7358
Fax 03/6471 7074
Email hellemanpaul@tassie.net.au
Web www.westcoasttourism.com.au
Gender Mixed
Choose between two self-contained colonial cottages (one sleeps two, the other sleeps four) decorated in period decor, with wood fires and breakfast provisions provided. The cottages are just 500m from the town centre, handy to restaurants and Macquarie Harbour. Smoking is permitted outside only.
Cost From $149 double ($28 each extra person)
Payment AmEx, Bankcard, MasterCard, Visa; cheque

PART TWO

contexts

pussy's bow

Fruit Salad

1998 Sydney Gay &

...POTE OF CONTEMPORARY GAY & LESBIAN WRITING

Queer screen culture

Queer representation has been present throughout Australia's **screen history**, from a sissy character in *Dad and Dave Come to Town*, a bush classic of early cinema, to the flamboyant commercial success of *The Adventures of Priscilla, Queen of the Desert*. An openly gay relationship featured in the 1970s sitcom 'No. 96', twenty years before Will and Grace graced US television screens. Amid much social consternation this risqué series flaunted hundreds of episodes between 1972 and 1977. The long-running series, 'Prisoner' (aka 'Cell Block H'), set in a women's prison, pointed heavily towards lesbian relationships. It screened from 1979 to 1987 and has made one of its leading actresses, Maggie Kirkpatrick, a gay icon.

Early last century Australia enjoyed a productive cinema scene. Predominant themes were rural endeavours – and consequently, the major relationships were often between man and the harsh environment, or man and his livestock. One **queer character** did appear, however, in Ken G. Hall's film, *Dad and Dave Come to Town* (1938), which features the high camp character Entwhistle. While often mistaken for a woman by other characters, which was all very humorous, Entwhistle was also depicted as a capable and beloved employee. The respect given by the lead characters and his importance in the plot, gives substance to Hall's claim that Entwhistle was a new kind of Australian character.

Meanwhile, female characters **cross-dressed** in several Australian films, some bearing stockwhips, as they took the macho culture in their stride. Louise Lovely, for example, masqueraded as a boy in *Jewelled Nights* (1925), in order to prospect for gold in Tasmania. In *Bitter Springs* (1950), Nonnie Piper is derided as 'a lady in trousers' which prompts her mother's comment, 'Well, you always wanted to be a boy'.

After a slump in the post-war period, Australian cinema enjoyed a government-funded revival in the 1970s. Public debate arising out of films such as *The Naked Bunyip* (1970), a semi-documentary exploring alternative sexual practices and lifestyles, led to some relaxation of censorship laws. A bawdy ocker genre emerged with films such as *The Adventures of Barry McKenzie* (1972) and *Alvin Purple* (1973), where **homosexual incidents** occur due to mistaken identities or misadventures, making the hero very nervous.

At much the same time there was a spate of period films, many becoming classics, which dealt with class, colonialism and the beauty of the natural landscape. Among them were Peter Weir's *Picnic at Hanging Rock* (1975) and Bruce Beresford's *The Getting of Wisdom* (1977), both of which were set in girls' boarding schools and featured crushes and relationships amongst pupils and staff. Although not overtly sexual, these films involved nuance, love letters and, in the case of *Picnic at Hanging Rock*, a group female ecstasy mysteriously leading to some schoolgirls' disappearances.

During this decade, many directors, some of whom would later gain international recognition, were making shorts and tele-movies dealing with **queer issues**. Among them were Paul Cox, *Skindeep* (1970); Phil Noyce, *Brad*; Chris Noonan, *Cass* (1978) and Gillian Armstrong.

Contemporary Australia has developed an active queer film culture. Apart from a large number of drama and documentary filmmakers, Australia is home to **Queer Screen** (see p.60), which presents the Mardi Gras Film Festival each February as part of the month-long Sydney Gay and Lesbian Mardi Gras Arts Festival – the largest of its kind in the world. Queer Screen also presents **QueerDOC**, the world's first film festival dedicated entirely to queer documentaries, and holds premiere screenings and special events throughout the year. Check their Web site for more information: www.queerscreen.com.au.

Although **gay Aboriginality** has been significantly celebrated in recent years in the visual arts, it has appeared rarely in film. Tony Ayres' documentary *Double Trouble* (1991) responds to the white Australian refrain: 'Lesbian and gay Aborigines? I didn't know there were any.'

Aussie ocker representation has come full circle with Geoff Burton's well-intentioned but unconvincing *The Sum of Us* (1994). Here, a suburban ocker gay male relationship is depicted between Jeff (Russell Crowe) and his new boyfriend (John Polson). The message is 'Ockers can be queers too'. This message is affirmed in *The Adventures of Priscilla, Queen of the Desert* (1994) where a transsexual (Terence Stamp) becomes involved with a married outback Aussie (Bill Hunter).

Queer Australian film will never be the same again after the 1990s. While Baz Luhrmann captured a **camp aesthetic** in *Strictly Ballroom* (1992), Stephan Elliot unshackled it completely in *The Adventures of Priscilla, Queen of the Desert* (1994). The work of Ana Kokkinos – *Only the Brave* (1994) and *Head On* (1998) – broadened the queer cinema experience by presenting dynamic urban realism.

LISTING OF QUEER AUSTRALIAN FILMS

This alphabetical list refers mainly to titles available on video, although a few are obscure and difficult to find. It also includes selected films from New Zealand – a cheeky cultural steal, but we Aussies can't help ourselves.

The Adventures of Priscilla, Queen of the Desert
Stephan Elliott, 1994
Starring gay icon Terence Stamp as a transsexual, and Guy Pearce and Hugo Weaving as drag queens in a cross-country musical romp. The girls manage to keep their feathers intact while travelling from Sydney to Alice Springs in a bus. Along the way they encounter hostility and occasional acceptance. Includes a cameo role by Margaret Pomeranz, one of Australia's most prominent film critics.

All Men Are Liars
Gerard Lee, 1994
Down-home comedy set in a country town. Mick, a teenage boy, cross-dresses in order to join an all-girl band. Fellow band member Angela falls in love with him.

Bloodlust
Jon Hewitt, Richard Wolstencroft, 1991
Violent, humorous and good-looking action thriller that borrows from the plot line of *Fatal Attraction*. Lear, Frank and Tad are modern-day vampires cruising nightclubs and getting up to all manner of trouble involving gangsters, religious fanatics and a drug-crazed sex orgy.

Break of Day
Ken Hannam, 1977
Set in a small rural community in Victoria which is rife with bigotry,

the story focuses on the relationship between a bisexual woman, an artist, and a returned soldier who is traumatized by his experiences at Gallipoli.

The Clinic
David Stevens, 1982
Comic day-in-the-life of a VD clinic. Starring Chris Haywood as a gay doctor concerned about meeting his lover's parents.

Crush
Alison MacLean, 1992
A dark, emotional thriller from New Zealand about a fifteen-year-old girl discovering her sexuality and a revengeful and jealous relationship between two women whose shared sexual past and present is ambiguous.

Cut
Kimble Rendell, 2000
A comic teen-slasher film that sends up horror and teen genres. Includes a token lesbian character involved in a teeny weeny girl–girl kiss. A group of students commit to finishing a horror film where the previous film makers perished. It becomes a question of whether they can finish the film before it finishes them. Starring Molly Ringwald, Jessica Napier and Kylie Minogue.

Dallas Doll
Ann Turner, 1994
In this comedy a happy, suburban family household is turned upside down when Dallas Adair arrives, played by Sandra Bernhard, and seduces most of the family members.

Dating the Enemy
Megan Simpson Huberman, 1996
A romantic comedy where a couple, played by Guy Pearce and Claudia Karvan, wake up one morning to find themselves in each other's bodies. They begin to see life through the other gender's eyes.

Desperate Remedies
Stewart Main, Peter Wells, 1993
Comedy drama from New Zealand featuring an overt lesbian relationship, this luscious period film is excellent viewing. Dorothea schemes to rescue her opium-addicted sister from a decadent rogue parading as a prince.

The Devil's Playground
Fred Schepisi, 1976
Powerful film set in a Roman Catholic school for boys, where pubescent boys react in various frightening ways to their sexuality and to their schoolmasters.

The Everlasting Secret Family
Michael Thornhill, 1987
Thriller/Drama. Based on a book of short stories, *The Everlasting Secret Family and Other Secrets* by Frank Moorhouse, this film depicts a fictional and sinister freemason-like sect of middle-aged homosexual men of influence, including a senator with an attraction for young schoolboys. The film follows one of these boys through the ranks and rigours of this secret society.

Feed Them to the Cannibals
Fiona Cuningham-Reid, 1993
An affectionate document of the twenty-year history of the Sydney Gay and Lesbian Mardi Gras from a small and illegal solidarity march to the present-day international tourist attraction. The title comes from a suggested early colonial solution to the homosexual 'problem'.

Felicity
John D. Lamond, 1979

A soft-porn 'how-to' coming-of-age story from the makers of *A–Z of Sex, Australian Style*. Includes some soft-focus lesbian scenes, but this intimacy is ultimately depicted as a warm-up to the 'real' thing – a loving, heterosexual relationship.

The Getting of Wisdom
Bruce Beresford, 1977

A refined period drama about a girl who is sent to an exclusive ladies' college in Melbourne and, despite many obstacles, wins a music scholarship. She falls in love with one of the other female students amidst a groundswell of schoolgirl crushes.

Ghosts of the Civil Dead
John Hillcoat, 1988

A violent and frightening tale of what men get up to in a high-security prison.

Head On
Ana Kokkinos, 1998

Based on Christos Tsiolkas's novel, *Loaded*, in which Ari, a young, confused and uptight Greek – Australian, tries to sort out tensions between his homosexuality and cultural upbringing. A dynamically directed back-lane drama, starring Alex Dimitriades and local and much-admired queer singer-entertainer Paul Capsis.

Heavenly Creatures
Peter Jackson, 1994

A superb and dynamic thriller/drama based on a true story from New Zealand, starring Kate Winslet and Melanie Lynskey. Two imaginative and intelligent girls form an obsessive relationship in which they share a dream world and passion for each other. Parental pressure to separate them provokes the girls to murder one of their mothers.

High Rolling (aka 'High Rolling in a Hot Corvette')
Igor Auzins, 1977

Starring Judy Davis, Grigor Taylor and Joseph Bottoms, this drama/thriller road adventure tells a tale of car (and marijuana) stealing, hijacking and getting drunk on the Gold Coast.

Holy Smoke
Jane Campion, 1999

A suburban Australian family try to save their daughter (Kate Winslet) from an Indian religious cult. Their crusade is helped and hindered by her gay brother and his lover.

Life
Lawrence Johnston, 1995

A film adaptation of John Brumpton's play *Containment*, this haunting drama is set in prison where Des, a tough crim, is placed in T2 Division after he tests positive to HIV.

Love and Other Catastrophes
Emma-Kate Croghan, 1996

A charming and energetic university comedy romance starring Frances O'Connor and Matt Day, follows a day-in-the-life of five students, including two lesbians.

Mary's Place
Melissa Lee, 1998

Powerfully moving documentary following the story of Mary, a lesbian who was raped by several men in a lane next to a popular gay venue. The lane was renamed 'Mary's Place' and the process of reclaiming it with brighter lights and community art works became a major step towards Mary's healing.

The Monkey's Mask
Samantha Lang, 2000
Starring Kelly McGillis (of *Witness* fame) and Susie Porter, this is an adaptation of Dorothy Porter's lesbian thriller verse-novel.

Only the Brave
Ana Kokkinos, 1994
Brilliantly performed and directed drama about two Australian–Greek wild girls who want to leave school and go north. Tensions between them build and when they learn the truth about each other it's too late. Kokkinos went on to direct *Head On*.

The Sum of Us
Geoff Burton, Kevin Dowling, 1994
Based on the play by David Stevens, this warm-hearted story is as much about love between father and son as it is about gay love. Jeff (Russell Crowe), a suburban good bloke, is sick of one-night stands and noisy gay bars and wants true love. His father approves of his son's sexuality and eggs him on into a relationship, but Dad's girlfriend is not so supportive.

The Sydney Gay and Lesbian Mardi Gras Parade
Recordings of parades over several years by various television networks. See all the tits, arses and feathers you were unable to view first-hand. Generally available in video stores.

Wake in Fright
Ted Kotcheff, 1971
This classic of the early 1970s tells the story of a young English school teacher who sets off across Australia, but loses all his money gambling in an outback town and ends up stuck in the middle of nowhere and falling prey to the drunken lechery of the town's male inhabitants.

Welcome to Woop Woop
Stephan Elliot, 1997
While this was a disappointing follow-up to *The Adventures of Priscilla, Queen of the Desert*, there can be no disputing how camp it is. It follows the adventures of a gorgeous New Yorker boy who, while travelling in the outback, is abducted by a sex-crazed girl and kept prisoner in a weird commune of kitsch inbreeds who make dog-food out of kangaroos and live off tins of pineapple and beer.

The Well
Samantha Lang, 1997
Starring Pamela Rabe and Miranda Otto, this is an adaptation of Elizabeth Jolley's novel of the same name. When an eccentric landowner falls for her lazy female housekeeper, she'll do anything to keep the girl on her remote country property. The housekeeper, however, hatches a terrible plan to steal her mistress's fortune.

The Year of Living Dangerously
Peter Weir, 1982
An Australian journalist (Mel Gibson) in Jakarta becomes involved with a British Embassy secretary (Sigourney Weaver). He befriends a Chinese–Australian dwarf, a fellow journalist, played by Linda Hunt as a man – an excellent performance, and inspired casting by Weir.

Grab a video . . .

For the more relaxed traveller with a bit of movie-watching time on their hands, we've listed a few video stores that have either a gay section or a more expanded Australian section:

Sydney

Video Drama
90 Oxford St, Darlinghurst
Phone 02/9331 3158

Metro Video
110 Darlinghurst Rd, Darlinghurst
Phone 02/9361 4887

Video Ezy
27 Macleay St, Potts Point
Phone 02/9331 0220

Dr What Video
562 Oxford St, Bondi Junction
Phone 02/9387 1100

Adelaide

Kino at Hyde Park
114 King William Rd, Hyde Park
Phone 08/8373 1635

Trak Video
367 Greenhill Rd, Toorak Gardens
Phone 08/8332 2120

Brisbane

Trash Video
709 Ann St, Fortitude Valley
Phone 07/3252 2650

Melbourne

Alternative Video
270–272 Glen Eira Rd, Elsternwick
Phone 03/9532 9404

Video Ezy
69 Brighton Road, Elwood
phone 03/9531 4165

Movietime
150 Barkly St, St Kilda
Phone 03/9525 5052

Perth

Planet Video
Cnr of Beaufort and Walcott streets,
Mt Lawley
Phone 08/9328 7464

Gay and lesbian music

Like mainstream music, gay and lesbian music in Australia revolves around the **big cities**, particularly Sydney and Melbourne. The national population is not big enough to support a large gay and lesbian music scene, and groups like Fruit, a popular world-music band, tour mostly overseas. While gay and lesbian performers contribute to every major type of music, the music scene as a whole is not universally gay- and lesbian-friendly and few stars are out (*Face* magazine learned some years ago how expensive it can be to go pointing the finger).

Major Australian bands and artists of gay and lesbian interest or content include **Kylie Minogue**, pop duo **Savage Garden**, boy band **Human Nature**, **Natalie Imbruglia**, **The Mavis's**, grunge group **silverchair** and **Killing Heidi**. Other moderate Australian camp/dance successes of late have been '**Joanne**' and **Vanessa Amorosi**. Two highly proficient dance outfits that have been greatly underrated in the 1990s are **Boxcar** and **Kiva**, though both have enjoyed some chart success.

In gay and lesbian music, some styles of music are popular and stand out. Female vocalists and acoustic groups flourish; there are small **cabaret** scenes in Sydney, Melbourne and Adelaide. The summer season of gay and lesbian festivals around the country provides a platform and a circuit for some performers, particularly in popular women's and popular music shows during the Sydney Gay and Lesbian Mardi Gras Festival. Many perform throughout the year in mainstream venues at regular gigs and are well worth catching.

At a semi-professional and community level, there are many gay and lesbian **choirs** and performing groups, and in Sydney and Melbourne up-and-coming queer performers are to be found at the inner-suburban hotel and café venues.

Perhaps the most successful queer music performer is **Pauline Pantsdown**, a drag impersonator of an infamous right-wing political figure. Pantsdown performs regularly in Sydney and has had Top 10 hits.

THE MAINSTREAM SCENE

Only in Sydney and Melbourne are there regular performances at an international standard of most styles of music, including opera, classical, dance, rock/pop, jazz, cabaret and musical theatre. In other cities there isn't the same range or depth, but performers and groups regularly tour state and regional capitals.

The main **arts festivals** (Sydney's is in January; Perth's in February; Melbourne's in October–November; Adelaide's is held every second year in February–March) all feature international performers, orchestras, groups and companies. There is also a **touring circuit** of international musicals (both new and revivals) to capital cities, and major theatre companies produce **musicals** from time to time. Often they are outstanding: *The Boy from Oz*, a Broadway-style musical based on the life of gay singer–songwriter Peter Allen ('I go to Rio'), has toured extensively.

Some cities are known for specific types of music. Go to Melbourne for **jazz**, Adelaide for **world music**, Sydney for **opera**, Tamworth (a town in northern New South Wales) for its week-long **country music** festival at the end of January. Melbourne is the **dance music** capital of the country with a greater variety of venues and DJs, and with more liberal licensing and entertainment laws than elsewhere. It also has a funkier rock-and-pop scene in hotels and other venues, with many of the best local singer-songwriters based there. Some vineyards and upmarket farms outside of Melbourne, Sydney and Adelaide offer music programs ranging from jazz to popular classics.

Now, a quiet word in your shell-like about the Sydney Opera House: it's a great building, however the acoustics in the Concert Hall and the Opera Theatre are not what they should have been. Some other venues occasionally used for live music are also architectural wonders: the Theatre Royal in Hobart is the oldest theatre in the country; and the State Theatre in Sydney and the Forum in Melbourne are both ornate 1930s movie palaces.

FEMALE VOCALISTS

Perhaps Australia's best-known gay pop icon is **Kylie** Minogue, the teen soap star who became a pop diva. Her big hits from the eighties include, 'I should be so lucky', and 'Locomotion', and from the 1990s 'the devil you know'. Kylie's album, *Impossible Princess*, was a huge success in Australia, and less dance-oriented than earlier albums. She has gone back to some of her dance basics in her latest album. Kylie regularly tours, performs and often appears at gay and lesbian events. Her sister **Dannii** (another pop and tabloid icon) also records and performs some very upbeat dance numbers.

Monique Brumby is a young solo acoustic performer with a strong lesbian and mainstream pop following. She writes sad romantic pop songs about love, break-ups and relationships. Brumby tours regularly to major capitals, frequently with all-women acoustic vocal groups such as Bluehouse.

Aboriginal singer Deborah Cheetham, trained for the opera, uses her voice to great effect in her one-woman show, *White Baptist Abba Fan*, and in solo performance.

Robyn Archer's work crosses the boundaries of cabaret, rock and music theatre. She has had an international, 25-year career, writing and performing her own shows, as well as classic cabaret in the style of Brecht and Weill. Her work has a political edge and some songs, like 'Lucky Country' have become classics.

Judi Connelli is Australia's queen of cabaret. She has a rich voice with a wide range, and performs distinctive takes of classics, pop covers and show tunes.

Emerging singers include: **Samantha Leith**, whose work is classic disco with a lemon lesbian twist; **Marie Wilson**, who does covers of Joan Armatrading songs, as well as performing her own songs; and **Kavisha Mazzella**, based in Melbourne, who sings and plays guitar, mandolin and piano accordion.

GIRL GROUPS

There are a range of girl groups on the music scene, generally acoustic, with outstanding harmonic singing. **Bluehouse**, an acoustic group with 'the best harmonies this side of heaven', combines influences from the Indigo Girls, kd lang and Suzanne Vega.

And a couple of off-beat duos are popular with lesbians: the **Topp Twins** from New Zealand, who tour regularly in Australia, displaying their country roots and mastery of yodelling; and Sisters **Vika and Linda Bull**, who were formerly with Australian band the Black Sorrows.

CABARET

There is a small but diverse gay cabaret scene in Sydney, Melbourne and Adelaide. **Paul Capsis**'s shows are stunning explosions of rock, camp and raunch. He began doing diva impersonations in gay pubs, but has branched out into mainstream theatre and concerts (as well as playing a Greek drag queen in the movie *Head On*). **John Breheny**, little known outside Melbourne, is the finest camp trash performer in the country. **Bob Downe** (aka Mark Trevorrow) is one of Australia's cheekiest and best-loved cabaret acts. He sings, dances and wears loads of polyester (even his wig is polyester). Modelled on daytime TV hosts from the 1970s, his shows are a riot of song and satire. **Phil Scott** performs satirical and humorous material, aided and abetted by his trusty piano. **Ignatius Jones** sings jazz-rock cabaret. **David Campbell**, now based in New York, and **Tim Draxl**, based in Sydney, also perform show tunes and classics to a broader audience, but have a large gay following. Adelaide-based performers to look out for include **David Gauci** and **Chris Maver**, as well as the group **Classic Cabaret**.

Cabaret venues include the Hopetoun Hotel and the Harbourside Brasserie in Sydney, and the Continental Cafe in Prahran, Melbourne.

FOLK SINGERS

Two fine folk singers who regularly perform on the gay and lesbian scene are **Margret Roadknight** and **Judy Small**. Small, often described as the finest folk singer in the country, has nine albums to her credit, and sings songs of peace, justice, love and hope. Among her most recent albums is *Judy Small, Out and Proud*. Roadknight, a veteran singer, became famous through the songs 'Girls in our town' and 'Menstruation blues', for her tough-edged voice and bluesy style of storytelling.

WORLD MUSIC

Every two years in March–April, Adelaide hosts **Womadelaide**, a world music festival. One local name to watch for there is Andrea Rieniets.

Unsurprisingly, perhaps the best gay and lesbian world music band in Australia is also from Adelaide. **Fruit** make upbeat acoustic pop. They've been together five years, the three frontliners write, and the whole band composes good-time dancing music.

CHORUSES AND CHOIRS

Most major cities with visible gay and lesbian communities have choruses or choirs with varying standards of performance, often depending on musical direction and whether or not they audition. The most prominent are the **Sydney Gay and Lesbian Choir**, the **Canberra Gay and Lesbian Quire**, the **Brisbane Pride Choir** and the **Melbourne Gay and Lesbian Chorus**.

In a more classical vein, the **Corinthian Singers** in Melbourne sing the repertoire of gay and lesbian composers.

An overview of queer art

There has always been a **strong queer presence** in Australian culture. Robert Hughes' *The Fatal Shore* made it clear that Australia's early settlement was something of a sodomite's paradise.

In the early nineteenth century there is little clear evidence of lesbian and gay artists, but there was a 'special relationship' between Lesueur and Petite, French botanical illustrators who came to Australia with La Perouse in the early 1790s. There are also rumours as to why Augustus Earle was dumped on the isolated island of Tristan da Cunha – being too free with his favours among the sailors!

The **colonial experience** and adventure encouraged different patterns of behaviour and survival quite separate from the far more decorous realities of 'home' in England or Ireland. Up until the 1860s there was a disproportionate population of men compared to women in Australia. This predominantly homosocial world must have led to deep relationships between men. Indeed, one of the great ideals of Australia, mateship, is about those deep bonds of care and concern. Quite likely some of these men were more than mates.

Generally, a queer presence in Australian art and urban culture is not clearly manifest until the 1880s when Australia's leading pictorial journal, *The Bulletin* (or *The Bushman's Bible*), delighted in deriding the urbane and citified effeminate male, in literature and cartoons. The queer presence was seen as an affront to the decorum of the colonies and was often linked to the effete ruling classes from England, as opposed to the strong and manly Australian-born.

As in other parts of the world at the turn of the **twentieth century**, the private spaces and socially acceptable intimate companionships of **women** allowed for relative freedoms for lesbians of means. Among artists of the early twentieth century was Eerie Mort ('the worst girl' at St Catherine's), who possibly had lesbian tendencies, although these are not clearly expressed in her prints. There was also the rich and somewhat imperious Janet Cumbrae Stewart who painted nude women for decades in Paris. Dora Olfsen was a sculptor who created exotic stories about herself, and finished up in Italy where she and her countess lover killed themselves when their hero, Mussolini, was executed. Agnes Noyes Goodsir, Bessie Davidson, Eveline Syme and Ethel Spowers were all Australian lesbian artists of the 1920s. Research is continuing to illuminate the lives and careers of these women.

Among **male artists** of the same period, there are similarly few clear-cut cases, though there is some suspicion about the desires of landscapist Arthur Streeton. Likewsie Adrian Feint – a student of Elioth Gruner, an important teacher in Sydney – who cut a fine figure in the smart set of Sydney's Potts Point. An etcher, graphic and interior designer and painter, Feint's work for *The Home* magazine is vital and energetic.

Donald Friend could be called the most outrageous homosexual Australian artist of the pre-war period. He made no bones about his proclivities and was reported in newspapers of the day as living 'in the Japanese style' with his companion in a renovated stable in Woollahra, an inner suburb of Sydney. Donald Friend said his first lover was Sid Long, an important decorative painter of the early 1900s.

Roi de Maistre and William Dobell went to London to escape the rigid cultural confines of Australia. There they learnt about modernist tendencies in art, as well as the **homosexual demi-monde**. (De Maistre was an important early influence on the famous Francis Bacon.) In the late 1940s Loudon Sainthill and a theatre-designer and painter David Strachan were members of the Merioola Group, known at the time for their wild 'bohemian ways'.

Despite the 1950s being a conservative period, Jeffrey Smart, Donald Friend and William Dobell continued to paint singularly homoerotic works. The first 'happenings' of the far more liberated and liberal-minded 1960s were organized by Vivienne Binns, who also made 'Vag Dens' (1963), a riotously colourful play of sexualized shapes.

In Australia, the legal proscriptions against homosexuality were not removed until the early 1980s. So, generally gay and lesbian art in Australia does not come out into the open until the late 1970s. The mantra 'the personal is political' still holds much weight. **Personal experience** is at the centre of much gay and lesbian visual art. The body is an iconic presence – certainly there is no shortage of dicks, clits, tits and bums on display at gay and lesbian arts events!

Contemporary gay and lesbian art is entwined in the genres of protest art; message art; feminism; pornographic and erotic art forms and art about health issues. The works of queer-labelled artists reflect current community concerns.

Censorship is always an issue. During the early 1980s a major exhibition by gay artist Juan Davila was closed and curtained off by the police in Roslyn Oxley Galleries in Sydney after complaints by the Festival of Light (a Christian activist group). Cath Phillips, a Sydney sculptor and writer, went to jail after refusing to take down her work in the Mildura Sculpture Triennial as a personal-is-public protest against the existing censorship laws in Australia. In 1998 the American artist Andres Serrano's 'Piss Christ' was taken down at the National Gallery of Victoria after violent threats from un-named extreme Christian groups. Australian artists are currently taking part in a number of Internet protests in an attempt to test the recently introduced draconian censorship laws regarding the broadcasting of information.

For a time, especially in the early 1990s, **Identity Art** was very fashionable. Now that HIV/AIDS is now becoming manageable with drug therapy, the limited legalization of homosexuality and the subsequent growth of the pink dollar and rampant commodification, gay and lesbian art per se has been seen to suffer from overexposure. The first government-sanctioned exhibition of HIV/AIDS-inspired art was held in 1995 at the National Gallery of Australia, Canberra. Curated by Ted Gott, 'Art in the Age of AIDS' encapsulated the wide range of community and artistic responses to the pandemic. Surprisingly, the exhibition created little controversy.

Gay and lesbian artists whose work has gained **mainstream** notice include Juan Davila, Linda Dement, Rea, Matthew Jones, Scott Redford, Neil Emmerson and Christopher Dean. Other mainstream survey exhibitions in the various state galleries have presented and collected the works of gay and lesbian artists. For example, most state and national galleries hold works by documentary photographer William Yang, who is widely considered to be the ultimate pictorial chronicler of gay life in Sydney. The Adelaide Biennale has included the work of gay Aboriginal artist Brooke Andrew and lesbian Aboriginal artist Rea. Perspecta, the state-sponsored survey and thematic exhibition held in Sydney and aimed at highlighting local artists and curators, presents the works of many gay and lesbian artists; and the Asia Pacific Triennial in Brisbane includes the works of gay and lesbian artists from Pacific Rim countries.

In Brisbane, the Institute of Modern Art has included the collaborative works of **multimedia artists** Jane Polkinghorne and Helen Hyatt Johnson; and the performance work of Luke Roberts in his drag character 'Pope Alice'. The Experimental Arts Foundation and the Contemporary Arts Centre in Adelaide have exhibited the works and writings of local queer artists such as Yanni Stephenson and Di Barrett. Artspace in Sydney has presented the work of Gary Carsley and his Ministry of

Public Art; and the collaborative installations and the multimedia-based works of VNS Matrix, a group of women artists whose work explores lesbian and fluid sexualities and power struggles. Lesbian photographer Kaye Shumack has exhibited at First Draft and Artspace in Sydney. Her manipulated images range across such subjects as simple home life and activities, to lesbian beats, cruising and body-enhancement games. Shumack works at the intersection of documentary, advertising, snapshot and staged narrative photography.

A major impetus for gay and lesbian art is the **Sydney Gay and Lesbian Mardi Gras Festival**. The Australian Centre for Photography often curates work in association with the festival, and the Art Gallery of NSW, the Australian Museum and the Museum of Contemporary Art have also organized exhibitions to coincide with the festival. The festival has made gay and lesbian artists, who are more usually marginalized, visible at mainstream events and venues. The most prominent artist to emerge in this way was Peter Tully, who designed numerous costumes and floats for the parade. His love of decoration is apparent in his Tribal Wear collection of objects of adornment; and his work has lived on powerfully since his death. Another artist who gained critical notice while working for the Sydney Gay and Lesbian Mardi Gras is glass artist and sculptor Philippa Playford, who now makes art for public places – including works for Liverpool, west of Sydney; The Entrance on the Central Coast of New South Wales; and the swimming pools at Cook and Phillip Park in the heart of Sydney. Also making permanent and temporary installations in public places is Lisa Anderson, best known for projection and sound work on the Sydney Opera House, the Harbour Bridge and the Australian Museum.

There is no **venue** exclusively devoted to gay and lesbian art in Australia. However, many of the **artist-run spaces** and contemporary art centres exhibit works by and about queer artists and their issues. Visiting these galleries and looking through their past catalogues, as well as current exhibitions, will prove fruitful in a search for queer art and artists. A useful guide to the art of the eastern states is *Art Almanac*, a monthly publication available at many newsagents and galleries for just a couple of dollars.

Gay & lesbian literature

Gay and lesbian literature has had a slow evolution in Australia, due largely to the fact that the **commercial viability** of the subject matter has not been seen as practicable given the nation's demographics. Consequently, small publishing companies like BlackWattle, Spinifex, Sybylla, and Hale & Iremonger emerged in the 1970s and 1980s in order that the previously unwanted and unheard voices of gay and lesbian experience could be read. BlackWattle no longer operates as a publisher and its demise must at least in part be due to **mainstream publishers** choosing to test the waters of gay and lesbian viability in the 1990s. With the loss of this valued imprint we have also lost many fine voices and publications and can only hope that some of these will resurface through more mainstream publishers. Great Australian authors such as Patrick White and David Malouf have tended to be published first in England, but gradually we hope that our presence in the community will be reflected in local publishers' lists.

TOP 10 GAY FICTION TITLES

Night Letters by Robert Dessaix
A fine literary work tracing in letters the journey of a dying man travelling through Italy.

Vanity Fierce by Graeme Aitken
Follows Stephen, one of Sydney's vainest young men, as he uses every hilarious trick in the book to get what he wants.

Loaded by Christos Tsiolkas
A gripping and savage tale about a young gay Greek–Australian torn between cultures.

Glove Puppet by Neal Drinnan
A sexually precocious young man embarks on a love affair that threatens to destroy everything he loves.

Beauty of Truth by Bruno Bouchet
Deals with the riotous pitfalls of vanity in the world of marketing.

Get Over It! by Phillip Scott
A detective tale with an opera-loving queen as Sherlock Holmes.

Medea's Children by Con Anemogiannis
A contemporary Greek–Australian odyssey through the experiences of

a sexually adventurous youth in working-class Sydney.

Fairyland by Sumner Locke Elliott
A semi-autobiographical novel by one of Australia's most famous authors.

Johnno by David Malouf
A semi-autobiographical account of wartime Brisbane.

String of Pearls by Tony Ayres
Tells funny and touching stories with an emphasis on culture shock and cultural collision.

TOP 10 LESBIAN FICTION TITLES

Set Up by Claire McNab
Australia's favourite lesbian crime writer proves time and time again that crime does pay.

Monkey's Mask by Dorothy Porter
Lesbian detective thriller verse-novel set in Sydney.

The Grass Sister by Gillian Mears
Follows the quest, both real and imagined, of a woman searching for her sister in Africa.

Passing Remarks by Helen Hodgman
Charts the romantic fortunes of a woman who has just won $30,000.

Working Hot by Kathleen Mary Fallon
A lesbian classic for over a decade, this wicked and riotous collection of poetry and prose is a sumptouos erotic feast of language.

Tasting Salt by Stephanie Dowrick
Portrait of a young New Zealander finding herself as a woman and an artist in England and Germany.

Blood Guilt by Lindy Cameron
A slick and suspenseful thriller.

Happy Families by Susan Varga
A panoramic story about the changing nature of families in Australia.

Heart on Fire by Diana Simmonds
Lesbian romance with verve and wit.

The Other Woman by Ann O'Leary
Infidelity can be more complicated than you think.

SIGNIFICANT NON-FICTION TITLES

Holding the Man by Timothy Conigrave
A beautiful biography of a gay love affair spanning two decades. The story begins in a Melbourne Catholic school and ends with Tim Conigrave's death from AIDS in 1994.

Homosexual: Oppression and Liberation by Dennis Altman
Written by one of Australia's premier gay academics, this was the first positive discussion of homosexuality published in the world (it was published in 1971).

Black Hours by Wayne King
A brilliantly moving story of a gay Aborigine's perspective on life in Australia, covering two generations.

The High Price of Heaven by David Marr
A powerful collection of journalism from Australia's most erudite and significant civil liberties advocate.

Everyday Passions by Dorothy McRae McMahon
A thoughtful biography from Australia's favourite lesbian member of the cloth.

Inside Out: An Australian Collection of Coming Out Stories edited by Erin Shale
Just as the title says . . .

Mardi Gras! True Stories: From Lock-Up to Frock-Up edited by Richard Wherrett
Stories by prominent Australians about Mardi Gras over the years.

Multicultural Queer: Australian Narratives edited by Peter Jackson and Gerald Sullivan
A broad look at the many different cultures that go to make up our queer communities.

City of the Plain: History of a Gay Sub-culture by Garry Wotherspoon
A comprehensive history of Australia's gay culture.

Sadness/Friends of Dorothy
by William Yang
Australia's most famous gay photographer reflects on AIDS, friendship and loss.

A Sydney Gaze: The Making of Gay Liberation by Craig Johnston
An academic look at the gay liberation process in Australia.

Ian Roberts: Finding Out by Paul Freeman
The coming-out story and biography of a leading Australian football player.

Mardi Gras: A History of the Sydney Gay and Lesbian Mardi Gras by Graham Carbery
Everything you always wanted to know abpout Mardi Gras, but were afraid to ask..

The Fall Upwards: Spirituality in the Lives of Lesbian Women and Gay Men edited by Dino Hodge
A survey of religious leanings in the queer community.

Being Different: Nine Gay Men Remember edited by Gary Wotherspoon
A collection of memoirs from pioneering gay men in Australia.

Theatre – an aside

Look out for plays by any of the following playwrights, who tend to tackle gay and lesbian themes in their work: Peter Kenna, Clem Gorman, Alison Lyssa, Eva Johnson, Alex Harding, Margaret Fischer, Sandra Shotlander, Michael Gow, Stephen House, Alana Valentine, Dorothy Porter, Christos Tsiolkas, Timothy Conigrave, Richard Barret, Stephen Carleton, Barry Lowe, and Campion Decent.

And for those in search of a historical perspective on plays in Australia, *Australian Gay and Lesbian Plays*, edited by Bruce Parr, and published by Currency Press, will be of interest.

index

IF KNOWLEDGE IS POWER, THIS ROUGH GUIDE IS A POCKET-SIZED BATTERING RAM

Written in plain English, with no hint of jargon, the Rough Guide to the Internet will make you an Internet guru in the shortest possible time. It cuts through the hype and makes all others look like nerdy textbooks

ROUGH GUIDES ON THE WEB

Visit our website www.roughguides.com for news about the latest books, online travel guides and updates, and the full text of our Rough Guide to Rock.

AT ALL BOOKSTORES • DISTRIBUTED BY PENGUIN

Rough Guides on the **Web**

www.travel.roughguides.com

We keep getting bigger and better! The Rough Guide to Travel Online now covers more than 14,000 searchable locations. You're just a click away from access to the most in-depth travel content, weekly destination features, online reservation services, and an outspoken community of fellow travelers. Whether you're looking for ideas for your next holiday or you know exactly where you're going, join us online.

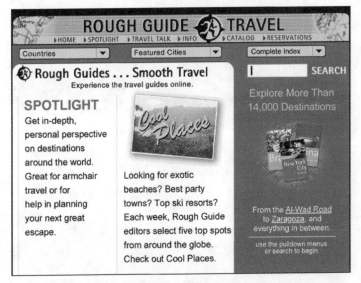

You can also find us on Yahoo!® Travel (http://travel.yahoo.com) and Microsoft Expedia® UK (http://www.expediauk.com).

Don't bury your head in the sand!

Take cover!

with ROUGH GUIDE Travel Insurance

UK Freefone 0800 015 09 06
Worldwide (+44) 1243 621 046
Check the web at
www.roughguides.com/insurance

ROUGH
GUIDES

Worldwide cover, for Rough Guide readers worldwide

Insurance organized by Torribles Insurance Brokers Ltd, 21 Prince Street, Bristol, BS1 4PH, England

Stay in touch with us!

ROUGH*NEWS* is Rough Guides' free newsletter.
In three issues a year we give you news, travel
issues, music reviews, readers' letters and the
latest dispatches from authors on the road.

I would like to receive ROUGH*NEWS*: please put me on your free mailing list.

NAME . . . .

ADDRESS . . . .

Please clip or photocopy and send to: Rough Guides, 62-70 Shorts Gardens, London WC2H 9AH,
England or

Rough Guides, 375 Hudson Street, New York, NY 10014, USA.

ROUGH GUIDES: Travel

THE ROUGH GUIDE TO

Australia

ROUGH GUIDES: Mini Guides, Travel Specials and Phrasebooks

MINI GUIDES

Antigua
Bangkok
Barbados
Big Island of Hawaii
Boston
Brussels
Budapest
Dublin
Edinburgh
Florence
Honolulu
Lisbon
London Restaurants
Madrid
Maui
Melbourne
New Orleans

St Lucia
Seattle
Sydney
Tokyo
Toronto

TRAVEL SPECIALS

First-Time Asia
First-Time Europe
More Women
  Travel

PHRASEBOOKS

Czech
Dutch
Egyptian Arabic
European

French
German
Greek
Hindi & Urdu
Hungarian
Indonesian
Italian
Japanese
Mandarin Chinese
Mexican Spanish
Polish
Portuguese
Russian
Spanish
Swahili
Thai
Turkish
Vietnamese

AVAILABLE AT ALL GOOD BOOKSHOPS

ROUGH GUIDES:
Reference and Music CDs

REFERENCE
Classical Music
Classical:
  100 Essential CDs
Drum'n'bass
House Music
Jazz

World Music:
  100 Essential CDs
English Football
European Football
Internet
Millennium

THE ROUGH GUIDE

Tango

Music USA
Opera
Opera:
  100 Essential CDs
Reggae
Rock
Rock:
  100 Essential CDs
Techno
World Music

**ROUGH GUIDE
  MUSIC CDs**
Music of the Andes
Australian
  Aboriginal
Brazilian Music
Cajun & Zydeco
Classic Jazz
Music of Colombia
Cuban Music
Eastern Europe
Music of Egypt
English Roots
  Music
Flamenco
India & Pakistan
Irish Music
Music of Japan
Kenya & Tanzania
Native American
North African

Music of Portugal
Reggae
Salsa
Scottish Music
South African Music
Music of Spain
Tango
Tex-Mex
West African Music
World Music
World Music Vol 2
Music of Zimbabwe

THE MILLION-COPY BESTSELLER

the
Internet

2001 EDITION · FOR PCs AND MACS

AVAILABLE AT ALL GOOD BOOKSHOPS